HISTORICAL
ATLAS
OF THE
PACIFIC
NORTHWEST

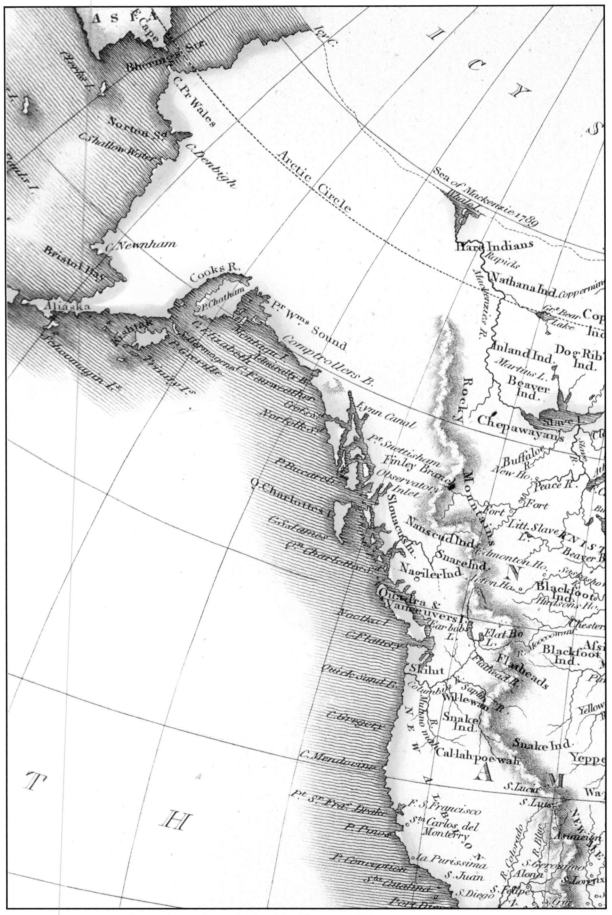

Map i *America*. From: *Thomson's New General Atlas*, John Thomson, 1817.
This map shows the northwest coast from George Vancouver's surveys of 1792 – 1794, and the Missouri, Columbia and Multnomah (Willamette) Rivers as mapped by Meriwether Lewis and William Clark in 1804 – 1806. Cook Inlet is shown as "Cooks R" despite being shown by Vancouver not to be a river. Vancouver Island is named "Quadra & Vancouvers I", the name given to the island by Vancouver after his meeting with the Spanish commander Juan Francisco Bodega y Quadra. This map is an aesthetically pleasing, typical atlas map of the early nineteenth century.

Geography writes history on the northwest coast of America

– George Bowering

HISTORICAL ATLAS

OF THE

PACIFIC NORTHWEST

MAPS OF EXPLORATION AND DISCOVERY

BRITISH COLUMBIA • WASHINGTON • OREGON
ALASKA • YUKON

DEREK HAYES

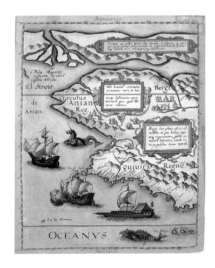

SASQUATCH BOOKS
SEATTLE

Map ii
Nouve Scoperte de' Russi al Nord del Mare del Sud si nell' Asia, che nell America Venezia 1776. Antonio Zatta, 1776.
(New Discoveries of the Russians in the North Pacific in parts of Asia and America.)

A strange but interesting representation of the Pacific Northwest coastline from Venetian mapmaker Antonio Zatta in 1776.
Before James Cook's third voyage took him to the Pacific Northwest in 1778, the outline of the coast was unknown except for a few points – and points do not a coastline make, as this map clearly demonstrates.
Early mapmakers often didn't like blanks on their maps, and so filled them with their imaginations. This is a particularly bizarre example.
The map shows the fictitious discoveries of a Spanish admiral named Bartholemew de Fonte in 1640 of a network of waterways leading from the Pacific Ocean to Hudson Bay – the Northwest Passage sought by so many.

For Carole

Published by Sasquatch Books, by arrangement with Cavendish Books Inc., Vancouver, B.C.

Printed in Hong Kong on acid-free Japanese art paper
03 02 00   5 4 3 2

Sasquatch Books
615 Second Avenue, Suite 260
Seattle, Washington 98104
(206) 467-4300
www.SasquatchBooks.com
books@SasquatchBooks.com

Library of Congress Cataloguing in Publication Data
Hayes, Derek. 1947–
        Historical atlas of the Pacific Northwest : maps of exploration and discovery
:   British Columbia, Washington, Oregon, Alaska, Yukon / Derek
Hayes
            p.   cm.
        Includes bibliographical references and index.
        ISBN 1-57061-215-3
        1. Northwest, Pacific--Discovery and exploration. 2. Alaska--Discovery and
exploration. 3. Yukon Territory--Discovery and exploration. 4. Northwest,
Pacific--Discovery and exploration--Maps. 5. Alaska--Discovery and
exploration--Maps. 6. Yukon Territory--Discovery and exploration--Maps.
        I. Title.
F851.H38   1999
979.5'01--dc21   99-10945

Acknowledgments

This book would not have been possible without the co-operation and assistance of many librarians and archivists in the institutions from which many of the maps were acquired, listed on page 196. I thank all of you. Thanks also to the many kind people who assisted me with the revisions for the second printing.

Derek Hayes
White Rock, British Columbia
May 2000

The author welcomes comments to: derek@cavendishbooks.ca

The map shown on the title page is Cornelius de Jode's 1593 map of the Pacific Northwest, the first map to show the region (see page 15).

CONTENTS

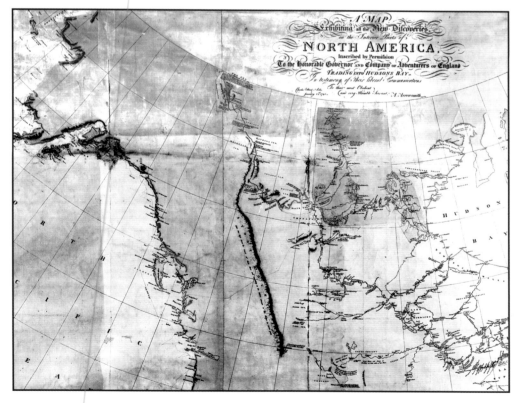

Map iii
A Map Exhibiting all the New Discoveries in the Interior Parts of North America. Inscribed by permission To the Honourable Governor and Company of Adventurers of England Trading Into Hudsons Bay. Aaron Arrowsmith, 1795.

This influential map was the most accurate map of North America when it was published. It shows Arrowsmith's concept of a single ridge of the Rocky (Stony) Mountains extending southwards only to about 49° N. They are marked *"3520 feet High above the level of their Base,"* which lent credence to the idea that the Rockies would be easy to cross, despite the fact that they are also marked *"according to the Indian account is five ridges in some places."* This concept was still in vogue when Captains Meriwether Lewis and William Clark set off on their westward trek in 1804. It was Lewis and Clark who would finally make geographers realize that there was a formidable mountain range with multiple ridges in the way of westward passage. The map also shows information from Samuel Hearne in 1770 – 72, and Alexander Mackenzie's expedition to the Arctic Ocean in 1789. The coast is according to James Cook and later fur traders such as George Dixon, but George Vancouver's epic survey is not yet recorded. As a result, Vancouver Island is not yet shown; both George Vancouver and Dionisio Galiano proved it was an island and mapped it as such in 1792, but the information would not be published until 1798 and 1802, respectively.

INTRODUCTION

Until the late eighteenth century, the Pacific Northwest of North America was a major blank on the world map and, with the exception of the two poles, the last major one. This was primarily the result of its location, which was to European explorers, exploiters, and colonizers the area of the world most remote to them. It was popularly known in England as "the backside of America." The region was reachable only by a long and dangerous voyage around the southern tip of South America, round Cape Horn or through the Straits of Magellan; by crossing the isthmus at Panama, involving transfer from sea to land and back again; or by an immensely long voyage eastwards, round the southern tip of Africa, across the Indian Ocean, and then across the Pacific Ocean northwards again.

Add to this the fact that the early mariners had to contend with other nations' control of parts of the routes, especially relevant when provisions and water were required, and the fact that we are talking of sailing ships here, at the mercy of wind and current, and it is easy to understand why the Pacific Northwest remained undiscovered for so long.

For the Russians, the route to the Pacific Northwest involved a long and difficult overland journey across Siberia to the Pacific coast, and before any voyage could be contemplated, you had to build your ship!

Even for the Americans, whose interest in the Pacific Northwest emerged after the War of Independence and the Louisiana Purchase in the early nineteenth century, the overland expedition to the west coast was an enormous undertaking, involving years of canoeing, portaging, and, most of all, finding a way across the multiple ranges of the Rocky Mountains.

It was not until after James Cook and George Vancouver in the late eighteenth century had accurately determined their longitude using chronometers that it was even realized how wide the North American continent actually was; up till that time it had been thought to be much narrower. One mid-seventeenth-century map even showed the Pacific coast only a matter of a ten-day march from the headwaters of rivers draining to the Atlantic! And the British, in what is now Canada, faced the same problems of distance, difficult country, and mountains. In addition to all this was the question of motivation.

Not until James Cook discovered, almost by accident, that the fur of the coastal sea otter was a valuable trade commodity was there much commercial reason for visiting the Pacific Northwest; before that the main reason was to pre-empt another power that was, or was thought to be, encroaching on the territory, a particular concern for Spain, which considered the Pacific a "Spanish lake" and had valuable territory to the south of the Pacific Northwest to protect. Spain was concerned from time to time about the Russians and the British.

A note on native maps

Many of the maps in this atlas were drawn by non native people "discovering" or exploring territory new to them. This is not to say that aboriginal people did not make maps; indeed they did, and sometimes these maps were given to, and used by, explorers in the construction of their own maps. But the predominantly oral tradition of the native peoples means that few native maps survive today.

There are many recorded instances of Hudson's Bay Company men using native maps. Perhaps the most famous example of native maps being given to explorers are the maps incorporated into the journals of Meriwether Lewis and William Clark. Nevertheless, most of the native maps were ephemeral, drawn with a stick on the ground, with charcoal on hides, or on bark – that is, with available materials. Thus, unless copied onto paper and preserved, these maps were usually lost.

For most of the period covered by this atlas, natives did not have the benefit of the more global perspective that the Europeans had, and hence, inevitably, their maps tended to be more local; they were not "filling in gaps" but recording ways of getting from one place to another, or other utilitarian information.[7]

A note on exploration and discovery

It is explicitly acknowledged that the terms "discovery" and "exploration" are used here in the sense of non-native, European or Asian discovery and exploration; there is no intention to diminish the fact of prior native occupation and knowledge of the lands. I have simply tried to put together a collection of what I felt were interesting historical maps, from the earliest to about 1900, and the maps that survived and are available are mainly those from non-native sources. It is a perhaps unfortunate fact that most of the maps tend to represent exploration, discovery, conquest of space and recording of political domination, but it was these maps that also recorded the emergence of modern knowledge of the geography of the Pacific Northwest.

A note on the choice of maps

While I have tried to assemble a representative collection of different types of maps from different sources, to illustrate the significant events in Pacific Northwest history, the choice is ultimately a personal one, tempered by availability.

Often, events now considered relatively significant have no contemporary maps to illustrate them, either because nobody drew any or because they have been lost. An example of the latter case is James McMillan's reconnaissance of Fort Langley in 1824. At least four people on this expedition are known to have produced maps, but none have survived. Peter Skene Ogden drew maps in his journal during an expedition to the Snake River country, but he lost them when his canoe overturned on his way back to Fort Vancouver. Thus the original maps perished, but since the explorer survived, he was still able to pass on the cartographic knowledge he had gained, and maps after that did reflect his discoveries.

In 1842, Charles Preuss, John Charles Fremont's mapmaker, lost his journal of astronomical and barometric observations, which he used to fix points on his maps and thus ensure their accuracy, when his boat overturned on the Platte River. Luckily, in this case, the journal was found downstream, soaked but still readable.

All maps first had to be brought back by the explorer himself, and later preserved by his successors, or by libraries, archives, or museums that *at the time* deemed the material to be important enough to preserve.

It must have been difficult to ensure that maps and charts and journals survived unscathed through perilous voyages under sail, often taking years to complete, or being packed across difficult country or in canoes on raging rivers. It is, perhaps, a wonder that many maps survived to the present day.

Sometimes maps that are artistically poor or that have deteriorated with age are included because they are historically significant or because the person who drew them was important to the history of the Pacific Northwest; sometimes maps that are historically of lesser significance have been included because they are artistically pleasing, and yet others have been included simply because I found them interesting.

Hand-drawn and printed maps

There are fundamentally two different types of maps reproduced in this atlas. The first type of map is that drawn by explorers or their men themselves, either during a voyage or expedition, or afterwards. These are typically one-of-a-kind maps (although often several hand-drawn copies were made, perhaps to guard against loss or to send to superiors). They may be the originals from which printed maps were later made, or may have been intended only for field or personal use.

The second type of map is the printed map, of which there may have been many copies originally, although often relatively few were printed and less survive today. For example, only a single copy of the 1773 Russian edition of the Müller map (Map 48, page 31) is now known; it seems the rest have disappeared. Many old printed maps are first engraved, which means that a different person has in effect copied the map so it can be printed.

Printed maps tended to have much wider circulation than hand-drawn maps and hence were more likely to influence public perceptions of the area depicted.

Geographical area covered

For the purposes of this book, I have defined the Pacific Northwest as the area now covered by the State of Alaska, Yukon Territory, the Province of British Columbia, and the States of Washington and Oregon, which was roughly the area that remained unknown on the maps of the world until the late eighteenth century.

A note on terminology and spelling

The geographical area covered by this atlas includes both American and Canadian territories that may not have been part of those countries during the historical period covered, and so spelling of names varies. As late as 1845, the American naval commander Charles Wilkes was using "English" spelling, referring, for example, to "Grays Harbour" rather than to the modern name of "Grays Harbor." In Canada, "railway" is commonly utilized rather than the American "railroad"; nevertheless, some American companies, such as the Great Northern Railway, did use the term "railway". I have attempted to use the spelling which is correct for the country and the time period being discussed, and the terminology and spelling which was being used at the time.

Map 1
Nova et Aucta Orbis Terrae Descriptio ad Usum Navigantium emendate accomodata
Gerard Mercator, 1569

The earliest maps of the Pacific Northwest were parts of world maps, and the outlines of the coast were based largely on speculation rather than facts. This map is part of the important 1569 world map by Gerard Mercator, the first world map to use his new projection, the Mercator projection. Here, straight lines on the map are lines of constant bearing, an exceptionally significant property for navigators. The map was ahead of its time; the significance of the projection was not realized until the next century, when the projection was used for sea atlases, collections of maps for maritime navigation (see Map 5, page 13). Mercator chose not to give detailed instructions for the plotting of his revolutionary new grid, and the mathematics involved was understood by few of his contemporaries. Even Mercator's son Rumold re-issued this map in a more familiar double-hemisphere form in 1587 (Map 7, page 14).

This map was intended to be read much as one would read a book, with blocks of texts expounding on subjects as diverse as the disposition of the earth's land masses and the technique of direction finding and measurement of distance. Note the Northwest Passage shown in the north, between Mercator's North American land mass and an Arctic land mass, the source of which was a medieval text.

EARLY APPROACHES TO THE NORTHWEST COAST

It is a near certainty that Japanese or Chinese people arrived on the northwest coast long before any European. Some may have come by accident rather than by choice, however. Chinese tradition tells of a junk that set out from China in 219 B.C. for the "Isle of the Blest", probably Japan, but the junk was driven eastwards for months by gales to a mysterious foreign land called Fu-sang or Fousang, possibly the northwest coast of America. "Fousang" shows up as late as the mid eighteenth century on a number of maps of the northwest coast where the geography was filled in by imagination (for example Map 43, page 30, or Map 56, page 35).

It is interesting to consider that if this tradition has any basis in fact, presumably some of the people in the junk must have returned to China to relate the tale.

There are several documented wrecks of oriental ships on the northwest coast, such as one at Clatsop Beach, just south of the mouth of the Columbia River, in 1820, and another near Cape Flattery in 1833. In the latter incident, Charles Wilkes of the 1841 U.S. Exploring Expedition (see page 119) reported that the Hudson's Bay Company was able to rescue three Japanese sailors and even send them to England so that they could find their way home from there.

The Spanish also quite likely came to the northwest coast involuntarily before any organized voyage. Since the discovery of the Westerly winds in the Pacific Ocean at about 40 – 44° N by the Spanish captain Alonso de Arellano in 1564, a galleon laden with spices, silver, and beeswax had made an annual voyage to New Spain from the Philippines. Some never made it. A number of items have been found on the beaches of Oregon which almost certainly came from Spanish galleons. Lots of beeswax from southeast Asia was imported for lighting as it was of a better quality and more long lasting than North American beeswax. Some of this ended up on the beaches of Oregon, and some was known to have been sold to the inhabitants of Fort Vancouver later. One such piece is illustrated here. It has numerals on it which could be "1679", and it has been carbon-dated to approximately that date.

There are numerous instances of castaways being assimilated by native people. It is interesting that the Clatsop native term for all whites was "Tlon-honnipts", meaning "of those who drift ashore".

If the first Europeans on the northwest coast were Spanish castaways, as seems likely, there were no consequences to their assimilators other than minor cultural and genetic effects. The Spaniards did not succeed in communicating with their homeland.

A large piece of beeswax from a Spanish galleon which was found on the Oregon coast. It has been carbon-dated to approximately 1679. This piece is on display at the Tillamook Pioneer Museum.

THE MAKING OF A SPANISH LAKE

In September 1513, the Spaniard Vasco Núñez de Balboa crossed the Isthmus of Panama and became the first European to see the Pacific Ocean. He waded into the sea and ceremonially took possession of the ocean *and any coasts that it might wash* in the name of Spain. This action was to be cited later as evidence that the entire Pacific coast of North America belonged to Spain.

News of Balboa's discovery reached a Portuguese navigator named Fernão de Magalhães, better known by his anglicized name of Ferdinand Magellan. He had the idea of sailing *west* to the Spice Islands, but the Portuguese king was uninterested. So Magellan entered the service of Spain and in 1519 was given command of a fleet of five ships. He discovered a way around the southern tip of South America, through the straits that bear his name. Having emerged into the new ocean on an unusually peaceful morning in November 1520, after a long struggle to get through the Straits of Magellan, he named it Mar Pacifica – the Pacific Ocean.

One of his ships, the *Victoria*, continued westward to become the first ship to circumnavigate the world – but without Magellan, for he was killed in the Philippines in a skirmish with natives.

THE FIRST SPANISH VOYAGES TO THE NORTHWEST COAST

After his conquest of central Mexico in the early sixteenth century, Hernando Cortés wanted to establish Spanish control to the north and also find a rumored strait to the Atlantic, which would soon become known as the Strait of Anian.

In 1539, Cortés sent Francisco de Ulloa northwards with three ships. After exploring the Gulf of California, which he named the Sea of Cortes, he rounded the tip of Baja California and sailed north, but he is thought to have reached only as far north as the Isla de Cedros, about halfway up the Baja peninsula.

In 1542, further ships were sent north. Juan Rodríguez Cabrillo sailed from the port of Navidad on the coast of New Spain in June 1542. The Spanish at this time had heard further rumor that the Portuguese had discovered a northern strait between two oceans. Cabrillo landed at Bahía de San Miguel, today San Diego, thus becoming the first European to land in Alta (Upper) California. He continued northward to just north of today's San Francisco, before returning southwards. On the return journey Cabrillo died, and in January 1543 his pilot, Bartolemé Ferrelo decided to turn northwards again, and he reached 44° N, the latitude of today's Eugene, Oregon, before abandoning the northward voyage due to the cold. The ships arrived back in New Spain in April 1543.

Although the Cabrillo-Ferrelo expedition described the coast and probably made charts, none appear to have survived. Spanish policy was to keep geographical details secret so that they could not be used by Spain's enemies.

THE ZALTIERI MAP OF 1566

This map of North America by Venetian mapmaker Bolognini Zaltieri was one of the first maps to show the Strait of Anian, thought to be a sea separating Asia from America, corresponding somewhat to today's Bering Strait. It was speculative, however, derived from an interpretation of Marco Polo's account of the land of Anian. The idea of a route around southern Africa to the Indies had been equally speculative the previous century and had proved to be correct, so why not the Strait of Anian, perhaps a Northwest Passage and itself a route to the Indies?

The title of this map is *...nova Francia* – New France, despite the fact that it shows the whole of North America and not just the area of eastern Canada which had been explored by Jacques Cartier in 1534 and claimed by France.

The land of Quivira, reputedly rich in gold, had been sought in the region of today's Kansas by the Spanish explorer Francisco Vasquez de Coronado in 1540 – 1542. It is shown by Zaltieri, but moved by him to the shores of the Strait of Anian. Quivira shows up on many later maps of the Pacific Northwest (see examples: Map

7, page 14; Map 8, page 15; and Maps 9 and 10, page 16). Baja California is recognizable, but much of the rest is conjectural.

The depiction of the Strait of Anian on Zaltieri's map is the same as that shown on a world map published a year later by another Venetian mapmaker, Giovanni Camocio. Mapmakers at this time, particularly where little real information was available, often copied each other. Thus the speculations of one were incorporated into other maps and soon became accepted as fact.

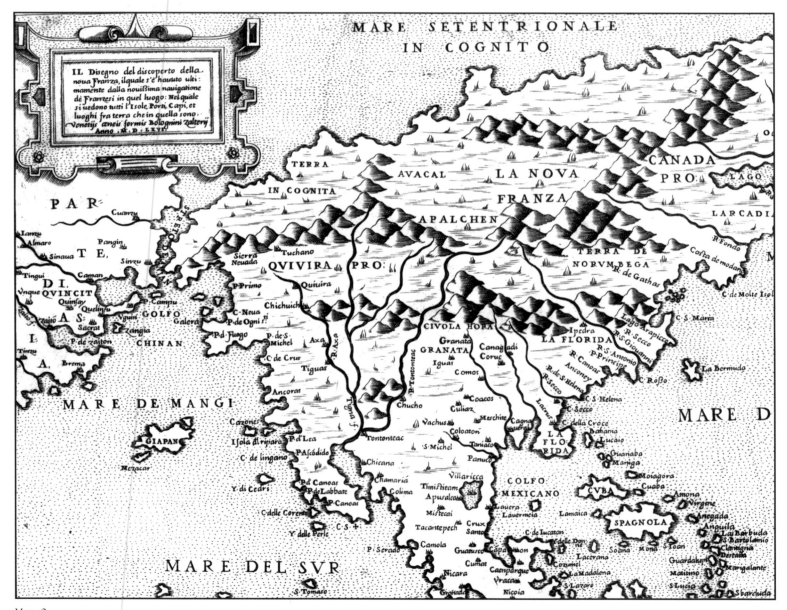

Map 2

Il Disegno del Discoperto della nova Franza, ilquale s'è havuto ultimanente dalla novissima navigatione de Franzesi; in quel luogo: Nel quale si vedono tutti L'Isole, Porti, Capi, et luoghi fra terra che in quella sono venetijs aneis formis Bolognini Zalterij Anno MDLXVI

One of the first maps to show the Strait of Anian separating North America from Asia. The map was published in Venice in 1566. The map has recently been attributed by some experts to Verona mapmaker Paolo Forlani rather than Zaltieri.

THE FAMOUS VOYAGE OF SIR FRANCIS DRAKE

The Englishman Sir Francis Drake is considered by many to have been the first European to have visited the Northwest coast of America, and to this day a debate continues among scholars as to precisely how far north he sailed and the location of a harbor he used and mapped. Whatever the truth, his voyage certainly had an effect on maps in the ensuing years. The "famous voyage," as it is commonly called, was the first circumnavigation of the world by an Englishman, the second ever (after Magellan), and the first in which the captain returned with his ship.

Drake left England in 1577, sailed through the Strait of Magellan and into the Pacific. There he took to attacking and plundering Spanish ships and towns whenever the opportunity arose. In early 1579, Drake attacked a Spanish galleon laden with silver and then sailed northwards towards the Pacific Northwest. He perhaps was searching for the Northwest Passage, but as this extract from the famous 1628 account of his voyage, *The World Encompassed,* makes clear, he didn't find it:

And alfo from thefe reafons we coniecture; that either there is no paffage at all through thefe Northerne coafts (which is moft likely) or if there be, that yet it is vnnauigable. Adde hereunto, that though we fearched the coaft diligently, euen vnto the 48. deg. yet found we not the land, to trend fo much as one point in any place towards the Eaft, but rather running on continually Northweft, as if it went directly to meet with Afia; and euen in that height when we had a franke wind, fo haue carried vs through, had there beene a paffage, yet we had a fmooth and calme fea, with ordinary flowing and reflowing, which could not haue beene, had there beene a frete : of which we rather infallibly concluded then coniectured, that there was none. But to returne.

This book was published after Drake's death by his nephew and namesake, but was compiled principally from the journals of Francis Fletcher, Drake's chaplain. It seems that Drake did reach 48° N, the latitude of the Strait of Juan de Fuca, but may or may not have seen it or entered it. One historian even calculated that Drake reached Vancouver Island on 10 June 1579, based on his analysis of all the accounts plus a knowledge of the winds and currents of the North Pacific.[11] If this was the case, then Drake was the first Englishman to reach what is now the west coast of Canada. However far north he did reach, it is better documented that when he returned south, he found a harbor, which he desperately needed in

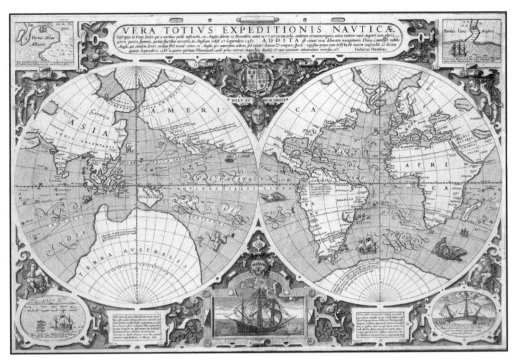

Map 3
Vera Totius Expeditionis Nauticae descriptio D. Franc. Draci....Addita est etiam viva delineatio navigationes Thomea Caundish... Joducus Hondius, Amsterdam, 1589.

Drake's harbor, which he found somewhere on the northwest coast, is shown as an inset, upper left.

order to careen his ship and repair leaks. This harbor was mapped by him and appears on the 1589 world map by Joducus Hondius (Map 3, above) as an inset map (Map 3A, below right). It was here that he took possession of the coast in the name of the Queen of England and named it New Albion. This name was to appear on maps for centuries, and later was often used to designate areas much further north.

As with the question of how far north Drake actually sailed, the location of the harbor, Portus Nova Albionis (in Latin), has been the subject of debate for years. Usually ascribed to bays in California, a recent suggestion, backed up by a lot of evidence, was that it was Whale Cove, on the Oregon coast just south of Depoe Bay. The problem is that all the evidence to date has been circumstantial. Although the map evidence seems to fit Whale Cove quite well, there are powerful arguments for a number of other locations. Unless archaeological evidence is unearthed at one of the locations, the controversy is likely to continue.

Whether Drake reached the coast as far north as the Strait of Juan de Fuca is also likely to remain a puzzle. There are

some interesting pieces of evidence, however. Just south of Cape Flattery, at the entrance to the strait, is an old Makah native village called Ozette, which was buried by a massive mudslide in about 1600. It was excavated by archaeologists in the 1970s, and a European bead and some brass tacks were among the items found. It is possible that the brass items and the bead came from Drake's ship; certainly the other possibilities seem relatively remote.

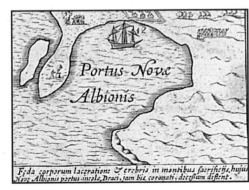

Map 3A
Inset in Map 3, above: *Portius Nova Albionis*

Drake's harbor on the northwest coast, the location of which has been the subject of debate for centuries.

On his return to England in 1580, Drake had presented Queen Elizabeth I with the chart of his voyage and his journal. Both of these have been lost, and it seems likely that the official policy of secrecy was the reason. Drake was considered a pirate by the Spanish, and Queen Elizabeth had to be careful when officially backing him. Drake brought back 10 tons of silver and 101 pounds of gold. In addition, if he had in fact "discovered" what he thought might be a Northwest Passage, then it would have been considered vital to keep this knowledge very secret indeed. Spain and England were at war until 1588, after which the need for secrecy declined.

One theory is that Drake actually did sail into the Strait of Juan de Fuca but did not continue eastwards or northwards because he was laden with treasure and expected, following the accounts of Sir Humphrey Gilbert, to encounter ice packs on the way through. He did not want to take that risk.

Following Drake's return to England, the official policy of secrecy meant that Drake's map was available only to a privileged few. The loss of the original since (it was thought to have perished in a fire in the late seventeenth century) meant that copies and derived maps are all we have left.

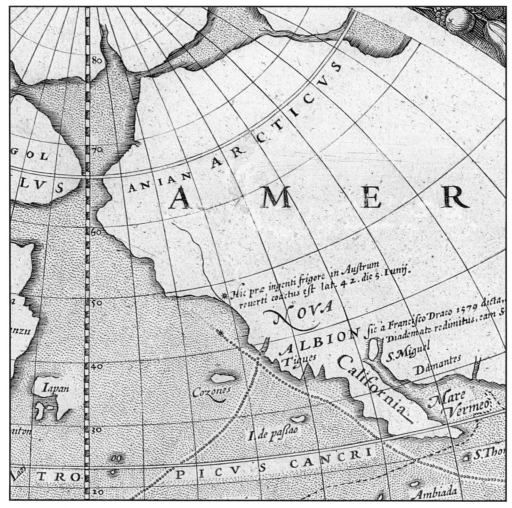

Map 3B (above)
Detail from *Vera Totius Expeditionis Nauticae descriptio D. Franc. Draci....Addita est etiam viva delineatio navigationes Thomea Caundish...* Joducus Hondius, Amsterdam, 1589.
Note the Strait of Anian forming a Northwest Passage to the eastern side of the North American continent.

Map 4 *(below)*
La Herdike [sic, Heroike] *Enterprinse Faict par de Signeur Draeck d'avoir Cirquit Toute la Terre*
Nicola van Sype, c.1583
"The French Drake Map"

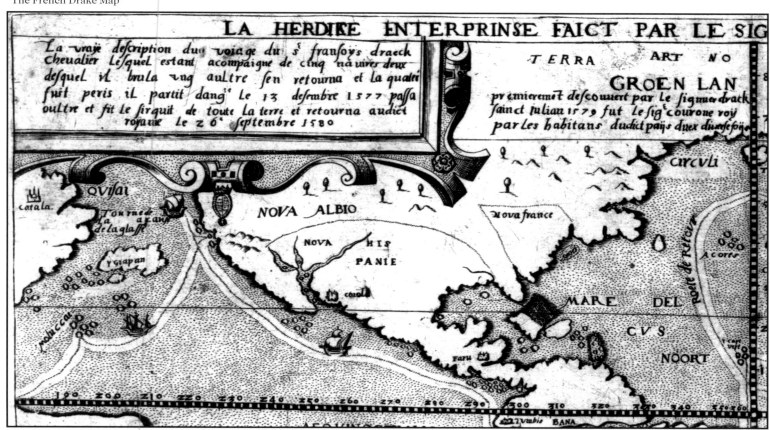

Three maps in particular are known to have been derived from the original, the so-called "Queen's Map". The first is a manuscript map now known as the Drake-Mellon map, dated September 1580, very soon after Drake's return, although other routes of Drake are also shown, indicating that it was not drawn until about 1586. An earlier map is one by Nicola van Sype, probably drawn in 1583 (Map 4). This map also shows Drake's track, and this time north of Portus Nova Albionis, but it conveniently disappears behind a cartouche! This map also shows "Novo Albio" stretching across North America. The map has a statement that it was seen and corrected by Drake. Presumably it was the original copied by van Sype that was seen and corrected, though it may be a second-generation copy.

A later printed map derived from the Queen's map is the 1589 world map by the famous mapmaker Joducus Hondius. This was reissued six years later surrounded by text, in Dutch, of an account of Drake's voyage, and for this reason is commonly known as the Drake Broadside map. This has the inset of Portus Nova Albionis in the top left-hand corner, and is virtually the same as the Hondius 1589 map (Map 3) shown on page 11.

In showing the world as a double hemisphere, using a stereographic projection recently made popular by Rumold Mercator with his 1587 world map (see Map 7, page 14), Hondius created room for decorative devices and pictures. This one includes a portrait of Queen Elizabeth I and a picture of Drake's ship, the *Golden Hind,* in the bottom center (Map 3, page 11). Hondius has marked on the coast of Nova Albion that Drake turned back at 42° N because of the cold (Map detail, Map 3B, opposite). There are indications on this map that the track was first marked continuing to about 48° N and was then partially deleted from the plate; an interesting correction indeed! Hondius may have corrected it after reading an account of the voyage by Richard Hakluyt, which itself may have been edited at the Queen's direction.

In 1647 the son of one of Drake's financial backers, Sir Robert Dudley, produced an atlas, *Dell Arcano del Mare,* which was published in Florence. Some of the coastal features on the map of the northwestern coast of America have been compared to modern coastal features, specifically Cape Flattery, Gray's Harbor, and the entrance to the Columbia River. Since Dudley's father was in a position to have had direct information from Drake this map is of particular interest.

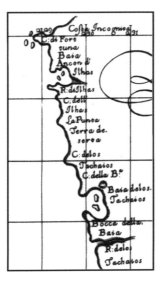

Map 5A (left) Detail from Map 5, the *Carta particolare,* below.

Does this show (from north to south) Cape Flattery, Grays Harbor, and the entrance to the Columbia?

Sir Francis Drake and world maps.

Map 5 (below)
Carta particolare della stretto di Iezo Pra l'America e l'Isola Iezo D'America Carta XXXIII Robert Dudley, 1647. From *Dell Arcano del Mare* (sea atlas), Florence, 1647. Engraved by Antonio Francesco Lucini.

Dell Arcano del Mare was a sea atlas, intended to be used for navigation. It was the first English sea atlas, the first sea atlas of the entire world, and one of the first, if not the first, on Mercator's projection, on which straight lines are lines of constant bearing. A massive undertaking, the atlas was made up of 146 charts, which took twelve years to engrave and utilized 5,000 lbs (2,270 kg) of copperplate.

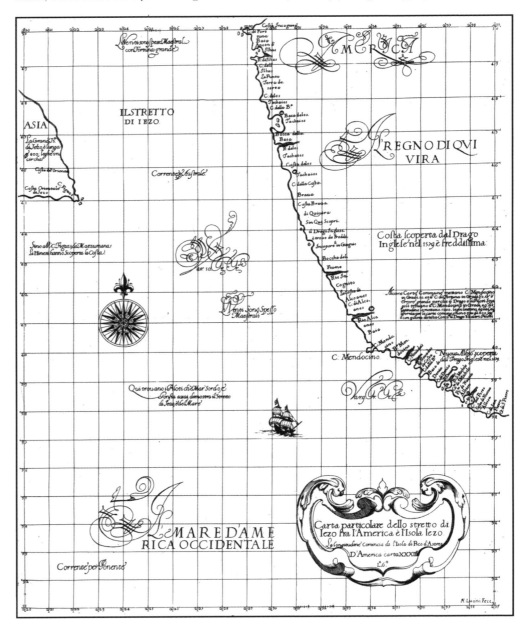

THE MICHAEL LOK MAP OF 1582

The first map to record the presence of Francis Drake on the west or northwest coast of America was published in a book by Richard Hakluyt in 1582. The map (Map 6) was by Michael Lok, of whom we shall hear more (see page 16).

The poor representation of the continent was based on a map Lok possessed which had been given by Giovanni da Verrazano to Henry VIII. Verrazano, who had sailed along the eastern coast of North America in 1524 had mistaken the waters over the sandbanks at Pamlico Sound in today's North Carolina for the eastern sea, the *mare orientale*. He otherwise produced a reasonably good map of the east coast, which was published by his brother, Gerolamo da Verrazano, in 1529. Verrazano Narrows in New York Harbor are named after Giovanni.

Lok showed the sea "discovered" by Verrazano as a gulf of the Pacific. The legend against the coast listing the voy-

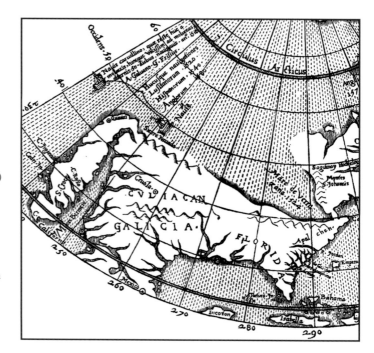

Map 6
Illustri Viro, Domino Philippo Sidnaes Michael Lok Civis Londinensis Hanc Chartam Dedicabat: 1582
(Michael Lok's map of 1582.)
From: Richard Hakluyt, *Divers Voyages touching the Discoverie of America,* London, 1582.

Anglorum navigationes 1580 on this map was the first record of Drake's voyage on a printed map.

ages to the region ends *"Anglorum navigationes 1580"*. Though Lok was out by one year, this is the first record of Drake's voyage on a printed map. The depiction of the Pacific Northwest has a long way to go from here!

The Lok map was intended to be given to English expeditions looking for the Northwest Passage. It was thought it might fall into the hands of the Spanish, and so New Albion or Drake are not mentioned on this map.

RUMOLD MERCATOR'S MAP OF 1587

This world map by Rumold Mercator (Map 7, above), published in Geneva in 1587, precedes the general knowledge of Drake's discoveries, showing the mythical Quivira, Anian, and Bergi but not yet Nova Albion. North America is *America sive India Nova*, "America or the New Indies". The general concept of the west coast separated from Asia by a strait is remarkably accurate considering it was totally speculative.

The shape of the west coast of North America on this map is derived from the 1569 world map by Gerard Mercator, Rumold's father (Map 1, page 8). This was the map in which Mercator first used his famous projection, the Mercator Projection, in which straight lines are lines of constant bearing, tremendously significant for navigators. However, Mercator's new projection was not widely accepted at first, and this lack of acceptance is underlined by the fact that when his son Rumold copied his map and republished it in 1587 (the map shown here), he replotted it as a more traditional double hemisphere.

The shape of the west coast shown in this map was copied by others as well, perhaps by Mercator's friend Abraham

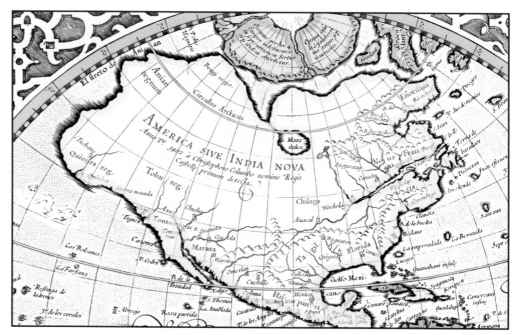

Map 7
Orbis Terrae Compendiosa Descriptio. Rumold Mercator, Geneva, 1587.

Ortelius in his *Theatrum Orbis Terrarum* (Theater of the World), published in 1570. In reality, as was common at the time, it is not clear who copied whom. Certainly the elder Mercator was greatly

respected in his day, and thus his maps were often not questioned the way they perhaps should have been.

THE FIRST MAP OF THE PACIFIC NORTHWEST

Ever since Francisco Vasquez de Coronado searched what is now the American southwest in 1540 – 1542 for a mythical city rich in gold called Quivira, the Spanish continued to speculate about such fabulous kingdoms to the north. Add to this the belief in a navigable strait to the Atlantic, the Strait of Anian, and you have the main ingredients for this map, which can be said to be the first map specifically of the Pacific Northwest.

Normally mapmakers tended to hide parts of the world when they had little information about them or to make them disappear off the edge or place them behind an illustrative engraving. Not so with the Dutch mapmaker Cornelius de Jode, who in 1593 produced this whole map of a relatively unknown part of the world – the Pacific Northwest.

The map combines the fantasies with the geographical knowledge of the day. Here is the mythical Quivira, plus Anian and Bergi, two kingdoms transplanted to the New World from Marco Polo's Asia. Cape Mendocino is shown at 40° N, close to its real location. The Arctic is shown according to an earlier map of Gerard Mercator, which showed only the Arctic regions, itself derived from a medieval text (see Map 1, page 8).

Map 8
Quivirae Regnu cum alijs versus Borea

From the second edition of a 1578 atlas of Gerard de Jode, *Speculum Orbis Terrae*, revised by his son Cornelius de Jode in 1593. This map appeared only in the 1593 edition and is the work of Cornelius.
Gerard and Cornelius de Jode were Antwerp mapmakers. A *speculum*, like a *theatrum*, was an early word used to describe a collection of maps. It was Gerard Mercator who first used the term we use today, the *atlas*.

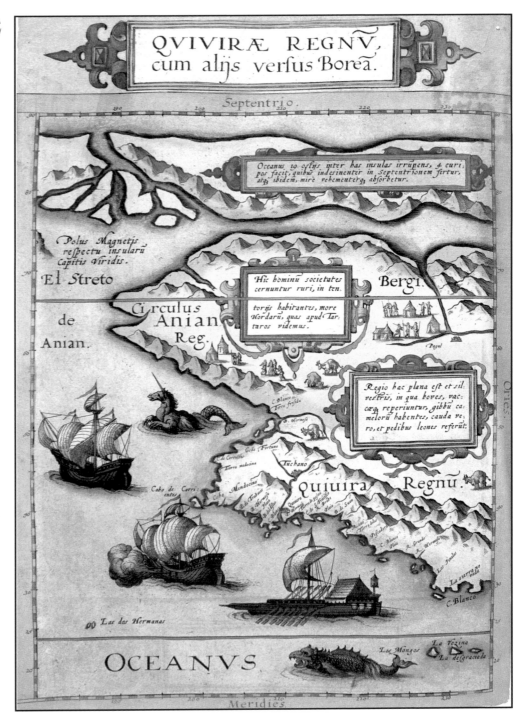

THOMAS CAVENDISH – THE SECOND ENGLISH CIRCUMNAVIGATION

For two decades after Drake's voyage, there is no documentation of any other Europeans visiting the northwest coast, but others may have, despatched by Queen Elizabeth to find the Northwest Passage or simply collect silver and gold from the Spanish. For instance, Drake's comrade Thomas Cavendish led a foray of two ships into the Pacific in 1587. Only one ship, the *Desire*, with Cavendish as captain, made it back to England, making

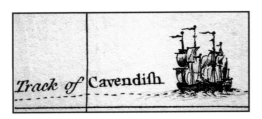

Track of Thomas Cavendish's ship *Desire*, a detail from the Pacific Ocean shown on a map from Thomas Jefferys' *American Atlas*, published in 1775 (see Map 56, page 35).

Cavendish the second Englishman to circumnavigate the globe. The other ship may have been lost when it deserted Cavendish to find a quicker way back to England via the Northwest Passage. A captive Spanish pilot on board Cavendish's ship *Desire* is reported to have stated that *"the other ship, as he supposed, was gone for the Northwest Passage, standing in 55°."* [15]

THE 1606 MAP OF JODUCUS HONDIUS

This part of a world map, published in Amsterdam by Joducus Hondius in 1606, shows the northwest coast and the Strait of Anian. Drake's Nova Albion is featured prominently. Hondius took over the Mercator map-publishing business at the end of the sixteenth century.

Map 9 (right)
Septentrio America. Joducus Hondius, 1606.

THE 1597 WYTFLIET MAP – THE FIRST AMERICAN ATLAS

Map 10

Limes Occidentis Quiuira et Anian 1597
From: Cornelius Wytfliet, *Descriptionis Ptolemaicae Augmentum sive Occidentis Notitia Breui commentario illustrata studio et opera...MDXCVIII,* 1597.
The first printed atlas of America.

This map of the northwest coast was only the second specifically of that region. It was published by Cornelius Wytfliet in 1597 in *Descriptionis Ptolemaicae Augmentum,* the first printed atlas of America. The atlas was intended to be a modern supplement to the *Cosmographia* of Ptolemy, the Alexandrian astronomer of the fourth century B.C. whose maps were rediscovered and printed from 1475 onwards. As Ptolemy's maps necessarily covered only the known world in his time, Wytfliet resolved to publish a western hemisphere addendum, a 192-page regional description of the Americas. This map was one of the maps in the atlas.

Cape Mendocino is correctly shown at about 40° N, the mythical Quivira in northern California, and the empty regions of Anian correspond to modern-day Alaska. A Northwest Passage above the Arctic Circle is perhaps suggested by this map.

THE VOYAGE OF JUAN DE FUCA – REAL OR IMAGINARY?

Juan de Fuca, after whom the Strait of Juan de Fuca was named by Charles Barkley in 1787 (see page 62), was the legendary Greek pilot of a Spanish ship. The story is that he sailed north to the strait in 1592. An account of his voyage was given to Michael Lok, an English promoter of the idea of a Northwest Passage (Map 6, page 14), and the account was published in Samuel Purchas' *Purchas His Pilgrimes* in 1625.

According to the narrative, Juan de Fuca sailed north

...untill he came to the Latitude of fortie seven degrees, and that there finding that the land trended North and North-east, with a broad Inlet of sea, betweene 47.

and 48. degrees of Latitude; hee entered thereinto, sayling therein more than twenty dayes, and found that Land trending sometime North-west and North-east, and North, and also East and South-eastward, and very much broader Sea then was at the said entrance, and that he passed by divers Ilands in that sayling.

This sounds remarkably like sailing through the Strait of Juan de Fuca and into the Strait of Georgia, past the San Juan Islands, but it could, of course, just be coincidence.

There was a pilot named Juan de Fuca in New Spain between 1588 and 1594. Other parts of his description of his voyage do seem correct; for example, he said

there was an *"exceeding high pinnacle or spired rock like a piller thereupon"* at the entrance to the strait, although he said it was on the north side rather than the south side, where there really is a pillar (see illustration at the bottom of Charles Duncan's map of the Strait of Juan de Fuca, Map 100, page 62).

Whether or not Juan de Fuca really did make this voyage is perhaps less significant than the fact that it was widely believed by mapmakers for centuries thereafter and an inland sea, later named The Sea of the West, was added to allow for the twenty days sailing de Fuca refers to in his narrative. This sea became an enduring myth shown on many maps (see, for example, Map 37, page 27).

THE VOYAGE OF SEBASTIÁN VIZCAÍNO

In 1602, the Spanish navigator Sebastián Vizcaíno sailed north from Acapulco, following the course taken by Cabrillo some sixty years earlier (see page 9). He did not appear to have Cabrillo's charts with him, however, because he rediscovered San Diego. He also discovered the harbor at Monterey. Vizcaíno, or at least his pilot or his cosmographer, made charts of the entire coast from Cabo San Lucas to Cape Mendocino, copies of which, made a year later by Enrico Martínez "cosmographer to his Majesty in this New Spain", have survived. One section, the northernmost chart of Cape Mendocino, is shown here (Map 12). It took another 200 years, however, for the summary chart of the entire voyage to be published by the Spanish in 1802 (Map 11).

The reports of the details of this voyage are often contradictory, but it appears that one of the ships, commanded by ensign Martín de Aguilar, after being separated from other ships in a storm, was forced northward beyond Cape Blanco and, on returning southward, came across a bay with a large river which they named Rio Santa Ines. This river, because of its strong current and east-west direction, was thought to perhaps be the fabled Strait of Anian.

Since the ship was by now undermanned, no exploration was carried out, but the resulting reports of the Rio Santa Ines revived interest in a passage from the Pacific to the Atlantic, and this concept was to confuse the cartography of the Pacific Northwest for almost two centuries. The "Entrada de Martín Aguilar", or "Opening discovered by Martin Aguilar" on English maps, was to show up on many maps for a long time after. Later, its supposed location somehow became about 43° N, and some thought it might be the Strait of Juan de Fuca.

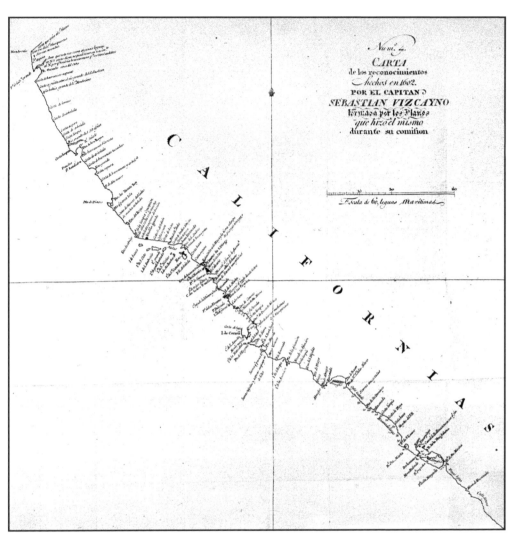

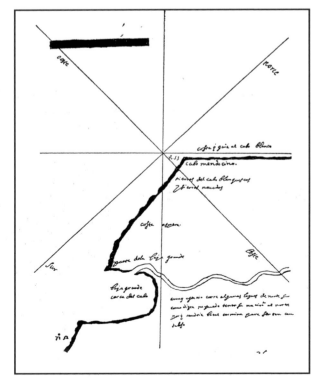

Map 12 (right)
Map of Cape Mendocino from Vizcaíno's 1602 voyage, perhaps by Fray Antonio de la Ascension. Copy by Enrico Martínez.

The most northerly of a series of coastal maps drawn soon after the 1602 voyage.

Map 11 (above)
Carta de los reconociemientos hechos en 1602 por El Capitan Sebastian Vizcayno Formaoa por los Planos que hizo el mismo durante su comision (Map of the reconnaisance carried out in 1602 by Captain Sebastian Vizcayno, made from his plans drawn during this voyage.)
From: *Relación del Viage...* Atlas No.4, 1802

This summary map showing the discoveries of Sebastián Vizcaíno took exactly 200 years to be published! Due to the Spanish policy of secrecy, the information was suppressed until the Spanish government belatedly realized that the published works of British navigators such as James Cook and George Vancouver were jeopardizing Spanish claims to the northwest coast by right of prior discovery. It was finally published in 1802 in the *Relación*, an important work described in more detail on page 79.

VIRGINIA TO THE PACIFIC?

In 1651, John Farrer, an agent of the Virginia Company, published a map of Virginia in which he also managed to show Drake's discovery of New Albion. It appeared in a sixteen-page booklet which described the travels of one Edward Bland, and others, in Virginia. The Pacific coast, complete with Drake's portrait, is shown as only ten days' march from the headwaters of the James River in Virginia.

This mistake came about from a continuing belief by some, following Verrazano over a century before, that the Pacific was very close to the east coast of America at this point, and the width of the North American continent was small. The underestimation of the width of North America, though not, of course, to this extent, was common on maps until those of James Cook and George Vancouver in the late eighteenth century, largely due to the problem of measuring longitude.

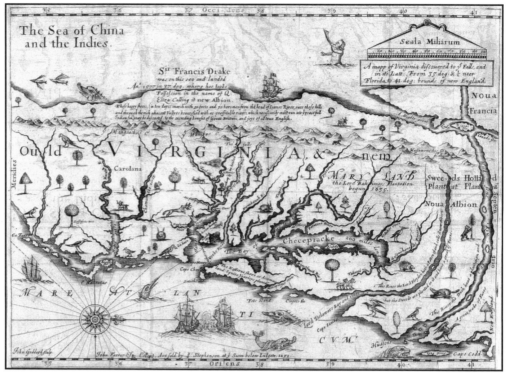

Map 13
A mapp of Virginia discovered to ye Falls and in it's Latt. From 35 deg. & ¹/₂ neer Florida to 41 deg. bounds of new England. John Farrer. From: Edward Bland, *The Discovery of New Brittaine,* 1651. The notation under Drake's picture, reads: *"Sir Francis Drake was on this sea and landed Ano 1577 in 37 deg. where he took Possession in the name of Q: Eliza calling it new Albion. Whole happy shores, (in 10 dayes march with 50 foote and 30 horsemen from the head of James River, over those hills and through the rich adjacent Valleyes beautyfied with as proffitable rivers, which necessarily must run into ye peaceful Indian Sea,) may be discovered to the exceeding benefit of Great Britain, and joye of all true English."*

THE VAN KEULEN SEA ATLASES

During the seventeenth and well into the eighteenth centuries, the Dutch were pre-eminent in the production of maps. One of the fields the Dutch were known for was the publishing of sea atlases, which focused on mapping the seas and oceans of the world. The most respected producers of these atlases were the van Keulens, Johannes and his son Gerard.

By this time the shape of much of the world was approaching what we today would recognize as correct. The major exceptions to this were Australasia and the Pacific Northwest, both in turn destined to have their outlines revealed by Captain James Cook. The map of the Pacific Northwest shown here was drawn by Johannes van Keulen about 1690, but the

map of this particular part of the world was virtually identical in their atlases into the 1760s, reflecting the dearth of real knowledge of the region until Cook. The company founded by Johannes and his son survived for two centuries, finally disappearing in the 1880s.

Map 14
Map of the Pacific Ocean. Johannes van Keulen. Amsterdam, c1700.

Shows the Straits of Anian – the Northwest Passage – north of California, which is shown as an island, as it was on many maps of this period. To the west are the mythical lands of Company Land and Esso. This early van Keulen map is a portolan-style map, using many rhumb lines, lines of constant bearing; the van Keulens were among the first to switch to the Mercator projection, in which straight lines are lines of constant bearing, as this was a particularly useful attribute for a navigational map.

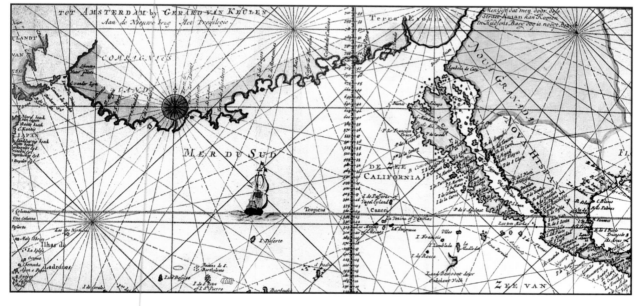

NICHOLAS SANSON'S MAPPE-MONDE

This map is part of a beautifully illuminated double-hemisphere world map published in Paris in 1705. It sums up the knowledge of the North Pacific at the time, which was, as can be seen, very little, erroneous, and mythical, but nevertheless generally believed. The western coast of North America ends at the northern tip of the island of California, itself another enduring myth. The mythical "Jesso or Company Land" fills the ocean. "Company Land" was supposedly a land discovered by a Dutch ship, captain unknown, named the *Castricom,* in the middle of the seventeenth century. "Gama Land", also reputedly discovered in the mid seventeenth century by Jean de Gama (again it is not known who he was), "Jesso," and "Company Land" are often shown and confused on maps of this period. Bering was to search for them in 1741; had he not been convinced of their existence, the 1741 expedition may well have had a less tragic end for him (see page 22).

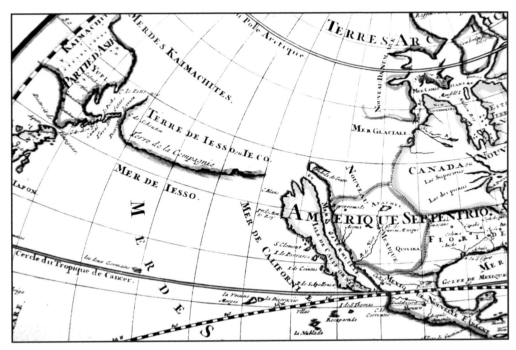

Map 15
Mappe-Monde geographique ou description general du globe terrestre et aquatique
Nicholas Sanson, c.1705. Pierre Mortier, Amsterdam.

GIANTS ON THE NORTHWEST COAST

The novelist Jonathan Swift used the lack of real knowledge of the northwest coast to construct his own version for his famous novel *Gulliver's Travels.* In the second book, published in 1726, Gulliver's ship is caught in a fearful storm, *"so that the oldest sailor on board could not tell in what part of the World we were."*

The novel included a map based on supposed reality but merging into fantasy north of what was known, for that is where he placed his land of the giants, Brobdingnag, complete with the notation "Discovered A.D. 1703".

South of Brobdingnag Swift placed the Straits of Anian, and further south yet New Albion and Port of Sir Francis Drake and Cape Mendocino. This interesting merging of fact and fiction was perhaps entirely reasonable given the state of geographical knowledge at the time – who was to say what was north of New Albion?

Map 16
The northwest coast according to Jonathan Swift in 1726.
From his novel *Travels... by Lemuel Gulliver;* from an edition between 1726 and 1766.

It is perhaps ironic that Swift, as the perpetrator of this and other maps which placed fictional lands in unknown parts of otherwise factual maps, was also the author of the famous quatrain, which made fun of the fact that mapmakers of the day often used pictures on their maps to fill in areas about which they had no information:

So Geographers in Afric-maps
With Savage-Pictures fill their gaps;
And o'er uninhabitable Downs
Place Elephants for Want of Towns. [19]

"*... it was ever my Opinion, that there must be a Balance of Earth to counterpoise the great Continent of Tartary; and therefore (geographers) ought to correct their Maps and Charts, by joining this vast Tract of Land to the North-west parts of America, wherein I shall lend them my Assistance.*" – Swift's Gulliver

VITUS BERING'S FIRST VOYAGE

In 1724 – 1725, Tsar Peter the Great decided that he wanted to know if and where Russia and America were separated, and how far north the Spanish might have encroached towards the far side of his domain. A Danish captain, Vitus Bering, was employed to lead an expedition to find out. Peter must have realized that Russia might even be encroaching on Spanish claims to the west coast of America. In February 1725, he instructed Bering:

[You are instructed] *to find out where it* [Asia] *joins America and ... seek out some city in European possession; or if a European ship is sighted, inquire of it what it* [the city] *is called and make a note of it; and go ashore on the coast itself and get first-hand information; and having put it on a map, return.*

Dispatched by Peter's widow, Catherine, it took three more years for Bering to actually reach the eastern shore of the Kamchatka Peninsula so he could begin his voyage, so bad were the travelling conditions in Siberia at the time. Just getting to the Pacific was a considerable feat.

Finally, in August 1728, Bering sailed his ship, the *St. Gabriel (Sviatoi Gavriil)*, into the strait which now bears his name. However, contrary to popular belief, he was not able to see the American side of the strait, due to fog, and went only as far north as 67° N, leaving open the possibility that the continents were joined above that latitude.

One of Bering's men, Petr Avraamovich Chaplin, compiled maps of the eastern part of Russia showing Bering's route and the presumed shape of the eastern coast; however, no American shore was shown, presumably simply because Bering had not seen it.

That was achieved four years later by Mikhail Gwosdev. In 1732 he reached what is now Cape Prince of Wales at the tip of the Seward Peninsula in Alaska, and, for the first time, produced a map showing the relationship of Asia and America (Map 18). The words east of Gwosdev's landfall read *"bolshaya zemlya"* (great land).

In fact, the first person to have proved that Asia and America were separate was probably an illiterate Siberian Cossack named Semen Dezhnev in 1648, eighty

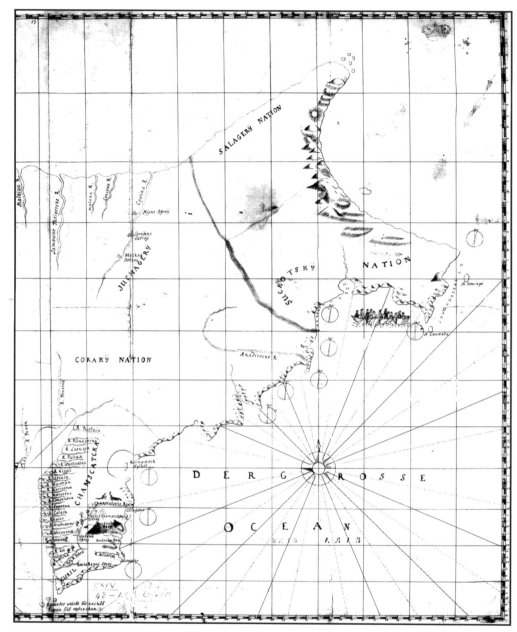

Map 17
Diese Charte uber Siberien nimt isren aufang zu Tobolske Ostwerts bis au die enferste Grentze von Sutotsky gemacst unter dem commendo des Capt Comandeurs Bering Ao 1729.
A German copy of 1729 map of Bering's discoveries, drawn by P.A. Chaplin, one of Bering's officers. It is significant that although this map shows that Asia has an eastern shore, it does *not* show the coast of North America.

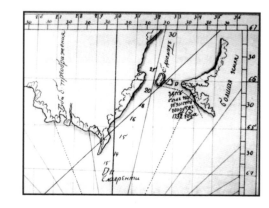

Map 18 (right)
Map by Martin Spanberg of the voyage of Mikhail Gwosdev, 1732.
This map does show the western shore of the North American continent, the land to the right in this map.

years before Bering. He sailed from the Kolyma River, which flows to the Arctic Ocean, round the eastern tip of Asia to a point near the Anadir River, which flows into the Pacific. However, he kept no journal and produced no maps, not a good way to preserve one's exploits for posterity! It was not until Gerhard Müller, a member of the Russian Academy of Sciences who himself was later to make a highly significant contribution to the emerging picture of what the northwest coast really looked like (see page 29), uncovered some reports in 1736 of Dezhnev's voyage that it was realized that what Bering had been sent to do had already been done. Müller published an account of the Dezhnev voyage in 1758, arousing considerable interest; it in fact became a factor in the decision to send James Cook to the north Pacific to look for a northwest, or northeast, passage between Europe and the Pacific.

Map 19
Sketch illustrating Bering's first voyage in 1728. Drawn by Joseph-Nicolas de L'Isle based on his conversation with Bering, c1732.

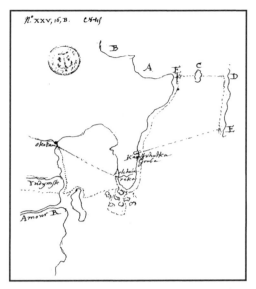

Map 20
Sketch illustrating Gwosdev's voyage in 1732. Drawn by Joseph-Nicolas de L'Isle, c1732. Finally, the coast of the North American continent is shown.

THE DU HALDE MAP REVEALS RUSSIAN DISCOVERIES

There was considerable secrecy surrounding the first Bering expedition in 1728. Russia wanted to keep its activities and discoveries secret from Spain in particular because of competing claims to the northwest coast. Apart from a small article in a St. Petersburg newspaper that slipped out, nothing was known about the expedition until 1735, when a book was published in France by Jean Baptiste du Halde which almost in-

cidentally, at the end of the four volumes, gives an account of Bering's voyage, accompanied by a map. This was translated into English and published the next year, 1736, with the catchy title of *A General History of China Containing a Geographical, Historical, Chronological, Political, and Physical Description of the Empire of China, Chinese Tartary and Thibet.* The map was also reproduced, and it is this map from the English edition, published

a year later, which is shown here (Map 21). Demonstrating as much of Bering's travails in getting to the Pacific coast as the voyage itself, the map was drawn by Joseph Nicolas de L'Isle, who was to feature large in future misleading maps of the north Pacific (see page 26), but who for once produced a reasonably accurate map. It was the first the world had noticed of Bering, and the first published map relating to his voyage.

Map 21
A Map of the Country which Capt.n Beerings past through in his Journey from Tobolsk to Kamtschatka.

Drawn by Joseph-Nicolas de L'Isle, based on a map by Jean-Baptiste Bourguignon d'Anville.
From: Jean Baptiste du Halde, *The General History of China,* London, 1736.
(English translation of 1735 French edition.)

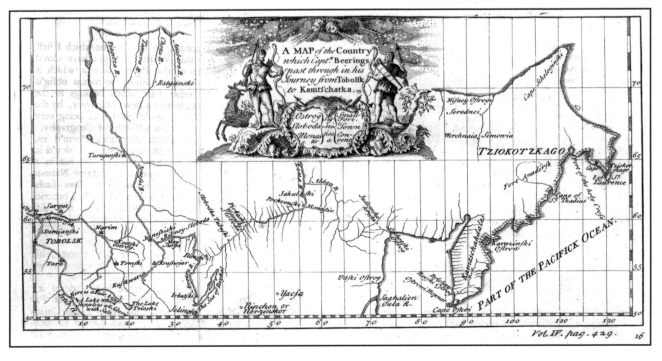

VITUS BERING'S SECOND VOYAGE

Vitus Bering was not pleased with the results of his first expedition, and in 1730 proposed to lead another which would go much farther eastward and discover more exactly the position of North America. It would be part of a larger scientific effort including the exploration of eastern Siberia, so that the whole scheme is often referred to as the Second Kamchatka Expedition, and this name appears on some of the maps. Bering's voyage would also discover whether the previously mapped (see Maps 14 and 15, pages 18 – 19) speculative lands of Esso or Jesso, Gama Land, or Company Land existed. These were lands claimed to have been sighted by various navigators in the seventeenth century, and they showed up on maps now and again either as islands or as part of North America as cartographers strove to reconcile conflicting accounts.

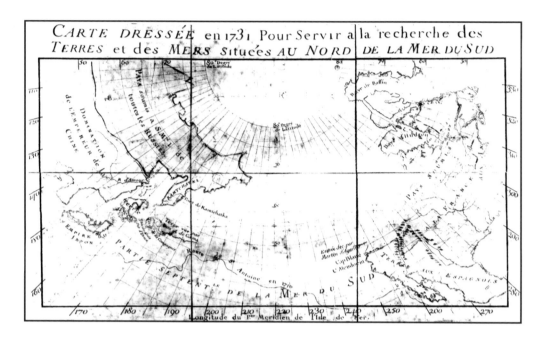

Map 23
Nova et Accuratissima Totius Terrarum Orbis Tabula Auctoribus R en I Ottens Amsterdam 1745. From Atlas van Zeevaert en Koophandel door de Geheele Weereldt, 1745.

A wide gulf of emptiness fills the space between Asia and America on this map, typical of maps of the period. The North American mainland ends at Cape Blanco. The map shows lands discovered by "Dom Juam de Gama" [sic] southeast of Kamchatka.
Reinier and Joshua Ottens were Dutch mapmakers. Compare this map with the similar map by Nicholas Sanson: Map 15, page 19.

After much preparation and years getting to Kamchatka again, two ships, the *St. Peter* and the *St. Paul (Sviatoi Petr* and *Sviatoi Pavel),* under the command of Bering and Alexei Chirikov, sailed from Petropavlovsk in the spring of 1741.

When Bering and Chirikov sailed, they used as their guide a largely speculative map which had been prepared by Joseph-Nicolas de L'Isle, who, as we will see later, was responsible for some of the worst – or most imaginative – of the speculative maps of the northwest coast. The map, drawn in 1731 and revised in 1733, was drawn, according to de L'Isle's own memoir, *"for the purpose of helping in the discovery of the shortest route between Asia and America"* (Map 22, above). The map mercifully showed a lot of blank space in the regions that Bering's expedition was about to sail to, blank being better than totally hypothetical. The maps did, however, show the speculative Gama Land – land supposedly seen by Jean de Gama – southeast of Kamchatka.

In seeking these imaginary lands, Bering's officers – including Joseph-Nicolas de L'Isle's brother-in-law Louis de L'Isle de la Croyère – decided, democratically, as was the custom at that time in such circumstances, to sail southeast towards this "land". The logic was that since the map had been provided to them by the Academy of Sciences, it must be correct!

The famous historian H.H. Bancroft put it succinctly:

The absurdity of sending out an expedition for discovery, requiring it to follow mapped imagination, seems never to have occurred to the Solons of St. Petersburg, and this when they knew well enough (from the first Bering expedition) that the continents were not far asunder toward the north. [22]

Of course the two ships found nothing, but as a result of this course, they ran into storms and became separated, never to find each other again. Each continued by itself towards North America.

On 17 July 1741 the log of Bering's ship *St. Peter* recorded sighting high snow-covered mountains, and among them a high volcano. This was Mt. St. Elias; Bering had finally reached the North American mainland. On 20 July, some of Bering's crew, led by Fleet Master Sofron Khitrov, were sent in the ship's longboat to land on an island, which Bering named St. Elias Island, as it was that saint's day. (Bering also named its most southerly point Cape St. Elias. Mt. St. Elias was given that name later. St. Elias Island is now called Kayak Island.)

Khitrov made a sketch map in his log book to show *"the position of the bay and the islands and their relation to the mainland"*. This was the first Russian map to show only part of the North American mainland. (Map 24). The representation of the mountains, as seen from the side, laid down on the coast, is unusual. The cloud-capped mountains shown on the mainland are Mt. St. Elias and adjacent peaks.

On the way back towards Siberia, Bering halted at the Shumagin Islands, on the east side of the Alaskan Peninsula; again Khitrov drew a map in his log book (Map 25). Nearing Petropavlovsk, Bering's ship was wrecked on an island now known as Bering Island, where Bering

Map 22 (page 22, left)
Carte Dressee en 1731 Pour Servir a la recherche des Terres et des Mers Situees Au Nord de la Mer du Sud
Joseph-Nicolas de L'Isle, 1731

A map that Bering carried with him on his 1741 voyage. Shows the imaginary lands of Yeso or Esso, Gama and Company, and the supposed route of *St. Antoine* to Baja California in 1710. The coast of North America north of Martín d'Aguilar's entrance (see page 17) is blank.

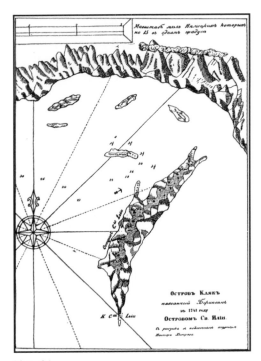

Map 24
Fleet master Sofron Khitrov's Sketch Map of St. Elias (Kayak) Island, 1741.

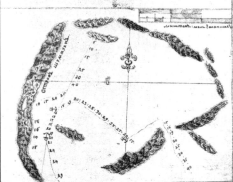

Map 25
Fleet Master Sofron Khitrov's Sketch Map of the Shumagin Islands, with log entries, 1741.

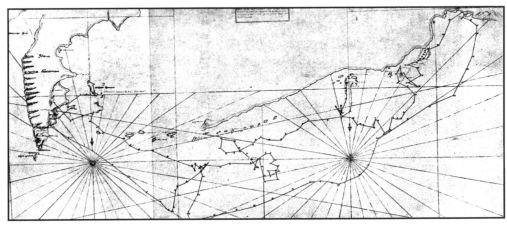

Map 26 (above)
Map of the known land of America, with the islands newly discovered under the command of the former Captain Commander Bering ... 1742.
A Russian map copy of Bering's voyage in 1741 and Waxell's continuation of the voyage after Bering's death in 1742.

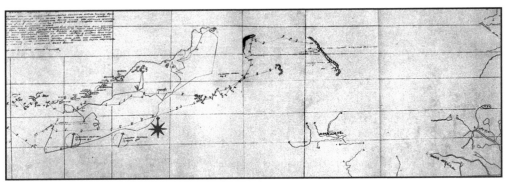

Map 27
Map of the voyage of Chirikov's expedition on the St Paul to America in 1741 and the discoveries of a number of Aleutian Islands and a part of the Alaskan coast, 1741

Note the correction of the position of the coast of what is today the Alaska panhandle as calculated onboard ship by dead reckoning and as observed once land was reached. This map was drawn in St Petersburg from the ship's logs.

and many of his crew perished. The survivors managed to make another ship from the wreckage of the first, and under Lieutenant Sven Waxell they finally made it back to Kamchatka in the spring of 1742.

Alexei Chirikov, with the *St. Paul*, fared better than Bering. He actually reached the North American coast ahead of Bering's landfall. He had a landfall just north of Dixon Entrance on 15 July 1741. However, in the ensuing days he lost both of his ship's boats and fourteen of his crew when they landed but did not return. Unable to land and unable to replenish his water supplies, he sailed for Petropavlovsk without touching land again.

The information gathered by Bering and Chirikov was significant. It allowed a considerable amount of the map of the northwest coast to be filled in, as the position of the mainland in relation to Asia was now reasonably fixed, as much as it could be in a time of dead reckon-

ing. Both Bering and Chirikov were out in their calculations of longitude. In addition, the fixing of points can still be, and was, misconstrued if the mapmaker wishes it. The map copied from Joseph-Nicolas de L'Isle of the northwest coast published in 1755 (see Map 34, page 26) marks the tracks of Bering and Chirikov reasonably accurately, but is still a hopeless speculation.

Chirikov's maps still show speculative geography south of his landfall (Map 27, above).

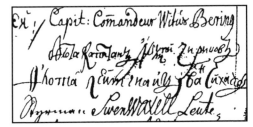

The signatures of Bering, Chririkov, Chikhachev, and Waxell, officers from the two ships, from a decision on which direction to sail. It was a Russian tradition that on voyages of exploration, the decision to sail a particular course was decided democratically.

JACQUES NICOLAS BELLIN'S ATTEMPTS AT REALISM

In contrast to the de L'Isle school of speculative geographers of the mid eighteenth century, the French cartographer Jacques Nicolas Bellin was one of the more responsible geographers of the day, publishing maps which were based on information available at the time, without embellishment.

That did not mean that all his maps were accurate, however, just drawn with a lot of gaps. His 1743 map of North America (Map 28, right) showed little of the northwest coast. The supposed position of Martín de Aguilar's Entrance (see page 17) was shown, and a River of the West was drawn flowing from a connection to Lake Superior nearly to the coast past the Mountain of Brilliant Stones. This mountain was an early name for the Rocky Mountains.

Bellin's 1763 and 1764 maps (Maps 29 and 30) have removed the River of the West but added the Sea of the West (Mer de l'Ouest). Obviously he did not want to discount all of de L'Isle's theories! Map 30 shows a western Alaskan coast with the notation that it was from discoveries in 1728; in fact Bering did not see the Alaskan coast. The outline of eastern Siberia is also relatively accurate, based on Bering in 1728. The map includes a note just south of the Arctic Circle that *"we don't know if this part is land or sea."*

The dates of these maps are confusing; both appeared in the same atlas published in 1764, yet obviously have differing dates. The information on Map 30 was present on Bellin's maps a decade earlier.

It is not surprising that Bellin endorsed the relatively responsible 1758 map of Müller (Map 40, page 29). In 1766, he essentially copied the Müller map in a map prepared for the French Depot de la Marine (Map 32, page 25). It connects the islands of the Aleutian chain with a tentative coastline as Müller had done, shows the landfalls of Bering and Chirikov in 1741 separately, as they were, and Bellin has now decided that the River of the West, excluded from his earlier maps, should flow to the Pacific via Martin de Aguilar's Entrance. This map was carried by the Spanish captain Bruno de Hezeta when he sailed to the northwest coast in 1775; he referred to it as his "principal guide" (see page 38).

Map 31 (above right) shows a later Bellin map which now incorporates information from Russian sources.

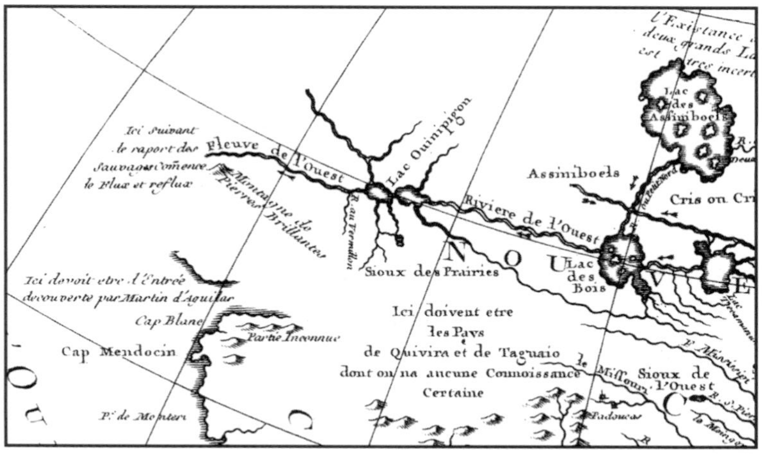

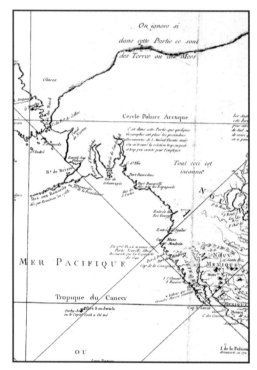

Map 28
Carte de L'Amerique Septentionale Pour servir a l'Histoire de la Nouvelle France
Jacques Nicolas Bellin, 1743

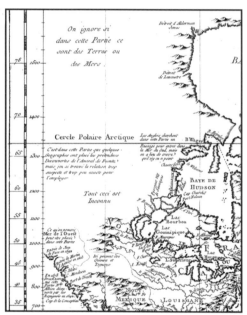

Map 29 (above)
Carte de Amerique et des Mers Voisines
From: J.N. Bellin, *La Petit Atlas Maritime Recueil de Cartes et Plans des Quatre Parties du Monde en Cinq Volumes, Vol 1, Amerique Septentrionale et Isles Antilles,* 1764, Map 2, 1763.

Map 31 (above)
Carte Reduite des Parties Connues Du Globe Terrestre Dressee au Depost des Cartes, Plans et Journaux de la Marine. Por les service des vaisseaux Du Roy
J. N. Bellin 1784.
Shows the Fox Islands in the Aleutians (Isles de Renards) as discovered by the Russian navigator "Krenitzin" [sic] in 1768 (see page 32), "Isles de Schumagin" as mapped by Khitrov (page 22), and the "Entree de Sandwich" (Cook's name for Prince William Sound), and there is still a notation about the supposed discoveries of Admiral Fonte (see page 26). Cook's King George's Sound (Nootka) is also shown.

Map 30 (left)
Carte Reduite du Globe Terrestre
From: J.N. Bellin, *La Petit Atlas Maritime Recueil de Cartes et Plans des Quatre Parties du Monde en Cinq Volumes, Vol 1, Amerique Septentrionale et Isles Antilles,* 1764, Map 1, no date.

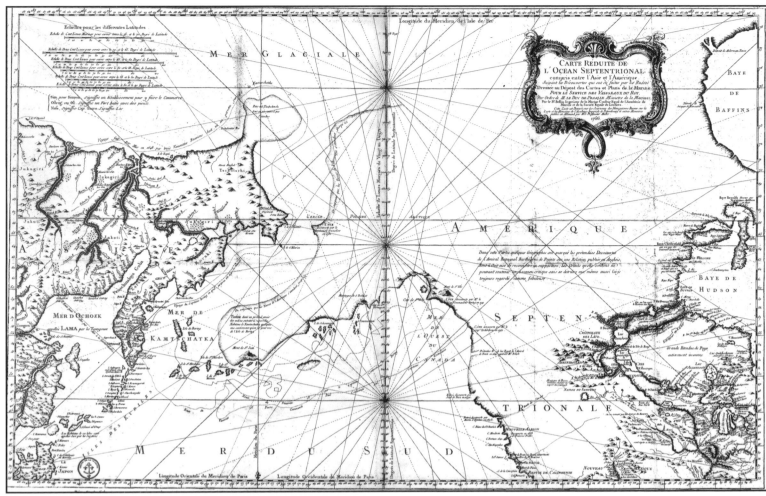

Map 32 (above)
*Carte Reduite de L'Ocean Septentriona*l. Jacques Nicolas Bellin, 1766.
Bellin's version of the 1754 and 1758 maps of Gerhard Müller (see
page 29). The north coast of the "Müller peninsula" is marked
"supposed land of America". Bering and Chirikov's tracks in 1741 are
marked. The "supposed river of de Fonte" (see next page) is marked.

THE LA FRANCE MAP OF 1744

This interesting piece of imaginary
cartography was constructed to satisfy
the wishful thinking of Arthur Dobbs, the
Surveyor General of Ireland, in 1744.
Dobbs was a promoter of the idea of a
Northwest Passage, and seemed to be pre-
pared to go to any lengths to prove that
one existed. Fleeing from the French, a
"French Canadese Indian" named Joseph
La France was taken to England in 1742,
and is reputed to have drawn a map for
Dobbs on the floor of a dining room in a
London tavern. It was this map, copied
and printed as evidence of Dobb's theory
that there was a Northwest Passage from
Hudson's Bay to the Pacific.

Map 33
*A New Map of Part of North America From The Latitude of 40 to 68
Degrees. Including the late discoveries made on Board the Furnace
Bomb Ketch in 1742. And the Western Rivers & Lakes falling into
Nelson River in Hudson's Bay as described by Joseph La France a
French Canadese Indian who Travaled into those Countries and Lakes
for 3 years from 1739 to 1742*
From: Arthur Dobbs, *An Account of the Countries Adjoining to
Hudsons Bay*, London, 1744.

THE MYSTERIOUS ADMIRAL FONTE –
THE MAPPING OF IMAGINATION

In 1708, a short-lived British magazine called *Memoirs for the Curious* published what purported to be a newly discovered account of a voyage into the northern Pacific Ocean by a Spanish admiral named Bartholemew de Fonte in 1640.

In sailing north along the coast, de Fonte was said to have entered a strait which led to a great inland sea and met a ship from Boston which had supposedly arrived through a Northwest Passage. Inconsistencies in this story plus modern geography show that this voyage was fictitious. Nevertheless, this account was widely read and was to have an effect on later explorers and mapmakers.

In 1744, the Surveyor General of Ireland, Arthur Dobbs, who was convinced of the existence of a Northwest Passage, used this account to bolster his case (see Map 33, previous page).

The chief culprit responsible for the introduction of the de Fonte account to the maps of the northwest coast of North America was the French geographer Joseph-Nicolas de L'Isle, the younger brother of the more famous French mapmaker Guillaume de L'Isle. Joseph-Nicolas spent twenty-one years at the Russian Academy of Sciences in St. Petersburg, and when he returned to Paris to join his brother-in-law Philippe Buache to produce maps, he brought with him some maps he had acquired from the Academy. In 1752 he published a map which showed previously unknown discoveries by the Russians. However, on the

northwest coast of America he constructed an elaborate speculative map using the de Fonte account as its basis (Map 41, page 29). Changed and further elaborated upon for a number of years, the imaginary part of the map was copied and again elaborated upon by others, most notably and spectacularly by Robert de Vaugondy, who in 1755 published another elaboration in Denis Diderot's *Encyclopedié, ou Dictionnaire Raisonne de Sciences, des Arts et des Metiers* (Map 34, below).

Another map published in the *Encyclopedié* was Philippe Buache's *Carte Des Nouvelles Découvertes* (Map 35), a

Map 34
Carte Generale Des Découvertes de l'Amiral de Fonte et autres navigateurs Espagnols Anglois et Russes pour la recherche du passage a la Mer du Sud par M. De L'Isle de l'Academie des Sciences etc. Robert de Vaugondy, 1755. From: Diderot's *Encyclopedié...* One of the most spectacular combinations of fact and fiction in a map of the Pacific Northwest. This map is also shown in the front endpaper.

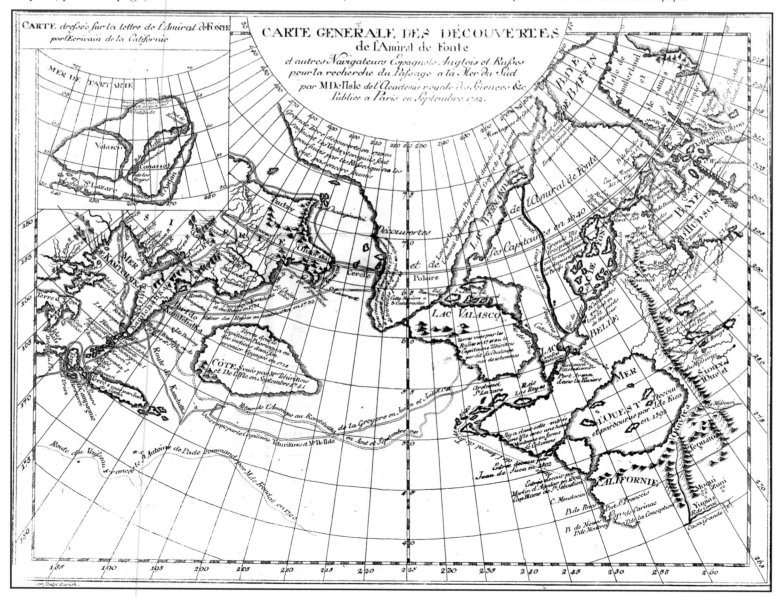

likewise fictitious and fantastic map of the northwest.

These maps demonstrate the extent to which total fabrications can become imbedded in knowledge, for the *Encyclopedié* was perhaps the most massive gathering of knowledge attempted in the eighteenth century, and was its most successful publishing venture. It had twenty-eight volumes, later expanded to thirty-five, with 8,000 articles and 3,000 plates, and represented the work of the leading French thinkers of the day, including, for example, Voltaire, Rousseau, Turgot, d'Holbach, and Quesnay. It was not only a comprehensive view of the knowledge of the day but also a manifesto of the Enlightenment, so much so that in 1759 it was banned by the King and the Church.

The maps show the supposed discoveries of Admiral de Fonte in the myriad of archipelagos and channels striking east towards Hudson's Bay. They also show the Mer L'Ouest (Sea of the West) supposedly discovered by Juan de Fuca in 1592 (see page 16). Kamchatka and the eastern coast of Siberia are shown relatively accurately, as is the track of Alexei Chirikov, who, with Vitus Bering, discovered the northwestern coast for Russia in 1741 (see page 22).

The reason for this relatively accurate track is that de L'Isle's brother-in-law, Louis de L'Isle de la Croyère, sailed with Chirikov as astronomer. Their landfall, however, was only a point, clearly easy to misinterpret in the context of a whole coastline.

The de Fonte myth showed up in many maps of this period. In 1776, the myth showed up in an Italian map by Antonio Zatta (Map ii, page 4), an artistically interesting but geographically appalling map. Another equally fantastic map by Amsterdam

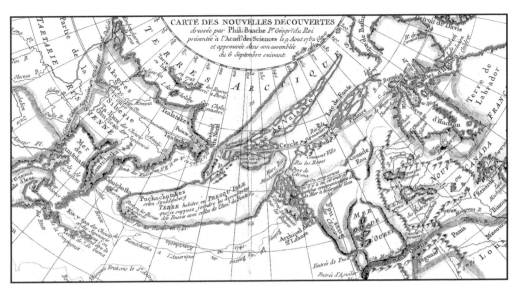

Map 35 (above)
Carte Des Nouvelles Découvertes dresse par Phil Buache, Pr. Geographer du Roi, presentee a L'Accad des Sciences le 9 Aoust 1752 et approuvee dans son assemblee de 6 Septembre suivant

Map 37
Mappe Monde ou Globe Terrestre en deux Plans Hemispheres. Dressee sur les observations de Mrss de L'Academie Royal Des Sciences.
Jean Covens and Corneille Mortier, c1780.
This superbly bizarre map shows a classic de Fonte Strait, a clear northwest passage to Hudson Bay. A huge Sea of the West stretches eastwards to Nebraska at about 98° W, Alaska is an island and Drake's New Albion is on a Californian peninsula!

Map 36
Carte Générale des Découvertes de L'Amiral de Fonte representant la grande probabilité d'un Passage au Nord Ouest par Thomas Jefferys Géographe du Roi à Londres 1768, French edition, 1780.
Thomas Jefferys was a believer of the idea of a Northwest Passage. This is his interpretation of the de Fonte myth.

mapmakers Jean Covens and Corneille Mortier (Map 37) dates from 1780, and also clearly shows the de Fonte strait.

James Cook's maps still left gaps in which the theoretical geographers could run riot, and it took the surveys of George Vancouver (page 85) finally to put an end to this cartographic nonsense.

JOHN GREEN TRIES TO SET THE RECORD STRAIGHT

The year 1752 had seen the publication in France of two of the more extreme interpretations of the geography of the Pacific Northwest, the Buache map (Map 35, previous page), and the de L'Isle map (Map 41, opposite).

A year later an Englishman, Bradock Mead, using the pen name John Green, produced a map of North and South America in six large sections in which he attempted to show the most recent discoveries of the Russians in the north Pacific in a much more responsible fashion.

These important maps were published by Thomas Jefferys in London in 1753, and the two sections relevant to the Pacific Northwest are shown here. Green also published at the same time a booklet called *Remarks in Support of the New Chart of North and South America in Six Sheets* in which he took the theoretical geographers to task.

He dissected the de Fonte story that de L'Isle had used to construct his map, maintaining that he had tried to *dazzle the Eyes of the Public with a grand Appearance of Rivers, Lakes, and Towns*", and concluded that

the discoveries ascribed to Admiral De Fonte have no real Existence in Nature; and that however commodiously they may help to fill-up a Map of the North-West Part of America, they ought in reality to have no Place there.

These parts, as yet wholly unknown are filled up, by Mess.rs Buache and Del'Isle, with the pretended Discoveries of Adm.l De Fonte and his Captains in 1640.

Notation on a later Jefferys map, also on Map 39 to the right of the margin, which says it all! (See Map 57, page 36, 1775.)

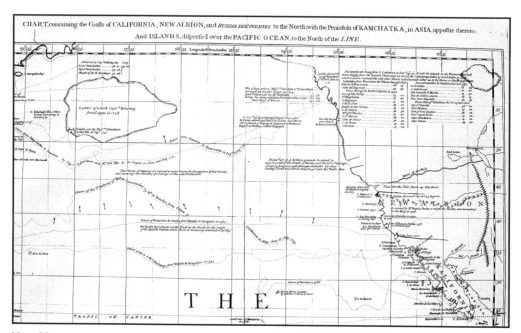

Map 38
A Chart containing the coasts of California, New Albion, and Russian Discoveries to the North with the Peninsula of Kamschatka, Asia, opposite thereto And Islands dispersed over the Pacific Ocean to the North of the line
John Green, 1753.
Published by Thomas Jefferys, London, 1753.

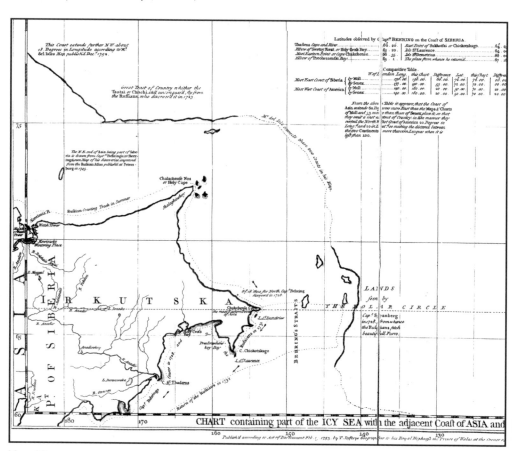

Map 39
Chart containing part of the Icy Sea with the adjacent coasts of Asia and America
John Green, 1753.
Published by Thomas Jefferys, London, 1753.

GERHARD MÜLLER AND HIS FAMOUS MAP

Gerhard Friedrich Müller was a German scholar who in 1725 left Leipzig and went to work at the newly formed Russian Imperial Academy of Sciences. In 1733 he was appointed head of the academic section of the Second Kamchatka Expedition, Vitus Bering's scheme to explore the whole of Siberia and the northwest coast of America, of which Bering's 1741 voyage was a part. Müller spent ten years exploring Siberia and was later appointed permanent secretary of the academy.

Müller is significant to the cartography of the Pacific Northwest because of a map he published in 1754, and which went through several revisions later, which made the then murky map of the region very much clearer. The 1758 edition is shown here (Map 40).

He had been encouraged to construct his map to correct mistakes on a map of the North Pacific published in 1752 by Joseph-Nicolas de L'Isle, about whose misleading maps we have heard (page 26).

Map 40
Nouvelle Carte des decouvertes faites par des vaisseaux Russiens aux cotes inconnues de l'Amerique Septentrionale avec les pais adjacents. St. Petersbourg a l'Academie Imperiale des Sciences 1758

Perhaps the most significant map of the Pacific Northwest of this period, it was widely copied. The large peninsula was the result of confusion between the islands of the Aleutian chain with mainland America. It reflected the official Russian view at this time.

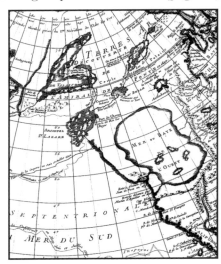

Map 41
Carte Des Nouvelles Decouvertes Au Nord De La Mer Tant a l'Est de la Siberie et du Kamtchatka Qu'a l'ouest de la Nouvelle France Dressee sur las Memoires de Mr Del'isle, Professeur Royale et de l'Academie des Sciences Par Philippe Buache de la meme Academie et Presentee a l'Academie, dans son Assemblee Publique de 8 Avril 1750 Par Mr Del'isle 1752

De L'Isle had returned to Paris after working with the Russian Academy and was accused of having stolen some information from the Russians. In fact, it was de L'Isle who upset the Russian policy of secrecy; like the first Bering expedition, the Russians wanted to keep their discoveries secret but they were upstaged by de L'Isle, who went back to his native France

and in April 1750 appeared before the French Royal Academy and read a report on the 1741 expedition. This report was accompanied by a map and was published in 1752 by Philippe Buache, who was in the mapmaking business with de L'Isle (Map 41).

Müller's 1754 and 1758 maps were an answer to de L'Isle's speculations. His map placed the discoveries of Bering and Chirikov on the map, but instead of connecting them with unsupported conjecture, Müller simply connected them with more or less straight dotted lines to indicate the most likely shape of the coast, a far more scientifically responsible way of showing the information.

The result was a map which bore a good resemblance to reality, bearing in mind the confusing effect of the Alaska Peninsula and the Aleutian Islands. It illustrated the official Russian view that most of the coastline seen by Bering and Chirikov on their return journeys was part of the North American mainland, hence the bloated Alaskan Peninsula. This map was widely copied, and translated into many languages.

An English translation of Müller's book was published in London under Tho-

mas Jefferys' name in 1761. Müller's book contained a copy of the de L'Isle map that prompted it in the first place (Map 42); in common with other maps of his, it has the discoveries of the mythical Admiral de Fonte front and center, blending truth and fiction in an intriguing fashion.

Map 42
A General Map of the Discoveries of Admiral De Fonte and other Navigators, Spanish, English and Russian in Quest of a Passage to the South Sea By Mr De L'Isle Sept 1752
From: Thomas Jefferys, *Voyages From Asia to America...* 1761. English translation of Müller's book.

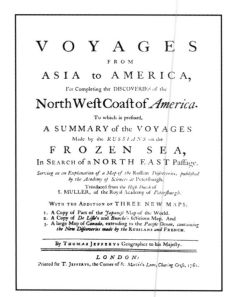

Title page of Gerhard Müller's book, published in 1761 in an English translation by Thomas Jefferys.

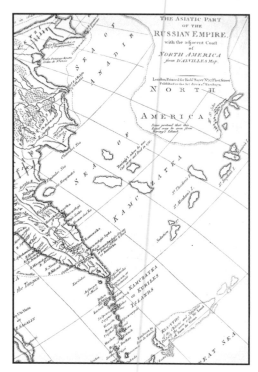

Map 44
The Asiatic Part of the Russian Empire with the adjacent coast of North America from D'Anvilles map. Robert Sayer, March 1772.

Map 43 (above)
An Exact Map of North America from the best authorities. J. Lodge, 1778.

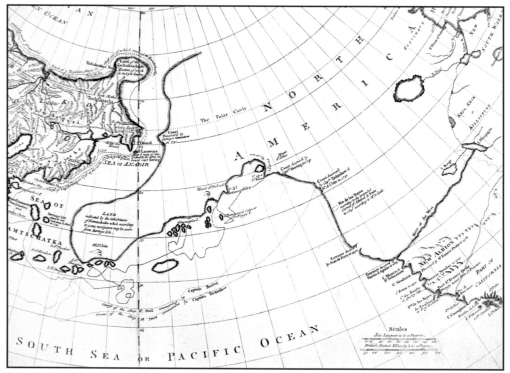

Map 45
A Map of the Discoveries made by the Russians on the North West Coast of America.
Published by the Royal Academy of Sciences at Petersburg London: Printed for Carington Bowles 1771
An English version of the map by Müller. Shows the coasts discovered by Bering and Chirikov; coast discovered by "surveyor Gwosdev in 1730 [1732]"; the "Rio de los Reyes", de Fonte's strait (see page 26); the "Entrance discovered by Juan de Fuca in 1592"; and the "Entrance discovered by Martin D'Aguilar in 1603." The "River of the West" flows to the sea at the latter, from a source in "L. Winipigon".

The large peninsula of Müller's map was copied by a number of mapmakers of the period. Map 43 shows it on a 1778 map by John Lodge.

After Catherine II came to power in Russia in 1762, she wanted to renew the strength of the Russian navy and had a renewed interest in discoveries in the north Pacific. In addition, she heard of the British dispatch of Commodore Byron to the north Pacific to seek a Northwest Passage (see page 32).

As a result, in 1764 Lieutenant Ivan Synd, who was one of the survivors of the 1741 Bering expedition, was sent on a

voyage into the Bering Sea. Although he produced maps and a journal, all but one seem to have been lost. His map showed that there was a strait, and showed that there was not a long peninsula from America almost to Kamchatka. The map he drew is shown here (Map 46).

On the basis of Synd's discoveries, Gerhard Müller modified his map (Map 48), and the overly long Alaskan Peninsula was shortened in favor of lots of islands, when reality lay somewhere between the two. The Russian version of this later map, dating from about 1773, is

notable claim to fame is that the largest island was given the name "Alaschka" and is the first reference to the modern name Alaska.

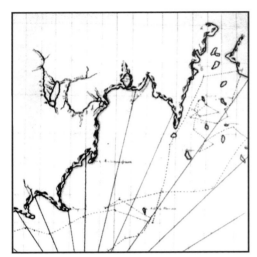

Map 46 (above)
Map of the explorations of Lieutenant Ivan Synd from 1764 to 1768.

shown here (Map 48, below).

Also based on Synd, Jacob von Stählin produced a map in 1774, which was hardly justified by Synd's own map. The latter showed fewer and much smaller islands in the northern Pacific. Perhaps its most

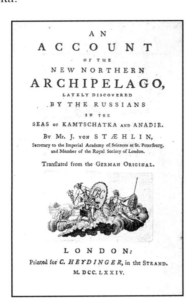

Title page of the English translation of von Stählin's book.

Map 47 (above)
A Map of the New Northern Archipelago discover'd by the Russians in the Seas of Kamtschatka & Anadir. Jacob von Stählin, 1774.

Map 48   Geographical map showing discoveries of Russian seagoing vessels on the northern part of America
           Gerhard Friedrich Müller, Imperial Academy of Learning, St. Petersburg. Russian edition c1773.
           Müller's maps of 1754 and 1758 were modified to incorporate the discoveries of Lieutenant Ivan Synd in 1764–1768.

These maps had an influence on later explorations. Both versions of Müller's map (1758 and 1773, Maps 40 and 48, pages 29 and 31) are known to have been carried by the Spanish explorer Juan Pérez in 1774, when the first Spanish voyage to the Pacific Northwest was made (see page 35). Ignacio de Arteaga carried the 1758 version with him in 1779 (see page 40), and James Cook had both Müller's and von Stählin's maps with him during his third voyage (see page 42). Von Stählin's map was destined to give James Cook some problems when he tried to follow it (see page 44).

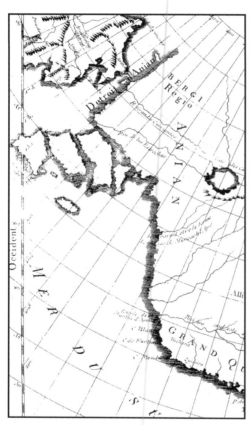

Map 49
Carte des parties nord et ouest de l'Amerique dressee d'apres les relations les plus authentiques par M en 1764. Nouvelle edition reduie pas M. de Vaugondy en 1772.
Note the "Rio de los Estrechos" (River of the Straits), which flows into "Detroit d'Anian" (Strait of Anian). The eastern shore of Asia is easily identifiable.

Interesting because of its resemblances to Müller's revised map (Map 48), Map 49 (above) is in fact a 1772 revision of a 1764 map drawn by Robert de Vaugondy. Like many of his maps, this one was published in Diderot's *Encyclopedié* (this one in the 1780 edition), which lent it credibility. Despite the similarities to Müller's revised map, it actually predated that revision and so is basically another de Vaugondy speculation, and quite a creative one. It was quite a change from his 1755 map for the *Encyclopedié* (Map 34, page 26)!

THE RUSSIANS DISCOVER THE ALEUTIANS

A new and top secret Russian expedition to North America was ordered in 1764. The Russians were concerned about possible Spanish designs on what, after Bering and Chirikov's 1741 voyages, they viewed as their territory. Concern about potential British interest in the region following the end of the Seven Years' War with France, which resulted in a strengthening of the British position in North America, may also have contributed to the reasons for a new Russian effort.

This was the expedition of Petr Krenitsyn and Mikhail Levashev. For secrecy, they were instructed only to actually build ships in Okhotsk, in Kamchatka, if they had no other alternative; otherwise they were to *"board a hunting ship or merchant vessel ... in the general capacity of passengers"* so they would attract as little attention as possible.

As it happened, there were no ships available, and Krenitsyn and Levashev had to build their own. Taking the maps of Vitus Bering and Petr Chaplin together with Bering and Sven Waxell's and Alexei Chirikov's journal, and a map of Bering and Chirikov's 1741 voyages (see page 22), they explored the North Pacific until 1769, becoming separated a number of times and overwintering three times.

They charted a number of the Aleutian Islands and the western part of the Alaska Peninsula, and added a little to Russian knowledge of the region. They produced maps such as the map of the Fox Islands, the easternmost of the Aleutians, shown here in a later English edition (Map 50). The secrecy obviously did not last very long! A map of the region incorporating their discoveries with those of Ivan Synd and the Müller maps was made in 1777 by V. Krasilnikov (Map 51).

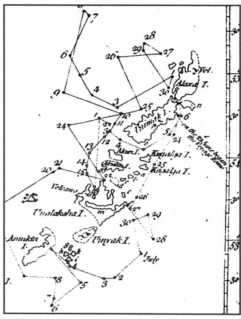

Map 50
Map of Krenitsin and Levashev's Voyage to the Fox Islands in 1768 and 1769.
Published April 13th 1780... by T. Cadell. Engr by T. Kitchin.
From: William Coxe, *An Account of the Russian Discoveries between Asia and America,* London, 1803.

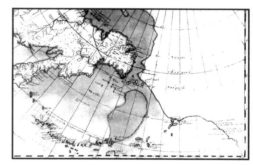

Map 51
Map of northeast Asia and northwest America. V. Krasilnikov, 1777.

BYRON'S PACIFIC VOYAGE

The voyage by Commodore John Byron that the Russian Empress Catherine heard about (page 30) took place in 1764 and 1765.

Byron, the grandfather of the poet, was sent on an exploring mission with specific instructions to sail to the northwest coast and find the Strait of Anian. If he found it, he was to sail through it from west to east.

However, once in the Pacific, in 1765, Byron never attempted to follow his instructions, and came nowhere near the Pacific Northwest. The instructions would be left for James Cook to follow.

JONATHAN CARVER'S TRAVELS

Jonathan Carver was a captain from Massachusetts who was sent in 1766 on a journey to explore "the uncharted western territories". He got only as far west as the Minnesota River, and on his return in 1769, Carver found that the officer who had sent him had exceeded his authority and hence he was not paid for his expedition. He therefore resolved to publish his journals, but it was not until 1778, after giving up in America and going to England, that they were published. His now famous *Travels Though the Interior Parts of North America in the years 1766, 1767, and 1768* was an immediate success, going through some thirty editions in several languages.

The details of Carver's book have been questioned, as it was probable that embellishments were added to make the book more attractive to his audience. As it relates to the west coast it is notable for the first published use of the name *Oregon*.

At the extreme western edge of a map of the "interior parts of North America" is shown a small lake with a river running westwards labelled "Heads of Origan" (Map 53, below).

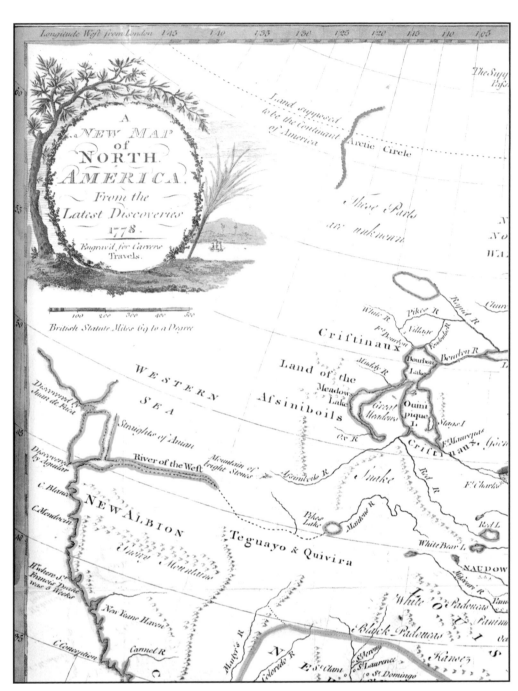

Map 52
A New Map of North America From the Latest Discoveries 1778 Engrav'd for Carvers Travels
From: J. Carver, *Travels through the Interior Parts of North America in the Years 1766, 1767 and 1768*, London, 1778.
The River of the West is shown flowing past the "Mountain of bright Stones" into the strait "Discovered by Aguilar" (from Vizcaíno's voyage in 1602, see page 17). The "Straights of Anian" connect it with the Strait of Juan de Fuca, and an inland "western Sea" covering an undefined area of the Pacific Northwest.

Map 53
The Heads of Origan. Detail from *A Plan of Captain Carver's Travels in the interior parts of North America in 1766 and 1767.*
From: J. Carver, *Travels through the Interior Parts of North America in the Years 1766, 1767 and 1768*, London, 1778.

The first known use of the word "Oregon".

This same area is also covered in another map in the book (Map 52) on which the river is called Mantons River and is shown as connected to the River of the West with a dotted line. This map may have been drawn by English mapmaker Thomas Kitchin and is unlikely to have been drawn by Carver himself, but in any case the western coast is almost certainly copied from another map; copying someone else's work was common at that time.

The confusion between the River of the West, the River Oregon, both nonexistent and both the Columbia River, shows in the text of Carver's introduction, of which a small piece is reproduced here.

Indians; particularly, the account I give of the Naudowesies, and the situation of the Heads of the four great rivers that take their rise within a few leagues of each other, nearly about the center of this great continent; viz. The River Bourbon, which empties itself into Hudson's Bay; the Waters of Saint Lawrence; the Mississippi, and the River Oregon, or the River of the West, that falls into the Pacific Ocean at the straits of Annian.

Another, later map by Jedediah Morse (Map 54) showed the "Oregan R" connected to the "River of the West".

Map 55 shows the same river labeled "River of the West according to some" flowing out of "Pikes Lake," as on Carver's map, but flowing to the Pacific south of Cape Blanco, while an alternate River of the West is shown flowing to the "Opening Discovered by Juan de Fuca in 1592." Despite the misinformation, Carver's book and its two maps had a considerable influence on the cartography of the western part of North America for the next twenty-five years.

(Far left and below)
Text and title page from Carver's book. There was a popular belief at this time that all the major rivers in North America had their sources very close to one another somewhere in the middle of the continent. This is the first reference to the name "Oregon."

T R A V E L S

THROUGH THE

INTERIOR PARTS

OF

NORTH-AMERICA,

IN THE

YEARS 1766, 1767, and 1768.

BY J. CARVER, Esq.

CAPTAIN OF A COMPANY OF PROVINCIAL TROOPS DURING THE LATE WAR WITH FRANCE.

ILLUSTRATED WITH COPPER PLATES.

LONDON:

PRINTED FOR THE AUTHOR;
And Sold by J. WALTER, at Charing-cross, and S. CROWDER, in Pater-noster Row.

M DCC LXXVIII.

Map 54 (above)
Map of North America Showing all the New Discoveries
From: *The American Gazeteer Exhibiting a Full Account of the Civil Divisions, Rivers, Harbours, Indian Tribes, etc. of the American Continent... Compiled from the best authorities by Jedediah Morse Author of the American Universal Geography.* Boston, 1804.
The *Gazeteer* contained a definition of the River of the West: *"River of the West, in the W, part of N. America, empties into the ocean in about lat. 43 17 30 N, and lon. 122 30 W. It is little known, except near its mouth."*
A similar River of the West, but flowing directly to the sea, is shown on a British map by R. Wilkinson published in 1794 (Map 320, page 204).

Map 55 (below)
A new map of the whole continent of America: divided into North and South and West Indies wherein are exactly described the United States of North America as well as the several European possessions according to the preliminaries of peace signed at Versailles Jan 20, 1783 compiled from Mr D'Anville's maps of that continent, with the addition of the Spanish discoveries in 1775 to the north of California and corrected in the several parts belonging to Great Britain from the original materials of Governor Pownall, M.P. London: Printed for Robert Sayer, 1786

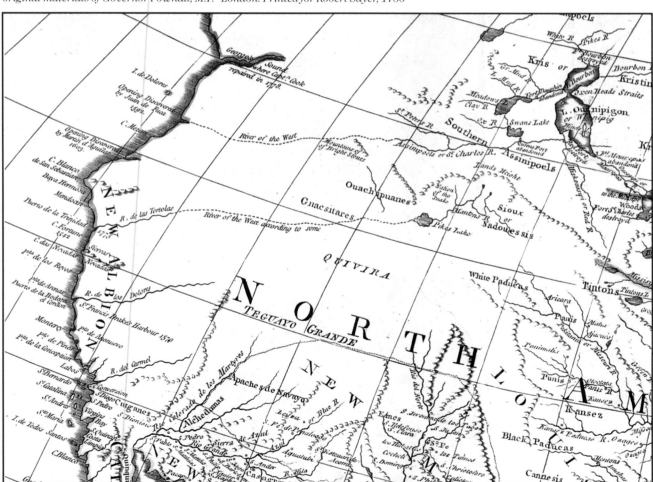

Note the River of the West *crossing* the Mountains of Bright Stones (the Rockies). Also shows "George's Sound where Cpt Cook repaired in 1778" (see page 42), the "Opening Discovered by Martin d'Aguilar in 1603" (see page 17), and "I. de Dolores" (sorrows), named by Hezeta in 1775 (see page 37, and also Map 63, page 40).

THE FIRST SPANISH EXPLORATIONS ON THE NORTHWEST COAST

By 1770, the Spanish knew that the Russians had brought a significant part of the northern northwest coast under their control. Maps such as Müller's convinced the Spanish that something should be done to try to ensure that the Spanish domination of the Pacific coast was not threatened. In 1773, instructions arrived in Mexico City from the Spanish king telling Viceroy Antonio Bucareli of the Russian threat and ordering him to make preparations to send ships northward.

Antonio Bucareli was the Spanish Viceroy in New Spain from 1771 to 1779 and was an unusually capable official. He was already responsible for the exploration of parts of California, and in 1776 was responsible for the establishment of a permanent settlement at San Francisco. He had also improved communications in the Pacific coast area. In 1773, Bucareli ordered Juan Pérez, the senior naval officer at the Spanish naval base at San Blas, to produce plans for the operation.

Juan Pérez was an experienced captain and explorer. He was the first Spanish captain since Sebastián Vizcaíno, 175 years before, to enter the harbors of both San Diego and Monterey. Pérez was given copies of the Müller Russian map in both its 1758 and 1773 versions (Map 40, page 29, and Map 48, page 31). Viceroy Bucareli wrote,

Notwithstanding that the charts published in St. Petersburg in 1758 and 1773, concerning the alleged voyages of the Russians, may be of little use to him, copies are included so that he may not be without this information.

Pérez left San Blas in his ship, the *Santiago*, in January 1774, and after calling at San Diego and Monterey, sailed north in early June. He kept well off-shore, and finally made a landfall on 18 July 1774 off the northwest coast of Graham Island, the northernmost of the Queen Charlotte Islands. They were visited by natives in canoes and the crew traded with the natives, but they did not land. Although Pérez' instructions had told him to proceed to 60° N, he turned south. Making another attempt to find the coast further south, he approached but probably did not enter Nootka Sound, on the west coast of Vancouver Island. His ship was again visited by native canoes. Pérez traded some silver spoons, perhaps the same as James Cook was to purchase from the natives four years later, recognize that they were Spanish, and realize thus that the Spanish must have been on this coast. Leaving the coast of Vancouver Island, Perez returned quickly to Monterey, arriving on 28 August 1774.

Map 56
A Chart Containing the Coasts of California, New Albion, and Russian Discoveries to the North with the Peninsula of Kamschatka, Asia, opposite thereto And Islands dispersed over the Pacific Ocean to the North of the line
From: *An American Atlas Engraved on 48 copper plates by the late Thomas Jefferys Geographer to the King, and others. London 1775*

At about 55° N, is the notation "*Here the Spaniards saw several White and Fair Indians in 1774*" and at about 50° N, presumably from Pérez's encounter at Nootka Sound, the map is marked "*Coast seen by the Spaniards in 1774 with inhabitants which go naked.*"

The two Jefferys maps (Map 56, right, and Map 57, overleaf) are a good summary of the knowledge of the northwest coast just before Cook's third voyage.

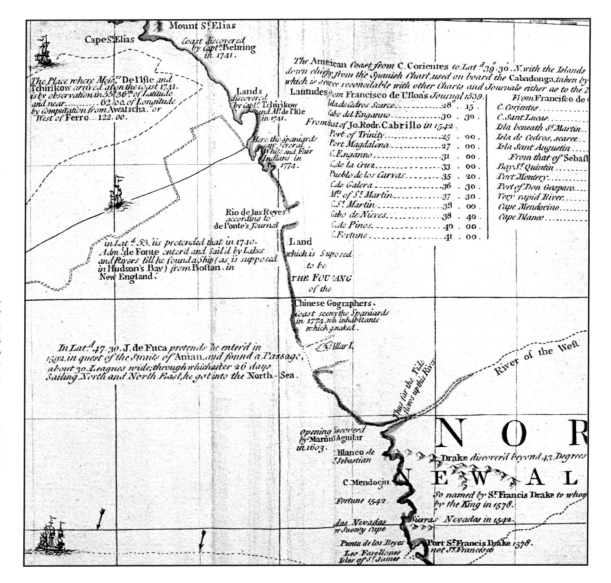

Although Pérez reached only 54° 40' N though his instructions were to sail to 60° N, he had carried out the first tentative but documented European reconnaissance of the northwest coast below 55° N.

Pérez' claim to have reached 54° 40' N was later used by the United States, having fallen heir to Spanish claims to the northwest by virtue of the 1819 Transcontinental Treaty. The United States pressed the Russians to accept 54° 40' N as the southern limit of their claims in North America, which they did. Later this latitude was made famous by the American slogan "Fifty-four-forty or fight!", as it was the division between the Oregon Country and Russian America, now Alaska (see page 133). Today 54° 40' N is, after slight later adjustments, the southern limit of Alaska.

And it all derived from the 1774 voyage of Juan Pérez!

THOMAS JEFFERYS'
1775 *AMERICAN ATLAS*

Cartographic information from Pérez' voyage showed up the next year in Thomas Jefferys' *American Atlas,* 1775 edition (Map 56, page 35). Quite how this happened has not been traced, since the Spanish were, as usual, very secretive about their discoveries, and in any case it usually took several years for new geographic information to find its way onto published maps.

Map 57 shows Alaska as an island, af-

Map 56A
Carta Reducida del Oceano Asiatico ō Mar del Sur que contiene la Costa de la California comprehendida desde el Puerto de Monterrey. hta la Punta de Sta. Maria Magdelena hecha segun las observaciones y Demarcasiones del Aljerez de Fragata de la R^l. Armada y Primer Piloto de este Departamento D^n. Juan Perez por D^n. Josef de Cañizares. 1774

Map showing the west coast of North America from Monterey to the tip of the Queen Charlotte Islands drawn by Pérez' pilot, Josef de Cañizarez. This map was found in 1989 in the National Archives, Washington, DC. It had previously been thought that no cartographic records from the 1774 Pérez voyage had survived.
It is the first map of part of the coast of BC to be drawn from actual exploration, as opposed to imagination.
Pérez' anchorage off Nootka Sound is shown as *Surgidero de S^n Lorenzo.* *P^ta de Sta Margarita* is the northern tip of Graham Island in the Queen Charlottes. *Cerro de Sta Rosalia* is Mount Olympus, Washington.

ter von Stählin's map of 1774, with the tracks of Bering, Synd, and others.

These two maps from the *American Atlas* (Map 56 and Map 57) are updates of John Green's 1753 maps (Maps 38 and 39, page 28).

The atlas was actually published by another London mapmaker, Robert Sayer, as Jefferys had recently died. The atlas also included a copy of the Müller 1758 map by Sayer (Map 58, right).

Map 57
Chart containing part of the Icy Sea with the adjacent Coast of Asia and America. Western half of: *A Chart of North and South America including the Atlantic and Pacific Oceans with the nearest coasts of Europe, Africa and Asia.*
From: *An American Atlas. Engraved on 48 copper plates by the late Thomas Jefferys Geographer to the King, and others. London 1775*

Shows Alaska as an island, as with von Stählin (Map 47, page 31), tracks of Bering and Synd, and the "Great Continent [North America] from whence the Russians fetch beautiful Furs, and seen by Capt Spangenberg in 1728". The latter reference is to Martin Spanberg, one of Bering's officers on his first voyage of 1728 (see page 20). Also marked is "Coast Discovered by Gwosdev in 1730" (actually 1732) on the western coast of the island of "Alaschka".

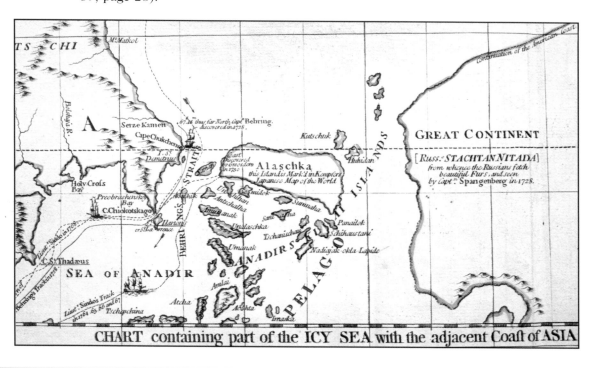

CHART containing part of the ICY SEA with the adjacent Coast of ASIA

Map 58
The Russian Discoveries from the Map Published by the Imperial Academy of St. Petersburg. London. Printed for Robt Sayer Map and Printseller No 53 in Fleet Street. Published as the Act Directs March 2nd 1775. From An American Atlas. Engraved on 48 copper plates by the late Thomas Jefferys Geographer to the King, and others. London 1775
Another example of a map with the Müller peninsula (see page 29). The "Entrance discover'd by Juan de Fuca in 1592" is shown at 47° N, while the "River of the West" runs from "L. Winipigon" to the "Entrance discover'd by Martin d'Aguilar in 1603" near 45° N. The "Rio de los Reyes according to the pretended Journal of Admiral de Fonte in 1640, according to Mr de Lisle" is also shown.

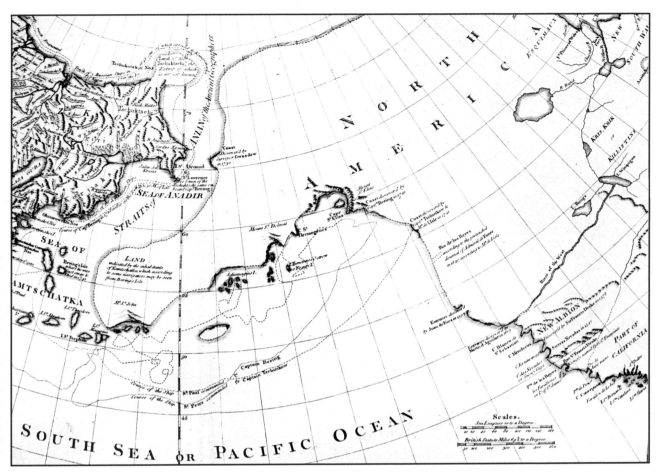

THE SPANISH MAP THE WASHINGTON AND OREGON COASTS

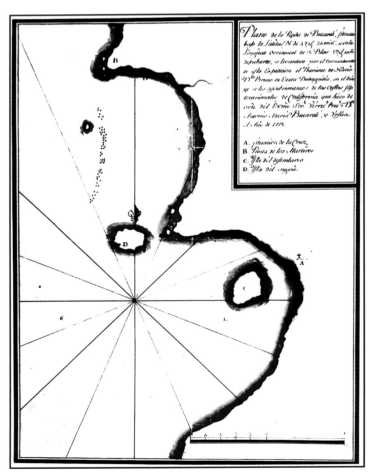

Map 59
Plano de la Rada de Bucareli situado...
Bruno de Hezeta y Dudagoitia, July 1775.

The first map of the Washington coast, showing today's Cape Elizabeth, the Quinault River, and Point Grenville.
In English, the map title is: *Map of Bucareli's roadstead, located below latitude N 47 24min and in longitude west of San Blas 19 40, discovered and charted by the commander of this expedition, first lieutenant Don Bruno de [H]ezeta Dudagoitia, on the voyage of discovery to the northern coasts of California, which was made by order of His Excellency, the Viceroy, Frey Don Antonio Maria Bucareli y Ursúa in the year 1775.* [37]

Although it seemed improbable that the Russians had settlements anywhere where they might threaten the Spanish, Viceroy Bucareli sent a second expedition northwards in 1775, with instructions to reach 65° N. There was the *Santiago*, with Bruno de Hezeta y Dudagoitia, commanding the expedition, and Juan Pérez, now demoted to second officer because of his failure to follow instructions the year before. The other ship to sail north was the *Sonora*, only 38 feet long, commanded by Juan Francisco de la Bodega y Quadra, who was destined to play a large part in the history of the northwest coast over the next twenty years; Francisco Antonio Mourelle was second officer.

Heading offshore to sail northwards, the two ships made a landfall at Trinidad Harbor just south of Cape Blanco, and on 14 July 1775 landed on the Olympic Peninsula near Point Grenville, several miles south of the Quinault River.

Here Hezeta performed a formal act of possession for Spain. Bodega y Quadra sent some of his men ashore again later to fill their water casks but they were all murdered by natives. Despite this and the short stay, Hezeta made a map of the area, which is shown here (Map 59).

Map 60
Plano de la Bahia de la Asunciōn...
Bruno de Hezeta y Dudagoitia, August 1775

Map of Assumption Bay or [H]ezeta's Entrance...
The first map of the mouth of the Columbia
River.

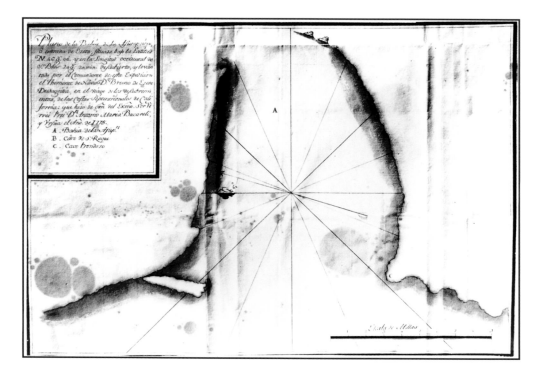

Naming the bay Bucareli's Roadstead
(Rada de Bucareli) after the viceroy of
Mexico, Hezeta also marked with letters:

A. Location of the cross (used in the act
    of possession ceremony)
B. Martyr's Point (after the murdered
    sailors; now Cape Elizabeth,
    Washington)
C. Landing Island
D. Deceit Island

The river shown is the Quinault, and the
dots extending south of Martyr's Point
show a reef on which the *Sonora* was temporarily stranded. This map is the first
known map of the Washington coast.

Leaving the coast and heading out to
sea again, the ships were separated in
heavy seas. Largely due to an outbreak
of scurvy, Hezeta decided to sail the *Santiago* south again, but followed the coast
closely.

On 17 August 1775, Hezeta came
across what appeared to be a large bay,
penetrating far inland. Hezeta tried to
sail into the bay, but the current was so
strong that he could not, even under a
full press of sails. *"These currents and
seething of the waters"*, he wrote in his
diary, *" have led me to believe that it may
be the mouth of some great river or some
passage to another sea."* [38] He decided it
was the strait discovered by Juan de Fuca
and that the latitude had been misjudged.
Hezeta named the bay Bahia de la
Asunciōn after a holiday two days earlier.

This is the earliest recorded sighting
of the mouth of the Columbia River by a
European, a feature which was destined
to be *missed* by many – including Cook
in 1778, Meares in 1788, Malaspina in
1791, and Vancouver in 1792 – until finally being found and entered by Robert
Gray, in the *Columbia Rediviva*, in 1792
(see page 82).

Map 61 (right)
Map of the northwest coast from the voyage of Juan
Francisco Bodega y Quadra, 1775.
Francisco Antonio Mourelle.
From: Daines Barrington, *Miscellanies*,
London, 1781, page 489.

This is a British copy of a Spanish map of Bodega y Quadra's
1775 voyage in the *Sonora* which was in Francisco Antonio
Mourelle's journal. The journal somehow found its way to
London. Given the Spanish policy of secrecy at the time, it
is particularly surprising that this occurred. Daines
Barrington translated and published Mourelle's journal in
1781 in a magazine called *Miscellanies*.

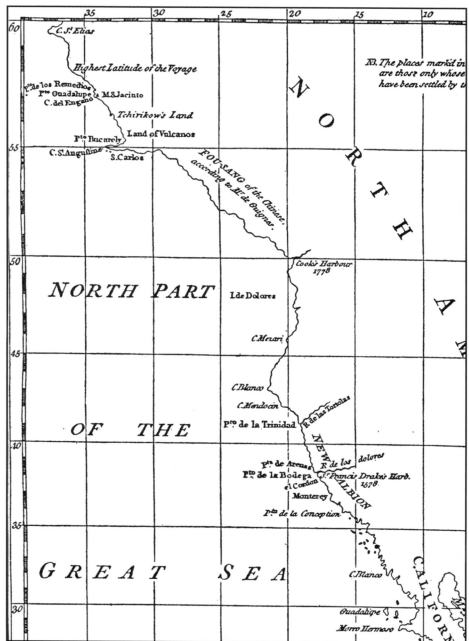

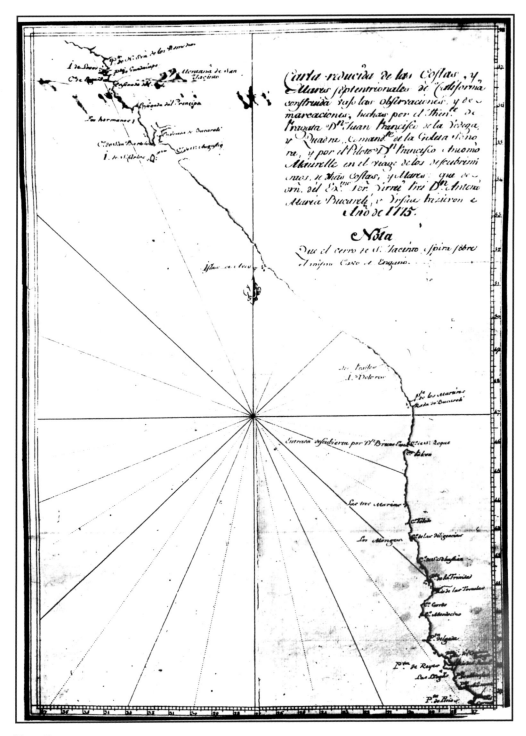

Hezeta was unable to anchor in the bay because he did not by this time have enough fit crew to handle the anchor, and he made directly for Monterey, reaching that port only twelve days later.

Hezeta did, however, prepare a map on the basis of what could be seen from outside the Columbia bar, and this is shown here (Map 60, page 38, top). This is the first map of the mouth of the Columbia.

The island shown at B and identified as Cabo de San Roque is Cape Disappointment, not in fact an island but a peninsula, and the point at C, Cabo Frondoso, is either Point Adams or Tillamook Head.[39]

After Hezeta, the Columbia River estuary appeared on many subsequent maps as "Entrada de Hezeta," "Rio de San Roque", or something similar. Had Hezeta been able to explore it farther, his discovery would have had a better chance of supporting Spanish claims to the area, but due to Spanish secrecy, their claims did not last long; after Gray's discovery of the river in 1792, his name, the Columbia, soon supplanted any other, even on Spanish maps.

Meanwhile, Bodega y Quadra in the little *Sonora* had decided after separating from the *Santiago* to attempt to follow their instructions, and so sailed northwards.

The *Sonora* made a landfall on 15 August 1775 at 57° N, near a snow-capped peak they named San Jacinto – today's Mount Edgecumbe, just west of Sitka. They eventually reached 58° N, just 2° south of the goal set for Pérez the year earlier. Bodega y Quadra examined the coast in the area quite extensively, as he expected to find the Strait of Bartholemew de Fonte (see page 26). They did locate a good anchorage on the west coast of what is now Prince of Wales Island, at a bay they named (and which is still named today) Bucareli Bay, after the Spanish viceroy who had sent them. Francisco Antonio Mourelle performed possession ceremonies there, Bodega y Quadra being ill that day; scurvy was beginning to take its toll on the *Sonora* as it had on the *Santiago*. They limped back to San Blas via Monterey, arriving on 20 November 1775. A number of the crew had died on the voyage, including Juan Pérez.

While Hezeta's voyage languished in Spanish secrecy, Bodega y Quadra's became known because a copy of Francisco Antonio Mourelle's journal of the voyage clandestinely found its way to London, where it was translated and published in 1781 (Map 61, left).

Map 62

Carta reducida de las costas, y mares septentrionales de California construida bajo las observaciones, y demarcaciones hechas por...de Fragata Don Juan Francisco de la Vodega y Quadra commandante de la goleta Sonora y por el piloto Don Francisco Antonio Maurelle en el viage de los descubrimentos de dichas costas que de orden de Exme...Don Antonio Alva Bucareli...hizieron el ano de 1775.

Bodega y Quadra's map of the northwest coast based on his discoveries and those of Hezeta. Detail is missing in the central part of the map due to the fact that Bodega y Quadra's ship was offshore at that time, a similar situation to that of James Cook in 1778, whose map of the northwest coast similarly shows little detail in the central part (see Map 67, page 43). Note the "Entrada descubierta por D[n] Bruno Ezeta", the entrance discovered by (Don) Bruno Hezeta, the mouth of the Columbia. Longitude is shown on this map, as it is on all Spanish maps of the period, as degrees west of San Blas, the Spanish naval port on the Mexican coast.

The first map of the northwest coast based on the discoveries of Hezeta and Bodega y Quadra is shown here (Map 62). Drawn in the portolan tradition, it shows the *Sonora*'s discoveries in southeastern Alaska, the Entrada of Hezeta (Columbia River), and Cape Blanco (Cabo de las Diligencias), plus the Rada de Bucareli (Grenville Bay) and Las Tres Marías (Three Arch Rocks) on the Washington coast. There is a gap in detail in the central area of the map due to the fact that the *Sonora* was offshore on the northward voyage, and unable to survey details, due to illness, on the return.

The 1774 and 1775 expeditions had found no Russian encroachment, and Viceroy Bucareli decided that Spanish claim to the northwest coast had now been secured by four formal acts of possession that had been performed.

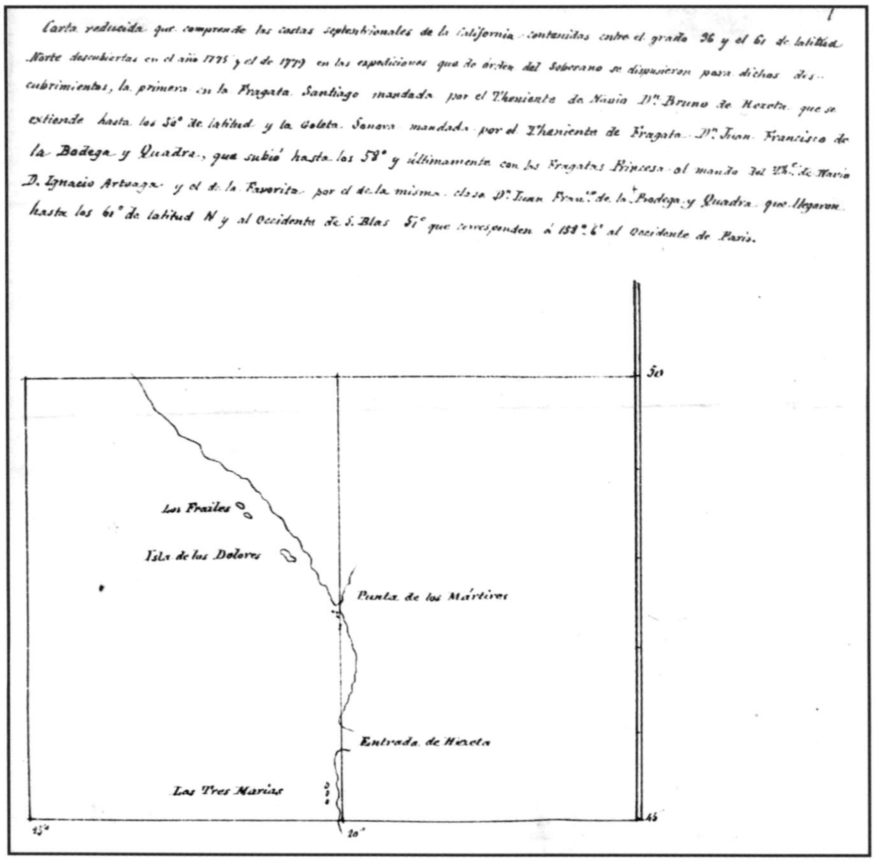

Map 63 (right)
Carta reducida que comprehende las costas septentrionales de la California...

This simple map of the southern part of the northwest coast is a British copy of one drawn by Arteaga in 1779. It shows features from the Hezeta voyage in 1775, notably the Entrada of Hezeta (the Columbia River); and the Punta de los Mārtires (Martyrs Point), near where Hezeta lost crew to an Indian attack. The river is the Quinault River in Washington.

IGNACIO DE ARTEAGA'S VOYAGE TO ALASKA

Several months before James Cook's ships left England for the Pacific in 1776, Spanish spies had learned that one of Cook's principal objectives was to visit the northwest coast in search of the Northwest Passage. Soon after, José de Gālvez, the Spanish minister of the Indies, responsible for the west coast of America, learnt of Bodega y Quadra's explorations in Alaska and Hezeta's discovery of a great river which might give access to the unexplored interior of North America. His immediate response was to order a third voyage for 1777. Lack of available ships and problems dealing with Indian uprisings in northwestern Mexico delayed the start of the expedition until 1779. In the meantime, Cook had come and gone.

Again two ships were sent north. The expedition was led by Ignacio de Arteaga, the ranking officer at the naval department at San Blas at the time, in the *Princesa*; and Bodega y Quadra again, this time commanding the *Favorita*.

Arteaga carried with him a number of maps, including Bellin's of 1766 (Map 32, page 25), the de L'Isle map of 1752 (Map 41, page 29), and the Müller map of 1758 (Map 40, page 29). He also made up another, a composite based on maps of the 1775 expedition, which seems to have been lost.

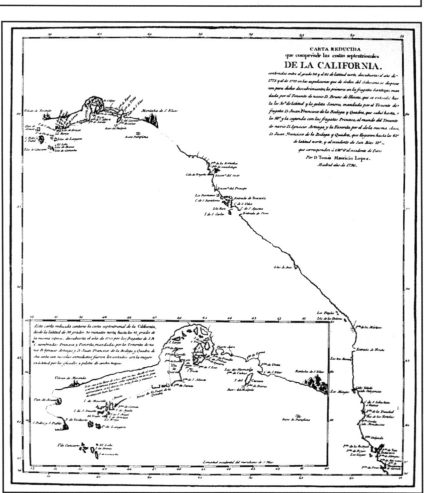

Map 64   *Carta Reducida que comprende las costas septentrionales de la California...*
Por D. Tomas Mauricio Lopez, Madrid, ano de 1796

A representation of Spanish knowledge of the northwest coast after Arteaga's voyage in 1779, though drawn much later. Lopez was a mapmaker in Madrid at the end of the eighteenth century.

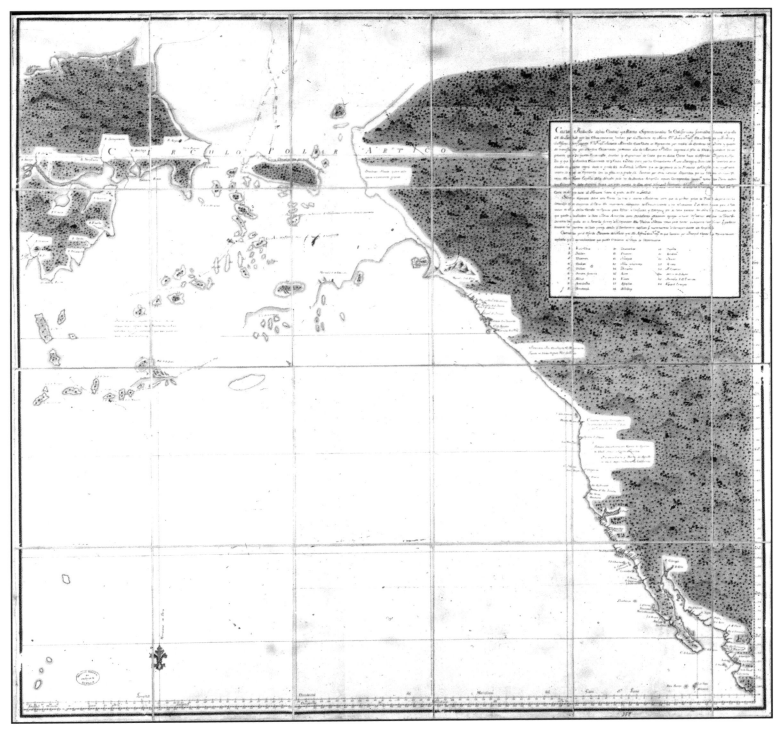

Map 65
Carta Reducida de las Costas y Mares Septentrionales de California... Watercolour, c1779.

This unique map from Spanish archives bears a close resemblance to the revised map of Gerhard Müller (Map 48, page 31) and shows part of Alaska as an island, reflecting the popular belief at the time. The southern coast of Alaska is also defined, incorporating the explorations of Bodega y Quadra in 1775 and Arteaga in 1779 with the knowledge the Spanish might have been able to acquire of Russian explorations. There is confusion, however, as to whether this is a continuous coast or a string of islands.

Arteaga was instructed to reach 70° N. He left San Blas in February 1779 and reached Bucareli Bay in early May. Near the entrance to Prince William Sound Arteaga took a party ashore and performed a formal ceremony of possession at a bay he named Puerto de Santiago de Apostól, today's Port Etches, on Hinchinbrook Island. This was the northernmost point at which possession was ever executed by the Spanish in America, and became the foundation for Spain's claims to sovereignty as far northwards as 61° N.

Arteaga found no evidence that James Cook had actually reached the coast the year before, and came to believe that the Russians had perhaps only penetrated as far east as the Aleutians. Because of this, the Spanish decided that it was unnecessary to continue to send expeditions northwards. It would be nine years before any further voyages would be ordered. The Spanish did not realize that Cook's voyage would expose to the world the possibility of trade in sea otter furs, and that a swarm of fur traders from several countries was about to descend on the northwest coast, challenging Spanish claims to sovereignty.

JAMES COOK'S THIRD VOYAGE REACHES THE PACIFIC NORTHWEST

James Cook, probably England's most famous explorer and navigator, and also a mapmaker *par excellence*, came to the northwest coast in 1778 with his ships the *Resolution* and the *Discovery*, straight from his discovery of the Sandwich Islands – today's Hawaii.

He reached what he called *"the long lost coast of New Albion"* near Cape Foulweather on the Oregon coast, which he named. Cape Foulweather is at 44° 33' N. Cook had been instructed to make a landfall at about 45° N, as this was north of any point which in British eyes could be considered subject to Spanish territorial claims. Britain had no wish to see the voyage cause an international incident. Bad weather did, however, force the ships southwards to about 43° N before they could begin to work their way northwards.

At about 48° N he located a headland south of Cape Flattery, which he named because it *"flattered us with the hopes of finding a harbour"*, but failed to find the entrance to the Strait of Juan de Fuca. *"It is in the very latitude we were now,"* Cook wrote in his journal, *"in where geographers have placed the pretended Strait of Juan de Fuca. But we saw nothing like it, nor is there the least probability that iver any such thing ever exhisted."* [42]

He did record *"a small opening in the land"* towards dusk. But darkness closed in, the weather deteriorated, and the ships were forced out to sea.

Much has been made of Cook's failure to find the strait, but he was just following his instructions, which stated *"(take) care not to lose any time in exploring Rivers or Inlets ... until you get into the before-mentioned latitude of 65"*. [42/2] It has even been suggested that Cook's health was failing at this point, but the real culprit was probably simply the weather, which forced Cook to sail further away from the shore than he would have liked.

If his instructions had not told him to not bother, his previous track record of meticulous exploration of coastlines suggests that he would have gone back to survey once the weather allowed.

Cook's ships eventually found a harbor further up the coast of Vancouver Island, at a place they called King George's Sound, later renamed Nootka by the British Admiralty. Nootka was to feature large in the history of the northwest coast

in the years before the end of the eighteenth century.

Cook stayed at Nootka for most of the month of April 1778, repairing his ships, surveying, and observing the natives. During this time he surveyed the sound in the ships' boats, producing a map of it (Map 69, page 44). Several of his crew made maps of Nootka in their journals as well as the official ones made by Cook. Perhaps more important, he fixed the position of Nootka so that henceforth other ships would be able to find it.

At the end of the month, he proceeded northwards towards Alaska, where he proceeded to map the coast in far greater detail than had ever been done before.

On his way, passing 50° N on 26 April, Cook noted in his journal that he regretted that again the weather was forcing him to stay away from the land, *"especially as we were passing the place where Geographers have placed the pretended Strait of Admiral de Fonte."*

Although Cook did not believe that such a strait existed, he wrote,

nevertheless I was highly desirous of keeping the Coast aboard in order to clear up this point beyond dispute; but it would have been highly imprudent in me to have ingaged with the land in such exceeding tempestuous weather...

The weather and Cook's instructions were the main reasons the maps of his voyage to the northwest are incomplete south of Alaska.

In Alaska in particular, Cook was looking for inlets that could be entrances to the Northwest Passage, and this was certainly the thought on his men's minds at this stage, because they would have shared in prize money – twenty thousand pounds – which had been offered by the British government for the discovery of such a passage.

Samuel Hearne's account of his 1771 journey to the Coppermine River was not published until 1795, but a copy of his journal and three of his maps were in the possession of the Admiralty before Cook sailed from England in 1776. They were loaned to the Admiralty by Samuel Wegg, a new Deputy Governor of the Hudson's Bay Company who was less secretive than his predecessors had been. Thus Cook knew that whatever inlets he discovered on the northwest coast could not extend

Captain James Cook

Nathaniel Dance's famous painting of England's foremost navigator with one of his maps hangs in the National Maritime Museum in Greenwich, England.

across the continent into Hudson's Bay because Hearne had not crossed any strait or great river.

South of Bering Strait, Cook reached a large, previously unmapped sound, which he named after the Speaker of the House of Commons, Sir Fletcher Norton. As the ships sailed up the sound, Cook noted a shoaling of the water which made him realize it was unlikely to be a passage. Nevertheless, it was explored and found not to divide Alaska from the rest of the coast (see Map 70, page 45).

On 9 August 1778, Cook reached the northwestern extremity of North America, which he named Cape Prince of Wales, after the heir to the British throne, despite the fact that it was already marked on Müller's maps of 1754 and 1758 (Map 40, page 29), which he carried with him, as "coast surveyed by surveyor Gwosdev in 1730," actually 1732 (see page 20).

Cook then sailed through Bering Strait and reached 70° 44' N before he was stopped by ice. This latitude was almost as far north as the equivalent southern latitude he had reached during his second voyage, 71° 10' S, in January 1773.

On 29 August he decided to return to Hawaii to refit for a second season. While mapping some of the Aleutian islands, Cook wrote in his journal,

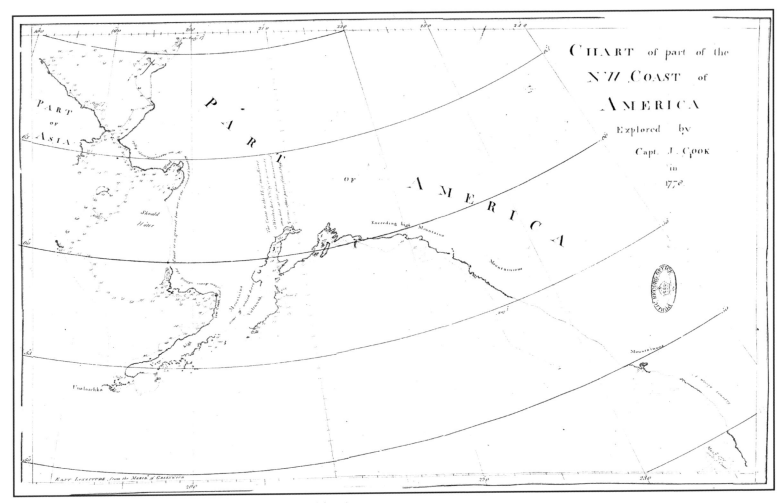

Map 66 (above)
Chart of part of the N W Coast of America Explored by Capt. J. Cook in 1778
Hand-drawn map enclosed with Cook's letter to Philip Stephens, Secretary of the Admiralty, from Unalaska, sent 20 October 1778 (21 in Cook's Journal) & received in London 6 March 1780.

In justice to Behrings Memory, I must say he has delineated this Coast very well and fixed the latitude and longitude of the points better than could be expected from the Methods he had to go by.[43]

On his way he called at the island of Unalaska, where he met Russian fur traders. Unalaska was the site of the first permanent Russian settlement in North America. The senior Russian officer there, Gerasim Grigorovich Ismailov, allowed Cook to copy two Russian charts, one of which showed

all the discoveries made by the Russians to the Eastward of Kamtschatka towards America, which if we exclude the Voyage of Behring and Tcherikoff [Chirikov], will amount to little or nothing.[43/2]

Cook in turn presented Ismailov with a map of his explorations to date.

The following day, 20 October 1778, Cook gave Ismailov a letter which contained a map, addressed to the British Admiralty, with the request that they be forwarded by him to London. Cook obviously felt that they had a good chance of reaching London overland via the Russians before he could otherwise get a communication through to the Admiralty.

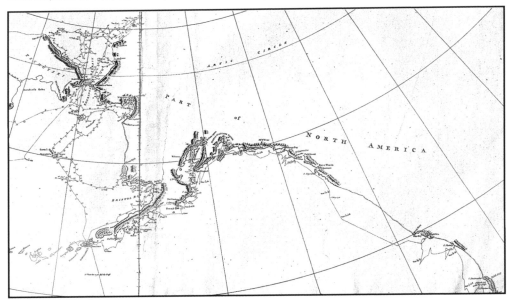

Map 67
Chart of the NW Coast of America and the NE Coast of Asia explored in the years 1778 and 1779
The unshaded parts of the coast of Asia are taken from a MS chart received from the Russians.
From: James Cook, *Voyage to the Pacific Ocean, 1784.*
The published map of the northwest coast. This map is also reproduced on the back endpaper.

The letter and the map did in fact get through, arriving at the Admiralty on 6 March 1780, and the map, probably drawn by Cook himself, is shown here (Map 66, above, top). This was the first map from Cook's third voyage, and the most com-

plete map of Alaska and the northwest coast to date. It was to be much copied.

At this time, an interesting comment appears in Cook's journal relating to the von Stählin map, which Cook had been using, or trying to use, up to this point.

Von Stählin's map showed the Alaskan region broken up into many islands, including one itself labelled Alaschka. Cook wrote:

... [the Russians] *assured me over and over again that they k[n]ew of no other islands but what were laid down on this chart* [the second of the two charts presented to Cook], *and that no Russian had ever seen any part of the Continent to the northward, excepting that part lying opposite the Country of the Tchuktschis* [across the Bering Strait]. *If M*ʳ *Staelin was not greatly imposed upon what could induce him to publish so erroneous a Map? in which many of these islands are jumbled in regular confusion, without the least regard to truth and yet he is pleased to call it a very accurate little Map? A Map that the most illiterate of his Sea-faring men would have been ashamed to put his name to.*[44]

Second Lieutenant James King wrote in his journal, *"... as far as we can judge, there never was a Map so unlike what it ought to be."*

Map 68
Chart of the New Northern Archipelago discovered by the Russians in the seas of Kamtschatka and Anadir. Jacob von Stählin, 1774.
Engraved for *Millar's New Universal System of Geography,* London, Alex Hogg, 1783.
A simplified edition; original is Map 47, page 31.

Cook also had Müller's map (Map 40, page 29) with him, but it proved to be not much better. King again wrote in his journal, on 23 July 1778:

as we have already Saild over a great space where Muller places a Continent, we can no longer frame any supposition in order to make our Charts agree with his...

Cook was killed by natives in Hawaii in February 1779, before he could return to complete the task he had been set. Captain Charles Clerke then assumed command, and the ships returned to Alaskan waters directly, principally to determine for sure that there was no practicable passage through Bering Strait. Clerke was already ill by this time and he died in August 1779, command then being taken over by John Gore, who guided the expedition back to London. Both Clerke and Gore received a great deal of help from William Bligh, later of mutiny on the *Bounty* fame, who was a brilliant navigator.

Map 69
*Sketch of Nootka Sound.
A. Ship Cove
1778*
From:
James Cook,
A Voyage to the Pacific Ocean,
1784.
The letter A, with an anchor, marks the position of Cook's Ship Cove. Today it is called Resolution Cove, after his ship.

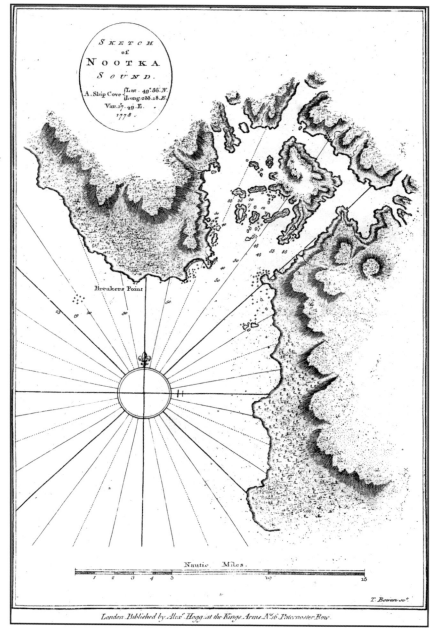

Nootka Sound. The view is to the north, about halfway between Friendly Cove and Resolution Cove, looking up Cook Channel. The Spanish Pilot Group of islands is to the right.

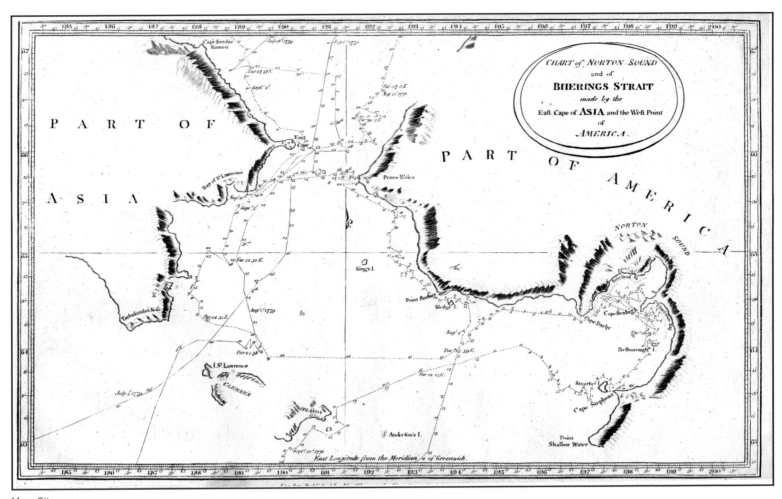

Map 70
Chart of Norton Sound and of Bherings Strait made by the East Cape of Asia and the West Point of America. 1778/1779.
From: James Cook, *A Voyage to the Pacific Ocean...,* 1784. Here at last the true relationship of America to Asia was defined.

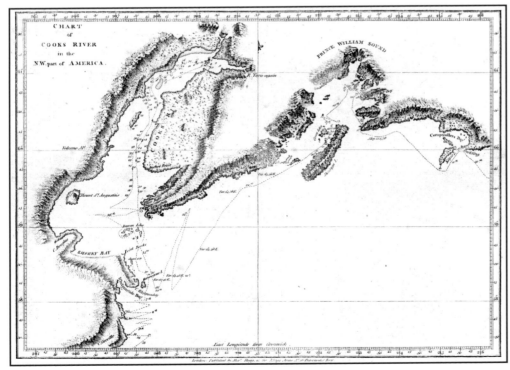

Map 71
Chart of Cooks River in the N W Part of America. 1778.
From: James Cook, *A Voyage to the Pacific Ocean...,* 1784.
Because of an incomplete survey of an extremity of Cook Inlet (Turnagain Arm), it was presumed that the inlet might lead to a river. This allowed continued speculation about a riverine Northwest Passage until George Vancouver finally surveyed it in 1793. Anchor Point, on the east side of the inlet, was named by Cook because he lost a kedge anchor there to the awesome tidal currents for which Cook Inlet is famous. Anchor Point today is the most westerly point in North America connected by road to the rest of the continent.

Arguably the most important map to result from Cook's third voyage was the map of Bering Strait and Norton Sound (Map 70, above). It shows for the first time the true relationship of America to Asia, ending once and for all the mystery of the existence and position of the "Strait of Anian." Bering had entered the strait in 1728 on his first voyage, but had not seen the American shore and so was unsure of its existence, and hence had not charted it. Cook sailed through the strait and into the Arctic Ocean before being stopped by pack ice at 70° 44' N. Both the American and the Asian shores were surveyed by Cook in 1778 and, after his death, by Clerke in 1779. The result was this map.

View across Cook Inlet
towards the Redoubt Volcano.

JOHN GORE'S HOPES FOR A NORTHWEST PASSAGE

John Gore, an American, was Cook's first lieutenant on board the *Resolution*. He was, to put it mildly, very optimistic about finding the Northwest Passage and collecting his share of a prize of twenty thousand pounds which had been offered by the British government. This is reflected in a chart he persuaded Henry Roberts to draw for him, which he included in his journal.

The map, shown here (Map 72), is untitled but shows Prince William Sound (Sandwich Sound) and Cook Inlet (The Gulf of Good Hope) and the track of the *Resolution* in May and June 1778.

At first, when the expedition explored Sandwich Sound, Gore supposed that this was to be the entrance to the Northwest Passage, so at the entrance he has marked *Cape Hold with Hope*. After this proved merely an inlet, they proceeded westwards, and Gore named the western end of Montague Island *Cape Lost Hope*. After being buffeted by gales for a few days, a large opening suddenly appeared. Gore named an island at the entrance *Hopes Return*.

More islands appeared, which Cook named the Barren Islands, but Gore named them the *Entry Isles*; he was sure this was to be the entrance to the Northwest Passage. Another headland Gore named *Cape Hope*, and the whole body of water, *The Gulf of Good Hope*. Further up the inlet, he saw *Nancy's Foreland*, "*a fair foreland for a favourite female acquaintance*," he wrote in his journal, in expectation of seeing her soon.

But, of course, it was not to be. Further explorations by two boats, one by William Bligh past the site of today's Anchorage, and the other by James King, showed that the water was turning fresh and the channels narrowing, so after sixteen days in this inlet, and the season running out on them, they left to resume their explorations westward.

The fact that Cook did not explore completely the northeastern end of Cook Inlet, and its naming as Cook's River instead of Cook's Inlet, left the possibility that a great river entered the sea here that penetrated the interior in such a way as to still provide a Northwest Passage by river, and this was postulated by some, notably Peter Pond (see page 64) until George Vancouver finally put the myth to rest. It was Vancouver who changed the name from Cook's River to Cook's Inlet.

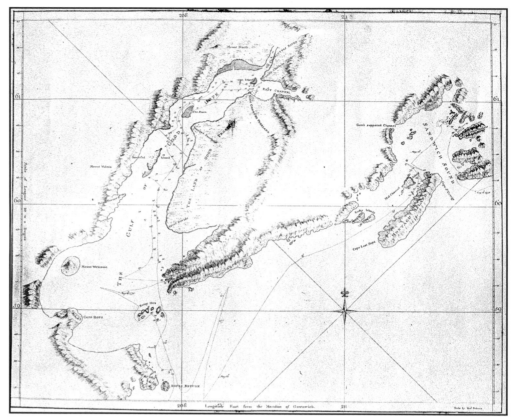

Map 72
Sandwich Sound and the Gulf of Good Hope (Prince William Sound & Cook Inlet).
Map by Henry Roberts for John Gore's journal, 1778.

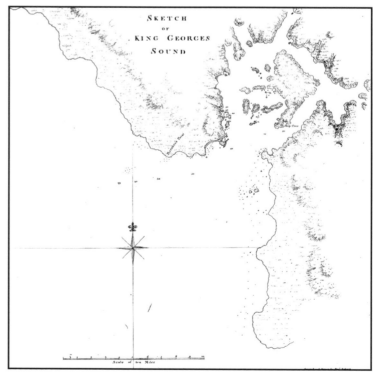

Map 73
Sketch of King Georges Sound
Map by Henry Roberts for John Gore's journal, 1778.

Nootka Sound and its approaches, on the west coast of Vancouver Island.

COOK'S LEGACY

The results of Cook's single season of exploration in 1778 were impressive. He had charted the American coastline from Mt. St. Elias northward, probed Bering Strait, determined that Alaska was not an island, and had touched on the coast of Vancouver Island.

Despite still thinking that the coast was mainland instead of a series of islands, he closed the gap between the Spanish voyages of the 1770s from the south, and the Russian voyages from the north, and established correctly the trend of the northwest coastline.

This was all summarized in the world map *General Chart exhibiting the Discoveries made by Capt, James Cook* (Map 74), published in 1784 by Henry Roberts, who had been Cook's principal mapmaker during the voyage.

Roberts had long been charged by Cook with making a world map with the tracks of all his voyages upon it; this was to be Cook's legacy to the world.

This map attempted to show the relationship between Cook's coastal explorations and those of Samuel Hearne in 1771 and 1772 in the interior. Hearne's discoveries were, however, placed too far north and too far west. Nevertheless, here we have for the first time a reasonably accurate map of all of North America.

Although, as we have seen, Cook himself knew of Hearne's discoveries and how they meant there could not be a temperate cross-continent strait, it is not clear whether Roberts knew this, though it seems unlikely that he would not have been privy to some conversation with Cook regarding it, considering that the pair were mapping together for a long period. At any rate, Roberts did find the Hudson's Bay Company maps of Hearne's discoveries and used them in his world map, thereby becoming the first to show Hearne's discoveries. This was eleven years *before* the publication of Hearne's report. Even the cartographer Aaron Arrowsmith ignored this, as he added it to his map of 1795 only *after* publication of Hearne's map.

It is interesting to note that the *Chart of the NW Coast of America and the NE Coast of Asia*, which was the map of the north Pacific published in 1784 with Cook's book, *Voyage to the Pacific Ocean*, and which was also prepared for publication by Roberts, does *not* show Hearne's discoveries (Map 67, page 43, and back

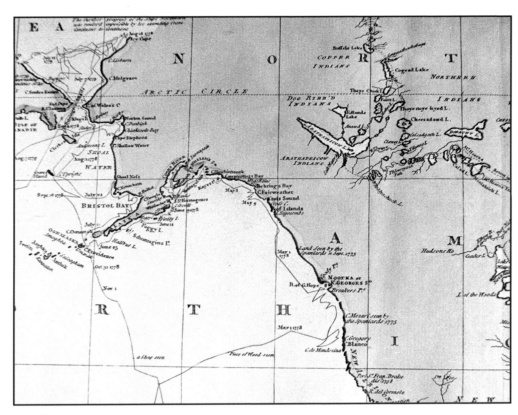

Map 74
General Chart exhibiting the discoveries made by Capt. James Cook in this and his preceding two voyages, with the tracks of the ships under his command. William Faden, 1784.

The Pacific Northwest part of Henry Robert's important map of the world, the result of the combined discoveries of Cook's three voyages. This map shows the interior discoveries of Samuel Hearne as well as the coastal ones of James Cook.

endpaper). This is because of a dispute with Cook's long-standing rival, Alexander Dalrymple, who, it seems, was unable to bring himself to accept the fact that Hearne's discoveries meant there could be no cross-continent strait. Roberts' original version was still published, however, a month after the "official" version, by William Faden, a well-known commercial map publisher of the time; this original version does show the Hearne material, similar to the world map, which was also separately published. Part of this map is shown here (Map 75).

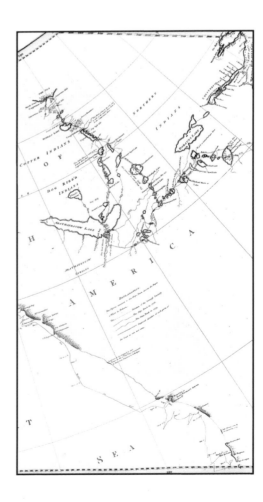

Map 75
Chart of the N.W. Coast of America and the N.E. Coast of Asia explored in the years 1778 and 1779. Prepared by Lieutenant Henry Roberts under the immediate inspection of Capt Cook Wm Faden 1784

Shows Cook's coastline and Hearne's discoveries. Cook's track is shown as a red line along the coast; Hearne's route is shown as a red line in the interior. Hearne's discoveries are placed too far west and too far north.

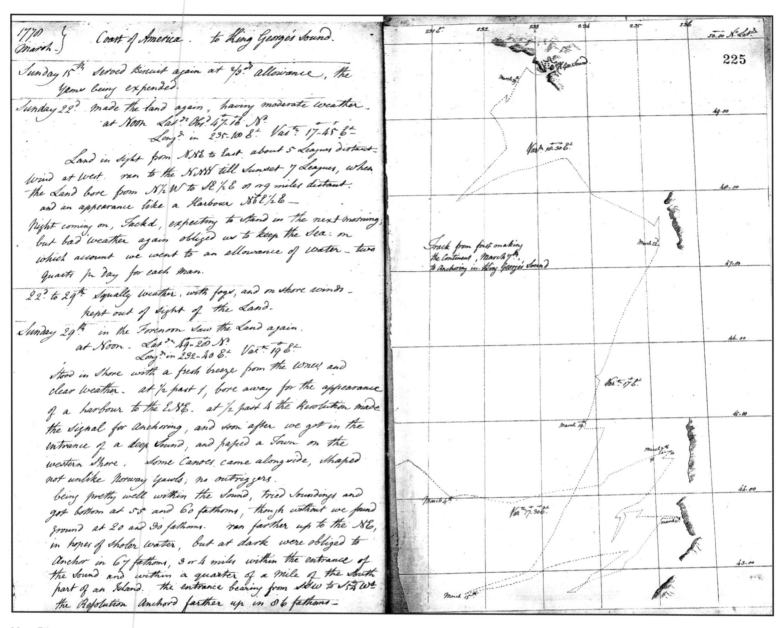

Map 76

Track from first making the Continent, March 7th, to Anchoring in King George's Sound. With facing page from the journal of James Burney, 1778.

This interesting little map was drawn by James (Jem) Burney, an officer on the *Discovery*. It vividly shows the erratic nature of the track of the *Resolution* and the *Discovery* caused by the weather. From an initial landfall near Cape Foulweather on 7 March 1778, the ships were driven south about 130 miles and offshore again by about 180 miles, before making any sustained headway north, a process which took over a week just to get back to the latitude of the initial landfall!

The further landfall near Cape Flattery at 48° N is shown, as is the discovery of King George's Sound – Nootka Sound, on Vancouver Island.

The page of Burney's journal opposite this map is also reproduced here, and the near miss of the Strait of Juan de Fuca is mentioned here:

...the land bore from N 1/2 W to SE 1/2 E 8 or 9 miles distant and an appearance like a Harbour NEE 1/2 E - night coming on, tackd, expecting to stand in the next morning, but bad weather again obliged us to keep the sea on which account we went to an allowance of water – two quarts per day for each man.

Finally, on 29 March, they saw land again, and Burney's journal relates how they sailed into King George's Sound, that some canoes came alongside, and how they anchored.

After the voyage with Cook, Burney went on to a successful naval career, and ended his life writing a monumental five volume book entitled *A Chronological History of the Discoveries in the South Seas.*

Map 77 (right, top) shows another page from Burney's journal, with a map of Nootka Sound.

SECRECY ON THE THIRD VOYAGE

As was normal at that time, Cook was instructed to ensure that all journals and maps made by any of his crew were gathered in before the end of the voyage. His instructions read:

Tak(e) care, before you leave the sloop to demand from the Officers and Petty officers, the Log Books and Journals they may have kept, and to seal them up for our [the Lords of the Admiralty] Inspection, and enjoining Them, and the whole Crew, not to divulge where they have been, until they shall have permission so to do...[49]

This was to try to keep information from the Spanish; as we have seen, Cook had no problem sharing information with the Russians.

There was a benefit likely unforeseen at the time which derived from this gathering of journals by the Admiralty; most were not returned to their writers and as a result stayed in Admiralty files, eventually to be preserved in archives such as London's Public Record Office or the Hydrographic Office of the Navy. Many probably would not have survived if they had stayed with their writers.

As might be expected, some crew members did not want to part with their work, and some escaped detection at the end of the voyage. Several unauthorized accounts of the voyage were published before the official one in 1784, including an anonymous one in 1781. Such was the journal of John Ledyard, an American from Connecticut who was a Corporal in the British Royal Marines, who in 1783 published an account together with a world map showing the tracks of Cook's ships (Map 78).

Sharing of information with the Russians was acceptable, unlike with the Spanish at this point in history. Map 79 is a copy of Cook's main chart of the north Pacific made by the Russians. It is probably a copy of a map given to the Russians by Charles Clerke, who had assumed command of the third voyage after Cook had been killed in Hawaii in early 1779. A map of the discoveries made by the English in the north Pacific had been presented to Lieutenant-Colonel Magnus Behm, the Governor of Kamchatka, at Petropavlovsk in May 1779.

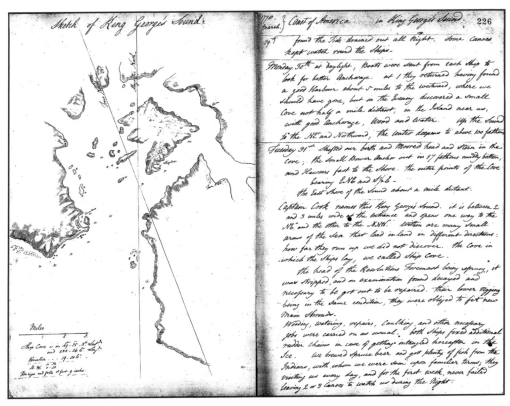

Map 77 (above)
Sketch of King George's Sound. With facing page from journal of James Burney, 1778.

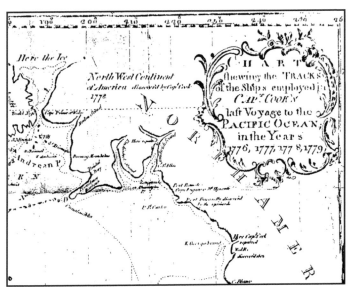

Map 78 (left)
Chart showing the Tracks of the Ships employed in Capt. Cook's last voyage to the Pacific Ocean in the Years 1776, 1777, 1778 and 1779 John Ledyard. From: *Journal of Captain Cook's last Voyage to the Pacific*, Hartford, 1783. (Probably copied from chart in Anon.: *Journal of Capt. Cooks Last Voyage*, Publ. E. Newbery, London, 1781.)

John Ledyard later led an expedition sponsored by Thomas Jefferson, who in 1786 was in Paris, to travel across Siberia to the Northwest Coast and then east to the United States. However, the expedition failed. The Russian Empress Catherine had him arrested and returned to Europe.

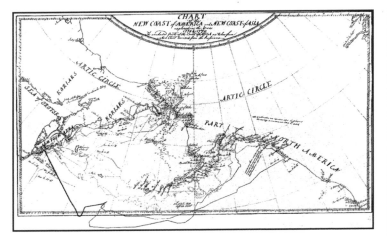

Map 79
Chart of New [sic] Coast of America and New [sic] Coast of Asia explored in the years 1778 and 1779...
Copy of Cook's chart by Russians; compare with Maps 66 and 67 on page 43.

The British ambassador to Russia had reported the official Russian attitude to Cook's voyage in a dispatch of January 1780: "(The Empress) *feels the great utility,*" he wrote, "*which must rest from such a voyage, and is anxious to promote its success...she expresst a very earnest desire of having copys of such Charts as may tend to ascertain more precisely the extent and position of these remote and unexplored parts of her Empire...*"
49/2

GEORGE VANCOUVER – MIDSHIPMAN

This map of Alaska and the northwest coast showing the track of Cook's ships between May and October 1778 was drawn by a midshipman on the *Resolution* who was destined to become much more familiar with the northwest coast in the future. The midshipman's name was George Vancouver. Vancouver sailed with Cook on both his second and third voyages. Midshipmen were young men in training to become full officers, and were required to do all the duties an officer might have to do, including keeping a journal and drawing maps. This is the only known map drawn by Vancouver on Cook's voyage to the northwest coast.

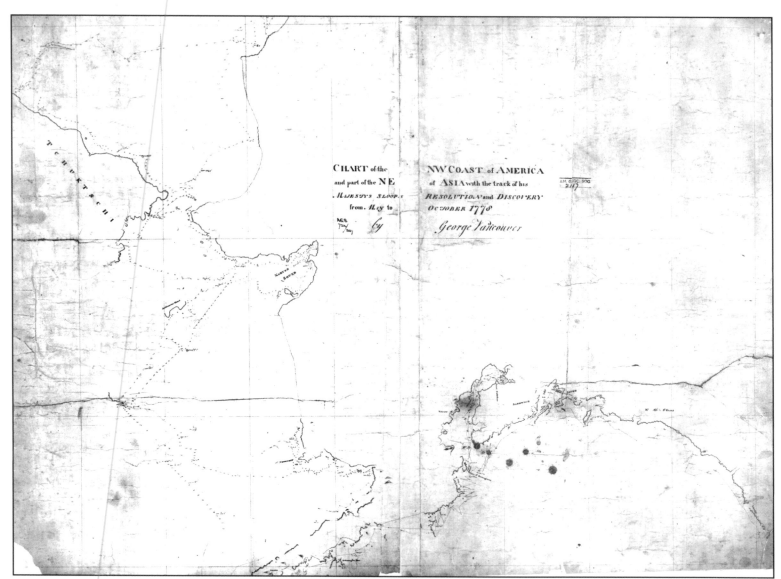

Map 80
Chart of the NW Coast of America and part of the NE of Asia (sic) with the track of his Majestys Sloops Resolution & Discovery from May to October 1778 by George Vancouver
This map was cut in half at some point in its history, so there are now two sheets, shown together here.

Russian Maps Used by James Cook

Maps that Captain James Cook is known to have carried with him on his voyage to the northwest coast are:

1. The map drawn by Petr Chaplin in 1729 showing the eastern coast of Siberia (Map 17, page 20)
2. Gerhard Müller's map showing the discoveries of Vitus Bering and Alexei Chirikov in 1741 (Map 40, page 29)
3. Jacob von Stählin's 1774 *Map of the Northern Archipelago,* which gave him so much trouble (Map 47, page 31)

PETER PALLAS MAPS COOK'S VOYAGE

Maps originating from Russia in the period just after Cook show many of the features Cook had plotted on his maps. One such map, published in 1781, was called *Map of the Discoveries between Siberia and America to the Year 1780* (Map 81).

It was contained in the first volume of a monumental seven-volume work published between 1780 and 1796 by Peter Simon Pallas, a German scholar who was a Professor of Natural History at the St. Petersburg Academy of Sciences. In 1768 he had been invited by Catherine the Great to take charge of a scientific expedition to Siberia, which lasted until 1774, and had seen the 1778 and 1779 despatches which Cook's expedition had sent to England as they passed through St. Petersburg.

It is perhaps not surprising then, that his map, published in 1781, bears a considerable resemblance to the one in the publication of Cook's voyage in 1784. It could also have been partly based on the outline map received from Cook by Gerasim Ismailov at Unalaska in October 1778 (see page 43).

What appears to be a Russian edition of the same map, though there are slight differences, is also shown here (Map 82). The Russian words at the top of the trace of the American coastline are *"The famous Captain Cook reached this vicinity in the year 1778".*

A map of Bering Strait was also prepared by Pallas, and appeared in volume four of his book in 1783. It is based on an earlier map by Ivan Kobelov, who in 1779 was sent to explore the area of the Chukchi, right across the Bering Sea from Cape Prince of Wales, and James Cook's map, as known to the Russians at that time (Cook's maps not being published until the following year), plus the Russian knowledge of the coast.

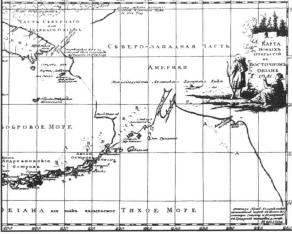

Map 81 (above)
Carte Der Entdekungen Zwischen Siberien und America bis auf das jahr 1780
(Map of the Discoveries between Siberia and America to the year 1780.)
Peter Simon Pallas, 1781.
From: P.S. Pallas, editor,
Neue nordische Beyträge,
St. Petersburg & Leipzig, Vol. l, 1781.

Map 82 (right)
Chart of the New Discoveries in the Eastern Ocean.
E. Khudyakov, 1781.

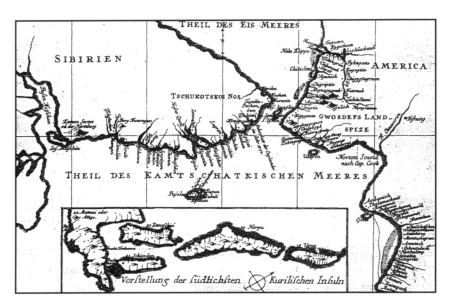

Map 83
Map of Bering Strait and adjacent coasts with inset: Representation of the Southernmost Kurile Islands.
From: P.S. Pallas, *Neue nordische Beyträge,* Vol.IV, 1783.

THE LOVTSOV ATLAS

Cook's mapping of the north Pacific was incorporated into a beautiful atlas of hand-drawn and colored charts in 1782 by Fleet Navigator Vasilii Fedorovich Lovtsov.

Although based principally on Russian sources, it also contains information from charts and notes left at Petropavlovsk by Captain Charles Clerke, who had succeeded Cook on the latter's death in Hawaii, and by Captain John Gore, who had taken over command of the expedition on Clerke's death in 1779.

The Lovtsov *Atlas* is somewhat of an enigma, in that it is more primitive than the information available to the Russians in 1782 would have permitted.

This one-of-kind, hand-drawn atlas is now in the British Columbia Archives.

Charts 11 to 14, of the northwest coast, in the atlas as individual pages, are displayed here overlapped to show the whole coastline (Maps 84A to 84E).

CHART 10 covers the Alaska Peninsula and the eastern Aleutians. As well as information from Cook, this map may incorporate information from Bering's second voyage and that of Krenitsyn and Levashev in 1766 – 1769. The cartouche contains a note about fog and storms precluding closer investigation.

CHART 11 is a rough outline of Cook Inlet, described as Big River, the Kenai Peninsula, and Sandwich Sound (Prince William Sound). It is based on descriptions from Cook's crew.

CHART 12 is the coast adjacent to the south. The inscription in the cartouche reads, *"Bay 58° 20', longitude 240° 45'. How far it stretches is impossible to ascertain because of shallowness of water"*. The latitude given suggests Cross Sound, the northern entrance to the Inside passage, but the reference to shallow water is puzzling.

Underneath this, the text reads, *"Captain Commander Bering was at this coast on the 20th day of July in the year 1741"*.

CHART 13, continuing south, two points separated by a break. The text in the cartouche reads, *"From the latitude 50° 07' to latitude 55° 23' and from longitude 249° 30' to longitude 243° 50' the land could not be seen because of fog and*

storms". The other text reads, *"Captain Chirikov was at this coast on the 15th day of July in the year 1741"*.

CHART 14 is the final map of the northwest coast, so schematic that one is led to conclude that if Cook's map was used as a basis for it, it must have been a outline map only, or perhaps a memory of a map seen but not retained.

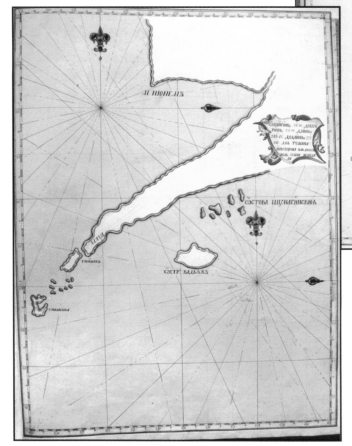

Map 84A. *Chart 10*

Map 84B *Chart 11*

The southernmost text is *"Novyi Albion"* (New Albion). The text in the cartouche reads, *"From the latitude 45° 00' to latitude 47° 00', longitude 253° 30' the land could not be seen because of fog and storms. Unknown if a bay or something else"*. [52]

Title Page from the Lovtsov *Atlas*

Compass rose from Lovtsov *Atlas*.

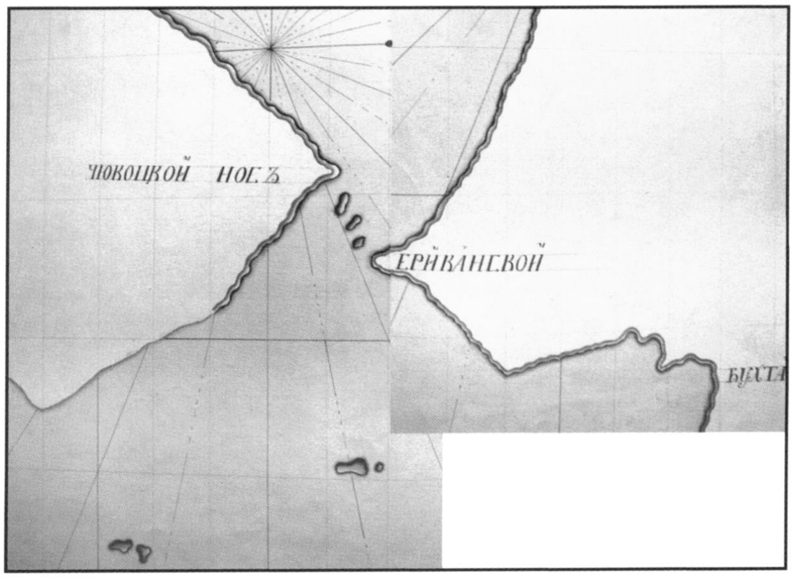

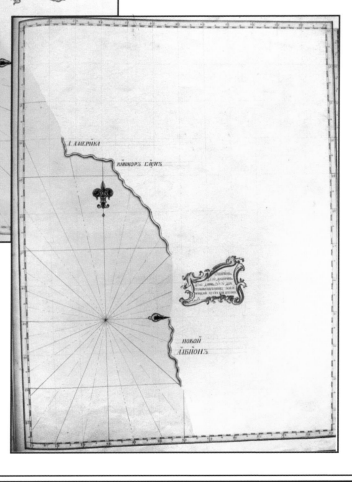

Map 85 (above)
Charts 8A and 8B, Bering Strait, from: Vasilii Fedorovich Lovtsov, *Atlas, by Navigator Lovtsov composed by him while wintering at the Bol'sheretsk ostrog in the year 1782,* watercolors, 1782.
The two charts are shown joined; in the atlas they are adjacent, but offset from each other.

This map was probably drawn with information given to Magnus Behm, the Governor of Kamchatka, by Cook's men in May 1779 (see page 49). At the top of the two sections of this map is a notation "along this line there was immovable ice". Cape Prince of Wales is labelled "American Cape". The cartouche reads, "From lat 68° to 69° and long 219° 30' fog and shallow water. Unable to sail [here] due to shallowness of water".

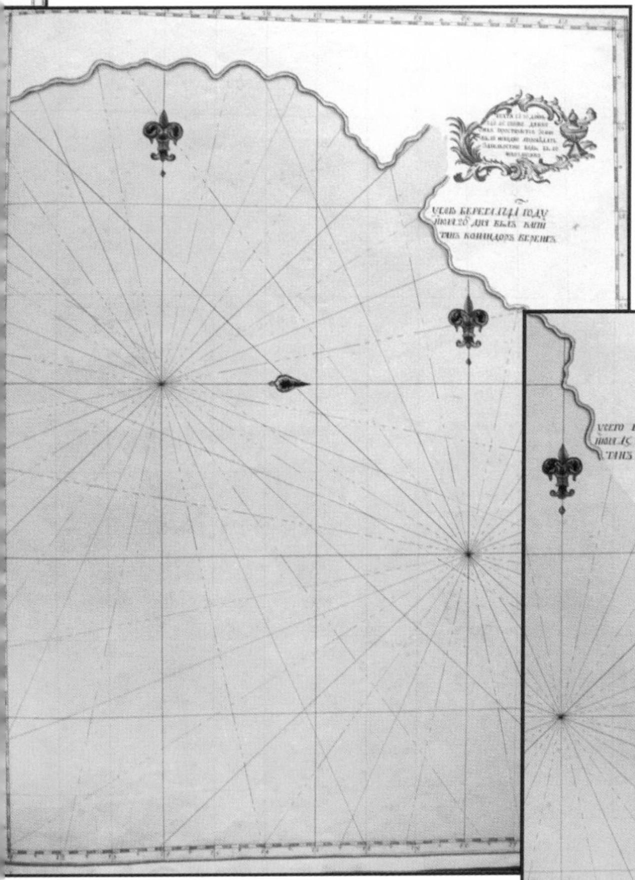

Map 84C *Chart 12*

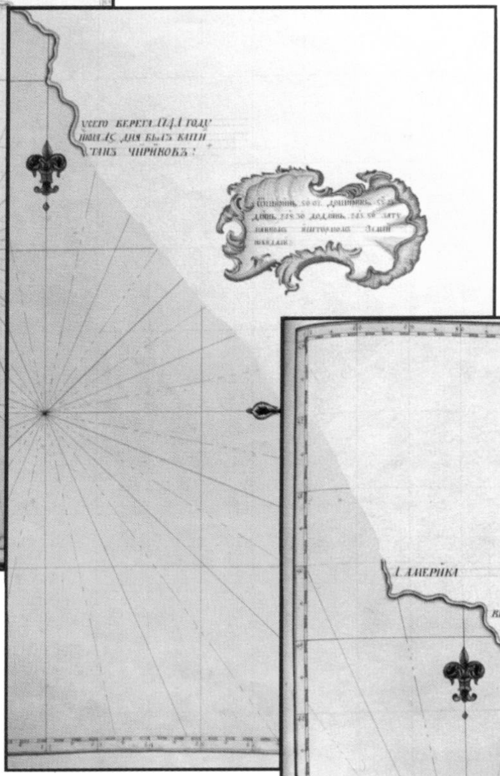

Map 84D *Chart 13*

Map 84 A–E
Charts 10, 11, 12, 13 & 14 from: Vasilii Fedorovich Lovtsov, *Atlas, by Navigator Lovtsov composed by him while wintering at the Bol'sheretsk ostrog in the year 1782,* watercolors, 1782.

Although the individual sheets in the *Atlas* are all the same size, Chart 13 (Map 84D) has been trimmed here so as not to obscure detail on overlapping charts.

Map 84E
Chart 14

WILLIAM FADEN'S MAP OF 1785

The year after the publication of the account of James Cook's third voyage, William Faden, who succeeded to Thomas Jefferys' business and as the geographer to the King, published a map of North America, part of which showed the north-west coast as revealed by Cook's maps.

Now Nootka Sound is shown, and the Alaskan coastline, following Cook, is quite well represented. Following the work Faden did with Henry Roberts on the preparation of the world map (Map 74, page 47), the discoveries of Samuel Hearne are shown. Further south, however, speculations continue to dominate. The River of the West is now suggested as flowing not only to the Pacific through the Strait of Juan de Fuca, but also, via the "Fair River", to Nootka or King George's Sound! This map is a reasonable representation of the state of knowledge of the Pacific Northwest, both coastal and interior, after James Cook but before George Vancouver.

Map 86
North America with the new discoveries, by William Faden, Geographer to the King. 1785

THE FUR TRADERS AFTER COOK

The crews of James Cook's ships had traded with the natives in Nootka Sound for sea otter pelts, which at the time they intended to use to keep themselves warm during the upcoming Arctic part of their voyage. However, when they reached Canton, they quickly found that the pelts had considerable value.

On the return of the third voyage to England, it did not take long for some of Cook's crew members to devise schemes to profit from this newly discovered commercial opportunity.

In 1783, there had been a general demobilization of the British Navy after the American Revolutionary War, with the result that there were many half-pay and retired officers available for voyages to wherever there was money to be made.

This led to a number of voyages to the northwest coast that despite the primary objective of making money, also produced significant mapping; after all, if you had discovered a good place to trade for furs, you would make a map to ensure that you could find your way back to the same location later.

JAMES HANNA

The first person out of the gate was a Scot named James Hanna, who sailed from Macao to the northwest coast in 1785 in a ship named, appropriately enough, *Sea Otter*, manned by only twenty men. They arrived at Nootka on 18 August. The natives were very willing to trade sea otter pelts, and Hanna quickly accumulated what he wanted.

During this time, however, after a so-called practical "joke" played on the chief, Maquinna (he sat on a chair under which was placed gunpowder and was blown into the air), the natives attacked the *Sea Otter* and were repulsed with considerable loss of life.

By the end of the year, Hanna was back in Macao with 560 sea otter pelts, which were sold for a good profit.

Encouraged by the money apparently to be made from this trade in sea otter pelts, Hanna and his supporters decided to try again the following year, and the *Sea Otter* arrived back at Nootka in August 1786. This time, however, he was disappointed to find two rival ships there ahead of him, and partly as a result of this obtained many fewer furs than on his first voyage, despite ranging up the coast as far as Alaska.

He intended to try yet again in 1787, but he died in Macao that year.

Hanna's discoveries added considerably to knowledge of some of the details of the northwest coast. The *Chart of Part of the N.W. Coast of America* shown here (Map 88) shows Cox's Island (named after Hanna's patron, John Henry Cox) as a separate island when in fact it is part of the northern extremity of Vancouver Island. The supposed channel making it an island is today's Quatsino Sound. Lance's Islands are the present-day Scott

Islands, and Fitzhugh Sound, also first mapped by Hanna, is so named today; it is part of the Inside Passage. The name was adopted by George Vancouver, who carried Hanna's maps with him in 1792. Hanna's map of St. Patrick's Bay (Map 87) is a detail of the first map.

The geographer Alexander Dalrymple made reference to Hanna's explorations when he was advancing British claims to the coast and to the fur trade; both of these maps were published by Dalrymple in 1789.

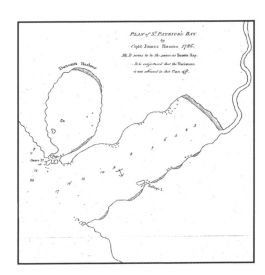

Map 87 (right, top)
Plan of St. Patrick's Bay by Capt. James Hanna 1786. Publ. by A. Dalrymple, March 29th 1789.
St. Patrick's Bay, just south of Cape Scott at the extreme northern tip of Vancouver Island, is today named San Joseph Bay, derived from the Spanish name Bahía de San José and shown on Spanish maps on pages 78 and 79 (Maps 128 and 129). Duncan's Harbour is today named Sea Otter Cove, which was the name James Hanna gave to it, but was not shown on this map, which was published by Alexander Dalrymple and not Hanna. It was shown with this name by John Meares in his book (see page 61). The promotory between San Joseph Bay and Sea Otter Cove is now named Hanna Point.

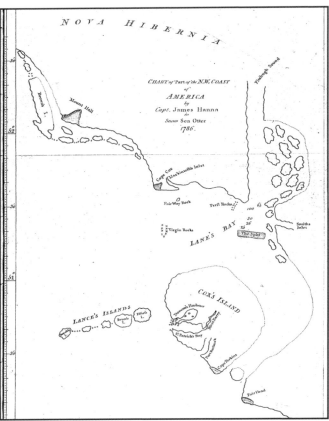

Map 88
Chart of Part of the N.W. Coast of America by Capt. James Hanna in Snow Sea Otter 1786 Publ. by A Dalrymple, March 29th 1789
Cox's Island is the northern part of Vancouver Island, north of Quatsino Sound.

JAMES STRANGE

The two rival ships that Hanna encountered when he entered Nootka for the second time, in 1786, were the *Captain Cook* and the *Experiment*, commanded by Henry Laurie and John Guise respectively; on board was a Scot named James Charles Stewart Strange, a godson of Bonnie Prince Charlie, and one of the financial backers of the expedition.

They had sailed from Bombay seven months earlier and arrived on the northwest coast on 25 June 1786. His expedition was an attempt by Bombay merchants, in conjunction with the East India Company, to expand British trade.

In Strange's instructions from David Scott, one of the Bombay merchants backing the voyage, the enterprise is grandiosely termed the "Exploring Expedition to the No. West Coast of America and towards the North Pole".

Strange is perhaps best known for his decision to leave the *Experiment*'s assistant surgeon, John Mackay, behind when he left the coast. This was in keeping with his orders to develop a trading relationship with the natives; Mackay was to record the language and customs of the natives, and compile a vocabulary.

Unfortunately for Mackay, Strange never returned, but luckily for him other traders were coming; he was rescued by Charles Barkley in June 1787.

Strange left Nootka on 28 July 1786 and four days later found islands off the northwestern tip of Vancouver Island – Hanna's Lance's Islands – and believing them to be a new discovery, named them Scott Islands, after David Scott. They are still called that today. Strange also named Cape Scott for the same reason.

Soon thereafter, Strange found a body of water running east and southeast which, because of its width and the tides and currents, he thought might be a strait or a river estuary, or even de Fonte's long-lost strait, although it was two degrees south of the latitude given to it in the printed account of de Fonte's voyage (see page 26). Strange called it Queen Charlotte's Sound; it is today's Queen Charlotte Strait, between the northern end of Vancouver Island and the mainland.

Two of Strange's maps are reproduced here. Map 90, drawn by S. Wedgbrough, (about whom little is known, but he may have been an officer on the *Experiment*) shows the northern end of Vancouver Island and parts of the mainland, plus the southern tip of the Queen Charlotte Islands, which Strange thought to be part of the mainland. The smaller scale map (Map 89) is actually the northeastern corner of a much larger map which shows the tracks of the *Captain Cook* and the *Experiment* from south-east Asia. As can be seen, Strange then proceeded to Prince William Sound, in Alaska. Here he met another ship, the *Sea Otter* (a popular name for obvious reasons, but not to be confused with Hanna's ship of the same name). This one was commanded by William Tipping, who had come to the northwest coast in company with the *Nootka*, commanded by John Meares, which had gone directly to Nootka Sound. Tipping found that Strange had not yet gone to Cook Inlet, and immediately set out for there; this pre-emption sealed the expedition's commercial fate.

Strange did not collect enough furs to pay the voyage's expenses, and for this reason never returned.

Map 89 (right)
Chart Exhibiting the Route of the Experiment Snow in the years 1785 and 1786
S. Wedgbrough.
From: *Strange's Journal and Narrative of the Commercial Expedition from Bombay to the Northwest coast of America. 1786 – 1787.*

The cause of all the sudden activity: the sea otter.

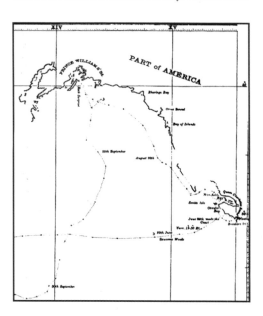

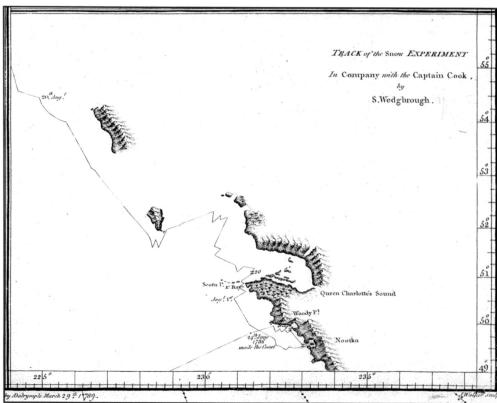

Map 90   *Track of the Snow "Experiment" In Company with the "Captain Cook" by S. Wedgbrough Publ. by A Dalrymple March 29th 1789*

COOK'S OFFICERS RETURN TO THE NORTHWEST COAST

Nathaniel Portlock and George Dixon were both veterans of Cook's third voyage who became involved with a British company formed in London to trade in Nootka Sound under the name King George's Sound Company, or Richard Cadman Etches and Company, after one of the principals.

Portlock sailed to the northwest coast in the *King George*; Dixon in the *Queen Charlotte*. They had official sanction from both the South Sea Company, which had by law a monopoly on trade in the Pacific, and the East India Company, so they could sell their furs in Canton. Most of the other traders after and concurrent with them did not bother with this nicety.

First on the coast in 1786, they achieved little, but the following year collected many sea otter pelts.

In the course of this trade, Portlock concentrated on the Alaskan coast, while Dixon went further south to the Queen Charlotte Islands, which he named after his ship. He was, in fact, the first European to realize that they were islands. He also named Dixon's Straits, now Dixon Entrance, which was the "Entrada de Pérez" that Juan Pérez had been puzzled about some thirteen years earlier.

Dixon concluded that the situation of the *"newly discovered"* Queen Charlotte Islands *"evidently show that they are the Archipelago of St. Lazarus, and consequently near the Straight of De Fonte."* [57] This archipelago had been shown on the maps purporting to show the discoveries of the mythical Admiral de Fonte in 1640 (see page 26).

Dixon published a map in a book after his return to London which shows Queen Charlotte's Isles and Dixon's Straits, but which showed the mainland coastline as continuous, though this was speculation, with dotted lines (Map 93, overleaf). No straits of de Fonte's here!

Portlock also produced a book on his return to London, and, not surprisingly, it contains some of the same ideas as Dixon's. He produced a map of the Alaskan coast and a number of detailed charts (Map 92, overleaf).

Map 91 shows the Pacific Northwest part of the great Arrowsmith world map of 1790, *as published in 1790*. It is important to note that this is the map as actually published in 1790, as several updated versions of this map exist, *without*

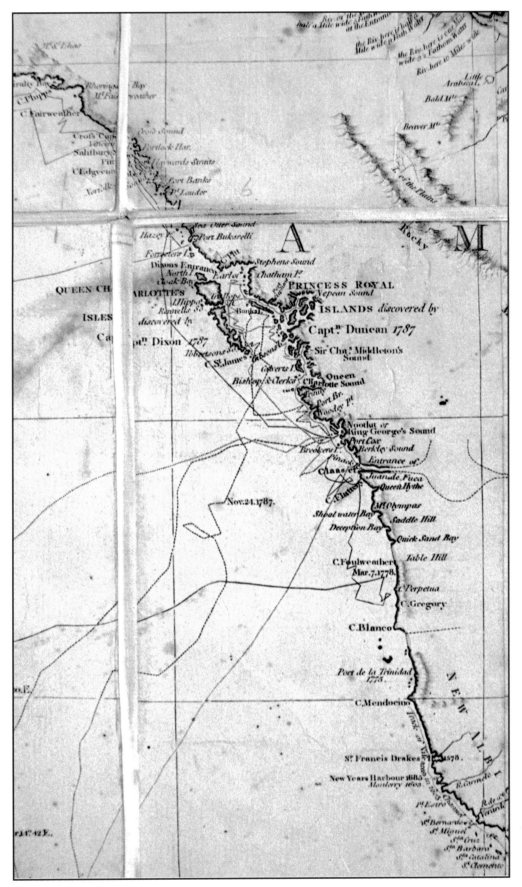

Map 91

Chart of the World on Mercator's projection, exhibiting all the new discoveries to the present Time, with the Tracks of the most distinguished Navigators since the year 1790, carefully collected from the best charts, maps, voyages, etc extant And regulated from the accurate astronomical observations made in three Voyages Perform'd under the command of Captn. James Cook, in the years 1768, 69, 70, 71, 72, 73, 74, 75, 76, 77, 78, 79 and 80.

Compiled & Published by A. Arrowsmith. London: 1st April 1790

The Princess Royal Islands (now Princess Royal Island) featured so prominently on this map were named by Charles Duncan in 1787, after his ship (see page 62).

The continuation of this map eastwards is shown in Map 159, page 97.

Map 92
*Chart of the North West Coast of America with the
Tracks of the King George and Queen Charlotte in
1786 – 1787*
From: Nathaniel Portlock, *Voyage around the
World but more Particularly to the North-West
Coast of America Performed in 1785, 1786, 1787
and 1788 in the King George and Queen Char-
lotte,* London, 1789.

the date changed. By far the most up-to-date map of its time, the atlas in which it appeared was London mapmaker Aaron Arrowsmith's first major work, which established his reputation as the pre-eminent mapmaker of his time. The map incorporated information from the voyages of Nathaniel Portlock and George Dixon, and also information from Charles Duncan, who was also on the northwest coast in 1787 and 1788 (see page 62). Note that Dixon's Queen Charlotte Islands are shown as two main islands on this map.

Many maps by the Arrowsmith firm appear in this atlas. Aaron Arrowsmith died in 1823, but his work was continued by his sons Aaron and Samuel until 1839, after which his nephew John Arrowsmith took over.

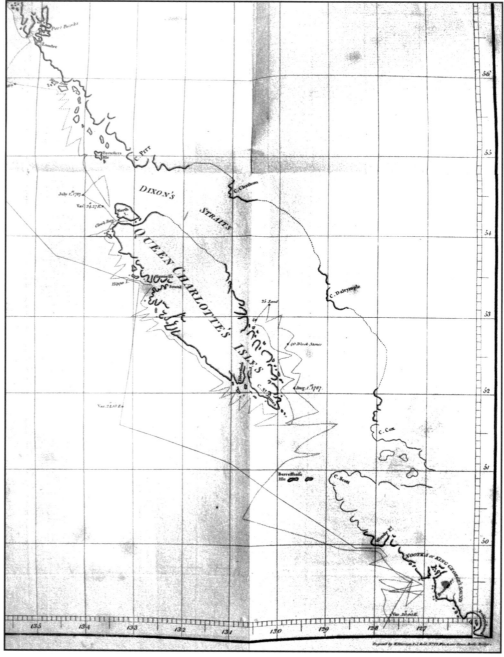

Map 93
*Chart of the North West Coast of America with Tracks of the King George and Queen Charlotte in 1786
and 1787*
From: George Dixon, *A Voyage Around the World,* 1789.
Note that Dixon shows only one large island for the Queen Charlottes.
Top: Title cartouche from the same map.

THE ILLUSTRIOUS JOHN MEARES

One of the more colorful figures in the early European exploration of the northwest coast was a former lieutenant in the British navy named John Meares.

Meares sailed to the northwest coast twice, in 1786 – 1787, and in 1788.

In 1786, after a voyage from India, Meares went straight to Nootka Sound while his partner, William Tipping, went to Alaska, where he outwitted James Strange (see page 56).

Later in the year, Meares, in his ship *Nootka*, sailed north to Alaska himself in search of furs and with the intention of establishing a permanent settlement. He found Russians occupying Cook Inlet on the site of modern Anchorage and pre-venting the natives from trading with any-one but themselves. However, before re-treating, he performed a possession cer-emony in the name of Britain at Point Pos-session. Then he went on to Prince William Sound, where there were no Rus-sians, and managed to obtain a consider-able quantity of furs. But Meares was very ignorant of Alaskan winter conditions and stayed too long; by November his ship was iced in. Twenty-three officers and crew died, killed by scurvy and alcohol.

Meares was eventually rescued by George Dixon and Nathaniel Portlock in May 1787; only Meares and nine of his crew were still alive. Given supplies by his rivals, he sailed back to Macao.

John Meares.

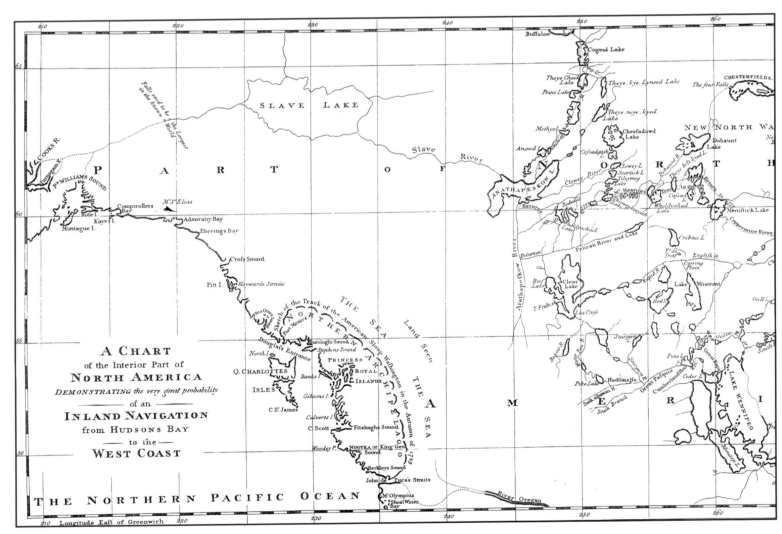

Map 94

A Chart of the Interior Part of North America Demonstrating the very great probability of an Inland Navigation from Hudson's Bay to the West Coast.
From: John Meares, *Voyages made in the years 1788 and 1789 from China to the North West Coast of America to which are prefixed An Introductory Narrative of a Voyage performed in 1786, from Bengal in the Ship Nootka; observations on the probable existence of a Northwest Passage and some account of the Trade Between the North West Coast of America & China, and the latter country & Great Britain,* 1790.
The "inland navigation" this map purports to show is from "Arathapeskow L." (Great Slave Lake; the latter and Lake Athabasca are confused) and the discoveries of Samuel Hearne in 1771 – 1772, to Cook Inlet or Prince William Sound on the Alaskan coast, through Slave River, Slave Lake, and "Cook's River". As such it mirrors the ideas of Peter Pond (page 64). A huge inland sea is shown from the Strait of Juan de Fuca to Dixon Entrance (shown here as "Douglas[']s Entrance) north of the Queen Charlottes. The "River Oregan" – the Columbia River – flows to the Strait of Juan de Fuca and Meares' inland sea.

In 1788, Meares was back. His ship, *Feliz Adventureira*, along with his partner William Douglas' ship, *Iphigenia Nubiana*, now carried Portuguese colors and even had a Portuguese captain, Francisco José Viana, to try to get around the East India Company monopoly in the Far East, where they hoped to sell their furs.

They had on board a copy of the Spanish map of Antonio Francisco Maurelle and Juan Francisco Bodega y Quadra (see Map 62, page 39).

In May 1788, Meares built a house at Friendly Cove in Nootka Sound, the first European to attempt any sort of settlement on the northwest coast.

He left one of his officers, Robert Funter, to build a smaller, shallower draft ship, and while it was being built, Meares sailed to the Strait of Juan de Fuca and traded along the coast as far south as Tillamook Bay in Oregon.

It was Meares who named Mount Olympus, on today's Olympic Peninsula in Washington; it had previously been named Sierra de Santa Rosalia by Juan Pérez.

At the latitude of the "Entrada de Hezeta", shown as "Rio de San Roque" on the Spanish map, Meares searched for, but could not find, the river's mouth.

"We can now with safety assert", he wrote, *"(that) no such river as that of the St. Roc exists, as laid down in Spanish charts."* By so missing the Columbia River, Meares considerably weakened later British claims to the area, particularly since Robert Gray, an American, located the river four years later, in 1792 (page 82).

Returning northward to Barkley Sound in July 1788, Meares sent Robert Duffin and thirteen men in a longboat to investigate the Strait of Juan de Fuca. Meares had acquired Charles Barkley's maps and journals (apparently now lost) in China, but still claimed discovery of the strait for himself. Duffin went as far as Port San Juan, an inlet on the north side of the entrance to the strait, where his boat was attacked by natives in two war canoes, and narrowly escaped death when his thick hat deflected an arrow.

In 1790, John Meares published an account of his voyages which suggested some affluent sponsorship, for the book was published in a deluxe edition accompanied by elegant maps and engravings. It purports to be the first extensive exploration of the northwest coast, but Meares had little respect for the truth,

and appropriated for himself discoveries made by Cook, Barkley, Dixon, Duncan, and some Spanish explorers. His book, *Voyages Made in the Years 1788 and 1789 from China to the North West Coast of America,* contained two now quite famous maps, the most significant feature of which was a depiction of the supposed track of the American sloop *Lady Washington*, commanded by Robert Gray.

These maps gave new credence to the idea of a Northwest Passage through one of the river-and-lake systems, an idea promoted by Meares in his book; one of these maps was one illustrating his ideas, with a map *"demonstrating the very great probability of an inland navigation from Hudsons Bay to the West Coast"* (Map 94, previous page).

This map shows Slave Lake connected to Arathapeskow Lake (Lake Athabaska) and with a suggestion, with dotted lines, of an outflow from Slave Lake to either Cook's River (Cook Inlet) or Prince William Sound. Interestingly enough, this was the same erroneous conclusion Peter Pond was coming to at about the same time, and it is quite possible that Meares was aware of Pond's maps (see page 64). The whole drainage system of the north-

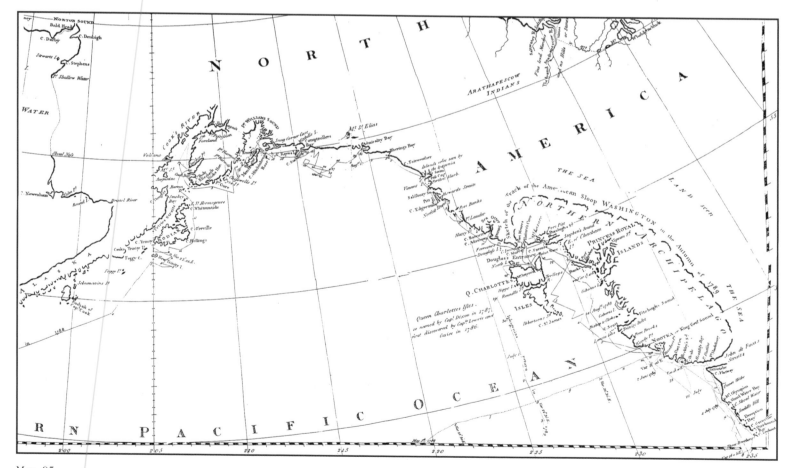

Map 95
Chart of the N.W. Coast of America and the N.E. Coast of Asia, explored in the Years 1778 and 1779 by Capt Cook and further explored, in 1788, and 1789.
From: John Meares, *Voyages*, 1790.

west territories was in fact shown substantially further west than it really was.

This map also shows the "River Oregan" with a suggested course either to the Strait of Juan de Fuca ("John de Fuca's Straits") or to the sea supposedly discovered by Robert Gray.

The main map of the northwest coast in Meares' book (Map 95) also shows the supposed track of Robert Gray's ship *Lady Washington*. Gray made no such voyage, and told George Vancouver so when he met with him later, in 1792.

It shows Meares tracks, and illustrates the fact that he did, in the time he was on the northwest coast, make a fairly detailed inspection of much of the outer coast from Kodiak Island to Oregon. With uncharacteristic modesty, his map does credit others for the discovery and naming of the Queen Charlottes, and is one of the earliest maps to show those islands as two main islands instead of one. This map shows longitude as degrees east of Greenwich, as is common for British maps of the period, during which the approach to the northwest coast was from the west (see, for example, all the maps of James Cook and those of George Vancouver); the international date line, with its meeting of 180° W and 180° E, had not yet, of course, been established. [61]

Several other detail maps from Meares' *Voyages* are also shown here.

A Sketch of Raft Cove (Map 96) was drawn by Robert Funter, the captain of *North West America*, the smaller ship built by Meares' men at Nootka, and the first

ship built on the northwest coast, other than small native craft.

A Sketch of Port Cox in the District of Wicananish (Map 97) is a representation of what is now Tofino, on the west coast of Vancouver Island. John Henry Cox was the merchant who helped finance the voyages of both James Hanna and John Meares. Today the island across the harbor from Tofino, in Clayoquot Sound, is named Meares Island, so named by Captain George Henry Richards in 1862.

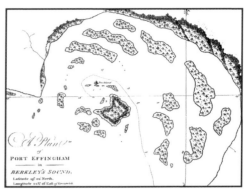

Map 98
A Plan of Port Effingham in Berkley's Sound
1787
The Broken Group of islands in today's Barkley Sound, on the west coast of Vancouver Island.

Map 97
A Sketch of Port Cox in the District of Wicananish
1787
The site of today's Tofino, on the west coast of Vancouver Island.

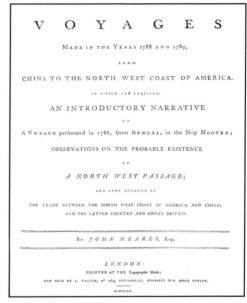

Title page of Meares' book.

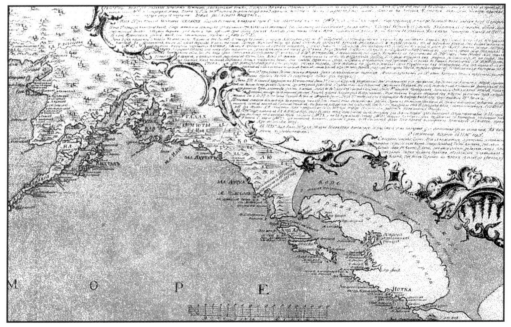

Map 96
A Sketch of Raft-Cove taken by Mr. Funter, Master of the North West American
1788
Raft Cove is on the northwestern coast of Vancouver Island, just south of Cape Scott.

Map 99
General map compiled under the direction of Grigorii Shelikov, c1793.
An interesting map related to Meares compiled by the Russian American Company, under Grigorii Shelikov, dated about 1793. Obviously the Russians had been sent a copy of Meares' book, for the island formed by the track of the *Lady Washington* looks remarkably similar to that on Meares' map.

CHARLES BARKLEY DISCOVERS THE "LONG LOST STRAIT"

In 1787, Captain Charles William Barkley came to Nootka in search of furs. His ship, the British *Loudoun*, had had its registry transferred to Ostend and its name changed to *Imperial Eagle*, under the Austrian flag, to escape the East India Company's monopoly at Canton, where Barkley hoped to sell his furs. He brought with him his seventeen-year-old wife, Frances, and she became the first white woman to visit the northwest coast.

As soon as the *Imperial Eagle* arrived, John Mackay appeared. He had been left behind by James Strange (page 56). He persuaded Barkley to take him on board. While on hunting parties with the natives the previous season, Mackay had come to believe that Nootka was on a large island, not on the mainland.

Barkley then sailed southwards to see if Mackay's beliefs were correct. At about 49° 20' N they discovered a large inlet to which they gave the name Wickaninnish's Sound, after the leasing chief in the area, and later explored another inlet to which they gave the name Barkley Sound. Further south, as Frances Barkley recorded later,

In the afternoon, to our great astonishment, we arrived off a large opening extending to the eastward, the entrance to which appeared to be about four leagues wide, and remained that width as far as the eye could see, with a clear westerly horizon, which my husband immediately recognized as the long lost Strait of Juan de Fuca, and to which he gave the name of the original discoverer, my husband placing it on his chart.[62]

Unfortunately, Barkley's chart did not survive, being confiscated in Canton when he sold his furs.

However, a chart drawn by Charles Duncan, another British fur trader some thirteen months later, did survive, and was published by Alexander Dalrymple in 1790. He had sailed south in the *Princess Royal*, much as Barkley had done, and drew a map of his discoveries.

His map is shown here (Map 100). Duncan's map shows a coastal view as an aid to finding the Strait, presumably because it had been so hard to find in the first place. It shows a pinnacle near the strait's entrance, which Duncan assumed was the pillar reported by Juan de Fuca in 1592 in the Michael Lok account (see page 16). The natives had told Duncan of a "great sea" – *A'ass toopulse* – to the east, undoubtedly the Strait of Georgia and Puget Sound. Duncan was convinced that this must be the Northwest Passage, so much so, that on his return to London, he commanded a Hudson's Bay expedition to find the eastern entrance to the Passage. After two attempts, which of course failed, he committed suicide.

Charles Duncan's map of the Strait of Juan de Fuca lived on to aid many navigators after that time, perhaps most notably George Vancouver, who had the map with him when he arrived on the northwest coast in 1792.

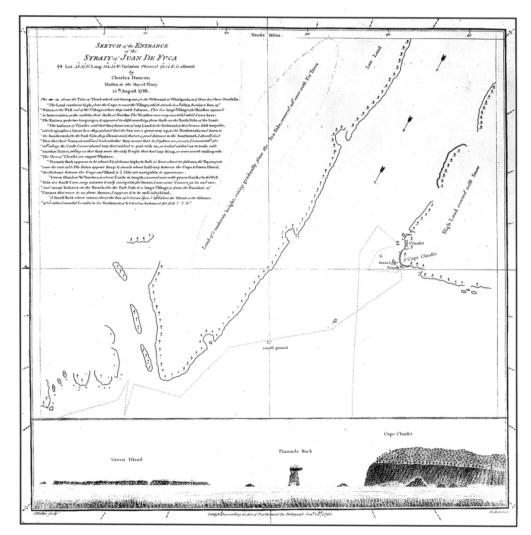

Map 100
Sketch of the Entrance of the Strait of Juan de Fuca
Lat 48° 37' N. 124° 54' W Variation observed 19° 14' E is allowed
by Charles Duncan Master in the Royal Navy 15th August 1788
Alexander Dalrymple, publ.

Part of the notation under the title reads, *"The Indians of Classet [Cape Flattery] said that they knew not of any land to the Eastward; & that It was A'ass toopulse, which signifies a Great Sea: they pointed that the Sea ran a great way up, to the northward..."* Enough to excite anybody about a Northwest Passage!

Some of the discoveries of Charles Duncan were shown by Aaron Arrowsmith on his 1790 *Chart of the World on Mercator's Projection...* shown on page 57 (Map 91).

WILBRECHT COMBINES THE DISCOVERIES OF COOK WITH THOSE OF THE RUSSIANS

This map by Alexander Wilbrecht was published in 1787. He combined the maps of Cook's third voyage drawn in 1778 and 1779 with the Russian maps from the voyages of Bering and Chirikov, and others. The coastline is more complete than Cook's maps published three years earlier. The inset map, of Kodiak and Afognak Islands near the entrance to Cook Inlet in Alaska, is probably copied from one drawn by Gerasim Ismailov, the Russian with whom James Cook had met at Unalaska in 1778 and exchanged cartographic information.

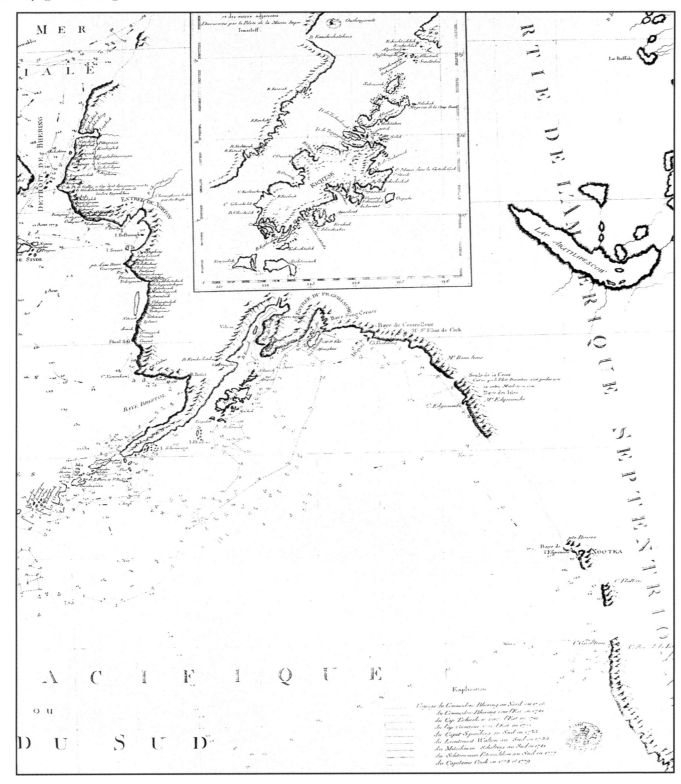

Map 101
Carte des Decouvertes Faites par Les Russes et par le Captaine Anglais Jacques Cook dans la Mer de Sud. Alexander Wilbrecht, 1787.
Lac Arathapescow (Lake Athabaska) is shown far too near to the Pacific, following the Roberts and Faden versions of James Cook's maps (see Maps 74 and 75, page 47). Nootka is prominently marked. More detail of the Alaskan coastline is shown than for most of the Pacific Northwest.

PETER POND AND HIS NORTHWEST PASSAGE

Peter Pond was an independent fur trader, later with the North West Company, who, in the period 1765 to 1788, ranged over vast tracts of what is now western Canada. Pond learned of James Cook's discovery of Cook's River, west of the Kenai Peninsula on the southern Alaska coast. Cook's River was later found by George Vancouver to be only an inlet (see Map 148, page 90). It was generally believed during the 1780s to be the mouth of a river, an illusion kept alive by the publication of various accounts of Cook's third voyage.

In the late 1770s, natives had told Pond of rivers flowing west fom Lake Athabasca to the sea, and by 1783 Pond was certain that one of those rivers was Cook's. A map he drew in 1785 shows the optimistic idea that the Great Slave Lake and Lake Athabasca are the source of the rivers for the entire northwest. The Mackenzie, Peace, and Athabasca do in fact flow north or west from the lakes. His 1785 map shows Cook's River flowing west to the Pacific.

Unfortunately, Pond was unable to make an astronomical observation to fix his position, and hence he relied on dead reckoning. This led him to produce maps which were distorted in their interpretation of distances. He located all his lakes and rivers too close to the Pacific on average by about 20° of longitude, about 1000 km (600 miles).

Pond's map of 1785 (Map 102) placed the Great Slave Lake at 135° W, 20° west of its true location. This placed it only 800 km (500 miles) from Cook Inlet, instead of the correct distance of almost 2,000 km (1,200 miles). It did, however, correctly show the Mackenzie River flowing to the Arctic Ocean.

While Pond wintered at Athabasca in 1787 – 1788, his wintering companion was a young Alexander Mackenzie. Pond's theories had a great effect; Mackenzie's 1789 and 1792 expeditions were both driven by Pond's ideas (see page 95).

Originally Pond was uncertain about the connections from the lakes to the Pacific, and confused Cook's River with the Mackenzie, but by 1787 he seemed to have become certain and drew maps showing Cook's River flowing from the Great Slave Lake to the Pacific.

In 1789, Pond talked about his ideas with a Quebec merchant named Isaac Ogden, who included notes of their dis-

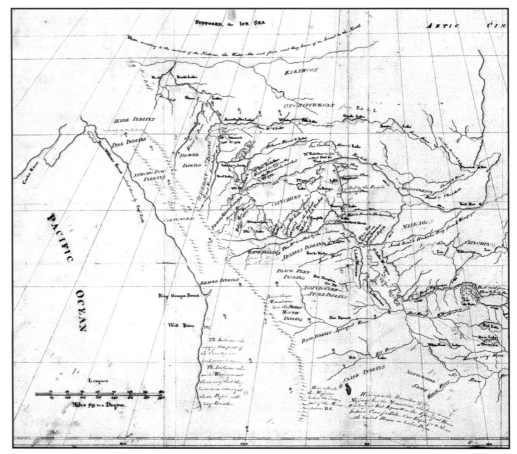

Map 102 (above)
Map of Western Canada presented to Lieutenant-Governor of Quebec, Lord Hamilton, in 1785 by Peter Pond.
Pond's map correctly places King George Sound (Nootka Sound) at about 126° W, but compresses the interior features between Hudson Bay, shown on the extreme right of this map, and the coast, are considerably compressed. The Rockies are shown not far from the Pacific coast. Great Slave Lake and Lake Athabasca are shown about 20° W of their true location, but correctly emptying into the Arctic.

Map 103 (right)
*A Map shewing the comm-
unication of the Lakes and
the Rivers between Lake
Superior & Slave Lake in
North America*
From: *Gentleman's
Magazine*, March 1790.

Pond now shows a river, labeled "Cook's or Slave R" flowing from the Great Slave Lake to Cook Inlet, then known as Cook's River. His dream of an inland Northwest Passage was complete!

First published in 1731, *Gentleman's Magazine* was the first to use the word *magazine* in the modern sense; it derives from the French for warehouse – a warehouse of essays.

cussion in a letter to his father in London. Included with the letter was a re-drawing of a map Pond drew in 1787, showing the Mackenzie, Great Slave Lake, and Cook's River and Prince William Sound as all connected. The letter and the accompanying map were published in a popular London magazine called the *Gentleman's Magazine* (Map 103). This

map caught the attention of government officials planning George Vancouver's expedition. Despite the fact that Mackenzie's 1789 journey was known by this time to have taken him to the Arctic Ocean, not the Pacific, Vancouver was instructed (failing discovery of a Northwest Passage to the south of Cook Inlet) to find Cook's River and evaluate its potential.

THE FRENCH SEND LA PEROUSSE IN COOK'S WAKE

La Perousse

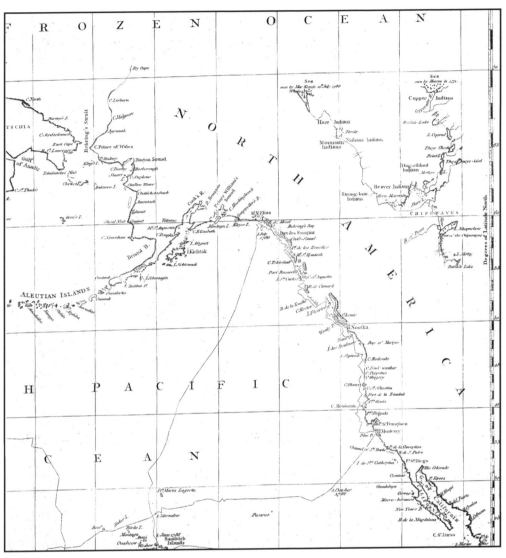

Map 104
Chart of the Coasts of America and Asia from California to Macao according to the discoveries made in 1786 and 1787 by the Boussole and Astrolabe
G G & J Robinson, November 1798.

From the English translation of the account of La Perousse's voyage. The map represents knowledge of the northwest coast in 1785. Inland, Mackenzie's 1789 expedition to the mouth of the Mackenzie River is shown, as are the earlier discoveries of Samuel Hearne. This was an excellent map for the time it was drawn, but out-of-date by the time it was published.

France and Britain had been at war since France sided with the United States in the American War of Independence, but in 1783, the year before Cook's journals were published, they signed a peace treaty. In August 1785, the French, not to be outdone by Cook, sent a distinguished naval officer, Jean François Galaup, Comte de la Perousse, on a similar scientific voyage around the world with two ships, *L'Astrolabe* and *La Boussole*.

La Perousse had orders to visit those parts of northwestern North America not visited by Cook, and also to search for the Northwest Passage, and to make scientific observations. But there were other considerations beyond discovery that motivated the French to dispatch La Perousse. He was to obtain information about the fur trade. The part of Cook's journals that mentions the possibility of developing a trade in furs had been studied in France particularly because France had recently lost her Canadian fur trade in the east, under the 1763 Treaty of Paris, and Britain was gaining considerable revenues from it through the Hudson's Bay Company.

In July 1785, La Perousse reached the northwest coast near Mt. St Elias in Alaska, and for the next three months sailed southwards to Monterey. Whereas Cook had sailed in almost a straight line between Nootka and Mount Edgecumbe in Alaska, La Perousse kept close to the outer islands and was able to chart precise reference points.

As a result, he produced what was an excellent map at the time he drew it (though he, like Cook, missed the Strait of Juan de Fuca), but it was not until as late as 1798 that the account of the voyage was published with this map, and by that time better maps had been produced by George Vancouver.

The delay was undoubtedly due to the fact that La Perousse never returned, both of his ships having been wrecked in the south Pacific in 1788. The maps survived only because he had entrusted them to the British in 1786 at Port Jackson, in Australia, to be forwarded to Paris.

The English edition of La Perousse's map of the North Pacific was also published on 1798, and a map from this edition is shown here (Map 104).

JOSEPH BILLINGS' RUSSIAN EXPEDITION

The Billings expedition of 1787 to 1793 was a Russian response to news of Spanish, British, and now French activity in what the Russians regarded as their sphere of influence. The orders for it were prepared within ten weeks of the sailing of the French expedition under La Perousse in August 1785.

Joseph Billings was a seaman who had sailed with James Cook. Several years after he had returned he offered his services to the Russians, who, because of the knowledge they assumed he would have from sailing with Cook, made him a lieutenant in the Russian navy, and when an expedition to the north Pacific was planned, he seemed to be the right person to lead it; after all, he had been there. Lieutenant Gavriil Sarychev was also appointed to the expedition, and his expertise in surveying and cartography were to prove useful; he ended his career an admiral and prepared an atlas in 1826.

Billings and Sarychev did cover a lot of ground in several years, reaching Kodiak Island to the east and even undertaking an overland march at one point, but the expedition is not viewed as particularly significant today. But it did fill in the Russian knowledge of some areas. Billings was not a writer, but Sarychev did produce a narrative of the expedition and a number of maps, of which the most important is the one shown here. This map finally rectified most of the blunders made by Synd earlier (see page 30), removing many nonexistent islands. Sometimes cartographic knowledge advances with removal of incorrect material instead of the addition of new!

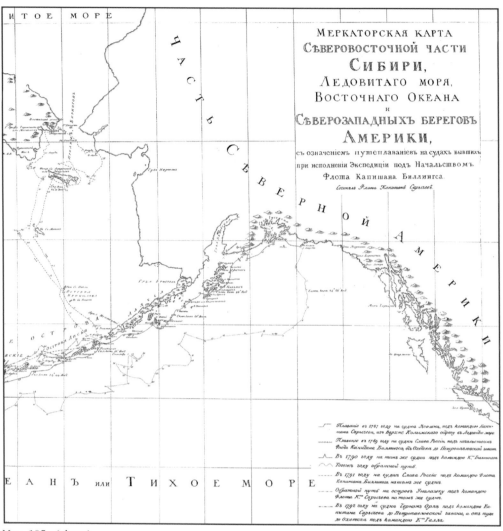

Map 105 (above)

Mercator Map Showing the Northeast Portion of Siberia, the Arctic Ocean, Eastern Ocean, and Northwest Coasts of North America. G.A. Sarychev, 1802.
From: *Puteshesvie flota kapitana Sarycheva po severovostochnoi chasti Sibiri ...* St Petersburg, 1802.

Map 106

Map of marine discoveries by Russian Navigators in the Pacific & Frozen Oceans, made in various years. Compiled & corrected according to the latest observations of foreign navigators & engraved in the year 1802 at the Map Depot of His Imperial Majesty.
Enclosure in Sir C. Bagot's Despatch no.56, Nov 17th 1821.
From: *British Case, Alaska Boundary Atlas,* 1903 (see page 188).

Sir Charles Bagot was the British ambassador to Russia in the period leading up to the 1825 Anglo-Russian boundary treaty regarding the territory which is now Alaska (see page 108). He utilized this 1802 map in those negotiations, and the map was again pressed into service in the Alaskan boundary negotiations between Britain and the United States which resulted in the boundary treaty of 1903 (see page 188).

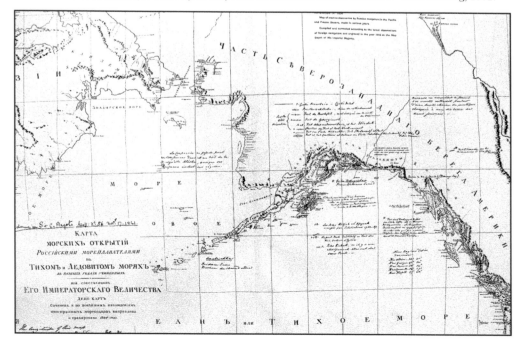

SPAIN ATTEMPTS TO SECURE THE PACIFIC NORTHWEST

The achievements of the Spanish in exploring the coast of the Pacific Northwest have been somewhat overshadowed by the British and the Americans, largely because it was the latter two nations which were destined to inherit the region, and, as always in history, the historical record is written by those who prevail. Famous west coast historian Henry Wagner reflected this view in 1933:

The great reputations attained by Captain James Cook and Captain George Vancouver for their work of exploration on the northwest coast of America have completely dwarfed in the mind of the public the achievements of the Spaniards during the same period.

The two isolated English voyages to the northwest coast appeared in England in large impressive folio volumes and each work was accompanied by a series of maps prepared with great care.

The Spanish officers who did far more work were not so fortunate. The Spanish government was not interested in furnishing the rest of the world with information about the northwest coast of America, which they claimed as their own, and it was not until Vancouver appeared on the scene with the obvious purpose of preparing a work for publication that the Spaniards awoke to the necessity of bringing their discoveries to light and thus of entering somewhat into the spirit of the times.[67]

The increased activities of Spain between 1788 and 1792 meant that a considerable number of maps were produced, some of of which were to be used by George Vancouver to assist his mapping efforts.

As we shall see, contrary to their previous policies of secrecy, the Spanish did share their cartographic knowledge with the British, but for reasons that remain obscure to this day, until 1802, when it was too late, they still chose not to publish their work, and so the world remained ignorant of what they had achieved. Ironically, free distribution of their maps and accounts of their explorations would have bolstered their claims to sovereignty on the northwest coast.

THE ALASKAN VOYAGE OF MARTÍNEZ AND HARO

In 1788, Esteban Jose Martínez and Gonzalo López de Haro were ordered north with instructions to reach 61° N, to claim possession for Spain wherever possible, and to produce charts in order to make it possible to find any place that they had visited should a decision be made later to colonize.

Arriving at Prince William Sound in May 1788, the expedition did not achieve a great deal due mainly to petty quarrelling instigated by Martínez, who had a volatile temper and often got drunk. They did, however, get as far west as Dutch

Harbor, on Unalaska Island, in the Aleutians, the furthest west the Spanish ever explored. López de Haro arrived after Martínez to find him feasting and getting drunk with the Russian trader there, Potap Zaikov, who liked Spanish brandy as much as Martínez liked Russian vodka. Martínez later performed a surreptitious ceremony of possession, without regard to the obvious Russian presence before them. Martínez and López de Haro returned separately to San Blas.

This expedition, despite the disagreements, added considerably to Spanish

cartographic knowledge of the Alaskan coast. López de Haro drew a map which showed the knowledge gained (Map 107). On his return from the 1788 voyage, Martínez recommended to the Spanish viceroy Flores that Nootka should be occupied to forestall any Russian expansion towards California.

THE SPANISH OCCUPY NOOTKA

The viceroy was convinced that Martínez was right and immediately put in hand plans to occupy Nootka. Martínez and López de Haro, despite their disagreements, were given this task, and they sailed north from San Blas in February 1789.

A day out of Nootka, Martínez met the American Robert Gray, in the *Columbia*, a sign that others were using Nootka. When they arrived, they found the *Iphigenia*, with Captain William Douglas, John Meares' partner, anchored in Friendly Cove.

Then began a series of events that almost led Britain and Spain to go to war against each other over the northwest coast.

Map 107
Carta reducida que contiene la costa septentrional de la California asta los 62 grados de latitud Norte correjida y en mendada en la expedicion que hicieron los dos buques de S.M. la fragata Princesa y el paquebot San Carlos desde el Puerto de San Blas asta las latitud Norte de 60 grados y 11 minutos en el ano de 1788
Gonzalo López de Haro, 1788

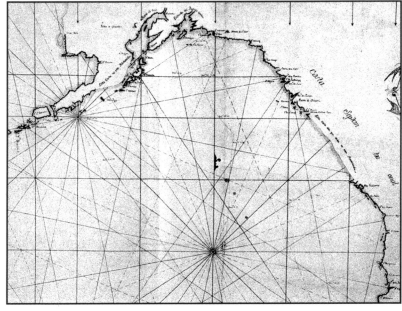

THE NOOTKA INCIDENT

In 1789, as Spain attempted to assert sovereignty over the northwest coast, a series of incidents occurred which almost led to war between Britain and Spain.

William Douglas, sailing under the Portuguese flag, had instructions in Portuguese which contained terminology which the new Spanish commander, Martínez, chose to find offensive. Among other things, the instructions claimed a right to be on the northwest coast because of the supposed discoveries of Bartholemew de Fonte (see page 26).

Martínez charged Douglas and the Portuguese captain Viana with having anchored in Spanish domain without a licence and possessing instructions violating Spanish sovereignty, and then arrested them. The Spanish seized Douglas' trade goods and furs, and his charts and journals. Douglas and his men were subsequently released on condition they leave the northwest coast; however, once released, they did not leave.

A few weeks later, another ship in the Meares trading group, the *Argonaut*, with its captain, James Colnett, entered Nootka Sound. Martínez picked an argument with Colnett. In response to Martínez' claim that he commanded the garrison at Nootka in the name of the King of Spain, Colnett replied that the northwest coast belonged to Britain, by virtue of the discoveries of Captain Cook. But the Spanish had the superiority in men and vessels at that point in Nootka Sound, and Martínez arrested Colnett and put a Spanish crew on board the *Argonaut*, sailing her to the Spanish naval port of San Blas, in Mexico.

The news of Douglas' arrest reached Britain in 1790, and John Meares presented a Memorial to Parliament which listed Spanish insults to the British flag.

The British prime minister, William Pitt, realized Britain could use this incident to extort from Spain assent to a principle never before conceded, that is, recognition of a British right to make settlements in any unpopulated area nominally claimed by Spain by right of prior discovery, but never colonized.

The principle of occupation, once recognized in a treaty, would not only provide unhindered access to the northwest coast but would also facilitate the achievement of a long sought-after British objective: the economic and political penetration of Spanish America. Pitt seized

on the Nootka incident despite the shady circumstances surrounding Meares' activities in 1788, using the Portuguese flag as a disguise.

The Nootka Convention, forced by England on Spain by threat of war, was signed in October 1790, *"a pact"*, as one writer put it, *"which in hindsight marked a watershed in Spanish history, the perceptible start of an ebb tide in Empire."* [68]

There were some ambiguities in the agreement, but after 1790 sovereignty became a matter of occupancy rather than prior discovery. This was a principle which would become very important later, when the United States inherited the Spanish claims (by the Transcontinental Treaty of 1819, Spain ceded her claims north of 42° N to the United States), and challenged Britain over the ownership of the Oregon Country (see page 131).

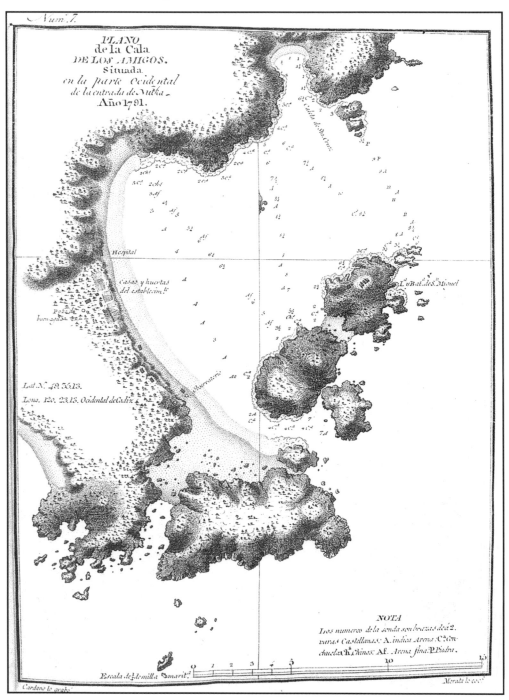

Map 108
Plano de la Cala De Los Amigos situada en la parte ocidental de la entrada de Nutka Ano 1791
From: *Relación.. Atlas, 1802.*

From 1790 onwards, British cartographers often showed British territory extending much farther south.

In late October 1789, the Spanish abandoned Nootka, but later the same year decided to re-occupy it. Early in 1790, three ships were dispatched from San Blas under the command of Francisco de Eliza, with Manuel Quimper and Salvador Fidalgo.

They arrived in early April, and, finding Friendly Cove empty, proceeded to build a settlement and fortifications. Seventy-five soldiers from the Company of Volunteers of Cataluña, under the command of Pedro Alberni (after whom Port Alberni and Alberni Inlet on Vancouver Island are named), were to be permanently stationed at Nootka. It was Alberni who cultivated the first garden in British Columbia here at Friendly Cove, where he carefully sowed a row of each of many different kinds of vegetables each week in order to determine the best sowing times. Clearly he expected Spain to be there for some time.

Map 108 shows the Spanish settlement at Friendly Cove, which they called Puerto de la Santa Cruz de Nuca, but on this map adopted the Spanish translation of the English name: Cala de Los Amigos. It shows the battery or fort they built on the first island at the entrance to the cove, which they called San Miguel.

THE FIDALGO EXPEDITION TO ALASKA IN 1790

Once ensconced in Nootka, Eliza dispatched Salvador Fidalgo to Alaska with the intention of countering the Russian presence in the area. Fidalgo explored Prince William Sound and took formal possession of a bay inside, which he called Córdova, from which the present city derives its name. He also entered Cook Inlet, but finding two Russian forts, sailed quickly for Kodiak Island, where he found yet another Russian post. From there he sailed south again, and unable to make Nootka due to winds, went back to San Blas. Fidalgo's explorations filled in Spanish cartographical knowledge of the Gulf of Alaska, which is evident on maps after that time, such as Map 109 here, but had little political consequence.

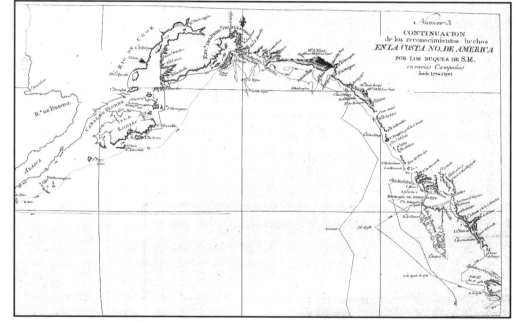

Map 109
Numero 3 Continuacion de los reconocimientos hechos En La Costa No. De America por los buques de S.M. en varias Campanas desde 1774 a 1792
From: *Relación...*, Atlas, 1802.

A Spanish stamp issued in 1967 to commemorate Spanish explorations of the Northwest Coast shows an almost identical map to Map 108.

This well-known view of Friendly Cove was the work of Spanish artist José Cardero. The ship at anchor is Eliza's frigate *Concepción*, covered up for a long stay. On the left is the battery of San Miguel, flying the Spanish flag.

MANUEL QUIMPER EXPLORES THE STRAIT OF JUAN DE FUCA

Manuel Quimper left Nootka on the last day of May 1790 to explore southwards. His ship was the *Princesa Real*, the *Princess Royal* confiscated from James Colnett's associate, Thomas Hudson. His pilot was Gonzalo López de Haro.

Quimper spent ten days in Clayquot Sound, and then sailed into the Strait of Juan de Fuca. He paid particular attention to possible harbors, charting and performing acts of possession in all he found. Maps were produced, two of which are shown here: Neah Bay (Bahía de Núñez Gaona), Map 110; and Esquimalt Harbour (Puerto de Córdova), Map 111. On 5 July 1790, just beyond the farthest point reached by the Quimper expedition, pilot Juan Carrasco also sighted an opening which he thought was a bay, and he named it Ensenada de Caamaño, after Jacinto Caamaño, one of the new naval officers serving out of San Blas. It was in fact Admiralty Inlet, the entrance to Puget Sound, which was to be discovered and named by George Vancouver only two years later. Quimper missed Admiralty Inlet despite the fact that natives had told him of a channel towards the south; he thought that the information was false.

Quimper named the circular "end" of the Strait of Juan de Fuca Seno de Santa Rosa, and came away believing it to be a more or less closed body of water. Carrasco also found Haro Strait (Canal de López de Haro), Rosario Strait (Boca de Fidalgo), and Deception Pass (Boca de Flon), but did not explore them enough to realize that this was just an archipelago, today's San Juan Islands, not a continuous shore. They did realize that Haro Strait was a channel (canal) rather than a bay (boca), but felt that they did not have enough time to explore it. Quimper spent eleven days at Neah Bay (Bahía de Núñez Gaona, Map 110) on the return trip to Nootka, where they also performed their possession ceremony for Spain.

The maps drawn during the expedition by Gonzalo López de Haro included a general map of the Strait of Juan de Fuca showing the closed-end basin that they believed formed its eastern end (Map 113). La Gran Montana Carmelo is today's Mount Baker. Map 112 is a British copy of this map which was sent to George Vancouver in 1792.

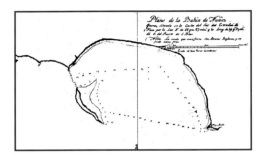

Map 110 (above)
Plano de la Bahía de Núñez Gaona, situada en la costa del Sur del Estrecho de Fuca por la lat. V de 48 gra 27 min y la long de 19 (?) 27 al O. del Puerto de S. Blas.
Manuel Quimper, 1790

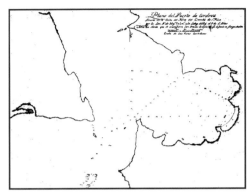

Map 111 (above)
Plano de Puerto de Córdova situado en la Costa del Nort del Estrecho de Fuca...
Manuel Quimper, 1790

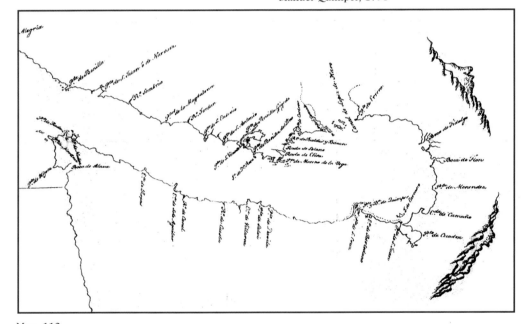

Map 112
Carta reducida que comprehende parte de la Costa Septentrional de California, corrigida y enmendada hasta la Boca de Estrecho de Fuca...Dn Manuel Quimper en el ano de 1790. Construida por su primer Piloto Dn Gonzalo Lopez de Haro 1790
Map sent to George Vancouver via the supply ship *Daedalus* in 1792. It arrived after Vancouver had already demonstrated that the Strait of Juan de Fuca did not have a closed eastern end, as this map suggests.

SPANISH BOUNDARY SUGGESTIONS

After the Nootka Convention had been signed, the Viceroy of New Spain, the Conde de Revillagigedo, considered that since Spain had agreed to return lands at Nootka that the British had never had, Spain should offer to cede the rest of Nootka and transfer her base to a port in the Strait of Juan de Fuca.

A royal order of December 1790 suggested a boundary line between British and Spanish territory be drawn from the entrance to the Strait of Juan de Fuca north to 60° N. By withdrawing a little,

Spain hoped to create a more defensible situation. The viceroy had a map drawn which showed this proposed boundary. Map 114 is this map. Written on the proposed boundary are the words *"Esta Linea puede ser la Demarcacion diverseria para precaver las Internaciones"* ("This is the line to provide a demarcation or division to guard against other nations"). Note that Vancouver Island is still shown as part of the mainland, and there is also a significant unknown part of the coast just below 55°N, where the Strait of de Fonte

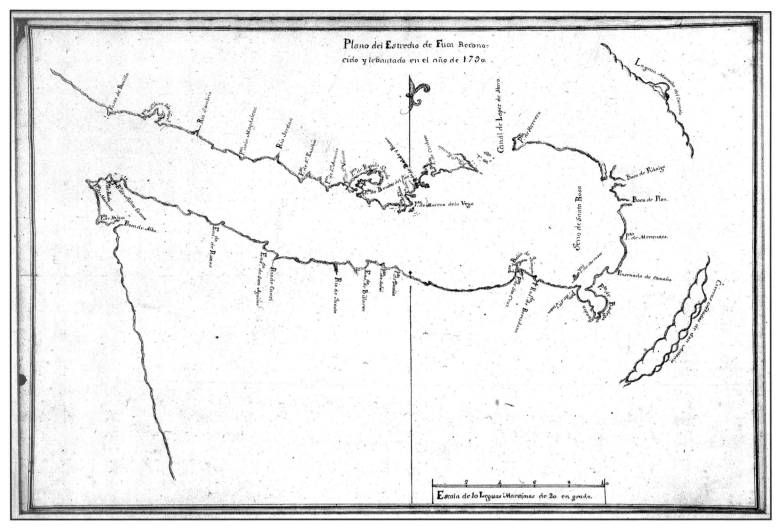

Map 113
Plano del Estrecho de Fuca reconicido y le bantado en el ano 1790. Attributed to López de Haro, 1790.
Graphically displays the state of Spanish knowledge of the Strait of Juan de Fuca in 1790. This knowledge was to improve rapidly as more expeditions were ordered.

was still thought to possibly lie, at the entrance seen by Juan Pérez in 1774 (now Dixon Entrance). Map 115 is a British copy of this map; it is not known how it was obtained, but it was found in British Foreign Office files.

Nootka Sound lay beyond the proposed boundary, and hence it became less important to the Spanish, but at the same time another base was needed south of the boundary. This led to the realization that the as yet unexplored interior waterways had better be explored. After all, the long-sought waterway to the continental interior might yet lie here. Hence the viceroy ordered another expedition, led by Francisco de Eliza, to explore eastwards from the Strait of Juan de Fuca.

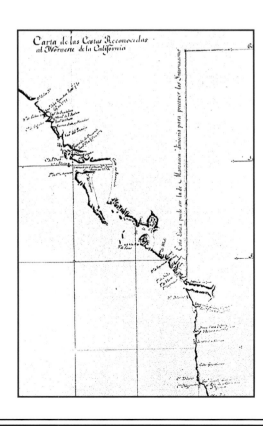

Map 114 (right)
Carta des las Costas Reconocidas al Norueste de la California, 1792.

A proposal by the Spanish Viceroy for a boundary line between Spanish and British territories.

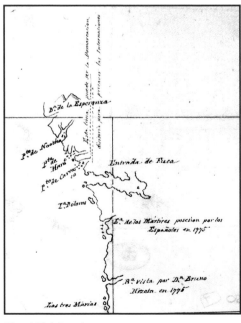

Map 115 (above)
Carta del la Costas reconocidas al Norueste de la California
A British copy showing the boundary line proposed by the Spanish.

FRANCISCO ELIZA'S EXPEDITION REACHES THE STRAIT OF GEORGIA

Francisco de Eliza was instructed to examine the remaining unknown areas of the northwest coast in 1791, but was unable to sail north at all so sailed south and into the Strait of Juan de Fuca. Contrary to what had been normal practice up till then, Eliza was given a map of the northwest coast which showed previous discoveries by the Spanish; Bodega y Quadra, then in charge at San Blas, had decided he wanted to end the renaming of the same place by successive expeditions. This was the same map as had been made to give to Alejandro Malaspina (see page 75).

Eliza left Nootka in May 1791 with two ships: the *San Carlos* and a smaller schooner, the *Santa Saturnina*, for exploring shallower waters. The *Santa Saturnina* was commanded by José María Nárvaez, with pilot Juan Carrasco.

The *San Carlos* explored and mapped Clayquot Sound (Archipelago de Clayacuat), and the *Santa Saturnina* Barkley Sound (Archipelago de Nitinat ó Carrasco), meeting the *San Carlos* later in Esquimalt Harbour (Puerto de Córdoba).

The longboat, commanded by ensign José Verdía, was then dispatched to explore northwards into Haro Strait (Canal de López de Haro), but returned quickly after being threatened by armed natives in canoes. Trying again, this time better armed, Verdía found that the channel opened out into an even wider body of water, which he named the Canal de Nuestra Señora del Rosario. This, of course, was the Strait of Georgia, named the Gulf of Georgia a year later by George Vancouver. (The remnant of the original Spanish name now applies to the easternmost main channel through the San Juan Islands: Rosario Strait.) Verdía returned in ten days.

Retiring to Port Discovery (Puerto de Quadra), Eliza then dispatched the *Santa Saturnina* northwards. They passed through Rosario Strait, past Bellingham Bay and into the Strait of Georgia, and for three weeks followed the strait north and northwestward. In so doing, they became the first documented European expedition to explore the area of what is now Vancouver, B.C.

Passing the Fraser River, they noted the fresh water and correctly believed that there was a large river discharging there. They named and mapped Point Atkinson (Punta de la Bodega), Howe Sound (Bocas del Carmelo), and sailed as far north as Texada Island (Isla de Texada), one of the few Spanish names retained today, before starting their return, as their supplies were running low.

The presence of whales made Eliza think that there may be another way in from the open sea, a belief in which he was correct, but he also thought that if any Northwest Passage existed it must be in this area. He reported to the viceroy:

...the passage to the Atlantic Ocean, which the foreign nations search for with such diligence on this coast, cannot, in my opinion, if there be one, be found in any other part...[72]

Returning to Nootka, Eliza anchored in Neah Bay (Bahía de Núñez Gaona), later to be a Spanish settlement. He arrived back at Nootka at the end of August 1791.

One of the maps produced as a result of this expedition is the *Carta que comprehende...* shown here (Map 117). It is the first map of the southern end of Vancouver Island and the shores of the lower mainland of British Columbia. It is believed to have been drawn by Nárvaez because Eliza transferred him to the *San Carlos* on the return to Nootka to draw up the maps.

With an eye to future patronage, perhaps, Eliza charted the archipelago they had explored as the Isla y Archipelago de San Juan, the San Juan Islands, after the viceroy, Juan Vicente de Guemes Pacheco

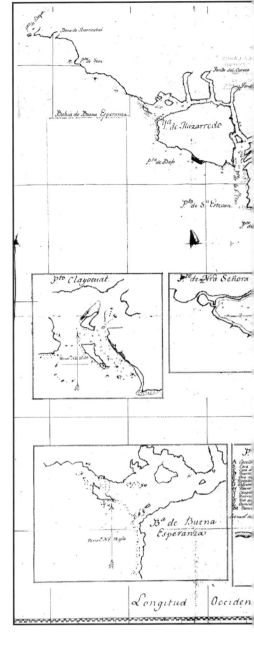

Map 116 (below)
Plano del Archipelago de Clayocuat...
Juan Pantoja y Arriaga, 1791
The Spanish map of Clayquot Sound.
Pantoja was Eliza's pilot on the *San Carlos*.

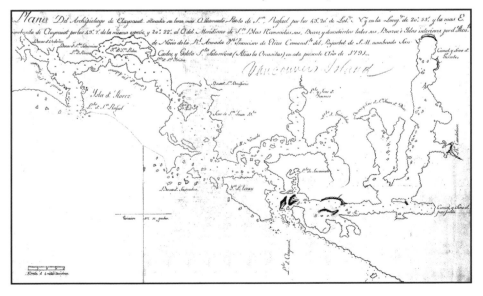

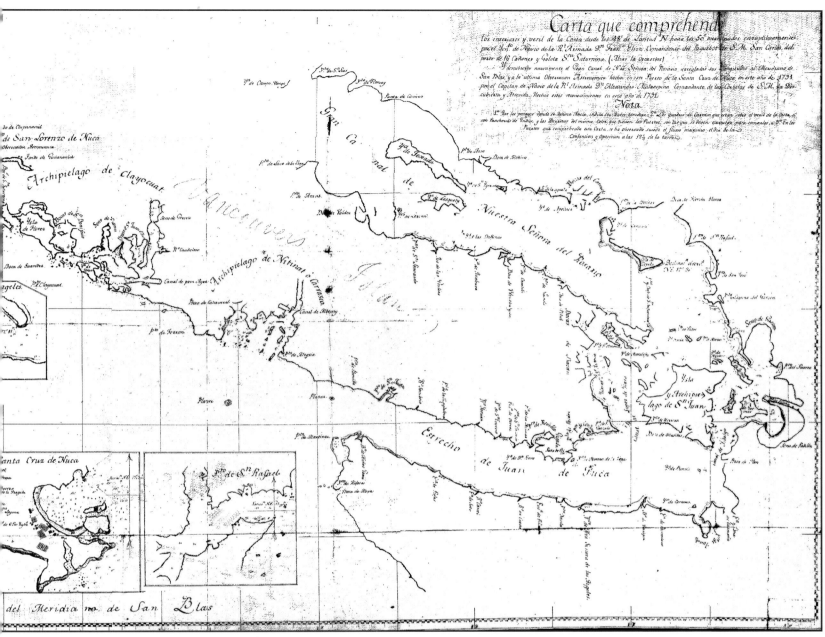

Map 117 (above)
Carta que comprehende los interiers y veril de la costa desde los 48° de Latitud N hasta los 50°...1791. José María Nárvaez, 1791.
The first map of the southern Georgia Strait region including the area which is now Vancouver, B.C., much of which is shown as water. Point Roberts (*Ysla de Zepeda*) is shown as an island. The western part of today's City of Vancouver is shown as a coastline only, labelled *Ys de Langara* (Island of Langara). This map has been attributed by some to Juan Carrasco, Nárvaez' pilot.

Padilla Horcasitas y Aguayo. Eliza sent this map to the viceroy later in 1791.

The next year, 1792, Galiano was to write in his diary of Nárvaez' map, as he passed the farthest northern limit of the area Nárvaez had mapped (Texada Island):

We must say about these in honor of the individuals who executed them that they labored with utility, as their map was found to contain good detail and good coastal trends. This was as far as the means with which they operated allowed them to reach; the latitudes and longitudes suffered from great errors, which they did not know how to remedy.[73]

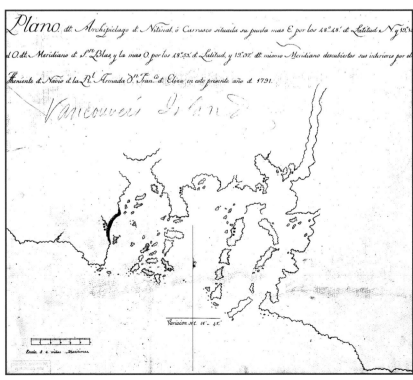

Map 118 (right)
Plano de Archipelago de Nitinat ó Carrasco...
José María Nárvaez, 1791

Today's Barkley Sound, on the west coast of Vancouver Island.

In 1792, a copy of the Nárvaez map was given to George Vancouver, who had one of his men make a copy of it (Map 119). This was sent to England with Lieutenant Broughton; it was found in the files of the British Hydrographer of the Navy.

Another copy of this map was later used in 1872 by the United States, having inherited Spain's territorial claims, as proof that Spain had discovered the San Juan Islands first, and that thus they should be American (see page 171).

The following January, another map was made by Gonzalo López de Haro, covering much the same area, listing geographical features at the top (Map 120). This was probably a copy intended for his own use.

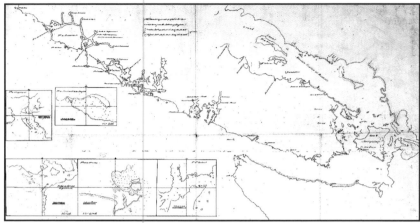

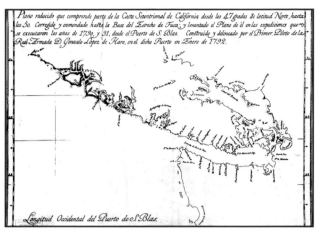

Map 119 (above)
A tracing by an English draughtsman of a Spanish survey of Vancouver Island from Nootka to Cape Classet and the Straight of Georgia; with plans of Pto. Clayocaut, Pto de Nuestro Sd de los Angles, Pto de la Sta Cruz, and Pto San Rafael.

Map 120
Plano reducida que comprehende parte de la Costa Septentrional... López de Haro, 1792.

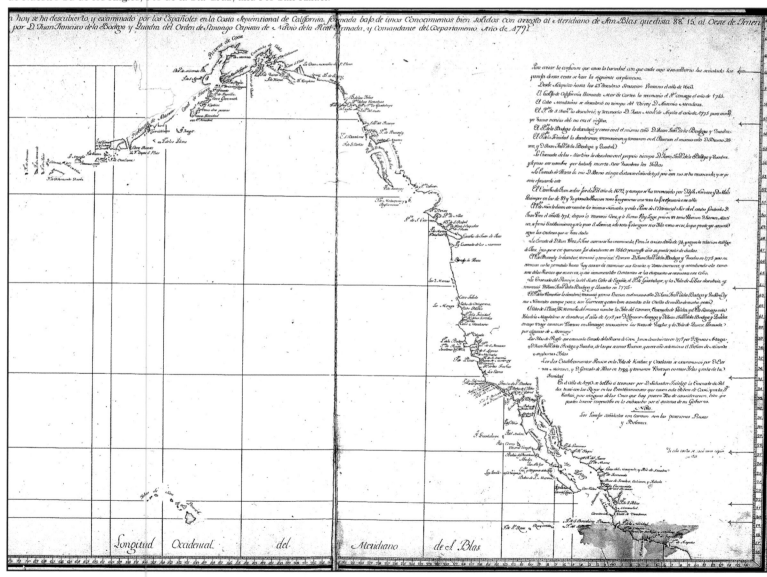

Map 121
Carta general de quanto asta hoy se ha descubierto y examinado por los Espanoles en la Costa Septentrional de California, formada...por D. Juan Francisco de la Bodega y Quadra...Ano de 1791. The second of Bodega y Quadra's small-scale summary maps of the west coast of North America. Compare the state of knowledge with his 1775 map (Map 62, page 39), and those of 1792 (Maps 130 and 132, page 80). Detail of this map is shown as Map 318, page 196.

IN COOK'S FOOTSTEPS –
THE MALASPINA EXPEDITION

The Malaspina expedition was an attempt by the Spanish to achieve the same kind of national glory that Britain had gained from James Cook's voyages. Conceived as a round-the-world voyage collecting scientific and geographical data, two ships had been specially built in Spain in 1789.

The corvettes *Descubierta* and *Atrevida* (*Discovery* and *Daring*) were manned by handpicked crews, and commanded by Alejandro Malaspina, a career naval officer who had completed a previous circumnavigation in 1784. Two of his officers were Dionisio Alcalá Galiano and Cayetano Valdes, who were destined to command another expedition to the northwest coast in 1792 (see page 77).

In 1770, another fictitious account of a voyage through the Strait of Anian was published; it had been found in the archive of the family of one Lorenzo Ferrer Maldonado, who was later shown to have been an inventive charlatan. The strait was said to be between 59° N and 60° N. However, this account had been endorsed in November 1790 by the French cartographer Philippe Buache, known to us as a maker of imaginary maps (see page 26), but this important fact was not known to the Spanish at that time. Hence the Spanish were prompted to send Malaspina, then in Acapulco, orders to explore the northwest coast between 59° N and 60° N with particular care to ascertain whether this alleged passage actually existed, despite all the previous exploratory voyages that had not found such a passage.

Malaspina had a map with him showing the combined knowledge of the coast at that time. It was based on maps from the published English works of Cook, Dixon, and Portlock, plus the Spanish voyages of Arteaga, Bodega y Quadra, Fidalgo, López de Haro, and Martínez.

Malaspina sailed directly from Acapulco to Yakutat Bay, at 60° N. This was Port Mulgrave, a name the Spanish accepted from fur traders. Here they stayed for more than a month, exploring channels and observing native customs. A map of Yakutat Bay was drawn, later engraved (Map 122). While the corvettes were anchored, two longboats were sent to determine whether some inlet contained a continental passage. Threading their way between the increasingly frequent pieces of ice in the water, they fi-

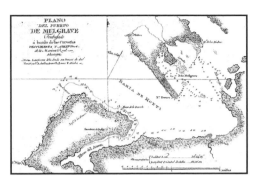

Map 122
Plano Del Puerto De Mulgrave Frabasdo a bordo de las Corvetas Descubierta y Atrevida de la Marina Real Ano 1791
From: *Relación...* Atlas, 1802
Yakutat Bay, Alaska.

nally reached the front of a glacier (the Hubbard Glacier), from which large pieces of ice were breaking off. Malaspina named this Bahía del Desengaño, Disappointment Bay, because it was not a Northwest Passage. An engraved map from the map the expedition drew of the bay is shown here (Map 123, below).

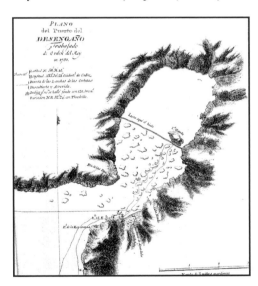

Map 123
Num 9 Plano del Puerto del Desengaño Trabasdo de Orden del Rey. From: *Relación...* Atlas, 1802. Clearly shows the front of the glacier (today's Hubbard Glacier) which led to Malaspina's "disappointment." This northeastern extension of Yakutat Bay is shown on modern maps as Disenchantment Bay.

After some more searching, Malaspina gave up and decided that no Strait of Anian existed, at least at the latitude in Maldonado's account.

The corvettes later explored Prince William Sound to the north and Bucareli Bay to the south, sailed back along the coast, and arrived in Nootka in August 1791.

At Nootka two longboats were sent to explore the interior channels. The result was the *Plano de los Canales Imediatos a Nutka* (Map 124); this was one of nine Spanish charts later given to George Vancouver and brought to England by Lieutenant William Broughton (see page 90).

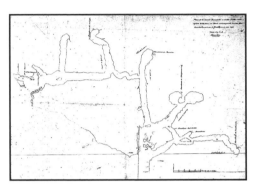

Map 124
Plano de los Canales Imediatos a Nutka y de la Navegation (sie) *hecha para su reconocimiento por las lanchos de las corvetas Descubierta y Atrevide en el Ano 1791 Pasa el uso de Mendendez*
This map was given to George Vancouver by Bodega y Quadra, and sent via Lieut. Broughton to England in 1792

The tracks of Malaspina's ships are shown, along with others, on a map published eleven years later (Map 109, page 69).

The extensive research carried out by Malaspina's scientists meant that the report on the voyage would have been very large, seven volumes with seventy maps and seventy other illustrations, and correspondingly expensive. Nevertheless, the Spanish government approved the expenditure, because they wanted a work which would, in the eyes of the international community, surpass the British publication of Cook's voyages. It was never published, however, because on his return to Spain, Malaspina became involved in a conspiracy against Manuel de Godoy, the Spanish prime minister, who threw him into jail and scattered his supporters and his work. A more general and less expensive account of all of the Spanish voyages, the *Relación del Viage...* (see page 79), was published by the Spanish government in 1802, still intended as a foil to Cook and to demonstrate to the world that Spain had legitimate claims to the northwest coast. By that time, however, it was too late; the star of Spain's empire was falling.

CAAMAÑO'S VOYAGE TO ALASKA

Jacinto Caamaño sailed his ship, the *Aranzazu,* into Nootka in May 1792. The Nootka commandant, Bodega y Quadra, decided to send him to survey the coast of the Alaskan panhandle from Bucareli Sound south to eliminate the last gaps in cartographic knowledge of the coastline in that region.

The Spanish by this time knew that there was a maze of islands and channels at that latitude (the Alexander Archipelago in the Alaskan panhandle), and thought there was an outside chance they could still hide the legendary Strait of Bartholemew de Fonte.

If such a passage existed, it was critical to find it before any boundary agreement was signed with Britain. The *Aranzazu* was too big to get into many of the inlets sighted; this was achieved using the ships longboat. Formal acts of possession, of which the Spanish seemed to be so fond, were performed on Graham Island, in the Queen Charlottes, on several other islands, and on the mainland. At one point, Caamaño entered a large strait and followed it north for 160 km (100 miles). It was the Inland Passage just north of Ketchikan, named Clarence Strait by George Vancouver a year later,[76] but Caamaño thought for some time it must be the de Fonte Strait. He followed it north to 55° 30' N, but was prevented by bad weather from going further. It did show, however, that much of what had previously been considered mainland (Prince of Wales Island, with Bucareli Sound on its west coast), was in fact an archipelago, so he did add considerably to Spanish cartographical knowledge. Caamaño returned to Nootka in September.

Map 125 is taken from Caamaño's journal, and shows the Queen Charlotte Islands more exactly than had previously been shown on Spanish maps. The presumed mainland coast, actually that of Vancouver Island, is named Nueva Cantabria (New Cantabria) by Caamaño after the region in northern Spain.

Map 126 is a British copy of a Spanish map which Bodega y Quadra gave to George Vancouver and which was sent to England with Lieutenant Broughton (see page 90). It is based mainly on the work of Caamaño. On both of these maps, the Queen Charlotte Islands are shown as one large island. The Spanish accepted the name given to the islands by George Dixon in 1786 (see page 57).

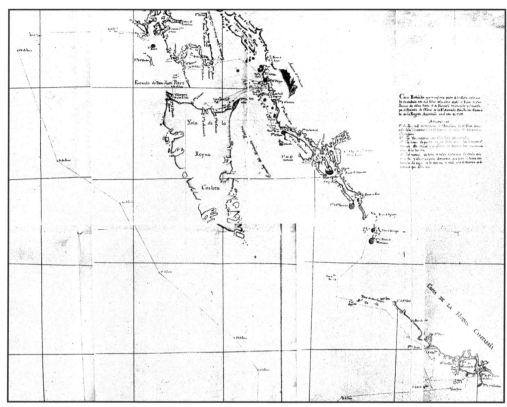

Map 125 (above)
Carta Reducida que manifiesta parte de la Costa de la nueva Cantabria con sus Yslas adjacenta... Don Jacinto Caamaño fio con la Fragata Aranzazu en el ano de 1792. From: Caamaño's Journal, 1792.

Map 126 (below)
Chart of the West Coast of North America, with the Isles adjacent from the Latde 50° 45'N & Longde. 30° (sic) copied from one constructed...by Dn. Caamano, a Lieutenant in the Spanish Navy in the year 1792 shewing the Straits said to be discovered by De Fonte in 1640... (Traced by an English draughtsman.)

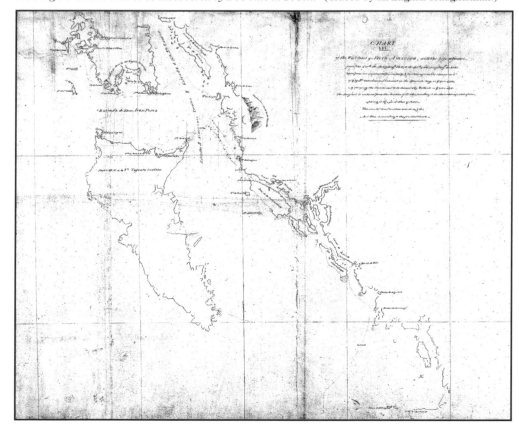

GALIANO AND VALDES – THE LAST SPANISH VOYAGE OF EXPLORATION TO THE NORTHWEST

While Malaspina was exploring Alaskan waters, the viceroy Revillagigedo was making plans for another voyage further to the south. It was originally intended to have been commanded by Francisco Antonio Mourelle, who had first been to the northwest coast in 1775 with Bodega y Quadra (see page 37), but he became ill and so command was given to two of Malaspina's officers, Dionisio Alcalá Galiano and Cayetano Valdes. Two ships were specially built, the *Sutil* and the *Mexicana*.

They sailed north from San Blas in March 1792, reaching Nootka in May.

It was four months before they were back at Nootka, having explored further north into the Strait of Georgia than any Europeans before, with the exception of George Vancouver, who was sailing a similar route at the same time and preceded the Spanish back to Nootka by a few days. However, Vancouver did not sail the part of the Vancouver Island coast south of Nootka to the Strait of Juan de Fuca, having entered the strait without going to Nootka first, so Galiano and Valdes became the first Europeans to circumnavigate Vancouver Island.

In June, Galiano and Valdes first sailed for Neah Bay, the recently founded Spanish settlement of Núñez Gaona. It had been founded by Salvador Fidalgo in May 1792. They learned from a visiting native chief from southern Vancouver Island, Tetacu, and to whom they gave a ride home, that there were already two large ships within the strait.

Galiano made the decision not to explore to the south, just as Eliza had done the previous year, and hence left the exploration of Puget Sound to Vancouver. Shortly after entering the Strait of Georgia (Gran Canal de Nuestra Señora del Rosario), Galiano and Valdes sighted the sails of the two other ships. Lieutenant William Broughton came aboard the *Sutil* and mutual assistance was offered.

On 14 June, Galiano and Valdes entered and anchored in the north arm of the Fraser River, becoming the first Europeans to find and enter this river.

A week later, on 21 June 1792, Galiano and Vancouver met off Point Grey, in what is now the City of Vancouver, near, but not at, the beach today called Spanish Banks. Vancouver had been surveying in a longboat. Galiano showed Vancouver their maps, including the *Carta que comprehende* summarizing information from the Eliza expedition of the year before (Map 117, page 72/73). No doubt these must have been of considerable interest to Vancouver, particularly since they showed mapped coastlines to the north, as yet unexplored by the British.

Following his instructions (page 85), Vancouver suggested to Galiano that they work together, and this they did, sailing northwards towards the northern end of the Strait of Georgia and into the many channels and islands separating the mainland from the northeastern part of Vancouver Island.

Galiano produced maps as a result of his voyage, which for the first time clearly demonstrated the insularity of Vancouver Island, and also proved that there was no entrance to a continental passage in this region. The map they produced of Vancouver Island and the surrounding mainland coast (Map 128, overleaf) is strikingly similar to that of George Vancouver (Map 153, page 93). Apart from details, the Spanish had finished their mapping of the northwest coast.

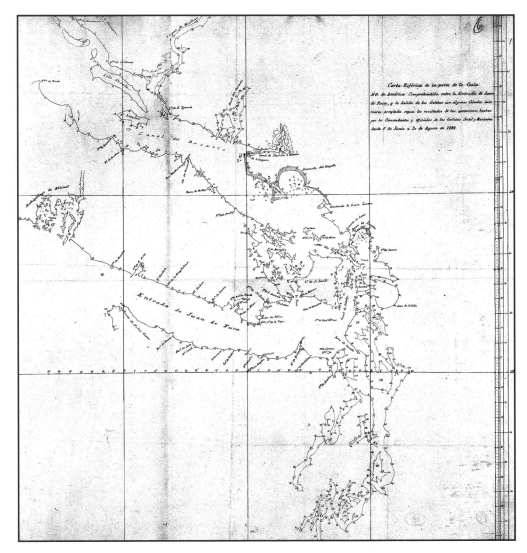

Map 127
Carta Esferica de la parte de la Costa No. de America Comprehendida entre la Entrada de Juan de Fuca, y la Salidas de las Goletas con algunos Canales interiores arroglada segun los resultados de las operaciones hechos por los Commandantes y Officiales de las Goletas Sutil y Mexicana desde 5 de Junio a 31 de Agosto de 1792
Dionisio Galiano, 1792

Note the San Juan Islands shown as one large island, plus a few much smaller ones. This particular map was one of the maps later used by the British in the arbitration of the San Juan boundary dispute in 1872 (see page 171).

78

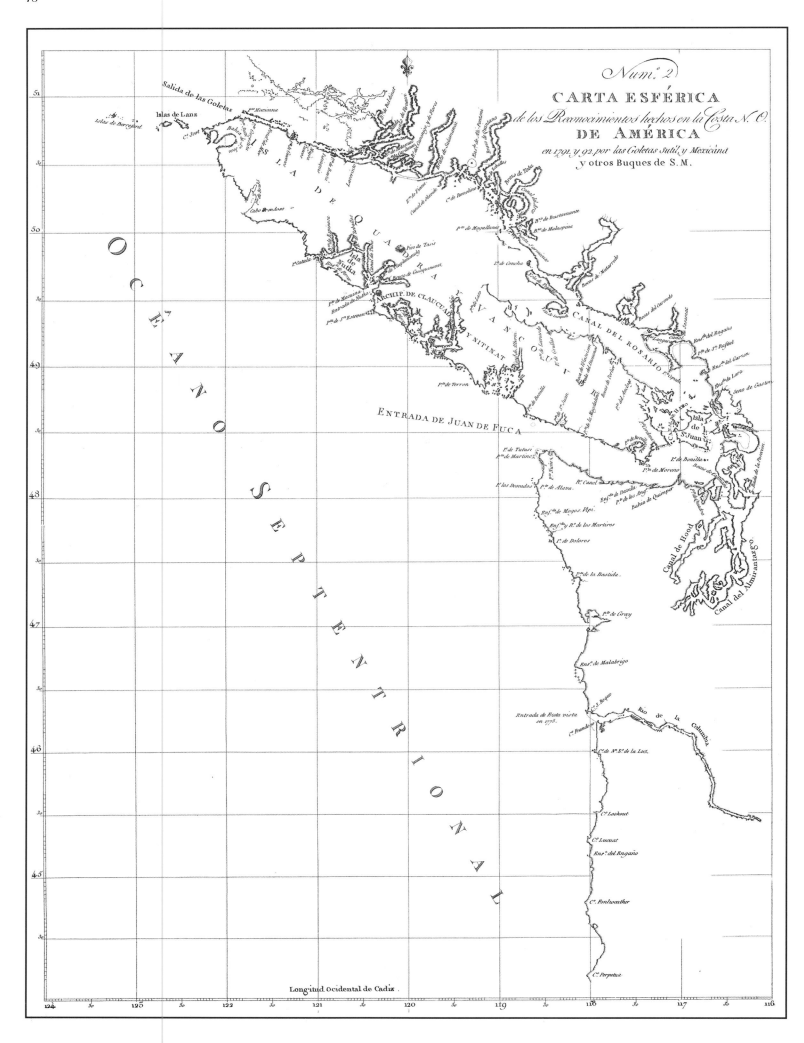

THE *RELACIÓN*

THE SPANISH POLICY OF SECRECY

In 1802, the Spanish government, still interested in maintaining claims to the northwest coast, officially subsidized the publication of an account of the explorations of Galiano and Valdes in 1792.

Although in title it was about the Galiano and Valdes expedition, it included an extensive introduction giving a history of Spanish voyages to the northwest coast, and attempted to vindicate Spain's territorial claims there by right of prior discovery and exploration.

It was perhaps also intended to clearly show that this area was not part of Louisiana, the territory which was to be ceded to France in 1803. The account was the *Relación del Viage hecho por las goletas Sutil y Mexicana en al ano 1792 para Reconocer el Estrecho de Fuca.*

The work was accompanied by an atlas with beautifully engraved maps and scenes, many of which are reproduced in this atlas. The map opposite is one such map. Others include Map 11, page 17, Map 109, page 69, Maps 122 and 123, page 75, and also the engraved view of Friendly Cove on page 69.

RELACION

DEL VIAGE HECHO POR LAS GOLETAS

SUTIL Y MEXICANA

EN EL AÑO DE 1792

PARA RECONOCER EL ESTRECHO DE FUCA;

CON UNA INTRODUCCION

EN QUE SE DA NOTICIA DE LAS EXPEDICIONES EXECU-
TADAS ANTERIORMENTE POR LOS ESPAÑOLES EN BUSCA
DEL PASO DEL NOROESTE DE LA AMÉRICA.

DE ÓRDEN DEL REY.

MADRID EN LA IMPRENTA REAL
AÑO DE 1802.

Title page of the *Relación,* an account of the history of Spanish explorations to the Northwest Coast, together with that of Galiano and Valdes, published in 1802 to belatedly counter the British publication of Vancouver's voyage.

For many years the Spanish were so concerned that other nations might discover a Northwest Passage before they did, hence endangering the Pacific as a "Spanish lake", that they treated the results of their expeditions, including their maps, as state secrets. Up to 1791, many successive Spanish voyages often took place without knowledge of the findings of their predecessors. Even the report of the scientific voyage of Alejandro Malaspina in 1791, which was intended as a counter to Cook's, was not published until nearly a century later, in 1885, because of his political downfall on his return to Spain. And as we have seen, the account of the 1792 voyage of Galiano and Valdes was only published in 1802 because the Spanish government decided that Britain was getting too much credit for prior discovery of the northwest coast, and was in response to the 1798 publication of George Vancouver's account. Despite the Nootka Convention, Spain still held to the idea that prior discovery was a claim to ownership, and so felt obliged to publish its own discoveries when there were other contenders.

Map 129 (below)
Carta esferica de la reconocimientos hechos en 1792 en la costa N. O. de America para examinar la entrada de Juan de Fuca y la internacion de sus Canales navegables levantada de orden Del Rey Nuestro Senor abordo de las Goletas Sutil y Mexicana Por D. Dionisio Galiano y D. Cayetano Valdes Capitaines de la Navio de la Rl. Armada Ano de 1793. 1795.

Map 128 (left)
Num. 2 Carta Esferica de los Reconocimientos hechos en la Costa N.O. De America en 1791 y 92 por las Goletas Sutil y Mexicana y otres Bruques de S.M. Dionisio Galiano, 1792.
From: *Relación...* Atlas, 1802.

The summary map showing the explorations of Galiano and Valdes in 1792.

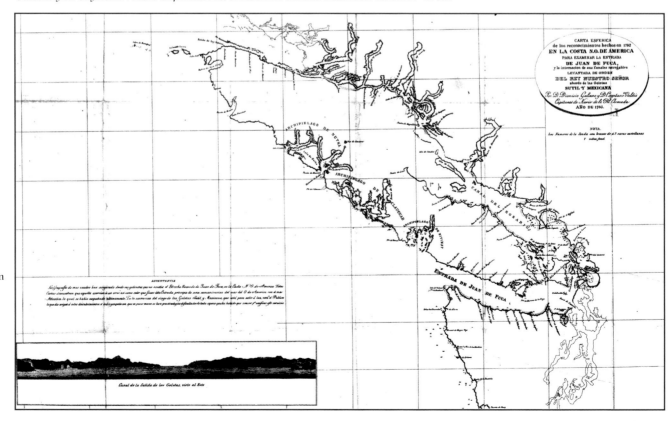

THE MAPS OF JUAN FRANCISCO BODEGA Y QUADRA

The Spanish commander at Nootka was Juan Francisco Bodega y Quadra, who had sailed to Alaska in 1775 on the *Sonora* (see page 39) and who had now been sent to negotiate with George Vancouver regarding the return of "British property" in Nootka under the terms of the 1790 Nootka Convention. He put all the new cartographic knowledge together to produce what can be considered the final Spanish maps of the northwest coast, which are more or less accurate, and more or less complete.

Some of his maps are shown here. Maps 130 and 132 were both drawn in 1792, but clearly Map 130 was drawn before the return of Caamaño, or the return of Galiano and Valdes, whereas Map 132 includes information from both of these voyages.

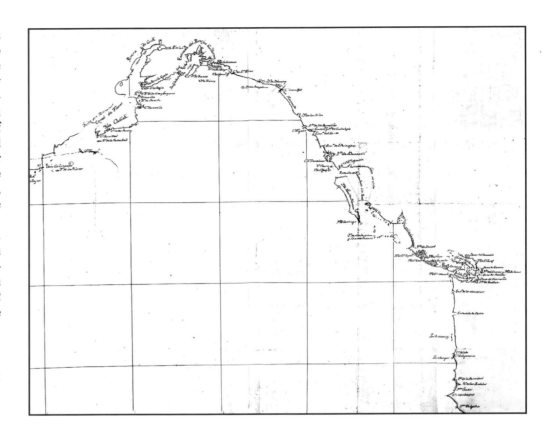

Map 130 (top right)
Carta Reducida de la Costa Septentrional desde el Puerto de Acapulco hasta la Isla de Unalaska
(Map of the northern coast between Acapulco and Unalaska.)
Juan Francisco Bodega y Quadra, 1792

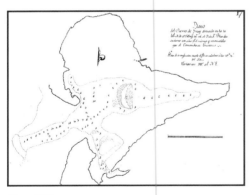

Map 131
Plano del Puerto de Gray...
Juan Francisco Bodega y Quadra, 1792
A map of Gray's Harbor, probably copied from George Vancouver.

Map 132 (bottom right)
Carta de los Descubrimientos en la Costa N.O. Americana Septentrional por las Embarcaciones de S. Blas y noticias adquirados en este viage
(Map of the discoveries made on the northern coast of America by the ships of San Blas and information acquired on this voyage.)
Juan Francisco Bodega y Quadra, 1792
Vancouver Island and the Queen Charlotte Islands are now shown, following the return of Galiano and Valdes, and Caamaño, from their expeditions of 1792.

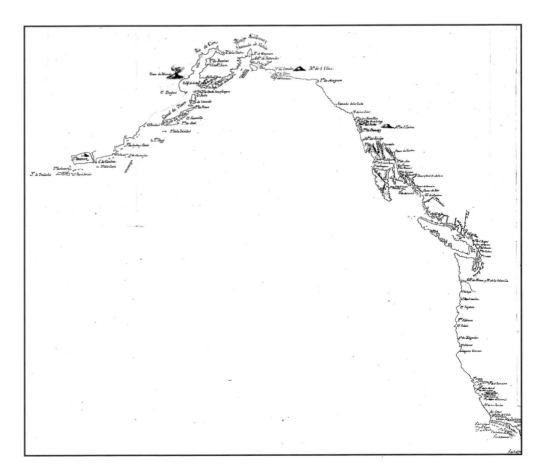

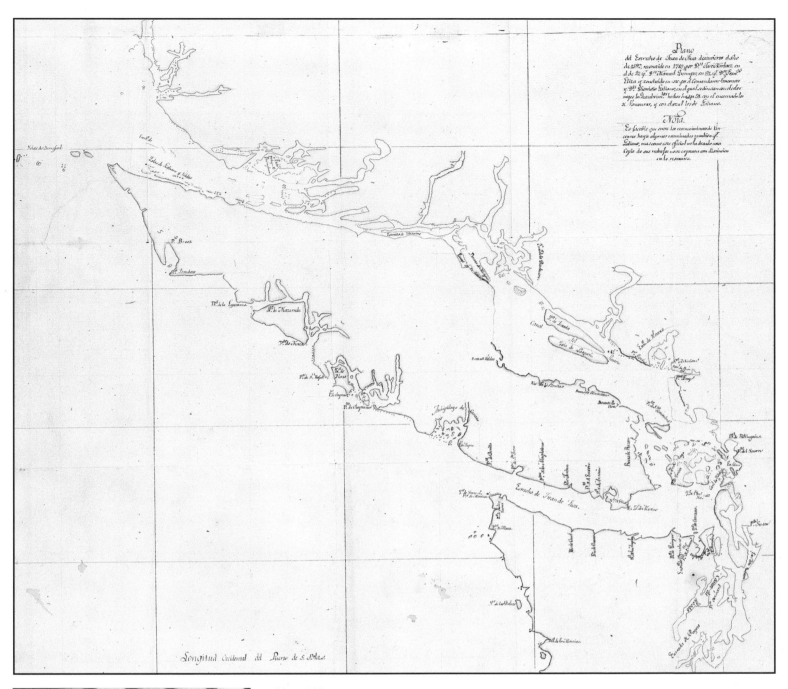

Map 133

Plano del estrecho de Juan de Fuca descuvierto el ano 1592, reconocido en 1789 por D[n] Jose Narvaez en el de 90...D[n] Manuel Quimper, en 91...D[n] Fran[co] Eliza y concluido en...el Comandame Vancouver y Dionisio Galiano en el qual sedenetan con el color negro los descubrim los hechos...con el ecarnado los Vancouver y con elazul los de Galiano. Juan Francisco Bodega y Quadra, 1792.

Bodega y Quadra recognizes the Spanish navigators and George Vancouver in the credits for this map; the brown/black lines represent coasts mapped by Galiano and red lines represent coasts mapped by Vancouver. The Spanish were likewise credited for information by Vancouver (Map 147, page 89).

Stained glass window in the church at Friendly Cove, showing a meeting in 1792 of Vancouver and Bodega y Quadra in Friendly Cove. The window was a gift from the Government of Spain in 1957.

Bodega y Quadra and one of his maps appeared on Spanish stamps issued in 1967 to commemorate the Spanish explorations of the Northwest coast of America. The map is similar to Map 121, page 74, and was drawn in 1791.

THE FIRST FRENCH FUR-TRADING VENTURE

Map 134
Hydrographical Chart of the Known Parts of the Globe Between the Seventieth Parallel North and the Sixtieth South to illustrate the Voyage round the world performed in 1790, 1791 and 1792 by Captain Etienne Marchand
From: Etienne Marchand, *Voyage Around the World...* (Translated from the French edition of C.P. Claret Fleurieu), London, 1801.

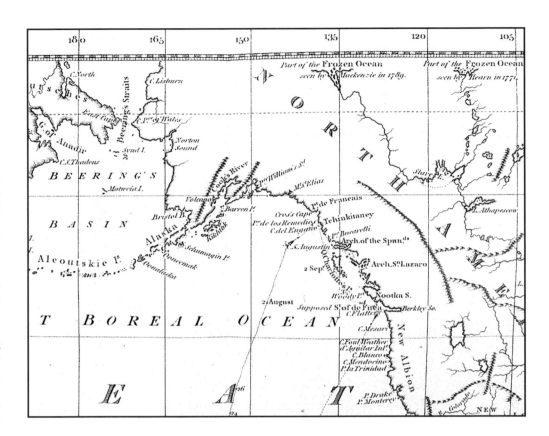

Etienne Marchand had met with Nathaniel Portlock (page 57) in 1788 on the latter's return from the northwest coast, and had become enthusiastic about mounting a French venture to the region. He managed to interest a group of Marseilles merchants in the idea, and in 1790, they equipped a ship, the *Solide,* which reached Nova Archangel'sk (Sitka) in August 1791, later sailing to the Queen Charlotte Islands and finally to Barkley Sound, in September 1791, before leaving for the Far East. From a fur-trading point of view, the expedition was only moderately successful, but the expedition did produce some maps.

Marchand's journal and maps were later published and translated into English in 1801. Marchand himself had died on another voyage soon after returning to France; the book was published by others, likely to show that revolutionary France was able to mount such voyages. Map 134 is a part of the world map that accompanied the book. It shows the Queen Charlottes; Vancouver Island is still shown attached to the mainland, reflecting what was known in 1791 but superseded by the time the book was published. The Strait of Juan de Fuca is confused with "Berkley" Sound.

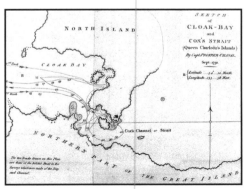

Map 135
Sketch of Cloak-Bay and Cox's Strait (Queen Charlotte's Islands) By Capt. Prosper Chanal, Sept. 1791
From: Etienne Marchand, *Voyage Around the World.*
Drawn from a survey of part of the Queen Charlottes in the ships boats by one of Marchand's officers, Captain Prosper Chanal. Cloak Bay had been named by George Dixon in 1787 from the prolific number of sea otter fur "cloaks" traded.

ROBERT GRAY DISCOVERS THE COLUMBIA

After the publication in 1784 of the details of James Cook's third voyage, a group of Boston merchants organized the first American voyage to the northwest coast. They purchased and outfitted two ships, the *Columbia Rediviva* and the *Lady Washington,* which left Boston in 1787. The captain of the *Washington* was Robert Gray; the captain of the *Columbia* was John Kendrick. They were instructed to act together, but once on the northwest coast, Kendrick treated the voyage as an enterprise for his own profit. He never returned to the United States. Gray swapped commands with him and did return via China to Boston in 1790, thus the *Columbia* became the first American ship to circumnavigate the globe, and Gray the first American captain to do so, albeit on two ships.

It was during this voyage that Gray entered the Strait of Juan de Fuca for a short distance, but the account of it was exaggerated by John Meares in his account and on his map (Map 94, page 59) to "prove" the insularity of Vancouver Island. The voyage was sufficiently promising that

the *Columbia* was immediately refitted and sent back to the northwest coast with Robert Gray as its captain. On 28 April 1792, Gray met with George Vancouver after encountering him at sea approaching the Strait of Juan de Fuca; this was when Vancouver learned that Meares' account of Gray's voyage around Vancouver Island was false, and also learned that Gray had discovered the entrance to the Columbia River, which Vancouver had uncharacteristically missed.

On 7 May 1792 Gray entered Grays Harbor on the Washington coast, naming it Bulfinch Harbor after one of the part owners of his ship. It was Vancouver who later chose to name it Gray's Harbour.

On 12 May 1792, Gray became the first to cross the bar of the Columbia and enter the river. Six days later, on 18 May 1792, Gray named the river after his ship, the *Columbia*. A chart Gray made of the entrance to the Columbia was copied by George Vancouver (Map 144, page 88), and was later used by Lieutenant Broughton as he began his survey of the Columbia River later in 1792 (page 88).

JOSEPH INGRAHAM AND THE JOURNAL OF THE *HOPE*

When Robert Gray returned to Boston in the *Columbia* in 1790, having completed the first American circumnavigation of the globe, other merchants were encouraged to send out their own ships to trade for furs on the northwest coast.

One of these was the *Hope*, commanded by twenty-eight-year-old Joseph Ingraham, who had been the first mate of the *Columbia*. He had been enlisted for the task by a Boston merchant acquaintance who was anxious to cash in on the newly discovered fur trade.

Ingraham arrived on the northwest coast on 2 July 1791, spent two months in the Queen Charlotte Islands gathering furs, and left for China in August. He was unable to sell his furs at a profit, however, because the Chinese had recently quarrelled with the Russians, and, believing that all furs somehow came from the Russians, had temporarily banned the import of furs.

Ingraham then returned to the northwest coast in 1792, but this time had no luck trading for furs. By July 1792, he was in Nootka Sound, where he found Bodega y Quadra, the Spanish commander, waiting for George Vancouver to arrive. Still having no luck finding furs, he returned to Boston, his voyage a commercial failure.

Joseph Ingraham did keep a journal, which has some interesting maps in it. Some of these are shown here.

The map of the coast south of Cape Flattery (Map 136), which is an inverted copy of the original in the journal, which has south at the top of the map (Map 137), is an interesting comparison with that of George Vancouver (Map 149, page 91) or Bodega y Quadra (Map 132, page 80), with which it is contemporary. Of course, some of the difference can be explained by the fact that Ingraham's was an entirely commercial venture, so much coastal detail was not important to him. This map shows both "Columbias River", and "Bulfinch Harbr", the locations of which Ingraham obtained from Robert Gray when he met him in the Queen Charlotte Islands on 23 July 1792.

Map 138, of Vancouver Island, originally called Vancouver and Quadra's Island, but not so named until *after* Ingraham had left the coast, must have been given the name Quadra's Isle by Ingraham following his visit to Nootka, where he was well received by Bodega y

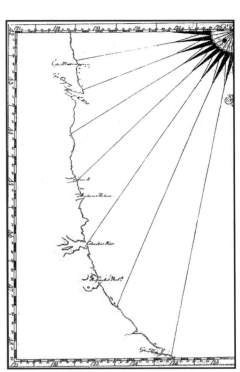

Map 136 (above left)
Chart of the N.W. Coast of North America from Cape Maddison to Cape Flattery.
Joseph Ingraham, 1792.

Map 137 (above right)
Chart of the N.W. Coast of North America from Cape Maddison to Cape Flattery, south at top of map.
From: Joseph Ingraham, Journal of the *Hope*, 1792.

Map 138 (right)
Quadra's Isles.
From: Joseph Ingraham, Journal of the *Hope*, 1792.

This intriguing map shows Vancouver Island, originally named Quadra and Vancouver's Island by George Vancouver. As the maps on this page illustrate, Ingraham did not hold with the convention that north should be at the top of the map!

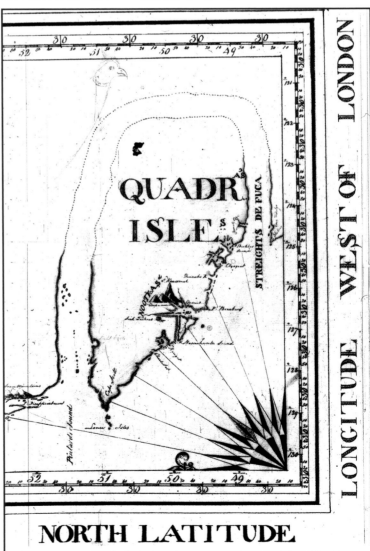

Quadra. Ingraham obviously believed that the Strait of Juan de Fuca connected with the ocean further to the north, as he has marked this on the map.

Washington's Isles (Maps 139 and 140) are the Queen Charlotte Islands; Ingraham believed them one main island at the time. On Map 139, the "Straight du Font" is marked, referring to the Strait of de Fonte, which Ingraham presumably still believed existed at that location.

The Queen Charlottes had been named Washington's Isles by Robert Gray in 1790. Washington seems to have been a popular name at this time; George Washington had been elected the first president of the United States in 1789. Early in 1791 Ingraham had visited part of what are now the Marquesas Islands in the south Pacific; these he had also named Washington's Islands. American traders continued to use the Washington name for the Queen Charlottes for many years after Gray and Ingraham.

Joseph Ingraham's journal is believed to have been obtained from his family in the 1830s by Robert Greenhow, a historian who was engaged in research on the bases of American claims to the Oregon Territory, and Ingraham is mentioned in his *Memoir*, published in 1840. Greenhow says of Ingraham's journal:

...it is illustrated by many charts and drawings, all serving to prove that the world is indebted to the efforts of the American fur traders for much information relative to the northwest coast, which is usually supposed to have been procured originally by the British and Spanish navigators.

Luckily for the United States, the American claim to Oregon was not based on the relative accuracy of Ingraham's maps compared to those of Vancouver and Bodega y Quadra!

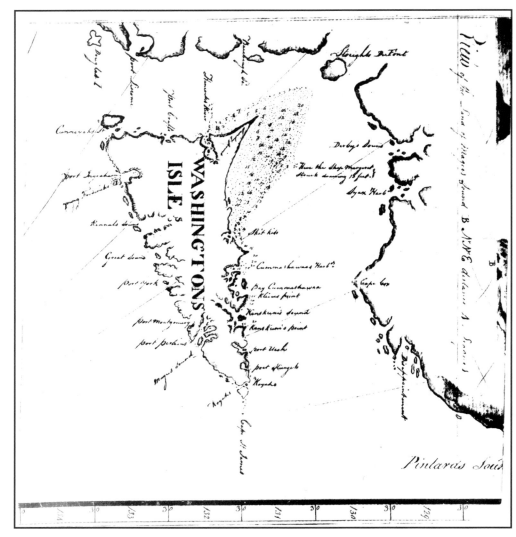

Map 139 (above)
Washington's Isles.   From: Joseph Ingraham, Journal of the *Hope*, 1792.
Note that on Ingraham's maps, the Queen Charlotte Islands are still shown as one island.

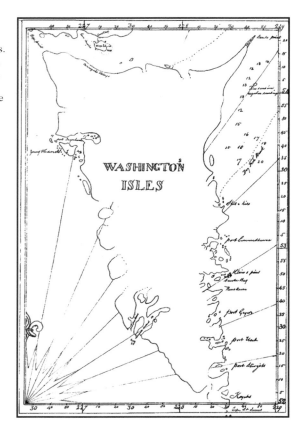

Map 140 (right)
Washington's Isles.
Joseph Ingraham,
September, 1791.
Another, slightly
earlier, map of the
Queen Charlotte
Islands.

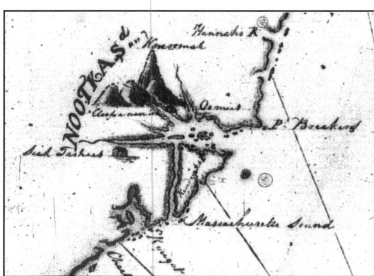

Map138A (left)
Nootka Sound and
Adjacent Coast.
Detail of Map 138
(Quadra's Isles,
previous page).
Joseph Ingraham,
1792.

GEORGE VANCOUVER'S VOYAGE OF DISCOVERY

George Vancouver was to have sailed to the northwest coast in April 1790, as second officer to Captain Henry Roberts, who, like Vancouver, had accompanied James Cook on his second and third voyages (see maps on page 47). The expedition was postponed by the British government when John Meares returned from Nootka with the news that Martinez had seized British ships and property there.

After the signing of the Nootka Convention (see page 68), the expedition was made ready to sail again, but Roberts had now been sent to the Caribbean, and so Vancouver was chosen to lead it instead.

Although only thirty-four, he was a seasoned sailor and an established surveyor and navigator, having sailed with Cook on his third voyage, also to the northwest coast, and had in fact already produced a map of the region (Map 80, page 50).

than it shall appear to be navigable by vessels of such burthen as might safely navigate the Pacific Ocean."

He was also directed to co-operate and treat in a friendly manner anyone they might meet from *"any other Power or State"*. In addition, should he meet any Spanish subjects, he was

to offer to him that they should make to each other reciprocally a free and unreserved communication of all Plans and Charts of Discoveries made by them in their respective voyages.

This was perhaps a tacit acknowledgement that any Spanish maps might well have more information on them than the British ones. Vancouver did precisely what he was instructed to do when he met with Galiano in the Strait of Georgia the next year.

Portrait of George Vancouver with John Cary's 12 inch Terrestrial Globe, about 1790.
There is some doubt as to the authenticity of this portrait, but the strong resemblance to Vancouver's brother, John, as well as other evidence, leads to the conclusion that it is George Vancouver's likeness. Vancouver is shown wearing a wig, which was out of fashion by 1790, but he was probably suffering from myxedema, which would have left him bald. The coat is considered to be the undress uniform of a captain of the day. "Cook Voyage" is on the bookshelf, and the globe is displaying the west coast of North America.[85/2]

VANCOUVER'S INSTRUCTIONS

Vancouver's instructions, contained in a letter from William Grenville, the British Secretary of State to the Lords of the Admiralty,[85] were twofold: Firstly, he was to formally *"receive from the Spanish officers such lands or buildings as are to be restored to His Majesty's subjects";* precisely what was to be received being uncertain. Secondly, Vancouver was to *"proceed in such course as he may judge expedient for the examination of the coast of North West America, comprized between Lat, 60° North, and lat. 30° North."* [from Baja California to Cook Inlet, the latter still thought to be Cook's River.]

One of the principal objects which Vancouver was to bear in mind was

the acquiring accurate information with respect to the nature and extent of any water communication which may tend in any considerable degree to facilitate an intercourse for the purpose of commerce between the North West coast and the countries upon the opposite side of the Continent, which are inhabited or occupied by His Majesty's subjects.

Vancouver was specifically directed *"not to pursue any inlet or river further*

VANCOUVER ON THE NORTHWEST COAST

George Vancouver arrived on the northwest coast expecting to secure Britain's rights to the entire coast almost from San Francisco to the Russian settlements in Alaska, despite the fact that he knew that the Spanish had been active in the region. Francis Drake's claim to New Albion was the basis for this expectation.

The *Discovery*, commanded by George Vancouver, and the *Chatham*, commanded by Lieutenant William Broughton, made their first landfall about 175 km (110 miles) north of San Francisco, on 18 April 1792, on the coast of Drake's New Albion.

Sailing north, surveying all the way, Vancouver somehow missed the mouth of the Columbia, even though he did recognize Cape Disappointment, the headland on the north side of the river, named by John Meares when he too could not find the river. Vancouver even noted the change in the color of the water, but thought it the probable consequence of some streams flowing into the bay.

"Not considering this opening worthy of more attention", he wrote, *"I continued our pursuit to the N.W...."* Thus he missed the first of the three major rivers of the northwest coast, and in so doing diminished British claims to the region.

Further up the coast, Vancouver met the *Columbia*, commanded by Robert Gray, who informed them that the Columbia River did indeed exist where Vancouver had just decided it did not. In fact, Gray entered the Columbia some thirteen days later, and named it after his ship. Gray was also able to inform Vancouver that he had not previously sailed in the *Lady Washington* to the east of what is now Vancouver Island, as was claimed by John Meares and shown in two of his maps (Map 94, page 59, and Map 95, page 60), both of which Vancouver had with him.

Soon after meeting with Gray, Vancouver passed into the Strait of Juan de Fuca, observing as he went some of the pillar-like rocks shown in the sketch under Charles Duncan's 1787 map of the strait (Map 100, page 62), which he also had with him. A rock off Tatoosh Island was named Rock Duncan (now Duncan Rock) by Vancouver.

In May and June 1792, Vancouver explored and surveyed Puget Sound, which was named after Peter Puget, one of his officers who did the surveying.

On 4 June 1792, he went ashore in the vicinity of Tulalip, near today's Everett, Washington, and claimed for

George III the coast south to 39° 20' N, which was his first landfall. Vancouver was convinced of the historical justification for his claim and his maps all show British territory from about 39° N northward. This performance of a formal ceremony of possession for Britain was not in Vancouver's instructions. He named the waters between the south end of Whidbey Island and the mainland Possession Sound, and it is still called that today.

Vancouver named the strait to the north of Puget Sound the Gulf of Georgia, after the British king, and also named the entire country south to 45° N New Georgia, a name which appeared on maps for some time, but did not persist.

While Vancouver was exploring Puget Sound, Lieutenant William Broughton in the *Chatham* explored and mapped the San Juan Islands. For the first time the principal islands were distinguished, whereas on the Nárvaez map of the year before they had been shown as one large island (Map 117, page 73).

On 11 June Vancouver sailed north into the Strait of Georgia, and anchored in Birch Bay. Joseph Whidbey, master of the *Discovery*, took two smaller boats south and found Bellingham Bay, named after Sir William Bellingham, controller of storekeeper's accounts of the British navy.

Vancouver then set out in longboats northward, round Point Roberts, which he named after Captain Henry Roberts, un-

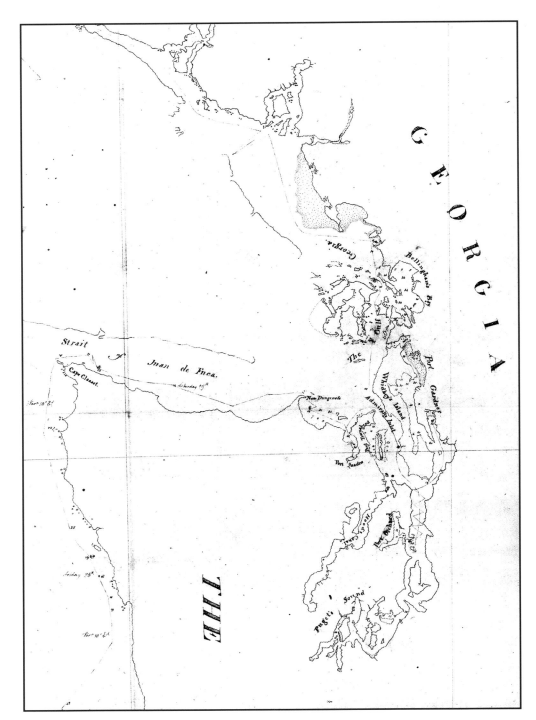

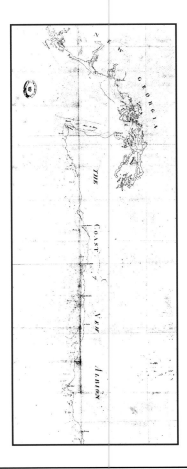

Map 141 (left), Map 141A (above)
Preliminary chart of N.W. Coast of America from George Vancouver's landfall to Cape Mudge.
From: Captain Vancouver's despatches, 1792.
The Columbia River is not marked; Vancouver missed it.
Map 141A, above, is a detail of Map 141, and shows the first mapping of Puget Sound. Note that the name Puget's Sound was applied by Vancouver only to the southern end of the inlet.

der whom he had almost sailed from England. Vancouver then inexplicably again missed a major river mouth, this time that of the Fraser. This seems to be partly explained by the presence of shoals off the coast at this point, necessitating keeping well out from the land, even in the smaller ship's boats. The Fraser was probably in flood, too; however, this did not prevent the Spanish ships under Galiano and Valdes from finding and anchoring in the north arm of the Fraser *the day after* Vancouver could not find it. Vancouver described the Fraser delta area

as a *"very low land, apparently a swampy flat, that retires several miles, before the country rises..."* [86]

Rounding Point Grey the boats then went up Burrard Inlet (which Vancouver named Burrard's Canal), and penetrated almost as far inland as today's city of Port Moody. Next was Howe Sound, where Vancouver named Point Atkinson and Point Gower (Gower Point) at its entrance, and Passage Island and Anvil Island within the sound. They then went north as far as Jervis Inlet before returning to the ships. On their way back they encountered

Galiano and Valdes (see page 77), from whom Vancouver was disappointed and alarmed to learn that the Spanish had already explored beyond where he had been, and had done so the year before, too.

Galiano showed Vancouver Nárvaez's map from the Eliza expedition (Map 117, page 73). Vancouver wrote,

I cannot avoid acknowledging that on this occasion I experienced no small degree of mortification in finding the external shores of the gulf had been visited, and already examined a few miles beyond where my researches during the excursion, had extended...[87]

Much has been made of the symbolism of this historic meeting, as a meeting of two destinies, the British star of empire ascending, and the Spanish one falling.

Vancouver learned from Galiano that Bodega y Quadra was waiting at Nootka for him, as his counterpart for the resolution of the 1790 Nootka Convention.

Later, the British and the Spanish ships sailed together northwards, into the channels north of the Strait of Georgia, examining the many channels and islands between Vancouver Island and the mainland. Usually Vancouver wanted to ensure that his men surveyed the inlets to ensure that they were closed at their ends and only rarely accepted the Spanish surveys. One of Vancouver's officers, James Johnstone, master of the *Chatham*, led many mapping parties to map the various inlets and ensure that they were not passages to the interior. One such map he produced was that of Loughborough Inlet, shown here (Map 143).

Finally, on one such expedition, Johnstone discovered a channel, now called Johnstone Strait, which led to the open sea, at last proving the insularity of Vancouver Island. "Johnson's Passage" is marked on the preliminary map produced showing the north end of Vancouver Island and the adjacent coastline (Map 142).

Here Vancouver's ships parted from Galiano and Valdes, and continued their northward surveying, almost to the latitude of Bella Bella, where they stopped the survey and made for Nootka.

On Vancouver's arrival in Nootka, he found that the storeship *Daedalus* had arrived carrying, amongst other things, a copy of a Spanish map made in 1790 by López de Haro (Map 112, page 70). This confirmed to him the extensive exploration work that the Spanish had carried out earlier on the northwest coast.

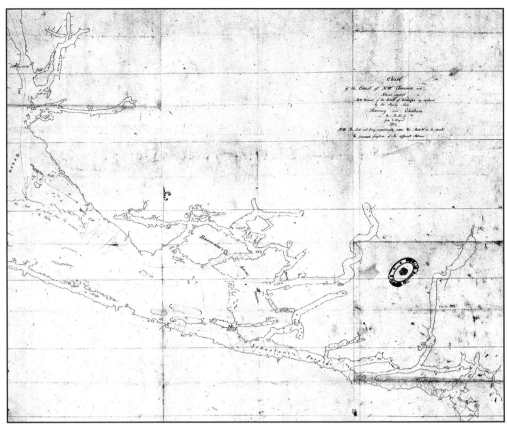

Map 142 (above)
Chart of the Coast of N W America and islands adjacent north Westward of the Gulf of Georgia as explored by His Majesty's ships Discovery & Chatham in the months of July & August 1792.
Preliminary chart, Cape Mudge to Queen Charlotte Sound. From Vancouver's despatches.

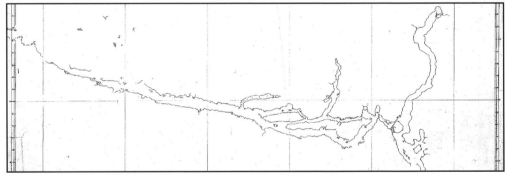

Map 143
James Johnstone's first survey of Johnstone Strait, with Loughborough Inlet at the right on the north side of the strait, 1792.

Captain George Vancouver's letter to the British Admiralty dated 28 September 1792 enclosing a number of new maps of the Northwest Coast. The letter and the maps were sent with his first lieutenant, Zachary Mudge, who left Nootka Sound on a ship sailing to China. Mudge delivered the letter and the maps to the Admiralty in June 1793.

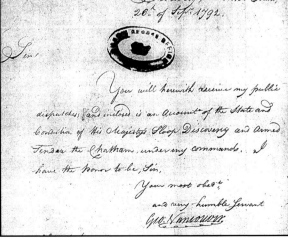

Here at Nootka Vancouver met with his Spanish counterpart, Juan Francisco de Bodega y Quadra, and began, as he thought, to carry out the second part of his instructions, that is, to receive back "British" lands under the 1790 Nootka Convention (see page 68). However, Bodega y Quadra was willing to give only a small area in Friendly Cove, and Vancouver was unwilling to accept such a small area. So, as gentlemen, they agreed to disagree, agreeing only to refer the matter once again to their respective governments for resolution. In fact, it would take two more Nootka Conventions and three more years for the dispute to be resolved, as it was in 1795 when both nations agreed to abandon Nootka.

At the end of September, Vancouver sent his first lieutenant, Zachary Mudge, to London, initially on a trading ship leaving Nootka for China. Mudge took with him reports, a request for further instructions, and copies of many of the initial surveys, including the maps shown on this and the preceding page.

The covering letter for this package is reproduced on page 87. Mudge arrived in London in June 1793.

In October 1792, Vancouver sailed south from Nootka with the *Discovery, Chatham,* and the *Daedalus.* Unable to enter the Columbia in the larger *Discovery,* Vancouver left William Broughton in the *Chatham* to enter and examine the Columbia River.

Broughton proceeded upstream in two smaller boats to a point 160 km (100 miles) inland, as far as a place he named Point Vancouver, near which, at Possession Point, he took formal possession for Britain. The clerk of the *Chatham,* Edward Bell, noted in his journal that the river *"might communicate with some of the Lakes on the opposite side of the continent,"* [88] and be of interest to the Hudson's Bay Company, an interesting remark given that the Columbia was the nearest thing to a continental waterway and would shortly become a major route for fur traders.

Broughton drew a map of the Columbia (Map 145) which was eventually copied on an engraved map by the British mapmaker Aaron Arrowsmith (Map 146). The *Daedalus,* now commanded by James Hanson, previously second lieutenant on the *Chatham*, with Joseph Whidbey, master of the *Discovery*, surveyed Gray's Harbor. The map was copied by the Spanish and is shown on page 80 (Map 131).

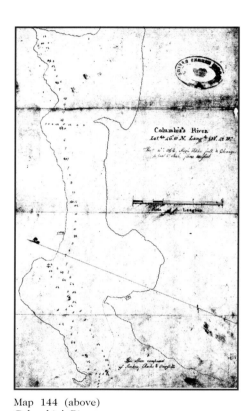

Map 144 (above)
Columbia's River
Chart of the entrance to the Columbia River; copy by George Vancouver of Gray's Chart, 1792. Taken to England by Zachary Mudge.
From: Captain Vancouver's despatches, 1792.
Covers only the area near to the mouth of the river. Gray originally named the river Columbia's River.

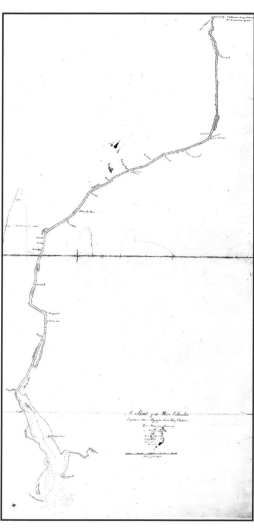

Map 145 (above)
A Sketch of the Columbia River Explored in His Majesty's Arm'd Brig Chatham Lieut Broughton Commander in October 1792

This was the map copied by Aaron Arrowsmith for Map 146.
Note the farthest upriver point reached by Broughton, which he named Point Vancouver.

Map 146 (left)
Plan of the River Oregan from an Actual Survey
London: Published 1st Nov 1798 by A. Arrowsmith

The engraved and published version of Lieutenant Broughton's survey of the Columbia.

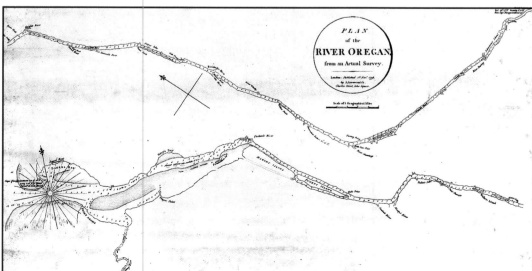

Title page of George Vancouver's book, published in 1798, after his death.

Map 147

A Chart of the Western Coast of N. America in which the continental shore from the Latde. of 42° 30' N and Longde. 230° 30' E. to the latde. 52° 15' N and longde 288° 03'; E. has been finally traced and determined by His Majesty's Sloop Discovery and armed tender Chatham under the Command of George Vancouver Esqr. in the Summer of 1792...The parts of the Coast red, are copied from Spanish Charts constructed by the Officers under the order of Senres. Quadra and Malaspina. Prepared by Lieut. Jos. Baker, under the immediate inspection of Captn. Vancouver.

This map was sent to England with Lieutenant William Broughton at the end of 1792. It was the first of George Vancouver's maps to incorporate information given to him by the Spanish. Vancouver sent Broughton from Monterey to England, after obtaining permission from Bodega y Quadra for Broughton to cross New Spain and then take a ship to England. As a result, he arrived in England in July, 1793, just one month after Zachary Mudge had arrived via China. As his ranking subordinate officer, Broughton was sent so that he could explain any details regarding the lack of agreement over the transfer of lands from the Spanish to the British under the Nootka Convention. Vancouver also required new instructions given the impasse that had been reached.

Map 148
A Chart showing part of the Coast of N.W.
America with the tracks of His Majesty's Sloop
Discovery and Armed Tender Chatham Com-
manded by George Vancouver Esq...The parts not
shaded are taken from Russian Authority.
Plate 12 of Atlas, *A Voyage of Discovery to the*
North Pacific Ocean and Around the World,
George Vancouver, 1798.
Shows Cook Inlet, including the site of today's
Anchorage.

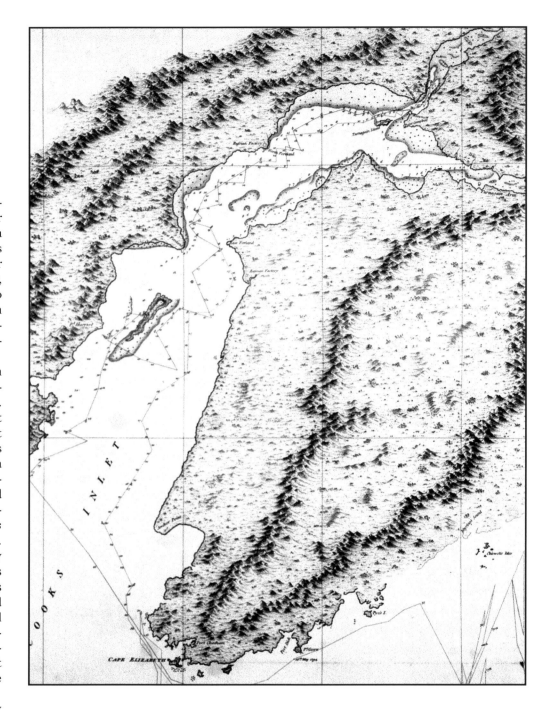

Vancouver proceeded first to San Francisco and then to Monterey to see if their respective governments had sent Bodega y Quadra and Vancouver instructions which would allow them to resolve their differences. None were received, however, so Vancouver sent William Broughton to London via Acapulco and Santa Cruz with reports and maps for the British government. Map 145 and Map 147 were delivered to London by this route.

In February 1793, Vancouver was in the Sandwich Islands (Hawaii) and returned to Nootka Sound in the spring. *Discovery* and *Chatham* spent the next four months surveying from the point they had stopped surveying the previous season, north to 56° N. Back in Nootka by October, the ships surveyed the southern California coast until December, and by January 1794 they were in the Sandwich Islands again to meet the *Daedalus* with supplies from New South Wales. Sailing again for the Alaskan coast, they surveyed the rest of the coast southwards from Cook Inlet, until then referred to as Cook's River, which Vancouver showed was not in fact a river at all despite all the speculation as to a possible route inland. Their survey southward that season linked up with their finishing point the season before, and their survey of the northwest coast was complete.

The last area surveyed was Admiralty Island, just south of today's Juneau, and their last major anchorage, from which boats surveyed, they named, appropriately enough, Port Conclusion.

Now Vancouver was able to state with certainty that no continental passage existed within the limits of his surveys. He wrote,

I trust the precision with which the survey of the coast of North West America has been carried into effect will remove every doubt, and set aside every opinion of a north-west passage, or any water communication navigable for shipping, existing between the North Pacific, and the interior of the American continent, within the limits of our researches.

Indeed it did.

GEORGE VANCOUVER'S MAPS

Comparisons of Vancouver's maps with modern ones show what excellent work he did. The only errors of consequence are where he had copied Spanish or Russian maps of some features of islands such as the Queen Charlottes or Kodiak Island, and his missing or not appreciating the significance of the three major rivers of the northwest: the Columbia, which he later found and had surveyed by Broughton, the Fraser, and the Skeena. He also missed the Stikine River.

Vancouver made a point of describing locations, sightings and soundings in detail, and his reports are as meticulous as his surveys. His book on the voyage, published in 1798, just after his death, ran to three volumes and an atlas. The maps on pages 90 – 92 are taken from that atlas.

Vancouver explained that it was his intention to make

the history of our transactions on the north west coast of America as conclusive as possible, against all speculative opinions respecting the existence of a hyperborean or mediterranean ocean within the limits of our survey.

No more would speculative geographers show northwest passages on their maps.

Vancouver's maps stood the test of time. As late as the 1880s, Vancouver's maps were still the best available for much of Alaska. And, of course, no one did make any serious attempt to find a western outlet to the Northwest Passage anywhere below the Arctic Circle. As one author wrote later:

No other man under analogous conditions has given to the world a detailed survey of equal excellence of so many miles of intricate coast.[91]

Many of Vancouver's surveys were reduced to smaller scale maps by Joseph Baker, one of his officers. While in the northern part of the Strait of Georgia, for instance, Vancouver had arranged his charts of the different surveys done so far in the order they had been made, and wrote in his account of the voyage,

These, when so methodized, my third lieutenant Mr. Baker had undertaken to copy and embellish, and who, in point of accuracy, neatness, and such dispatch as circumstances admitted, certainly excelled in a very high degree.

Map 149
A Chart shewing part of the N.W. Coast of North America with the Tracks of His Majesty's Sloop Discovery and Armed Tender Chatham...
Plate 14 of Atlas, *A Voyage of Discovery to the North Pacific Ocean and Around the World,* George Vancouver, 1798.
The summary map of the entire west coast of North America, the work of three years of surveying. At last the map of the Pacific Northwest looked much like reality.

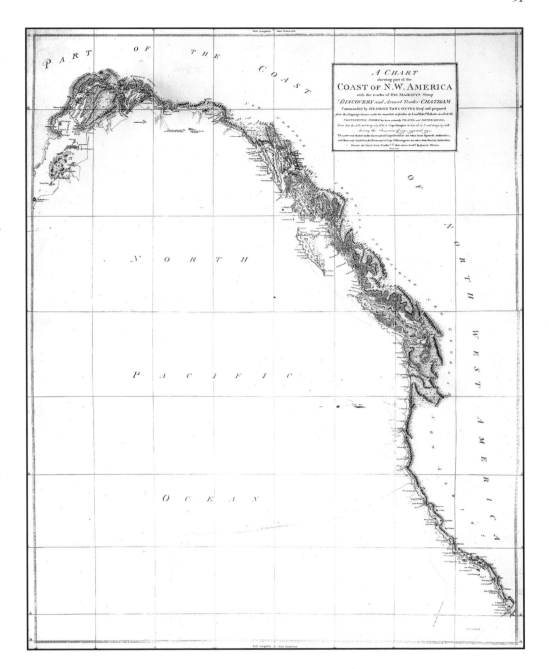

VANCOUVER'S SURVEYING INSTRUMENTS AND MAPPING METHODS

George Vancouver was initially supplied with two chronometers for determining longitude. They were made by the leading chronometer makers, Larcum Kendall and John Arnold. Kendall's chronometer, K3, was the same one that had been carried by James Cook on his voyage to the north Pacific.

Vancouver used these chronometers and three others which were later sent to him via the supply ship *Daedalus,* to fix longitude, but also used other means when possible, such as observing eclipses of Jupiter's moon and a method called lunar distances, which involved painstaking observations and calculations using tables called a nautical almanac.

Vancouver used a running survey for much of his mapping work by which "ship stations" would be established from time to time and the bearings to all prominent coastal features observed. Then the distance to the next "ship station" would be determined using a log line to measure the speed of the ship, which, in conjunction with the time taken to get to the next station, would give the distance. Vancouver was very good at this method of survey, having used it with James Cook before. Augmented with more precise positional fixes using instruments and carefully done, as it was by Vancouver, the results were excellent.

When Vancouver met Dionisio Alcalá Galiano, he was surprised to find that they were also well equipped for surveys; they had two chronometers by John Arnold on board their ships.

Vancouver's latitudes were very close to their actual values, but his longitudes were not as accurate, despite the chronometers. His errors in lunar distance observations for longitude can be attributed to the inherent difficulty of the method itself, and even to errors in the tables he was using, which, of course, were at the time all calculated manually by astronomers. Galiano had determined that the tables did have errors and was ahead of his time in partly rejecting this method in favor of chronometers. By the time Vancouver was in his final season of surveying, in 1794, his chronometers had developed errors. Nevertheless he did a superb surveying job considering the technology with which he had to work.

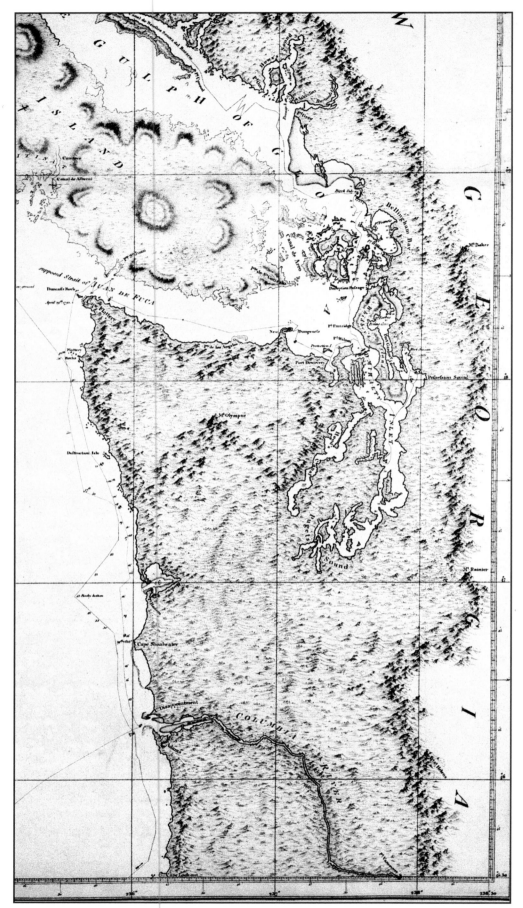

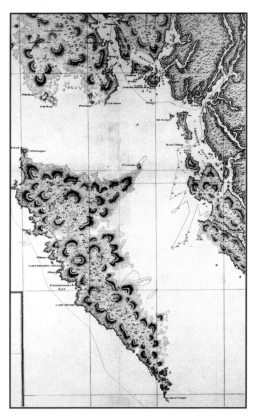

Map 151 (above)
A Chart shewing part of the Coast of N.W. America...
Plate 7 of Atlas, *A Voyage of Discovery to the North Pacific Ocean and Around the World,* George Vancouver, 1798.
The Queen Charlotte Islands and the adjacent coast.

Map 152 (below)
A Chart shewing part of the Coast of N.W. America...
Plate 11 of Atlas, *A Voyage of Discovery to the North Pacific Ocean and Around the World,* George Vancouver, 1798.
Prince William Sound.

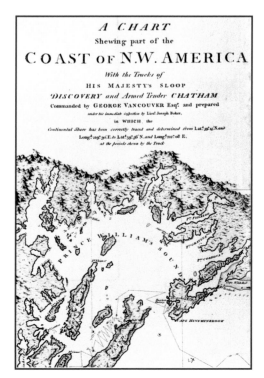

Map 150
A Chart shewing part of the Coast of N.W. America with the tracks of His Majesty's Sloop Discovery and Armed Tender Chatham Commanded by George Vancouver Esq....The parts not shaded are taken from Spanish Authorities. Plate 5 of Atlas, *A Voyage of Discovery to the North Pacific Ocean and Around the World,* George Vancouver, 1798.
Detail of northwestern Washington and southwestern British Columbia. Puget Sound is shown on a published map for the first time, as is much of the Strait of Georgia; although the Spanish had mapped the area first, they did not publish their maps until 1802 (see page 79).

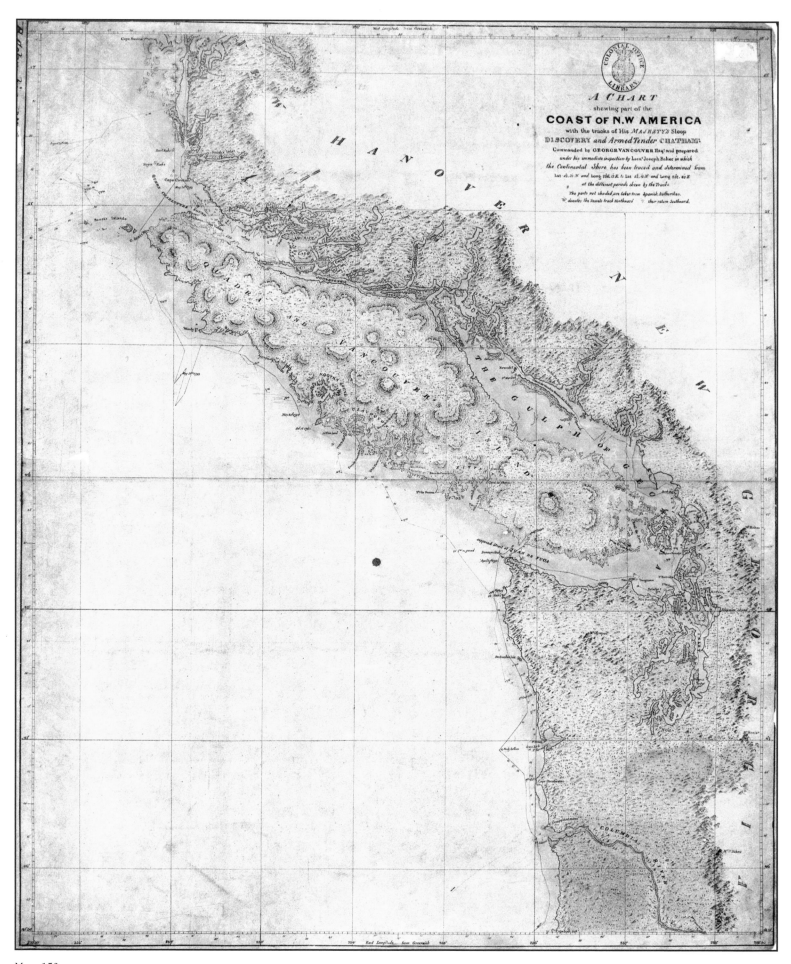

Map 153
A Chart shewing part of the Coast of N.W. America with the tracks of His Majesty's Sloop Discovery and Armed Tender Chatham Commanded by George Vancouver Esq. and prepared under his immediate inspection by Lieut. Joseph Baker...The parts not shaded are taken from Spanish Authorities.
Compilation chart for Plate 5 of the Atlas for *A Voyage of Discovery to the North Pacific Ocean and Around the World,* George Vancouver, 1798.

THE LAST SPECULATIVE MAP

George Vancouver thought his surveys would put an end to speculative maps, but that did not even begin to happen until his work was published.

William Goldson was an English physician who followed every geographical theory pertaining to the northwest coast and, in particular, the Northwest Passage.

Unwilling to discard virtually any supposed discovery, he produced a speculative map of his own in 1793, at the very same time that George Vancouver was surveying the Pacific Northwest so accurately that such maps would no longer be possible. Goldson attempted to reconcile every theory and fact he knew about the northwest. The result was a very interesting but wildly inaccurate map of the Pacific Northwest, the last truly speculative map of the region that would ever be produced.

Goldson's Strait of Anian was actually Prince William Sound, where in 1778 Cook's officer John Gore had noticed an opening to the northeast which had not been explored.

AC KO MOK KI'S MAP

This intriguing map shows a large area of western North America. It is a copy by Peter Fidler, a Hudson's Bay Company surveyor, of a map drawn at his request by Ac ko mok ki, a Blackfoot chief. It was drawn at Chesterfield House, at the junction of the Red Deer and South Saskatchewan Rivers, on today's boundary between Alberta and Saskatchewan. The Rocky Mountains are shown as a double line drawn horizontally across the upper middle of the map, and beyond them, towards the top on this map, is the Pacific Northwest. The detail shown in that region is that of two rivers, labelled by Fidler the "Big River" and the "Red Deer River" which have variously been interpreted as the Columbia, the Snake, or the Fraser. The Red Deer River west of the Rockies, and many features east of them, showed up on Aaron Arrowsmith's updated maps of North America by 1802.

The location and sizes of some thirty-two native tribes are also shown on this map, which clearly shows that the native knowledge of the land was extensive, long before it was mapped by Europeans.

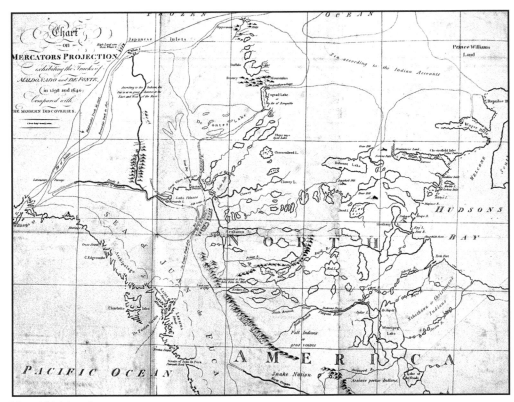

Map 154 (above)

Chart on Mercator's Projection, exhibiting the track of Maldonado and De Fonte in 1598 and 1640, compared with the modern discoveries. William Goldson, *Observations on the Passage between the Atlantic and Pacific Oceans,* 1793. A vast inland "Sea of Juan de Fuca," sweeps down from Alaska, relegating all the sightings of coastal lands to that of an archipelago, ironically close to reality in many parts of the coast.

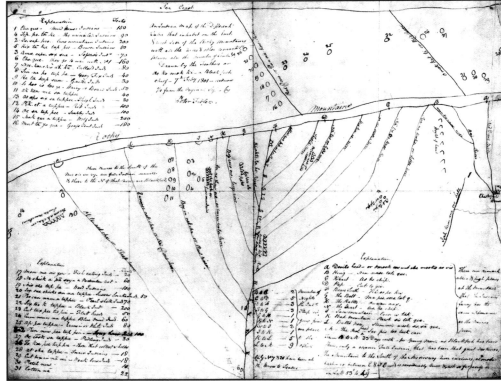

Map 155

An Indian map of the different tribes, that inhabit on the East and West side of the Rocky Mountains with all the rivers and other remark[bl] places, also the number of Tents etc. Drawn by the Feathers or Ac ko mok ki a Blackfoot chief 7th Feby 1801 – Reduced ¼ from the Original Size – by Peter Fidler. 1801.

This map is oriented with the *west at the top.* It shows a huge area of western North America from Wyoming and Alberta west to the Pacific. The Rockies are the horizontal double line, with eleven peaks marked (keyed bottom right). The tributaries to the Missouri are shown, with the Missouri itself drawn down the center of the map. The "Sea Coast" at the top edge is the Pacific. In the area above (west of) the double line of the Rockies, two rivers are shown, the Red Deer and the Big, which Fidler thought might be north and south branches of the Columbia River. They may have been the Snake or Columbia and the Fraser. The small circles with numbers are the locations of native tribes; the table in the top left of the map is the key, giving populations in numbers of tents. Chesterfield House, the Hudson's Bay Company post where the map was drawn, is shown on this map near the right-hand margin, about halfway down.

ALEXANDER MACKENZIE – THE FIRST CROSSING OF NORTH AMERICA

Alexander Mackenzie was a partner of the North West Company at Fort Chipewyan on the southwest shore of Lake Athabasca. In 1789 he set out, he hoped, to trace a river from Great Slave Lake to the Pacific. From his conversations with Peter Pond, Mackenzie thought it was Cook's River, flowing into today's Cook Inlet (see page 64). Instead he found the river now named after him, and traced it to its mouth in the Arctic Ocean.

"I went [on] this expedition", Mackenzie wrote in his journal, *" in hopes of getting into Cook's River, tho I was disappointed in this it proved without a doubt that there is not a North west passage below this latitude."*

In October 1792, carrying James Cook's map of the northwest coast, he set out again. Overwintering on the way, he ascended the Peace River for more than 1450 km (900 miles) from its mouth in Lake Athabasca. Near the source of the Parsnip River, a headwater of the Peace, natives told Mackenzie about a short portage to water flowing south. Here he crossed the Continental Divide and found a creek that flowed into a larger river, and then into a yet larger river, which the natives called Tacoutche-Tesse, or Tacoutche-Desse, today's Fraser River.

Mackenzie's trek to the Pacific was made much easier by native guides and others who often drew maps for him.

In his search for the way across the Continental Divide Mackenzie was aided by a native who said he knew of *"a large river that runs towards the midday sun"* and drew a map for him. On 10 June 1793 Mackenzie wrote,

I desired him to describe the road to the other river [the Fraser] *by delineating it with a piece of coal, on a strip of bark, which he accomplished to my satisfaction.*

Mackenzie then travelled downstream on the Fraser and its tributaries, which he believed were the Columbia River, for 400 km (250 miles).

Mackenzie was able to avoid the difficult sections of the Fraser by striking westward along the valley of the West Road River. He was advised to do this by natives, one of whom drew him another map of the Fraser south of where he was at the time. Another drew him a map of the West Road River route. Mackenzie wrote again,

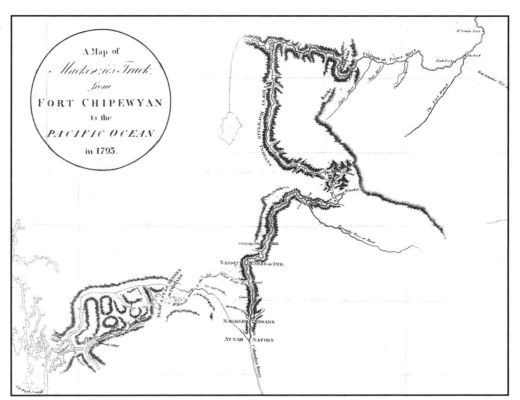

Map 156
A Map of Mackenzie's Track from Fort Chipewyan to the Pacific Ocean in 1793
This map shows detail of Mackenzie's route west of the Continental Divide. The whole map shows the route from Fort Chipewyan, in northern Alberta. The title cartouche has been moved on this reproduction. Mackenzie's 1792–1793 overwintering place, Fort Fork, is shown in the top right-hand corner, so this portion of the map represents the 1793 westward part of his journey. A "height of land" is marked on the Continental Divide, between the Parsnip River, which flows into the Peace, and James Creek (the "Bad R."), which flows into Herrick Creek, the McGregor River, and the Fraser. Mackenzie received considerable assistance from native guides and other native people in the regions through which he traveled. Maps were produced by natives to describe the country to him, and a note in Mackenzie's journal suggests maps were often made. On 21 June 1793, when trying to determine whether to continue down the Fraser or take some other route Mackenzie wrote *"My first application to the native... was to obtain from him such a plan of the river* [the Fraser] *as he should be enabled to give me; and he complied with this request with a degree of readiness and intelligence that evidently proved it was by no means a new business to him."*

I now proceeded to request the native...to commence his information, by drawing a sketch of the country upon a large piece of bark, and he immediately entered on the work, frequently appealing to, and sometimes asking the advice of, those around him.

Following established native trails for the most part, Mackenzie traveled westward for 300 km (200 miles), until he came to an inlet of the Pacific Ocean, North Bentinck Arm, at Bella Coola, east of King Island, and finally, threatened by coastal natives, towards the open sea at Dean Channel. On 22 July 1793, despite difficulties caused by the increasing belligerence of natives, and the urging of his men to leave, Mackenzie fixed his latitude at 52° 21' N (which compares well with the actual 52° 22' 30" N), and in the evening observed Jupiter's moons to fix his longitude at 128° 02' W (the actual is 127° 26' W).[95]

This is where Mackenzie left his famous inscription on a rock, painted in vermilion and melted grease: *"Alexander Mackenzie, from Canada, by land, the twenty-second of July, one thousand seven hundred and ninety-three".*

Mackenzie thus became the first documented person to cross North America.

Mackenzie's journey proved beyond a doubt that the North American continent reached at least as far west as 128° W, undivided by any water passages to Hudson Bay, at least south of 52° N.

He had reached the coast at the same time that George Vancouver was surveying it; in fact, one of *Discovery's* boats had been in Dean Channel only six weeks before.

In 1801, Mackenzie published maps illustrating his travels in his book *Voyages from Montreal...* (Map 156, above, and Map 173, the general map, on page 105).

The Tacoutche-Tesse was thought for many years after Mackenzie to be the upper reaches of the Columbia River, and it is shown as such on a number of maps at this time. It was not until 1808 that Simon Fraser traced it to the sea in the Strait of Georgia, and in so doing proved that it was not the Columbia, but the river known today as the Fraser, so named by David Thompson in 1813.

THE FIRST RUSSIAN CIRCUMNAVIGATION

Urei Lisianskii was a Russian naval captain, who together with Ivan Kruzenstern embarked upon the first voyage around the world to be undertaken by the Russian government. This was perhaps, rather belatedly, the Russian answer to the scientific circumnavigations executed by most of the principal maritime powers before the end of the eighteenth century – Cook for England, Malaspina for Spain, and La Perousse for France.

The voyage took from 1803 to 1806 and explored many parts of the world and in particular the south Pacific, but Lisianskii, in his ship *Neva*, was sent to the northwest coast ahead of Kruzenstern, who went to Kamchatka, in 1804.

The voyage was largely at the instigation of the Russian American Company, which had been reorganized and given a monopolistic mandate under Grigorii Shelikov in 1799. The voyage was essentially a feasibility study of a fundamental change of strategy for the company. This was the idea of supplying their settlements in Alaska and the northwest coast from the south, by ship around Cape

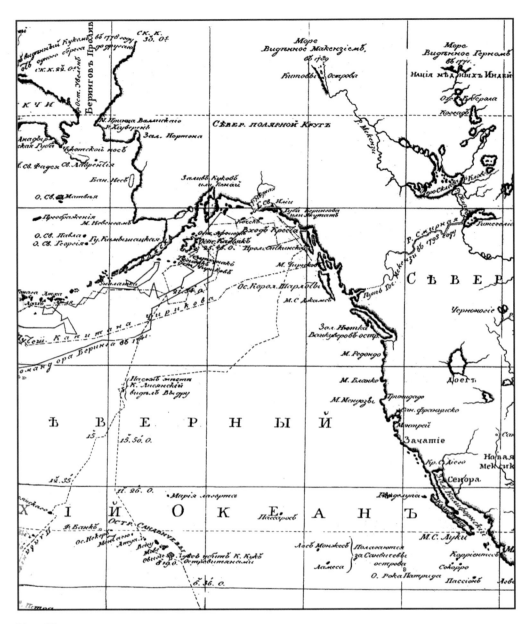

Map 158
Map of the Globe, incorporating the latest descriptions from the Lisianskii fleet, with a display of the route of the Neva from 1803 – 1806
From: *Collection of Maps and Drawings Relating to the Voyage of the Fleet of Captain (1st Order) and Gentleman Urei Lisianskii of the ship Neva*, St Petersburg, 1812.

The northwest coast part of Lisianskii's world map, showing the route of the *Neva* during the first Russian voyage of circumnavigation. Alexander Mackenzie's routes of 1789 to the Arctic Ocean and 1793 to the Pacific are clearly shown.

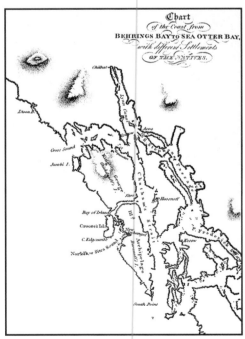

Map 157
Chart of the Coast from Behrings Bay to Sea Otter Bay with different settlements of the natives. Surveyed by Captain Lisiansky. (1804) Engr. under the direction of Mr. Arrowsmith.
From: Urey Lisianskii, *Voyage Around the World in the Years 1803, 1804, 1805 and 1806*. London. English translation published by John Booth, 1814. Shows the northern part of the Alaska panhandle centered on Novo Archangel'sk.

Horn, as opposed to from the north or east, across land through Siberia, as it had been done up to that time.

The voyage was approved by a new Tsar, Alexander the First, who was much more interested in the naval power and Russian expansion in the north Pacific than his murdered predecessor, Paul I.

Lisianskii's book, from which these maps are taken, was dedicated to the Tsar *"under whose auspices the Russian Flag was first carried around the globe."*

The Russians at this time had been engaged in warfare against the Tlingit, who had destroyed the initial Russian settlement on Sitka Sound, Mikhailovsk, in 1802, killing 400 people. While Lisianskii was in Sitka Sound, he assisted the manager of the Russian-American Company, Aleksandr Baranov, fight a major battle against the Tlingit to regain possession of the sound by using the ship's cannons for bombardment (see page 111). This was close to the site of Novo Archangel'sk, which later became Sitka.

Map 157, from the English translation of Lisianskii's book, shows the northwest coast centered on Novo Archangel'sk, while Map 158 shows the northwest coast part of a world map showing Lisianskii's track around the world, which was not published until 1812.

LEWIS AND CLARK'S OVERLAND TREK TO THE PACIFIC

In 1773, Samuel Hearne had advanced the idea of a Continental Divide, a range of mountains beyond which all rivers ran west. Following this idea, Aaron Arrowsmith, a London mapmaker, drew on his maps of North America a single ridge of western mountains. His 1790 map showed them only as far south as about 48° N, with the "River Oregan" flowing west (Map 159), suggesting easy passage to the coast from the head of the Missouri. His 1795 map (Map iii, page 6) shows this single ridge to about 49° N.

By about 1798, his maps extended the Stony or Rocky Mountain ridge south to about 38° N, as shown in Map 160. This map, like several others, noted that the mountains were only *"3520 feet high above the level of their Base."* This gave credence to the idea that they would not be a formidable barrier to westward movement, despite the fact that on the 1795 map Arrowsmith also wrote *"according to the Indian account is five ridges in some places."* Map 160 shows the headwaters of the Missouri flowing from the mountain ridge. William Broughton's mapping of the Columbia to Point Vancouver (Map 145, page 88) is also shown. Later, Arrowsmith has con-

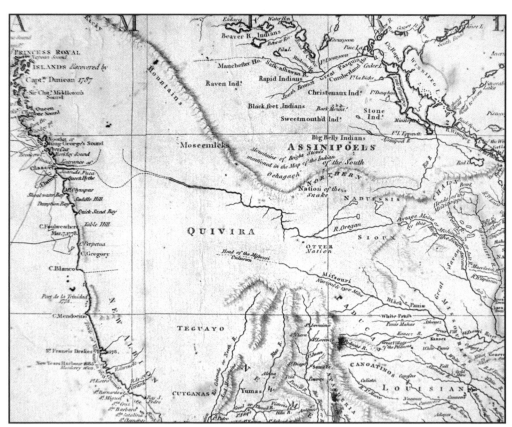

Map 159 (above)
Chart of the World on Mercator's projection, exhibiting all the new discoveries to the present time, with the track of the most distinguished navigators since the year 1790, carefully collected from the best charts, maps, voyages, etc extant and regulated from the accurate astronomical observations perform'd under the command of Captn. James Cook, in the years 1768, 69, 70, 71, 72, 73, 74, 75, 76, 77, 78, 79 and 80. Compiled & Published by A. Arrowsmith. London: 1st April 1790.
Shows "Head of the Missouri...Unknown"; and the "R. Oregan" flowing to the Pacific at the "Entrance of Juan de Fuca". The map is suggestive of an easy route from the United States (shown east of the Mississippi, on the right-hand edge of this map). The coastal part of this map is shown as Map 93 on page 58.

nected the "R. Oregan or Columbia R." with a dotted line to the other side of the single mountain ridge, suggesting an easy connection between the two (Map 161, page 98). The Columbia River had recently been discovered, by Robert Gray in 1792 and was known to have a latitude virtually the same as the headwaters of the Missouri. Perhaps portage between the two would be possible? So the Americans thought they might be on the verge of discovering a "Passage to India."

This, together with another myth in vogue at the time, that the American West would become the "Garden of the World", provided impetus for Thomas Jefferson's long held plan for a transcontinental expedition.[97]

In 1803, formal instructions were given to the man chosen to lead the expedition, Jefferson's secretary, Captain Meriwether Lewis. Lewis was ordered to

explore the Missouri river, and such principal streams of it, as, by its course and communications with the waters of the Pacific ocean, whether the Columbia, Oregon, Colorado, or any other river, may offer the most direct and practicable water communication across the continent, for the purposes of commerce.[97/2]

Map 160
Part of double hemisphere world map.
Aaron Arrowsmith, 1794, updated to c1798.

This map now shows the route of Alexander Mackenzie, and the coastal features mapped by George Vancouver. The Missouri rises at the single mountain ridge, but there is no suggestion of the direction of the "R. Oregan or Columbia R."

98

The expedition was also to fix geographical points by astronomical observations specifically so that an accurate map of the region could be made.

The Corps of Discovery, as they were called, left St. Louis in May 1804 under Meriwether Lewis and William Clark to begin their famous overland trek to the Pacific. Ascending the Missouri, they wintered at Fort Mandan, a camp they built in what is now North Dakota, and spent four months getting over the *unexpected* multiple mountain ranges of the Rockies.

On 7 November 1805, Clark was able to write the famous entry in his journal: *"Ocian in View! O! the joy."* The expedition had arrived near the Pacific coast.

On 3 December 1805, William Clark emulated Alexander Mackenzie, whom he had read and admired, when he carved into a large pine tree the words: *"Capt William Clark December 3rd 1805. By Land. U. States in 1804 – 1805".*

The expedition explored the Columbia estuary, establishing a camp for the winter which they called Fort Clatsop, just south of what is now Astoria, Oregon. They remained there from December 1805 to March 1806.

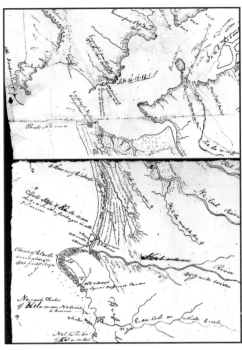

Map 162 (above)
Sketch map of the mouth of the Columbia River, northern and southern parts.
William Clark, 1806.

Many of the Clark maps were drawn initially on pages of a small handbook. These maps are no exception. Viewing these two pages as one, as we have shown them here, Cape Disappointment is at the top left-hand corner, with the Columbia River flowing to the south west.

Map 161 (above)
Chart of the World on Mercator's projection...
(Title as Map 159) A. Arrowsmith.
The map is dated London: 1st April 1790, but is in fact updated to c1800. Now a dotted extension of the "R. Oregan or Columbia R." has been made to the vicinity of the headwaters of the Missouri. Note also the tentative connection of Mackenzie's river (the Fraser) to the Columbia, labelled "Tacoutche or Columbia R."

Map 163 (below)
Page 152 from William Clark's journal, showing Cape Disappointment and the north shore of the Columbia River. 19 November 1805.
On this day, Clark headed his journal entry *"Cape Disapointment at the Enterance of the Columbia River into the Great South Sea or Pacific Ocean. Tuesday November the 19th 1805".*

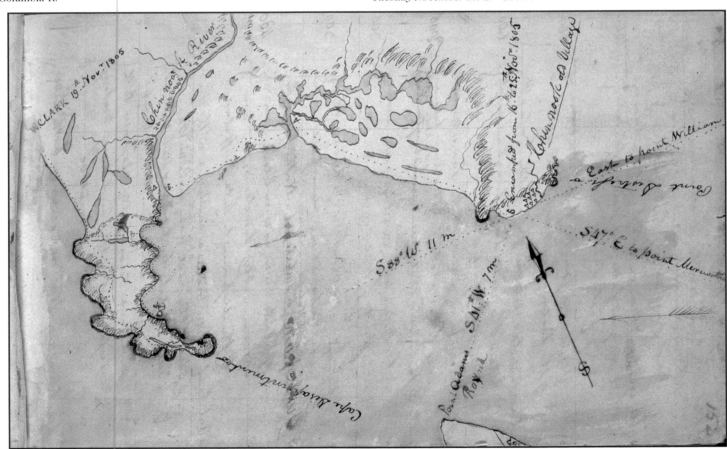

Lewis and Clark drew many sketch maps of the areas they passed through. Some of the original maps of the mouth of the Columbia and the area just south of it, drawn by Clark, are shown here (Maps 162 and 163).

Once at Fort Clatsop, confined in his makeshift hut while it poured with rain outside, Clark began the task of converting his smaller maps and his daily "courses and distances" (that is, his compass readings and dead reckonings) into a larger, smaller-scale general map. He added information about areas he had not seen from information gained from others such as fur traders and natives. On 14 February 1806, Clark was finished:

I compleated a map of the Countrey through which we had been passing...We now discover that we have found the most practicable and navigable passage across the Continent of North America.

Map 164 (below) is part of Clark's hand-drawn general map. On his return to St Louis, he kept it in his office until 1810, updating it some more as he could when he received more information. This was the basis for an engraved map, which is generally thought of as being "the" Lewis and Clark map, in 1814 (Map 168, page 101). This was published with the book entitled *History of the Expedition under the Command of Captains Lewis and Clark*. Now, for the first time, there was a reasonably accurate map of the region west of the Mississippi.

Meriwether Lewis died in 1809 from suicide or murder, leaving Clark to finish the work of creating a final map. Clark left the actual drafting of the map to Philadelphia mapmaker Samuel Lewis.[99]

Lewis and Clark laid to rest the dreams of a navigable water route to the Pacific. They did, however, find several routes through the mountains which could be used by future explorers or emigrants going to the Oregon country. In addition, they established another base for the future American claim to Oregon.

They also made cartographers realize that the Rocky Mountain range was wider and further from the Pacific than had been previously thought.[99/2] Clark had calculated the distance they would have to travel: from St Louis to Fort Mandan, his estimate of 2,400 km (1,500 miles) had been very close to the correct distance, but further west, from Fort Mandan to the Pacific his estimate of 2150 km (1,350 miles) was quite wrong; the real distance is 4050 km (2,550 miles). This error was due to incorrect positioning of Fort Mandan and the Rocky Mountains on previous maps and not, as has often been stated, to a lack of knowledge of the width of the continent; the latter had been well established by the surveys of Cook and Vancouver. The longitude of the Pacific coast is clearly marked on a map drawn by Meriwether Lewis about 1803 (Map 317, page 195), which was copied by him from George Vancouver.

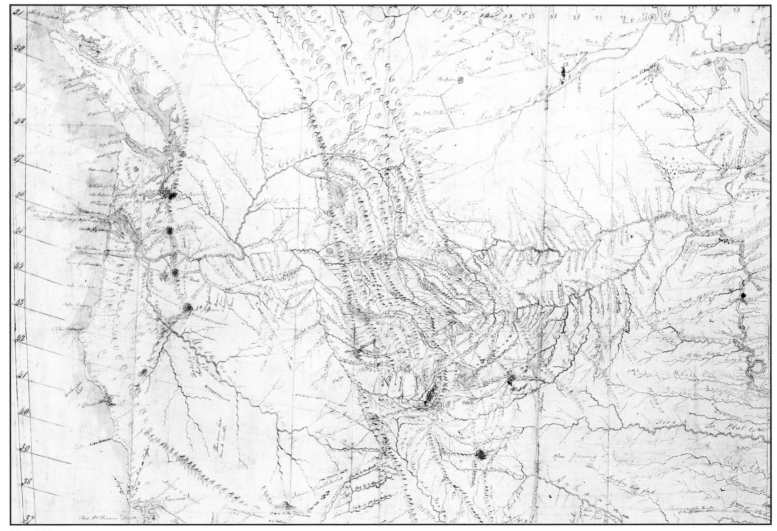

Map 164
A Map of part of the Continent of North America From Longitude...W of Washington City to the Pacific and between Latitudes 35 and 52 North. Compiled from the information of the best informed travellers through that quarter of the Globe...shewing Lewis and Clarks rout over the Rocky Mountains in 1805...to the Pacific from the United States. William Clark. 1810.

Elliott Coues called Clark *"one of the greatest geographical geniuses this country ever produced."* [99/3]

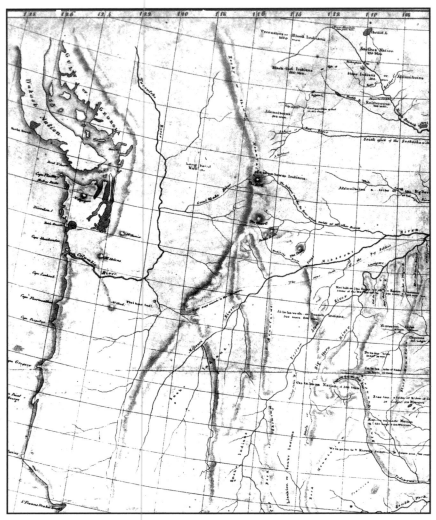

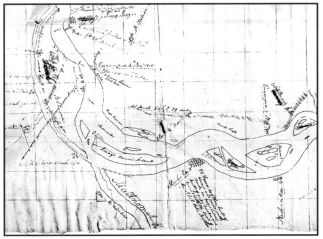

Map 166 (above)
Sketch of the Columbia River from the forks, & the 19th of October 1805 to the 1st of Jan[y] *on the Pacific Ocean.* William Clark, 1806. The part shown is of the Columbia River at its confluence with the Multnomah, including the sites of today's Vancouver, Washington, and Portland, Oregon. This and other maps in the possession of Clark's granddaughter were rediscovered by Reuben Gold Thwaites in 1903 and incorporated into his publication of the original journals in 1904.

Map 165 (above)
A Map of part of the Continent of North America, Between the 35th & 51st degrees of North Latitude, and extending from the 89 degrees of West Longitude to the Pacific Ocean. Compiled from the Authorities of the best informed travellers, by M. Lewis 1805–6
Copied by Nicholas King, 1808
Nicholas King was a Philadelphia mapmaker who came to the United States from England in 1796.

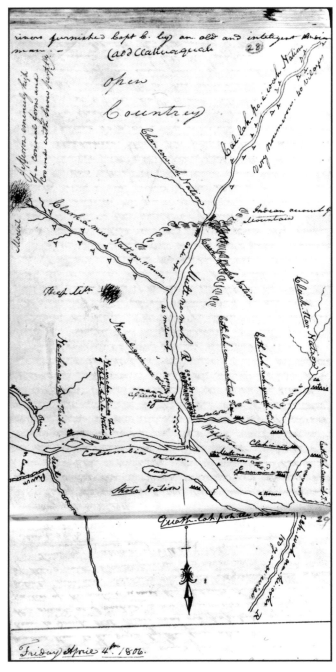

Map 167 (right)
[Map of the Multnomah and Columbia] *rivers furnished Capt C. by an old and inteligent Indian.* Meriwether Lewis, 3 April 1806.
This map is a copy of *A Sketch of the Multnomah River given by several different Tribes of Indians near its entrance into the Columbia,* from William Clark's journal of the same date. Lewis and Clark incorporated into their maps a lot of information given to them by natives. They had missed the Multnomah – today's Willamette – on both their westward and return journeys, despite that on their return they were looking for a south bank tributary of the Columbia which they thought was necessary to "balance" those they had already found on the north side. They found the Quicksand River (the Sandy River, on the left side of this map), but soon realized it was very short and not the larger river they were expecting. Natives told them of the existence of the Willamette, and Clark returned to investigate. Several natives who lived near the mouth of the Willamette visited Clark's camp and drew a map for him with lumps of coal on a grass mat; others were reported to have drawn a map with a finger in the dust. Clark copied it onto paper. This map is Lewis' copy of this map. It has no title in his journal, but the map is essentially the same as one in Clark's journal with the title given here.

Turning this map upside down so that north is at the top may aid in viewing. The convention of having north at the top of a map derives from Ptolemy, and hence was not followed by natives of North America.

The Willamette or Multnomah Valley, between the Cascades and the coastal ranges, was termed "the Columbian Valley" by Lewis and Clark. According to their estimates, the region was capable of maintaining an agricultural population of 40,000 to 50,000 people. Lewis wrote in his journal that it was the only desirable situation for a settlement which he had seen on the western side of the Rocky mountains.[100]
It was principally because of Lewis's description that later supporters of American settlement in Oregon such as Hall Jackson Kelley (page 115) promoted the region without even having visited it, nevertheless having a considerable effect in spurring western migration.

Map 168
A Map of Lewis & Clark's Track, Across the Western Portion of North America from the Mississippi to the Pacific Ocean; By Order of the Executive of the United States, in 1807, 5 and 6 Copied by Samuel Lewis from the original drawing of Wm Clark. 1814.

The engraved and published version of the final Lewis and Clark map, by Philadelphia mapmaker Samuel Lewis, copied from William Clark's hand-drawn map of 1810 (Map 165, page 99).

These engraved portraits of Meriwether Lewis (right) and William Clark (left) were specially drawn for the first annotated history of Lewis and Clark's expedition, prepared by Elliott Coues in 1893. It is still in print today. Coues rediscovered and used the original journals of Lewis and Clark from the American Philosophical Society in Philadelphia, where they had been deposited on Clark's instructions by Nicholas Biddle, the editor of the 1814 edition.

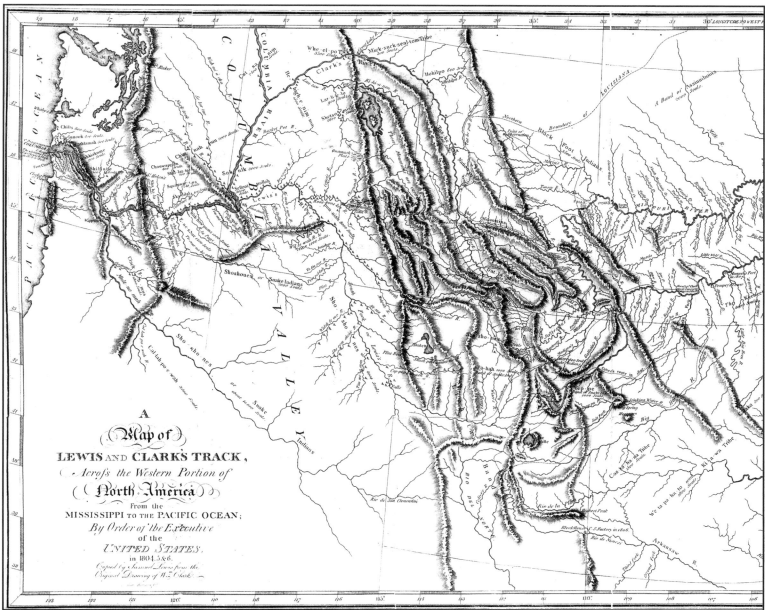

SIMON FRASER FOLLOWS HIS RIVER TO THE SEA

The news of the Corps of Discovery had a major effect on the British fur traders. It was the final incentive for the North West Company to establish a permanent trading post in the Pacific Northwest.

The company's famous explorer Simon Fraser began the process of opening up New Caledonia, the region of the upper Fraser River, by building Fort McLeod, on McLeod Lake in 1805, and followed this up by building Fort St. James, on Stuart Lake, and Fort Fraser on Fraser Lake on the Nechako River in 1806, and Fort George at the confluence of the Fraser and Nechako Rivers in 1807.

At this time, there was considerable confusion between the Columbia and the Fraser, and the headwaters of the Fraser were often shown either positively or tentatively flowing to the sea at the Columbia estuary (Map 171, page 103, is an example of a tentative connection).

In 1808, Simon Fraser mistook the river that was to bear his name for the Columbia and became the first to follow it to its mouth in the Strait of Georgia. He was disappointed to find that the river was not navigable through the Fraser canyon; because of this it was to play a lesser part in the fur trade.

ASTORIA – THE FIRST AMERICAN SETTLEMENT

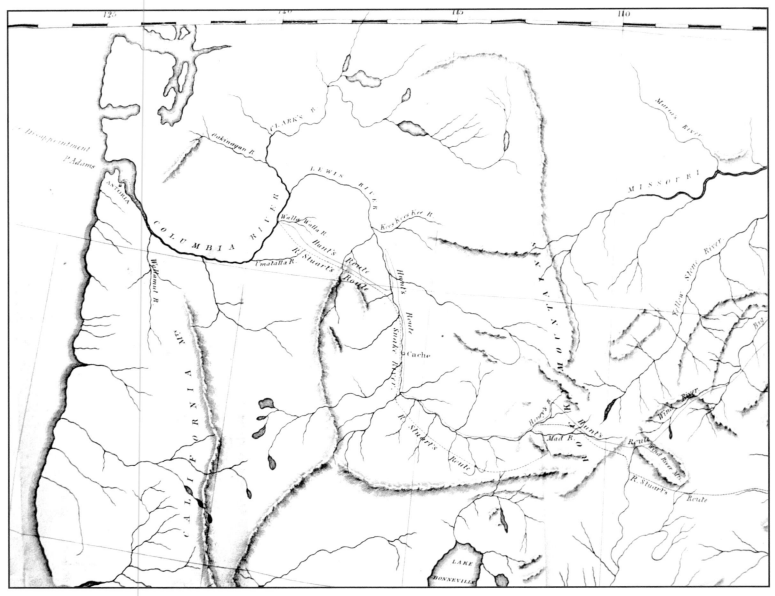

Map 169
Sketch of the Routes of Hunt & Stuart. From: Irving Washington, *Astoria*, 1836.

In 1811, the first of the American fur traders arrived on the west coast. They were from John Jacob Astor's Pacific Fur Company, and they built Fort Astoria, at the mouth of the Columbia. Astor intended to collect the furs of the Oregon country, pay for them with his own trade goods, and sell them in China, using his own ships.

To establish his trading post, he sent two expeditions, one by sea and one by land. His ship, the *Tonquin*, was commanded by an autocratic naval officer on leave, Jonathan Thorn. In March 1811, *Tonquin* arrived at the Columbia, but lost seven men attempting to sound out a channel across the Columbia bar before successfully crossing it. Fort Astoria was

built by Thorn and his men on the south bank of the Columbia, near what is now Smith Point, in Astoria. While the settlement was being constructed, Thorn took the *Tonquin* up the west coast of Vancouver Island to begin acquiring furs, but the ship was attacked in Clayquot Sound by natives, in retribution for some natives recruited by a previous captain, G.W. Ayres, but not returned. All the crew were killed except a native interpreter. One man managed to ignite the *Tonquin's* powder magazine, blowing up himself, the ship, and some two hundred natives.

The overland expedition also ran into trouble. Under the leadership of Wilson Price Hunt, it left St. Louis in March 1811, late. Hunt was not a good leader. His

expedition got lost, two men died, and others became temporarily deranged before arriving at Fort Astoria, in February 1812. This was the second American transcontinental crossing.

In May 1812 Fort Astoria was reinforced with the arrival of a supply ship, and the Pacific Fur Company began to consolidate and develop its territory. They had established Fort Okanagan, at the junction of the Columbia and Okanagan Rivers, in 1811, and other forts and seemed ready to challenge the North West Company when in 1813 came news of the outbreak of the War of 1812, between Britain and the United States. Astor's men at Astoria were already considering abandonment when this news arrived, as they had learned of the loss of their annual supply ship, which meant that they had no trading goods. Because of the war, they now feared capture by a British ship, so in October 1813 the Pacific Fur Company sold out to the North West Company. Most of the Astorians simply changed allegiance from one company to the other.

Indeed, a few months later a British navy ship, the *Raccoon*, did arrive at Astoria. Its captain, William Black, was annoyed that the settlement had simply sold out to the North West Company, and decided to hold a formal ceremony to establish conquest rather than simply a sale; in a dramatic gesture he smashed a bottle of Madeira against the flagpole and claimed Astoria by right of wartime conquest. This was later to be used by the United States as part of their claim to the Oregon country. The American Astoria was renamed Fort George by the British.

Astoria in 1812.

Robert Stuart, who had arrived at Astoria on the *Tonquin* in 1811, accomplished what turned out to be the most significant exploration that the Astorians achieved, by discovering South Pass, in Wyoming's Wind River Range. This was the easiest route yet found across the Continental Divide, and led Stuart to claim that *"a journey across the continent of North America might be performed with a wagon."*

South Pass later became an essential part of the Oregon Trail, which in the 1840s led to a major in-migration of American settlers and ultimately was one of the reasons the southern part of the Oregon country became American (page 133). South Pass was rediscovered in the 1820s by "mountain man" Jedediah Smith.

In retirement, John Jacob Astor wanted to secure his place in history and offered many original journals of the Astorians to a well-known author of the time, Washington Irving. Irving produced a book in 1836 called *Astoria; or, Anecdotes of an Enterprise beyond the Rocky Mountains,* which was a wild success, and in fact became what one writer termed *"an American literary perennial."* [103]

The book contained a map of the routes of Hunt and Stuart (Map 169), based on information from B.L.E. Bonneville, another western explorer. It perpetuated the image of the Rocky Mountains as narrow, easily crossed on foot or by wagon, even showing one branch of the Missouri crossing the Continental Divide! The map was poor cartographically in that the information was out-of-date, but *Astoria* was so popular that as a result, many settlers coming to Oregon later would have a poor perception of the magnitude of the journey ahead of them.

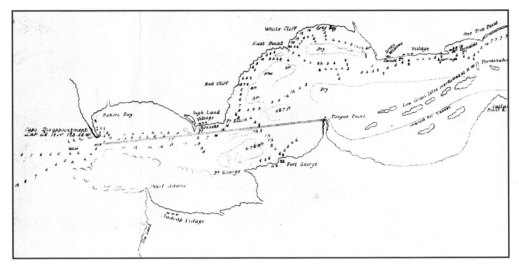

Map 170 (above)   *Columbia River 1825. British War Office, 1826*
This map shows the location and approaches to Fort George, Astoria renamed by the British.

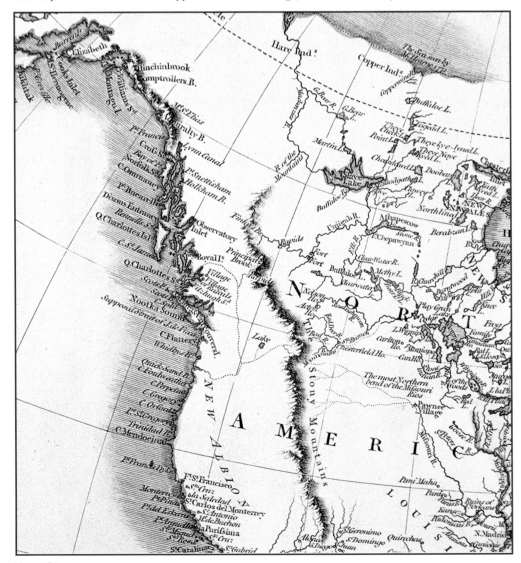

Map 171
A New Map of America from the Latest Authorities. John Cary, Engraver, 1803.

DAVID THOMPSON – CANADA'S GREAT MAPMAKER

David Thompson was undoubtedly one of Canada's greatest explorers and mapmakers, perhaps rivaling on land the surveying ability of James Cook on the sea. Through more than six decades, beginning when he came to Canada in the employ of the Hudson's Bay Company in 1784, he traveled well over 128,000 kms (80,000 miles) by foot, canoe, and horse, surveying, taking astronomical observations to fix his position, and noting the natural history. Thompson also gathered information from natives, who often drew maps on the ground with sticks for him. In this way, he accumulated geographic information for areas he had not visited.

His maps were forwarded to the company in London, where they were also seen by the British cartographer Aaron Arrowsmith. Thompson's early explorations and Arrowsmith's maps became one of the sources of inspiration of President Thomas Jefferson, leading him to conceive of what became the Lewis and Clark expedition of 1804 – 1806 (see page 97).

Thompson left the Hudson's Bay Company in 1797 to join the Northwest Company, which encouraged exploration and mapping, whereas the Hudson's Bay Company was more interested in fur trading alone.

Thompson was the first European to discover the Howse and Athabasca Passes through the Rockies, and to find the upper Columbia River and its branches and source, and first to explore the Kootenay River, Kootenay Lake, and much of what is now southeastern British Columbia, northeastern Washington, and northern Idaho.

Thompson is best known for his journey in 1811 down the Columbia to the Pacific, arriving just after Astoria had been established by John Jacob Astor's Pacific Fur Company; this timing was later to weaken the British claim to Oregon. During this expedition, he became the first European to follow the Columbia downstream from Kettle Falls to its fork with the Snake River, following Lewis and Clark's route of six years earlier downstream to Astoria. He mapped the full length of the Columbia.

On arriving at the mouth of the Columbia, Thompson wrote,

Thus I have completed the survey of this part of North America from sea to sea, and

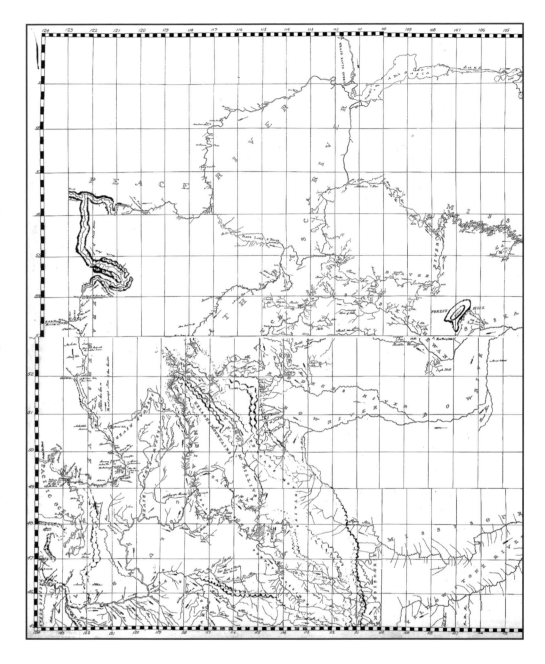

Map 172

Map of the North-West Territory of the Province of Canada from actual survey during the years 1782 to 1812. This map, made for the North West Company in 1813 and 1814 embraces the region lying between 45 and 60 degrees North latitude and 84 and 124 West longitude comprising the surveys and discoveries of 20 years, namely the discovery and survey of the Oregon Territory to the Pacific Ocean, the survey of the Athabasca Lake, Slave River and Lake from which flows Mackenzie's River to the Arctic Sea by Mr. Phillip Turner the route of Sir Alexander Mackenzie in 1792 down part of Frasers River together with the survey of this river to the Pacific Ocean by the late John Stewart of the North West Company, by David Thompson, Astronomer and Surveyor. Sgd. David Thompson

by almost innumerable astronomical Observations have determined the positions of the Mountains, Lakes, and Rivers, and other remarkable places of the northern half of this Continent; the Maps of all of which have been drawn, and laid down in geographical position, being now the work of twenty-seven years.[104]

Thompson left the west in 1812 and worked in eastern Canada for the rest of his life, surveying, among many things, what is now the Ontario section of the boundary between Canada and the U.S. Such was his reputation as a surveyor of reliability and integrity that Thompson was accepted by the Americans as the boundary surveyor.

David Thompson was responsible for many maps and much geographical information which is shown on maps as early as 1801 and as late as 1857, information for which he often was improperly credited.

Thompson is thought to have drawn, without being credited for it, the map in Alexander Mackenzie's book *Voyages from Montreal to the Frozen and Pacific Oceans*, published in 1801 (Map 173). It showed not only Mackenzie's explorations but also those of David Thompson to 1800.

In 1813, after his return to Montreal, Thompson drew a map of the west which was sent to the North West Company. It showed a nonexistent Caledonia River flowing into the Pacific in Puget Sound south of the Fraser. Thompson temporarily thought this was correct based on native accounts. A copy of this map was published in 1816 in a pamphlet of the North West Company, without permission, and was a prime source of other maps for about twenty years after that, all showing this error! A North West Company map of 1817, based on the 1813 map and showing the "Caledonia River" is shown here (Map 174).

In 1814, Thompson corrected the fictitious river when he drew another, more accurate map of the west for the North West Company. A copy of it was later sold, probably by one of his sons, to the Government of Canada West (Ontario) and it formed the basis for a map of western Canada published for settlers in 1857 which became the basic map of the west for almost another fifty years.

The fictitious Caledonia River persisted on some maps for many years, reflecting the scarceness of information and the degree to which maps were copied. Map 176 (page 107), an 1824 Aaron Arrowsmith map, still shows this river.

In 1826 Thompson sent a set of revised maps to the British government to assist them in one of the negotiations that was then taking place to determine a boundary line between the U.S. and British territory in the Oregon Country. Astonishingly, the British government sent

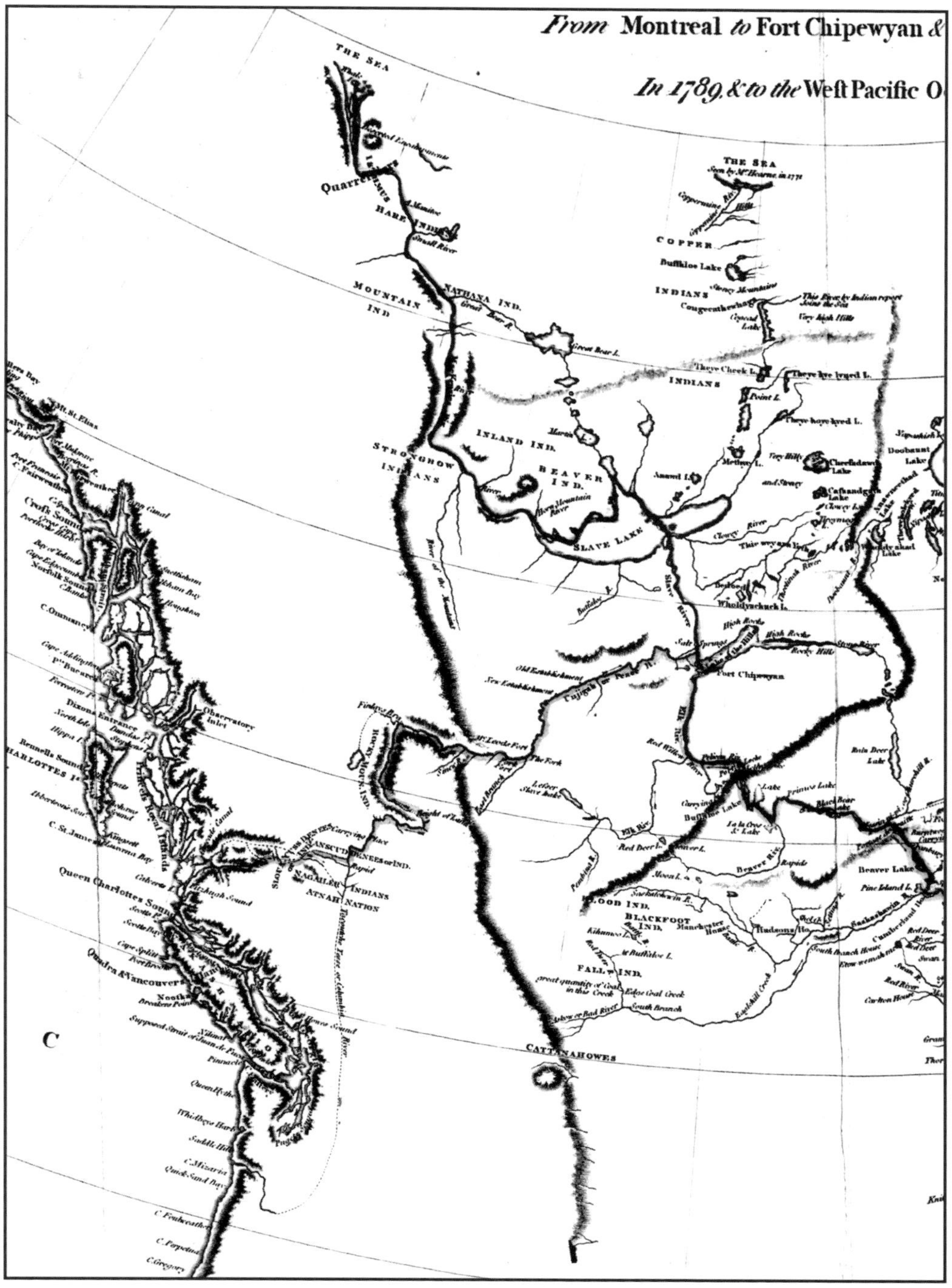

Map 173 (top right)

A Map of America between the latitudes 40 and 70, and longitudes 45 and 180 west Exhibiting Mackenzie's Track from Montreal to Fort Chipewyan and from thence to the North Sea in 1789 and to the West Pacific Ocean in 1793

From: Alexander Mackenzie, *Voyages from Montreal on the River St. Laurence through the Continent of North America to the Frozen and Pacific Oceans; In the Years, 1789 and 1793,* 1801.

The original of this famous map is thought to have been drawn, uncredited, by David Thompson. It shows Thompson's explorations to 1800 as well as those of Mackenzie.

Mackenzie wrote in the preface to his book: *"The general map which illustrates this volume, is reduced by Mr. Arrowsmith from his three-sheet map of North America, with the latest discoveries, which he is about to republish. His professional abilities are well known, and no encomium of mine will advance the general and merited opinion of them."*

From **Montreal** *to* **Fort Chipewyan** &

In 1789, & *to the* **West Pacific O**

Map 174

A Map of America between Latitudes 40 and 70 North and Longitudes 80 and 150 West Exhibiting the Principal Trading Stations of the North West Company. Drawn by David Thompson, 1812, but uncredited. The fictitious Caledonia River flows into Puget Sound south of the mouth of the Fraser River.

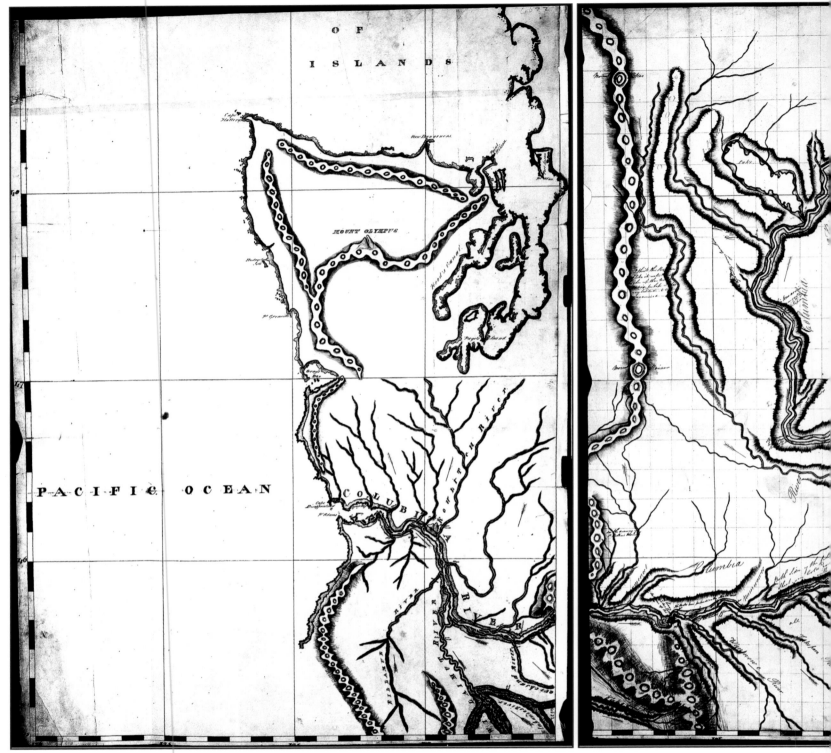

Map 175
Untitled hand-drawn map of part of western British North America by David Thompson, 1843.
Four of the numerous large-scale sheets. Perhaps due to loss of glued parts originally joining the
sections of this map, many of the sheets do not fit together, as here.

them back, saying that the Hudson's Bay Company had already supplied them with maps! The maps that the Hudson's Bay Company supplied were of course also Thompson's, from the one published in 1816 in the North West Company pamphlet. The Hudson's Bay Company and North West Company had merged in 1821.

In 1843, Thompson again sent the British government maps; this time revised maps, again for use in boundary ne-

gotiations, leading up to the 1846 boundary treaty (see page 131). Again, however, they were not used by the British.

Both the 1826 and 1843 maps, plus the 1813 one, were all pirated and incorporated into other maps, without any acknowledgment, by the Arrowsmiths, the London map-publishing company, and in this form became the standard for the rest of the century.

Some western sections of the 1843 map are shown here (Map 175).

A stamp showing David Thompson and one of his maps, issued by Canada in 1957 to commemorate the centennial of Thompson's death in 1857. The map is clearly one of western Canada.

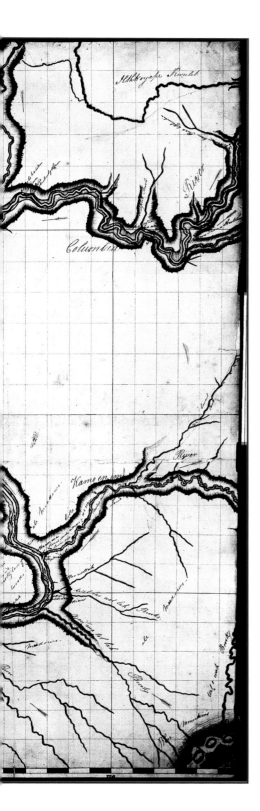

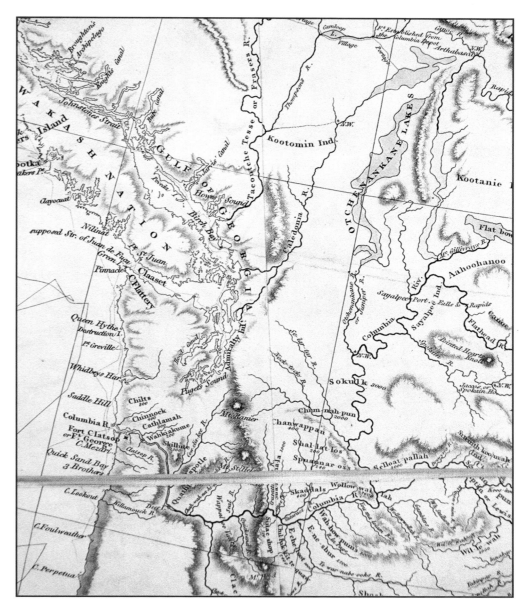

Map 176

A Map Exhibiting all the New Discoveries in the Interior Parts of North America. Inscribed by Permission to the Honourable Governor and Company of Adventurers of England Trading into Hudson Bay.
In testimony of their liberal Communications To their most Obedient and Humble Servant. A. Arrowsmith
Jan 1 1795 Additions to 1811, 18, 19, 20, 24. 1824.

Clearly shows Thompson's phantom Caledonia River, a mistake Thompson himself corrected in 1814. Note the ingratiating dedication; Arrowsmith owed some of his early success to the willingness of the Hudson's Bay Company to let him see their maps.

WHY WERE THOMPSON'S MAPS SO ACCURATE?

Latitude can relatively easily be fixed by observing the angle of the noonday sun. Longitude, however, requires other methods, some of which involve knowing the local time, again observable from the sun, and comparing it to the time at some other point, in Thompson's case Greenwich Observatory in England, today's 0°. Chronometers, to keep Greenwich time, such as had been used by James Cook and George Vancouver, were, in Thompson's

time, too fragile to be carried across a roadless country. Because of this, surveying wilderness lands presented far greater problems than at sea.

Two methods were used by Thompson, both of which took a lot of time. One was to observe Greenwich time, derivable from tables, from the moment of an eclipse of one of Jupiter's moons, observed through a telescope, but considerable time had to be spent peer-

ing through the telescope so as not to miss the exact moment of the eclipse.

The other method involved observations of the angle between the moon and two fixed stars, and then reference to a set of astronomical tables, a reliable method but one which took about three hours to perform. This was called the method of lunar distances.

Thompson spent endless hours making thousands of observations for latitude and longitude by these methods. But through this work, he was able to accurately fix the position of thousands of points on his travels, and they are the framework of his maps and the reason why they were so accurate.

RUSSIAN AMERICA

Life at the main Russian settlement in North America, Novo Archangel'sk (today's Sitka, Alaska), was often difficult. By November, everything was rationed, birds and rats were eaten, and it was impossible to fish due to threat of attack by native Tlingit. In March 1806, Nikolai Rezanov, a visiting senior official with the Russian-American Company, went to Spanish California for food. The ship's captain, N.A. Khvostov, used George Vancouver's charts for the first time; they had arrived in Novo Archangel'sk with Lisianskii. The ship arrived in San Francisco Bay in April. The Russians were taking a chance. Trade with them was forbidden to the Spanish, and the Russians did not even know that the two countries were not at war with each other. However, luck was on their side, and they were able to trade for all the provisions they needed.

Rezanov noted during his Californian sojourn that the Spanish had no settlements to the north of San Francisco, and this, plus the initial trading success, set in motion the idea of founding a permanent Russian settlement in Upper California to supply the northern settlements with food. The plan made a great deal of sense, given the difficulty keeping the Russian-American settlements supplied from their traditional sources.

After some more reconnaissances and a lengthy process of obtaining Imperial permission (which was given on condition that all expenses be met by the Russian-American Company), company manager Aleksandr Baranov finally sent his associate Kustov south to establish such a permanent settlement late in 1811.

The site they selected was eighteen miles northwest of Bodega Bay on the coast north of San Francisco, at latitude 38° 33' N. During 1812, the Russians built a log fort, with ten cannon, and during the next two years they completed a settlement, which they named Slaviansk, Fort Rossiia, or Ross. In so doing, the Russians rejected the contention that the Spanish had exclusive rights to all of New Albion, as they claimed. It was to be a more lasting challenge than Nootka; the Russians did not finally withdraw from California until 1842.

In a ukase, or edict, of September 1821, the Russians claimed sovereignty over territory on the North American continent south to 51° N, approximately the latitude of the northern tip of Vancouver Island. This sovereignty was to be exercised by the Russian-American Company. All foreign ships were forbidden to come within "100 Italian miles" of this territory. Within a year, the British and the Americans had issued formal protests, and the Hudson's Bay Company had resolved to approach Russian territory from the land.

Map 177, prepared by Captain-Lieutenant Vasili Berkh in 1821, shows no apparent eastern boundary to Russian territory as well, stretching as it does to Hudson's Bay, albeit depicted too far west.

By 1824, the Russians were prepared to concede that they could not hold dominion over so large an area. In April 1824 they signed a convention with the United

States in which they abandoned claims to the area south of 54° 40' N.

In February 1825 they signed a convention with Britain which established a boundary no more than 50 km (30 miles) inland from tidewater in what is now the Alaskan panhandle, and 54° 40' N was established with the British as the southern limit of Russian territory. The 141st line of longitude was also established as the eastern boundary of Russian territory with British territory.

It was this convention which established the approximate boundaries that

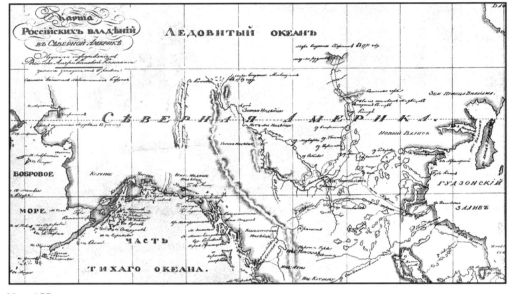

Map 177
Map of Russian Possessions in North America
From: Vasili Nikolayevich Berkh, *Atlas geograficheskikh otkrytii v Sibiri i v Severo-Zapadnoi Ameriki,* 1821.
Berkh had served with Lisianskii on the *Neva*, and produced this map as part of an atlas accompanying the account of the Lisianskii and Kruzenstern circumnavigation of 1803 to 1806 (see page 96). The map is based on Mackenzie's 1801 map (Map 156, page 95); little updating has been done.

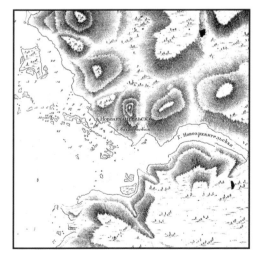

Map 179
Gulf of Sitka as described under the observations of the fleet of Urei Lisianskii, Captain and Gentleman, 1805 Novo Archangel'sk
From: *Collection of Maps and Drawings Relating to the Voyage of the Fleet of Captain (1st Order) and Gentleman Urei Lisianskii of the ship Neva.*
St Petersburg, 1812.
The immediate area around the Russian capital Novo Archangel'sk, shown in the middle of this map protected by many small islands.

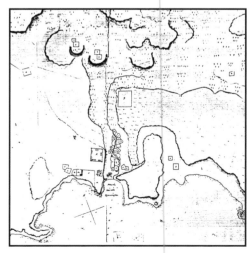

Map 178 Map of the Fort Ross area, 1817.

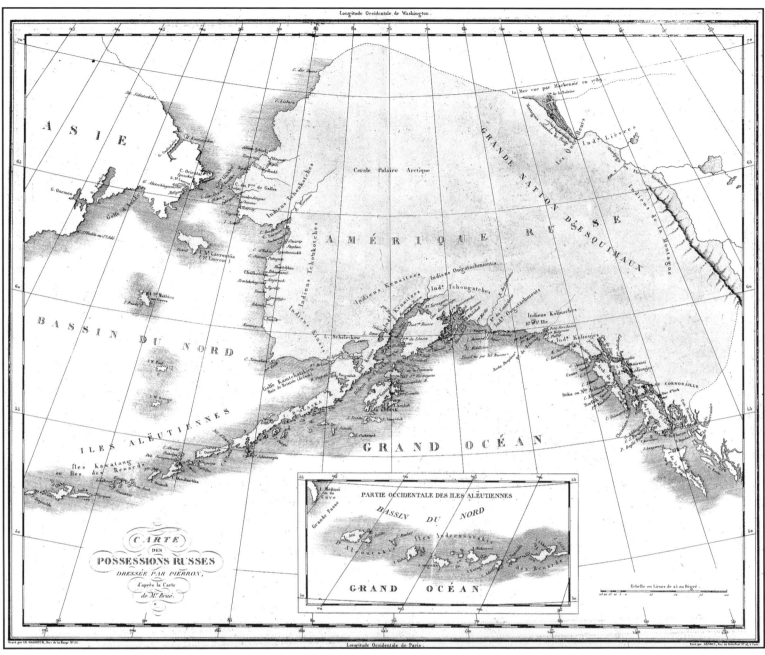

Map 180
Carte des Possessions Russes, dressee par Pierron, d'apres la carte de Mr. Brue. 1825.
A French map showing, not very accurately, the extent of Russian territory in North America.
Russian possessions extend eastwards, across the Rockies.

Alaska has today, although there was to be considerable bickering over details almost a century later (see page 188).

A French map which purports to show the new boundary according to the treaty is shown as Map 180, though it is inaccurate as far as the boundary is concerned. A much more accurate boundary was marked on the Arrowsmith map of North America published in 1825 (Map 181).

A British map published in 1829 (Map 182, overleaf) shows the southern boundary of Russian possessions at 54° 40' N, and extending eastwards to the Rocky Mountains.

Map 183, overleaf, drawn by J. and C. Walker and published in Britain in 1834, is much more accurate. The boundary is shown clearly as 141° W longitude plus the panhandle; "Columbia" is shown stretching from there to the 42° N line of latitude, the boundary with Mexico, which had become independent from Spain in 1819.

Map 181 (right)
North America
A & S Arrowsmith 1825
Samuel and Aaron Arrowsmith, 1825

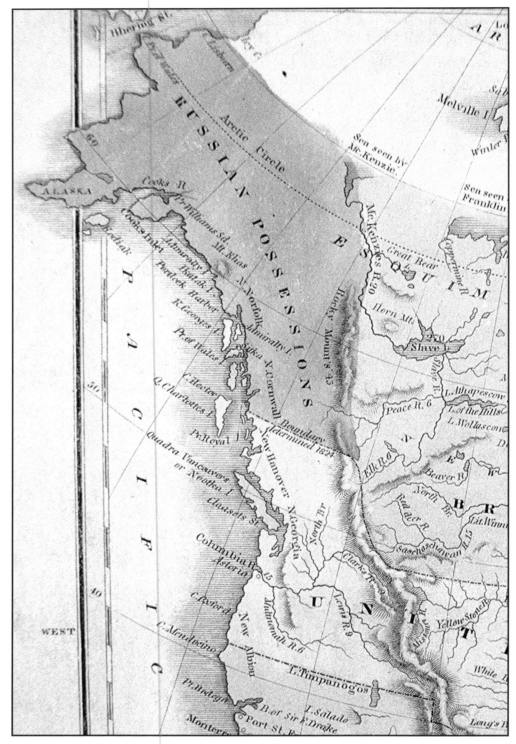

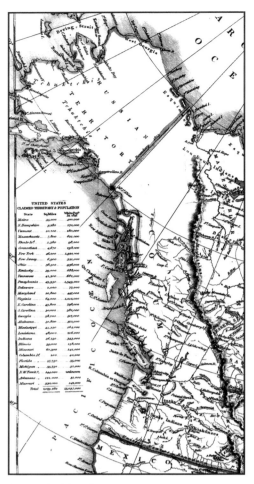

Map 183 (above)
British Possessions in North America
For Montgomery Martin's *History of New British Colonies Vol III – Possessions in North America.* Drawn & Engraved by J. & C. Walker, 1834. Shows quite accurately the newly established 141° W boundary between Russian and British territories, and that of the Alaska panhandle.

Map 182
North America, D.F. Robinson, 1829.
In this interesting map, Russian possessions are shown as reaching as far east as the Rocky Mountains and as far south as 54° 40' N, despite the fact that in 1825 the British and the Russians had signed a treaty establishing 141° W as the eastern boundary (the Alaska boundary of today), and restricted south of Mt. St Elias to the coastal strip today referred to as the Alaskan panhandle.

Islands in Sitka Sound viewed from Sitka. These islands protect Sitka, making it an ideal harbor.

Reconstructed blockhouse at Sitka, formerly Novo Archangel'sk. Built on the same site as the original, which formed part of the stockade the Russians erected to keep out the Tlingit.

Map 184 (right)
*Map of the Frozen Ocean & the Eastern Ocean.
Compiled from the latest documents in the
Hydrographic Department of the Ministry of
Marine 1844.*

From: *British Case, Alaska Boundary Atlas,* 1903.
This 1844 Russian map was used in boundary
negotiations between Britain and the United
States over the details of the boundary between
Alaska and British Columbia in 1903 (see page
188).

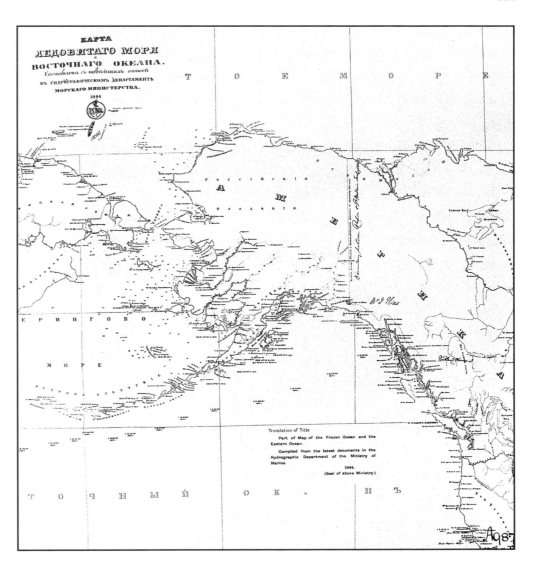

The Russian Orthodox Cathedral
of St. Michael, Sitka, Alaska.

NOVO ARCHANGEL'SK – THE CAPITAL OF RUSSIAN AMERICA

Novo Archangel'sk, often anglicized as New Archangel, was Russian America's chief settlement from 1804 to 1867, when Alaska was purchased by the United States (see page 168). It was situated on Sitka Sound, on the west coast of Baranov Island. This was a good harbor, with shelter being provided by numerous islands, which nevertheless required careful navigation. Map 185 shows the approaches to the Russian settlement taken from Mikhail Tebenkov's 1850 atlas (see page 143) and the photograph opposite shows a view of them from today's Sitka.

The first settlement the Russian-American Company established on Sitka Sound was in 1799, at a location a few miles north of the current city. It was destroyed by the native Tlingit in 1802. By 1804, the Russians were back, defeating the Tlingit with the help of Urei Lisianskii and his ship *Neva*, which was on a voyage of circumnavigation, the first the Russians achieved (see page 96). Lisianskii's maps of Sitka Sound are also shown.

By 1808, Novo Archangel'sk was the capital of Russian America and a port of call for merchant vessels from all over the world.

Although most of its inhabitants lived in crowded, damp houses, top officials lived relatively well. Under the Tsar's patronage, clergy of the Russian Orthodox Church built schools and churches and spread Russian culture. For a long time, Novo Archangel'sk was known as "the Paris of the Pacific," and was easily the most important city on the west coast of North America.

In 1867, Novo Archangel'sk, in future to be known as Sitka, was the scene of the official handover of power from Russia to the United States.

*Map 185
Map of the
approaches to
Novo Archangel'sk,*
Mikhail Tebenkov,
1850.

Another map, also
by Tebenkov, of
the larger area of
Sitka Sound is
Map 245, page
144.

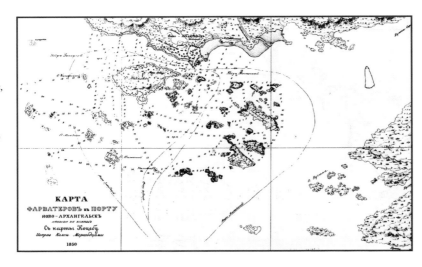

THE HUDSON'S BAY COMPANY AND FORT LANGLEY

In the early 1820s, the uncertainty of the political future of the country north of the Columbia led the Hudson's Bay Company governor, George Simpson, to support the idea of a new interior supply line to New Caledonia using the Fraser River, with a new marine depot to be established somewhere in the lower reaches of the Fraser Valley, which had not been explored by fur traders since Simon Fraser in 1808.

James McMillan was chosen to lead an expedition to report on the navigability of the lower Fraser, the route from the mouth of the Columbia, and the possibility of trading with the natives.

The expedition set out in late fall, 1824, and reached the site which McMillan recommended for a new fort, that of the original Fort Langley, by canoeing up the Nicomekl River in what is now Surrey, B.C., and portaging to a small river flowing into the Fraser.

Several members of the expedition are known to have prepared maps, because this was recorded by the Hudson's Bay Company, but all have been lost.

In 1827, on Governor George Simpson's recommendation, the Hudson's Bay Company decided to go ahead with the establishment of a new trading post on the lower Fraser, to be called Fort Langley, after Thomas Langley, a director of the company.

James McMillan was to establish this new post. A new company schooner, the *Cadboro*, under Captain Aemilius Simpson, had just arrived on the coast from England, so it was decided to use this vessel to transport supplies and then stand guard while the new fort was built.

Getting into the Fraser, with its sandbars and shoals, and then sailing upriver was not an easy task. Some indication of the difficulty they were having entering the Fraser is shown in the entry for Tuesday 17 July in the journal of one of the expedition's members:

Another attempt was made this morning to beat up the entrance of the Channel into Fraser's River but without preceding any distance, for the wind fell and about 7 am anchor was again cast on the edge of the south Sturgeon Shoal. Captain Simpson and Mr. Annance were off twice in a Boat during the day to sound for the Channel; but returned after nine at night without having discovered one.[112]

Map 186 (right) Northwest coast of America from Lat 52° to Lat 57° 30'. A Hudson's Bay Company map; the mapmaker is unknown, but it may have been Aemilius Simpson. It shows the northwest coast from halfway up the Alaskan panhandle to the southern tip of the Queen Charlottes, which are still shown as one island.

Map 187 (below) *Fraser River from a drawing by Mr. Emilius [sic] Simpson in HBC Schooner Cadboro 1827* London: Hydrographic Office 1849, Chart 1922. Islands in the Fraser named after members of McMillan's party sent to establish Fort Langley include Barnston Island (George Barnston); Annacis Island (François Annance); and McMillan Island (after James McMillan himself).

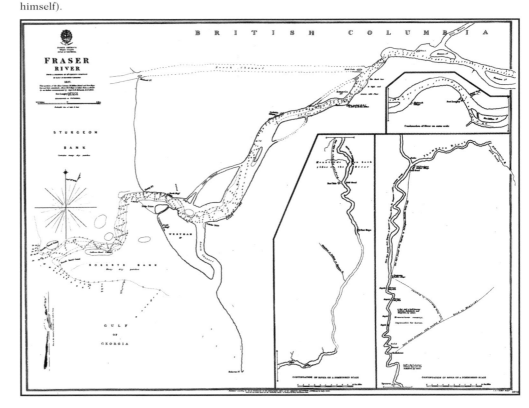

Reaching the site of the new fort at the end of July 1827, Fort Langley was quickly built, and the new fort was officially christened on 26 November.

Aemilius Simpson drew a map of the lower Fraser based on his experiences, and although his original map has been lost, the British navy presumably had it in 1849, when they published an engraved version (Map 187). Simpson continued to command the *Cadboro* until his death in 1831, during which time he sailed up and down the coast mapping and investi-gating new opportunities for trading in furs. He died at Fort Nass, which Simpson had established with Peter Skene Ogden in 1831; the post was then renamed Fort Simpson. The settlement was moved to Port Simpson in 1834.

Simpson was probably responsible for the map of the northern coast, drawn about 1829, which is a Hudson's Bay Company map (Map 186). In the late 1820s, the Hudson's Bay Company extended its trade to what is now the northern British Columbia coast and the Alaska panhan-dle. It did this to compete with American fur traders. This undated Hudson's Bay Company map, thought to have been drawn about 1829, still shows the Queen Charlotte Islands as one island.

Plaque marking the site of the original Fort Langley.[113]

Fort Langley building today.

THE FIRST MAP OF THE BRITISH COLUMBIA INTERIOR

This was the first map of the whole southern interior of British Columbia, drawn by Archibald McDonald of the Hudson's Bay Company in 1827. It was drawn to illustrate his district report to the company. This map collected what knowledge there was of the region together and fixed the position of several places on it. He showed the region's connection to the Fraser River, now known; Thompson's River is correctly shown flowing into the Fraser. McDonald had fixed the position of the confluence of the Fraser and the Thompson the year before; it is shown on this map a degree too far west. Kamloops is shown, located between the Columbia River and the Hudson's Bay Company's district of New Caledonia. A fort had been built there in 1812 by David Stuart, of the Pacific Fur Company, based in Astoria.

It must have been considered a good location, for later the same year the North West Company built Fort Thompson on the other side of the river.

Map 188
A Sketch of Thompson's River District 1827 by Archibald McDonald
The first map of the whole southern interior of British Columbia.

JEDEDIAH SMITH, MOUNTAIN MAN

One of the greatest explorers of all the American "mountain men" was Jedediah Smith. Most of his explorations were in the great basin of today's Utah and Nevada, but he did explore in Oregon in 1828.

While camped at the Umpqua River in southern Oregon in July 1828, his party was attacked by natives and only four men survived, one of them Smith. Heading into the woods, Smith and the others eventually made it to the Hudson's Bay post at Fort Vancouver, where they stayed until they headed eastwards in March 1829. While at Fort Vancouver, he was treated well by Chief Factor John McLoughlin and also met Governor George Simpson, and they all exchanged information; surprising perhaps, given the fact that the two groups were competitive rivals.

Some of the information Jedediah Smith gave to McLoughlin was sent to London, and eventually found its way onto the maps of John Arrowsmith (Map 189).

This was the map that would be copied by Washington Hood (see Map 197, page 118) to illustrate a bill introduced by Senator Lewis Linn, which authorized the president to occupy Oregon. This was also the first map to show correctly the relative positions of the Columbia and Snake Rivers, based on information obtained by Peter Skene Ogden.

A copy of a Smith map was given to David Burr, who was the official mapmaker to the House of Representatives, and this information was included in a map Burr produced in 1839 (Map 190). The Oregon rivers flowing into the Pacific were all named by Smith and are shown on this map. Some were shown also on the 1845 map of John Charles Fremont, actually drawn by Charles Preuss (Map 205, page 123). Also shown on this map was the important South Pass, which Smith characterized as being able to accommodate loaded wagons with ease. This report added to the perception that the Rockies would be easy to cross via this route and was a major contributing factor in encouraging migration of settlers to the Oregon country.

Jedediah Smith was killed in 1831, at the age of only thirty-two, by Comanche in the southwest.

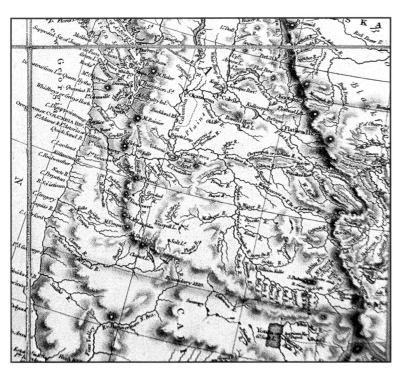

Map 189
British North America by permission dedicated to the Hon. Hudson's Bay Company containing the latest information which these documents furnish. By their obedient servant J. Arrowsmith. Pub^d 15 Feb 1832 by J Arrowsmith.
The Oregon rivers flowing to the sea are now correct, as is the position of the Snake River, based on information from Jedediah Smith.

Map 190
The Northwest Coast of North America and adjacent Territories Compiled from the Best Authorities under the direction of Robert Greenhow to accompany his Memoir on the Northwest Coast published by order of the Senate of the United States drawn by David H. Burr 1839.
From: Robert Greenhow, *Memoir, Historical and Political, on the Northwest Coast of North America and the adjacent territories,* 1840.

THE TRAVELS OF PETER SKENE OGDEN

In 1823, Governor Simpson of the Hudson's Bay Company put Peter Skene Ogden in control of the Snake River brigade of fur trappers. Ogden was to trap out the entire watershed of the Snake River, to render it a "fur desert", so that it would be unattractive to American trappers and traders coming from St Louis.

The idea was to avoid a challenge to the Hudson's Bay Company in the Oregon country. The policy appeared to work, and the American trappers tended to stay in the Rockies, earning them the appellation "mountain men". Ogden became, in his trapping efforts, the first explorer to cross the Rockies from north to south. His reports and maps of his travels increased the knowledge of the interior of Oregon.

On a later expedition south to the Gulf of California, Ogden lost all his maps and journals in a whirlpool on the Columbia River. There were some maps that didn't make it!

HALL KELLEY AND THE AMERICAN SETTLEMENT OF OREGON

After Jedediah Smith, the next Americans to arrive in Oregon were a party of more than a hundred men led by Captain Benjamin Bonneville, who arrived at Fort Walla Walla in 1832, with plans to enter the fur trade. He got no co-operation from the British, who wanted no competition, and as a result the venture did not succeed. Bonneville did, however, show that the overland trek to Oregon was possible for settlers, using the Oregon Trail. In 1829, Hall J. Kelley founded an organization called the "American Society for Encouraging Settlement of the Oregon Territory", and devised and announced a plan to move three thousand New England farmers to the banks of the Columbia. Much of his sight-unseen optimism derived from his readings of Lewis and Clark's endorsements of the agricultural potential of the region (see page 100).

In 1830 Kelley published what became a very influential book entitled *A Geographical Sketch of that Part of North America, called Oregon*, despite the fact that it would be another five years before Kelley actually got to Oregon. The title page of the book is reproduced here.

The book contained a somewhat exaggerated account of the wonders of the west, and is more famous for its effects in spurring migration than for its factual accuracy.

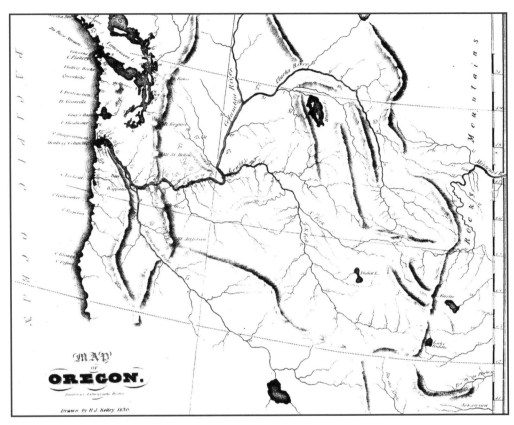

Map 191
Map of Oregon   Drawn by H.J. Kelley 1830
From: Hall J. Kelley, *A Geographical Sketch of that part of North America, called Oregon*, 1830.

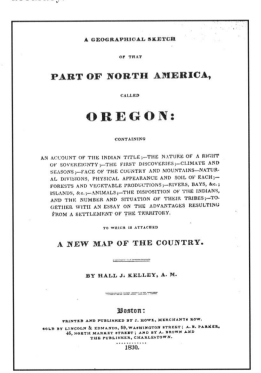

Title page of Kelley's influential book.

Kelley flooded the United States Congress with appeals for immediate American occupancy of the territory of the Columbia. He hoped to found a settlement at the mouth of the Willamette River, close to the site of today's Portland. This map was shown in a pamphlet Kelley drew up for his promotions and included in his book (Map 192).

Map 191 was included in Kelley's book. It is thought to be the first printed map specifically of Oregon. The numbers on the map refer to features mentioned in the book. Kelley marked the 49th parallel on the map, extending across Vancouver Island to the Pacific. Also marked is the 42nd parallel, the boundary with Spanish California. The Multnomah River is marked, today's Willamette. The Fraser River is shown entering Puget Sound below the 49th parallel. And in a glaring inconsistency, the Missouri River is shown crossing the Rocky Mountains!

One of the readers and believers in Kelley's book was Nathaniel Wyeth, a Bostonian intent on making his fortune in Oregon. He twice tried to establish

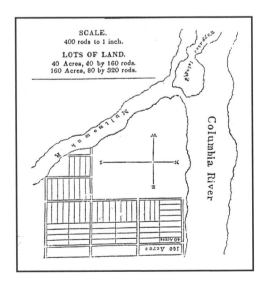

Map 192
Site plan of Hall J. Kelley's proposed city at the confluence of the Multnomah (Willamette) and Columbia Rivers.
From: Hall J. Kelley, *General Circular*, 1830.

The site of Kelley's proposed city was given the name Kelley Point in 1926. It is the north point of Pearcy Island. The City of Portland acquired the site, and more, for a park in 1979; it is today's Kelley Point Park.

trading enterprises in Oregon. In 1832 he failed because his supply ship was wrecked; after going back to Boston he returned in 1834 to set up the Columbia River Fishing and Trading Company, but his attempts at salmon fishing on a commercial scale failed. He returned to Boston, but several members of his party, including missionaries Jason and Daniel Lee, stayed in Oregon and established themselves in the Willamette Valley. At a place called Willamette Falls, they had opened a general store. At this location in 1842, the Hudson's Bay Company Chief Factor at nearby Fort Vancouver, John McLoughlin, laid out Oregon City, now a suburb of Portland.

Map 194 is a map of Oregon City surveyed in 1844 by Adolphus Lee Lewes of the Hudson's Bay Company. In 1844, Oregon City became the first incorporated U.S. city west of the Rocky Mountains.

Near Oregon City, at Champoeg, in July 1843, American settlers resolved to form the first government for Oregon. All this was happening despite the fact that the area would not be officially ceded to the United States for another two years.

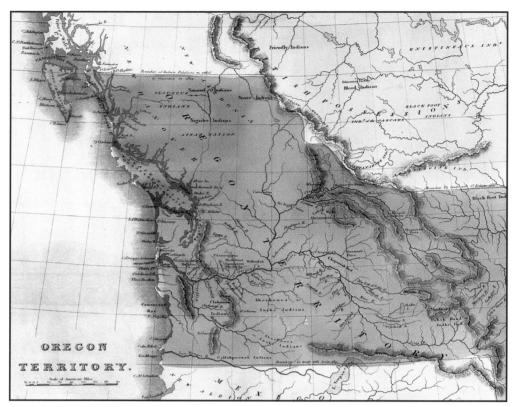

Map 193 (above)
Oregon Territory Entered according to act of Congress in the year 1833... David H. Burr, 1833. Oregon is shown as extending from about 54° 05' N in the north ("Boundary of Russian Possessions settled by Convention in 1825") to 42° N in the south ("Boundary by treaty with Spain 1819").

View of Oregon City in 1845, by Henry Warre (see page 129).

Hall Kelley's dream was to recreate New England in Oregon. Ignoring the native presence, he wrote,

When improved and imbellished by the white man, Oregon will become the loveliest and most envied country on earth. Oregon cannot be outdone whether in wheat, oats, rye, barley, buckwheat, peas, beans, potatoes, turnips, cabbages, onions, parsnips, carrots, beets, currants, gooseberries, strawberries, apples, peaches, pears or fat and healthy babies.

By such words were settlers induced to move west!

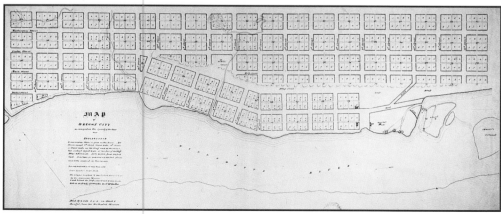

Map 194
Map of Oregon City as surveyed in the spring of the year 1844. Adolphus Lee Lewes, 1844.

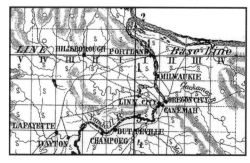

Map 195
Map of Oregon Territory West of the Cascade Mountains. Surveyor General's Office, Salem, O.T. Oct. 1st 1855 C.K Gardiner, Surveyor General... This 1855 map shows the locations of Champoeg, Oregon City, and Portland and Linn City (named after Senator Lewis Linn; see page 118).

Map 196
*The United States and the Relative Position of The Oregon and Texas
by James Wyld, Charing Cross East. 1845*

In support of British claims to Oregon was this map by James Wyld. It was published with a little booklet, part of which is shown, listing historical events which supported both the British and the American cases, called *"Comparative Chronological Statement of the Events connected with the Rights of Great Britain and Claims of the United States to the Oregon Territory."* The bias is clearly revealed in this title; Britain has "rights", whereas the United States has "claims".

The map shows the "Supposed Boundary of Ancient Louisiana, according to the Patent of Crozat, 1712, Purchased fom France in 1805" (purple line); the northern boundary of Spanish territory according to the Treaty of Florida, between the United States and Spain, 1819 and 1828 (now the 42° N southern boundaries of Oregon and Idaho), and the boundary between the United States and British territory according to the Convention of 20 October 1818 (the 49th parallel east of the Rockies) (orange lines); the boundary line proposed by the United States in 1824 and 1825 (green line); and the boundary proposed by Britain in 1826 (red line). Just south of San Francisco Bay is the "line proposed to Mexico by the United States" (brown line).

COMPARATIVE

CHRONOLOGICAL STATEMENT

OF THE EVENTS CONNECTED WITH THE

RIGHTS OF GREAT BRITAIN

AND THE

CLAIMS OF THE UNITED STATES

TO THE

OREGON TERRITORY.

ENGLAND.	AMERICA.
578-81. Sir Francis Drake discovered the north west coast of America, from Cape Mendocino to the 48° of north latitude.	
	1712 Louis XIV. granted a patent to Antoine Crozat for the exclusive trade to Louisiana. The patent states, " that the territories possessed by the King are bounded by New Mexico and by the lands of the English in Carolina, and

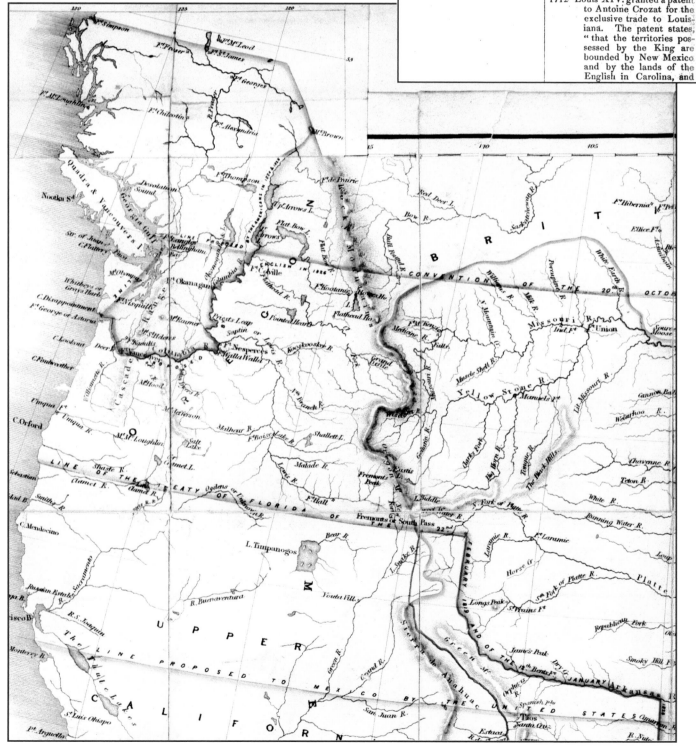

SENATOR LINN'S BILL TO OCCUPY OREGON

Senator Lewis F. Linn of Missouri was an ardent Oregon booster who in February 1838 introduced a bill into the United States Senate

authorizing the occupation of the Columbia or Oregon River, establishing a territory north of latitude 42 degrees, and west of the Rocky mountains, to be called Oregon Territory; authorizing the establishment of a fort on that river, and the occupation of the country by the military forces of the United States...

Accompanying the bill was a map which had been essentially copied from John Arrowsmith's 1832 map of British North America (Map 189, page 114) by Captain Washington Hood (Map 197). The boundary between British and American territory was shown as the 49th parallel, continuing through Vancouver Island.

In the bottom left-hand corner of this map is the wording of an ultimatum given during negotiations in June 1826 by Henry Clay, the U.S. Secretary of State, to Albert Gallatin, special commissioner of the United States in London. He was to offer the 49th parallel, but to *"consent to no other line more favorable to Great Britain."*

These negotiations resulted only in the indefinite extension of the joint occupancy arrangement of 1818.

Lewis Linn's bill was a little before its time, but not much. In 1841 he tried again, this time with a 54° 40' boundary line, but again did not succeed. But it was only a matter of time.

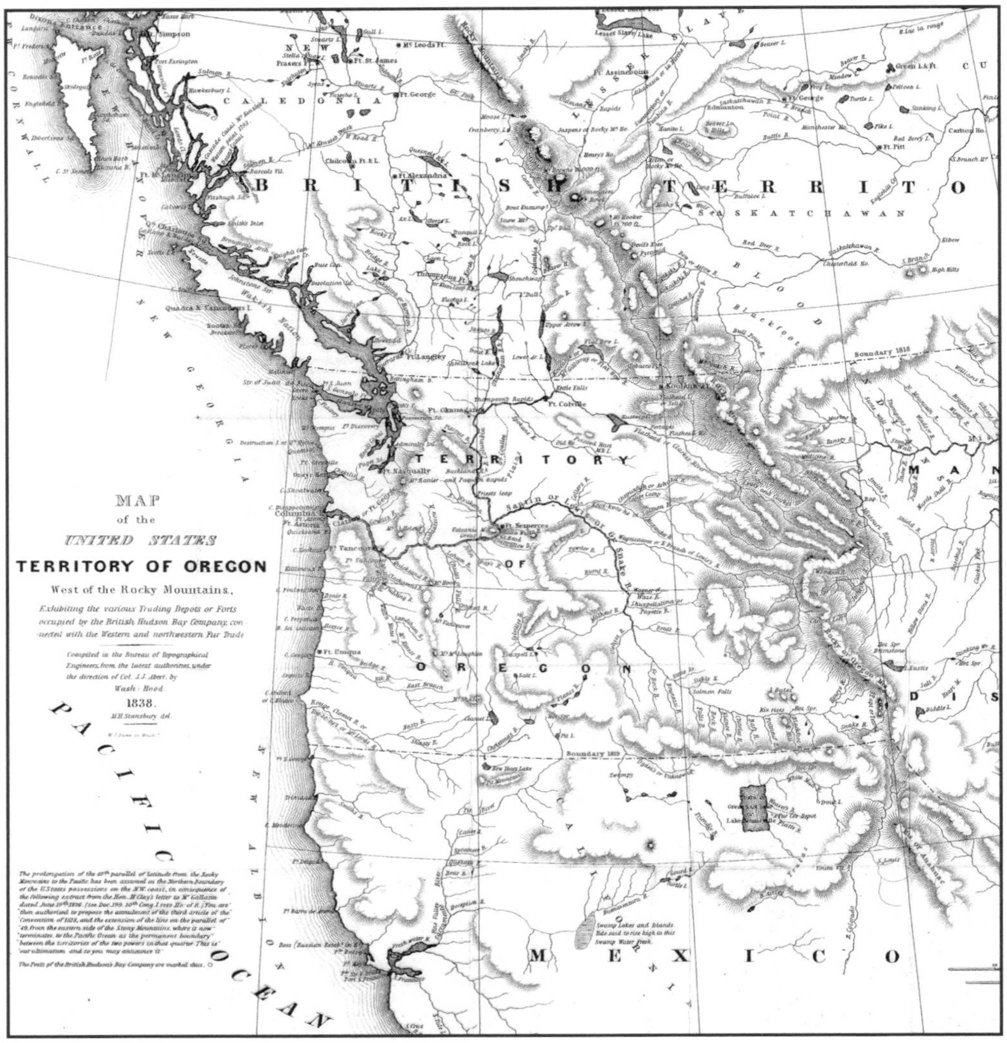

Map 197 (top)
A map of the United States Territory of Oregon West of the Rocky Mountains Exhibiting the various Trading Depots or Forts occupied by the British Hudsons Bay Company, connected with the Western and northwestern Fur Trade
Captain Washington Hood 1838

Copied from Arrowsmith's 1832 map of British North America, and used to illustrate Senator Linn's bill.
Note the boundary between the United States – the "Territory of Oregon" – and British Territory is shown as the 49th parallel, extending westwards to the Pacific – right through Vancouver Island.

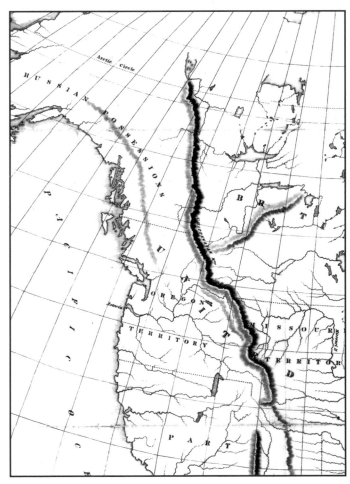

Map 198 (right)
Map of North America
Publ. by R. Cadell Edinburgh 1833

An interesting 1833 map which shows no territory on the Pacific coast as British, despite the fact that the map originated in Britain. The United States is shown extending to a boundary line at the 54° 40' N. The southern boundary of Oregon Territory is 42° N, the boundary with Mexico, inherited from Spain after the Mexican revolution in 1819. Russian possessions are shown north of the 54° 40' N line, despite the negotiation of an eastern boundary with the British in a 1825 treaty.

CHARLES WILKES AND THE U.S. EXPLORING EXPEDITION

With the growth of the United States came growth in national pride, and in the mid-1830s a decision was made to send a major, government-sponsored scientific expedition on a voyage of discovery around the world. After all, Britain (Cook), Spain (Malaspina), France (La Perousse) and Russia (Kruzenstern and Lisianskii) had all done it, so why not the United States?

Not coincidentally, as part of its itinerary the expedition was to explore the Oregon Country to which the United States laid claim, but was currently sharing with Britain under the joint occupancy treaty of 1818.

Chosen as the leader of this effort, dubbed the United States Exploring Expedition but almost always abbreviated as the "U.S. Ex. Ex.", was a naval commander named Charles Wilkes. He was a temperamental man whose bad habits tended to overshadow his good qualities.

The expedition, which lasted from 1838 to 1842, visited and explored for the first time the part of Antarctica south of Australia today called Wilkes Land. In addition they visited some 300 Pacific islands and arrived in Oregon in 1841.

The expedition did a lot of quite accurate hydrographic surveying in the Strait of Juan de Fuca and along the Washington and Oregon coasts, including the mouth of the Columbia. One of the expedition's ships, the *Peacock*, was wrecked as she attempted to cross the notorious Columbia bar, despite the fact that they had the published version of Lieutenant Broughton's 1792 map with them (Map 146, page 88).

Charles Wilkes

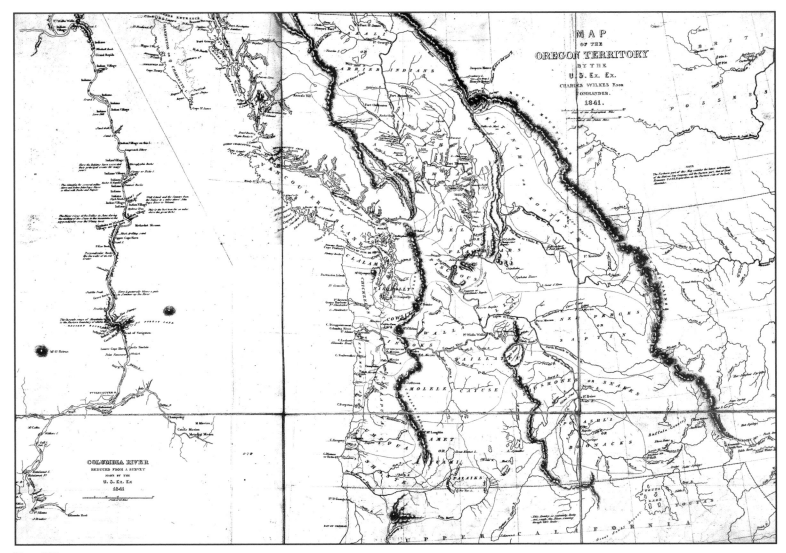

Map 199
Map of the Oregon Territory by the U.S. Ex.Ex. Charles Wilkes Esq. Commander 1841. Inset: *Columbia River, Reduced from a Survey Made by the U.S. Ex.Ex. 1841.* Charles Wilkes, 1845.

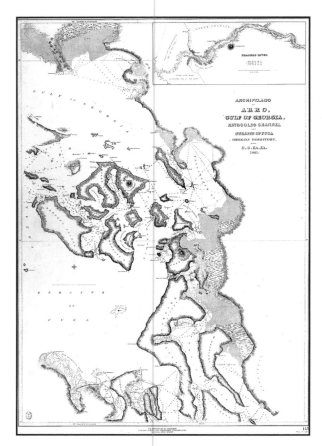

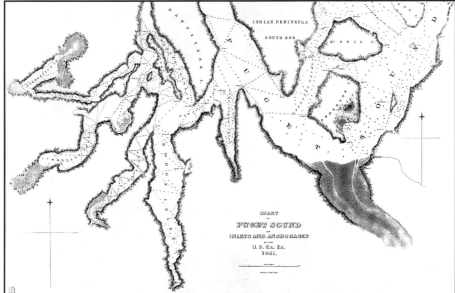

Map 200 (left)
Archipelago of Arro, Gulf of Georgia, Ringgolds Channel and Straits of Fuca Oregon Territory By the U.S. Ex. Ex. 1841 Charles Wilkes, 1845. Rosario Strait.

Map 201 (above)
Chart of Puget Sound Its Inlets and Anchorages by the U.S. Ex. Ex. 1841 Charles Wilkes, 1845.
This shows the site of today's Olympia. All of the inlets and islands shown on this map were named by Wilkes after his officers; Drayton Passage was named after the expedition's artist.

Referring to the many explorers before him who had missed the mouth of the Columbia, Wilkes wrote,

I am at a loss to conceive how any doubt should ever have existed, that here was the mouth of the mighty river, whose existence was reported so long before the actual place of its discharge was known...

Wilkes' *Narrative of the United States Exploring Expedition* was published in five volumes in 1844.

Also published were a number of maps of the northwest, including one map of the whole Oregon Territory (Map 199, previous page), which contains an inset map of the Columbia River. Another map was of the southern part of Georgia Strait (Map 200). Ringgolds Channel, named after one of Wilkes' officers, is today's Rosario Strait. A map of the southern part of Puget Sound (Map 201) shows the site of today's Olympia.

Wilkes supported the view of Senator Lewis Linn that the boundary of the American claim to the Oregon Country should be 54° 40' N. His map of Oregon Territory (Map 199) was used to support his claim, which was on "topographical" grounds. He particularly liked the harbors in the Strait of Juan de Fuca and Puget Sound and thought it essential that the United States include at least this territory in its claim, particularly considering the lack of good harbors to the south; even the Columbia River had its notori-

ous bar, the dangers of which had been emphasized by the embarrassing loss of the *Peacock.*

The *Narrative* was published just over a year before the division of the Oregon Country between Britain and the United States, and was instrumental in setting the scene for American interest in Oregon.

The "U.S. Ex. Ex." also helped establish the United States as a credible scientific power, and the tens of thousands of specimens that the expedition collected around the globe were one of the first collections of the Smithsonian Institute, founded in 1846.

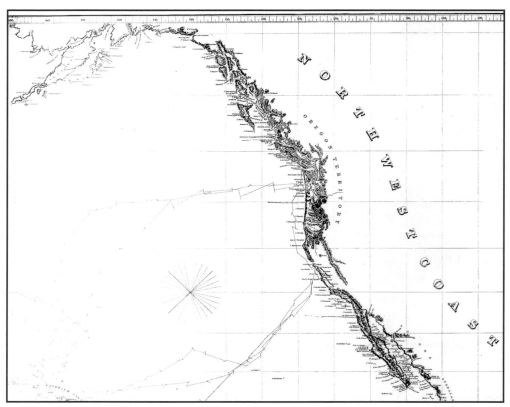

Map 202
Chart of the Pacific Ocean, Exhibiting the Tracks & Researches of the U.S. Exploring Expedition With Corrections to the Year 1844. Charles Wilkes, 1845.
Wilkes' summary map in the tradition of Cook, Vancouver, and Bodega y Quadra.

JOHN CHARLES FREMONT AND THE OREGON TRAIL

From 1838 until the Civil War, a small elite branch of the U.S. Army called the Corps of Topographical Engineers was responsible for much of the exploration and mapping of the American West. The most famous of this group was John Charles Fremont, who led three separate exploration and surveying expeditions to the west.

At the beginning of his first expedition, in 1842, Fremont hired a melancholy German immigrant mapmaker named Georg Carl Preuss. He had been a surveyor for the Prussian government and had immigrated to the United States in 1834. In the process he became known as Charles. Charles Preuss turned out to be a brilliant cartographer who helped Fremont produce maps of the American west that were unsurpassed in their time.

The first Fremont expedition was directed to map the country between the Missouri River and the Rocky Mountains, including a route which had become known as the Oregon Trail and was already being used by settlers travelling to Oregon. It was Fremont's task to chart the trail, determine where to establish forts, and find usable passes through the Rocky Mountains. From a mapping point of view, this first expedition was not a great success, unaccountably failing to pinpoint the exact location of South Pass, the Oregon Trail's main route though the Rockies and one of the expedition's main mapping objectives.

In the spring of 1843, Fremont was again sent west, and again took Preuss with him. This time his orders were to connect the reconnaissance of 1842 with the surveys of Charles Wilkes on the Pacific coast, (see page 119) so as "to give a connected survey of the interior of our continent." One of the more famous "mountain men" that Fremont hired to help him was Kit Carson.

Reaching Oregon, Preuss, never a particularly cheerful person, complained about the damp and the cold of the Northwest. *"It is certainly terrible,"* Preuss wrote in his diary at Walla Walla on 27 October 1843, *"what a poor devil has to contend with in this country in order to make an honest living."*

Late in 1843, Fremont and Preuss reached Fort Vancouver by canoe, thus achieving the objective of linking up with Wilkes' coastal surveys. Instead of returning the way he had come, Fremont headed south first, and in the process disproved the existence of a river called the Rio Buenaventura, which, like the River of the West, was another legendary river thought to flow westwards at least from the Rockies to the Pacific. He also defined, mapped and named the Great Basin of what is now Nevada and Utah.

Back in Washington, D.C., in 1845, Preuss produced a major summary map to accompany Fremont's report to Congress. The map is shown below (Map 203).

Map 203
Map of an Exploring Expedition to the Rocky Mountains in the Year 1842, and to Oregon & North California in the Years 1843 – 1844
Drawn by Charles Preuss, 1845.
From: *Report of the Exploring Expedition to the Rocky Mountains in the Year 1842, and to Oregon & North California in the Years 1843 – 44.*

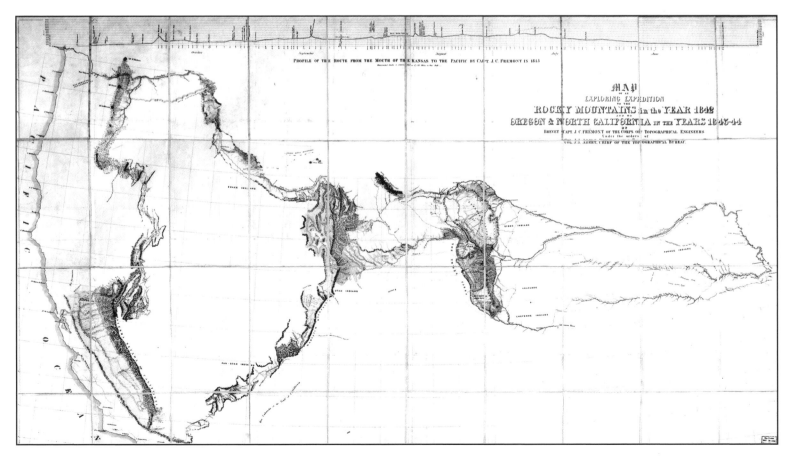

The Oregon Trail

The Oregon Trail was the foremost, and certainly the most famous, route used by immigrants to Oregon in the mid nineteenth century.
It originated with a series of accidental discoveries by Astorians led by Robert Stuart returning east from the Columbia River in 1812 (Map 169, page 102). After 1824, Jedediah Smith (see page 114) publicized South Pass, in today's Wyoming, as an easy crossing of the Rocky Mountains.

In 1836, a missionary group led by Marcus Whitman which included his wife Narcissa and Eliza Spalding (massacred in 1847 by Nez Perce natives) made the first westward journey with women, and served to enhance the route as easy to travel for families. The Whitman farm is shown near Fort Wallah-Wallah on the map below. The first family to move to Oregon for the express purpose of establishing a home, as opposed to a mission, used the Oregon Trail in 1840, and in 1842 came the first of the wagon trains, when eighteen wagons led by Elijah White moved westward. After 1842, a growing wave of settlers moved to Oregon, making it more and more difficult for the British, in the form of the Hudson's Bay Company, to hold on to the region.

Migration became an annual event, and increased after Oregon became American territory in 1846. Some four thousand emigrants headed west along the Oregon Trail in 1847. Between 1840 and 1860, about 53,000 people traveled the Oregon Trail.

The Trail remained the principal highway to the Pacific Northwest until the Northern Pacific Railroad was completed in 1883.

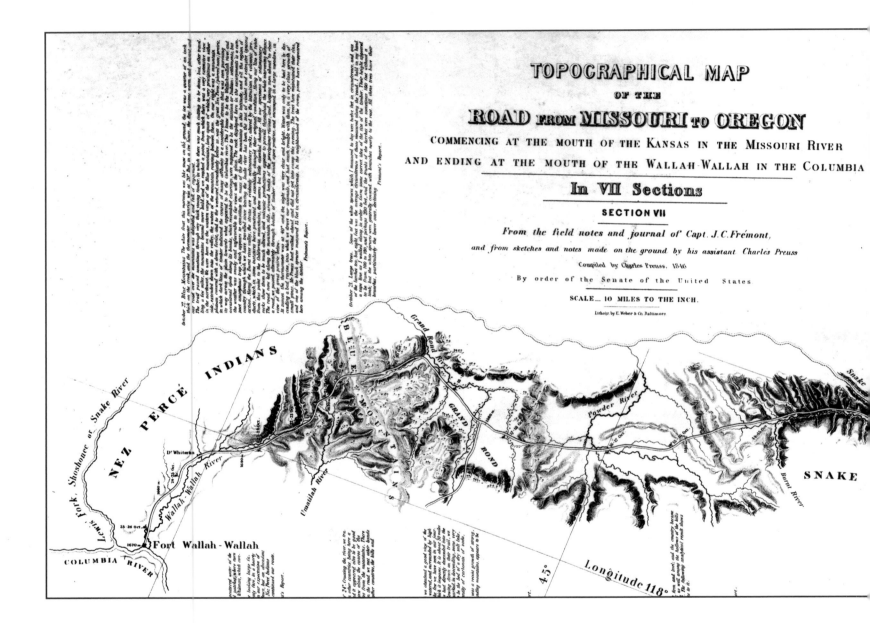

Preuss was very conservative in his work, as was typical. With a few exceptions, such as the coastal surveys of Wilkes, he incorporated only the information that had been collected by the Fremont expeditions. His positions were carefully computed from astronomical observations and elevations from his pioneering use of barometers, or even, when those had been broken, from the temperatures of boiling water, which vary with height. This map showed the Columbia to be the only river that flowed from the Rockies to the Pacific. The 1845 Preuss map is considered by most experts to have changed the entire picture of the western interior of what is now the United States and to be a landmark in the progress of geographical knowledge and a lasting contribution to cartography.

Preuss' next map was a map of the Oregon Trail, 10,000 copies of which were ordered by Congress to facilitate migration to Oregon (which became part of the United States in 1846 with the demarcation of the boundary with British posses-

Map 204

Topographical Map of the Road from Missouri to Oregon Commencing at the Mouth of the Kansas in the Missouri River and Ending at the Mouth of the Wallah-Wallah in the Columbia
10 miles to 1 inch
The Oregon Trail.
Drawn by Charles Preuss in 7 sections. Sheet 7, Wallah-Wallah, 1846.

Note the Whitman mission near the western end of the map. Marcus and Narcissa Whitman had traveled what would become the Oregon Trail in 1836. They were killed by Cayuse in November 1847, the infamous Whitman Massacre.

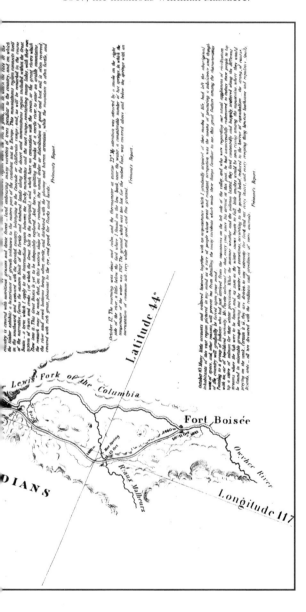

In 1845, Fremont again headed west, this time without Preuss, which was probably just as well for Preuss, since Fremont got himself involved in military action when war broke out with Mexico in 1846. Fremont got into a dispute with General Stephen Kearny which later led to Fremont's dismissal from the army.

Preuss meanwhile produced his third important map, the *Map of Oregon and Upper California,* completed in 1848 (Map 205, below). Apparently the first map to apply the name Golden Gate to the entrance to San Francisco Bay (not shown on the part illustrated here), this map, like the 1845 *Map of an Exploring Expedition...* (Map 203) was widely used for many years after as a base map for railroad route planning, and by settlers and gold seekers.

The map shows the newly determined boundary with British possessions, and shows the San Juan Islands as British (see also detail, Map 284, page 172). It was the most accurate general map of the west for its time.

John Charles Fremont

Preuss committed suicide in 1854, but Fremont built on his fame as an explorer. He became a senator from the new state of California, was the Republican presidential nominee in 1856, a general in the Civil War, made millions from mining, lost millions in investments in railroads, and was the territorial governor of Arizona.

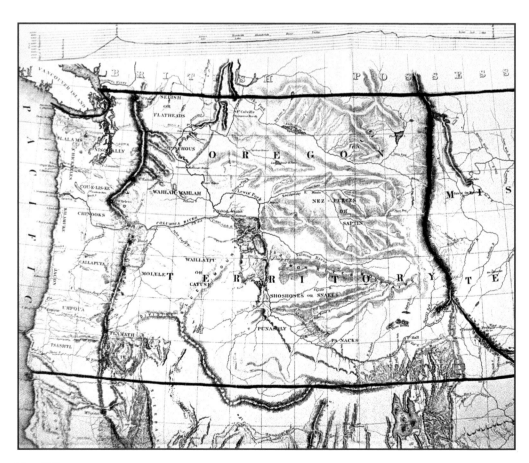

Map 205
Map of Oregon and Upper California From the Surveys of John Charles Fremont And other Authorities. Drawn by Charles Preuss Under the order of the Senate of the United States, Washington City 1845. From: John Charles Fremont, Geographical Memoir Upon Upper California in Illustration of His Map of Oregon and California, 1848.

sions (see page 131). Published in 1846 in seven sections and at a scale of only ten miles to the inch, the map, entitled *Topographical Map of the Road from Missouri to Oregon...* (Map 204) was essentially the first road map of the west.

FORT VANCOUVER

Fort Vancouver, in today's Vancouver, Washington, across the Columbia River from Portland, was established in the winter of 1824 – 1825 by the Hudson's Bay Company. They had decided to move the headquarters of their Columbia Department from Fort George, the Astoria of the Pacific Fur Company, because the opportunities for agriculture were much greater around the Fort Vancouver site. In 1843, seeing the likelihood diminish that the British would retain their claim to Oregon, the Hudson's Bay Company established Fort Victoria, at the southern tip of Vancouver Island, and in 1849, moved their headquarters there.

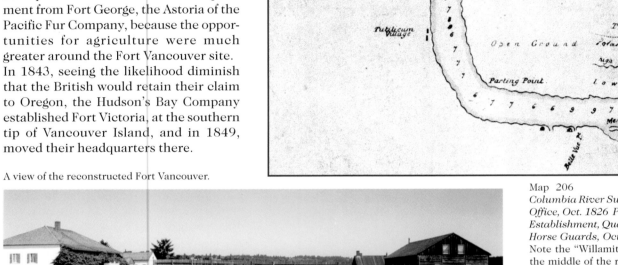

A view of the reconstructed Fort Vancouver.

Map 206
Columbia River Surveyed 1825. British War Office, Oct. 1826 Printed at the Lithographic Establishment, Quarter Master Generals Office, Horse Guards, Oct. 1826 (eastern part)
Note the "Willamitte Riv", the soundings along the middle of the river's channel, and the "Potatoe Grounds" just north of the fort.
This map was made soon after the establishment of Fort Vancouver, and may be the first map drawn which shows it. The survey was probably made by the Hudson's Bay Company despite being printed by the British War Office.

The treaty which gave the region south of the 49th parallel to the U.S. in 1846 also allowed the Hudson's Bay Company to continue operations at Fort Vancouver, but by 1860, trade had been reduced to a trickle, and they abandoned the fort. By 1866, fires and decay had destroyed all the structures.

The fort was reconstructed in 1966 at its original location, revealed by excavations, and is now a National Historic Site.

Fires had threatened Fort Vancouver a number of times during its thirty-five-year life. One was in 1844, which was shown in a map by Henry Peers, a Hudson's Bay Company clerk (Map 207). It shows Fort Vancouver at the height of its development as a British settlement.

Another map of Fort Vancouver was made in 1845 by Mervin Vavasour, a British officer assessing the defenses in preparation for a possible confrontation with the United States; this map is shown on page 129 (Map 216).

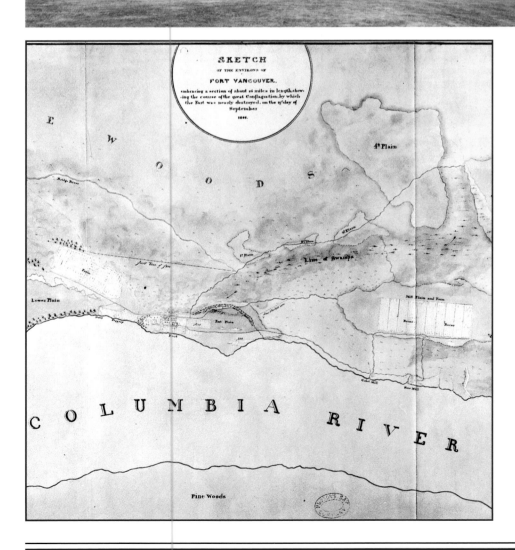

Map 207
Sketch of the Environs of Fort Vancouver embracing a section of about 16 miles in length, showing the course of the great Conflagration, by which the Fort was nearly destroyed, on the 27th day of September 1844. Henry Newnsham Peers, 1844.

JAMES DOUGLAS
AND THE ESTABLISHMENT OF FORT VICTORIA

The situation of the Hudson's Bay Company post at Fort Vancouver had often proved difficult, being 145 km (90 miles) upriver from the sea. Despite better maps, the treacherous bar at the river entrance continued to claim ships, such as the U.S. Ex. Ex.'s *Peacock* in 1841.

Fort Vancouver was not considered to be a very healthy location, presumably because it was too low-lying. There was also the awareness that Fort Vancouver might one day be lost to the Americans.

These factors led as early as 1832 to the consideration of a number of potential sites further north for a new depot, including Cowlitz, Dungeness, Whidbey Island, Lulu Island (today's Richmond,

B.C.), Birch Bay, and Fort Langley. By 1836, the Company had decided that Vancouver Island would be the best strategic location for a new fort, because of the fact that it was an island.

Chief Factor John McLoughlin visited Puget Sound in 1835, but could find no suitable place. Following further more urgent requests from Governor Simpson and the Hudson's Bay Company board, McLoughlin instructed Captain William Henry McNeill of the *Beaver* to examine the southern end of Vancouver Island, which he did in the summer of 1837. McNeill examined three harbors, Sooke, Esquimalt, and Victoria, and selected Victoria as the most promising. McLoughlin

and James Douglas visited the site later in 1837. Douglas wrote in an 1838 report to Simpson,

I am persuaded that no part of this Sterile and Rock bound coast will be found better adapted for the site of the proposed Depot or to combine, in a high degree, the desired requisites, of a secure harbour accessible to shipping at every season, of good pasture, and, to a certain extent, of improvable tillage land.

McLoughlin continued to prefer Fort Vancouver, but Governor Simpson, seeing the writing on the wall, was sure that a depot on Vancouver Island was necessary.

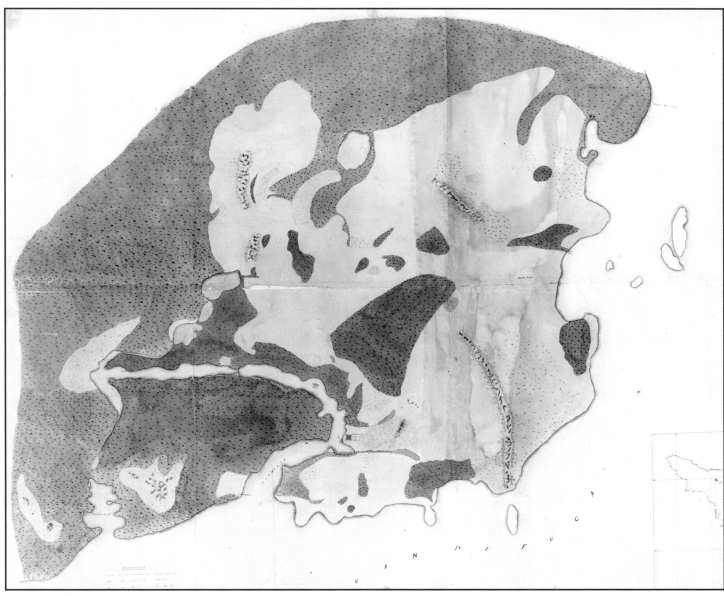

Map 208   *Ground Plan of Portion of Vancouvers Island Selected for New Establishment Taken by James Douglas Esqr.*
James Douglas and Adolphus Lee Lewes, 1842. The site proposed for the new Fort Victoria is shown as a red square.
This map is essentially a land-use map, allowing Douglas to show why the site was a good one for a new settlement.

In 1842, he sent James Douglas, accompanied by Adolphus Lee Lewes as surveyor and mapmaker, to report on a specific site for a fort.

Douglas recommended Camosack, or Camosun Inlet (today's Victoria Harbour) as the best harbor, and a site on the eastern shore of this inlet for the fort. He wrote that

the place itself appears a perfect Eden, in the midst of the dreary wilderness of the Northwest coast, and so different is its general aspect from the wooded, rugged regions around, that one might be pardoned for supposing it had dropped from the clouds into its present position.

The map that Douglas and Lewes drew on their return to Fort Vancouver to illustrate their choice is shown here (Map 208, previous page).

The colors on this watercolor map from the Hudson's Bay Company Archives are quite well preserved. It is essentially a land-use map, with dark green showing the forested areas, light green what Douglas refers to as "plains," with marshy areas in a less well preserved yellow, and lakes in blue. The site chosen for the fort is shown in red.

On the basis of this map and the accompanying report by Douglas, a decision was made by the Hudson's Bay Company to establish their new depot at this site. One of the reasons why it was chosen over other harbors, such as the adjacent Esquimalt Harbour, is that it had "*a great extent of valuable tillage and pasture land*" around it. This map is essentially the first map of Victoria, which was to be the capital of the future colony of Vancouver's Island.

On 13 March 1843, Douglas was back in Victoria Harbour aboard the Hudson's Bay Company's steamer *Beaver* with fifteen men to begin the construction of the new fort.

Map 209
*Victoria Harbour
Henry Kellett
1847
London:
Hydrographic
Office. 1848*

Henry Kellett was the captain of HMS *Herald*, and surveyed the waters of the northwest in 1846 and 1847.
The position of Fort Victoria is marked, as is James Bay, where the Empress Hotel now stands. James Bay was named by Kellett after – who else – James Douglas, and is shown on this map for the first time.
Kellett and the *Herald* were ordered to leave their surveying work and join the search for Sir John Franklin, lost in the Arctic.

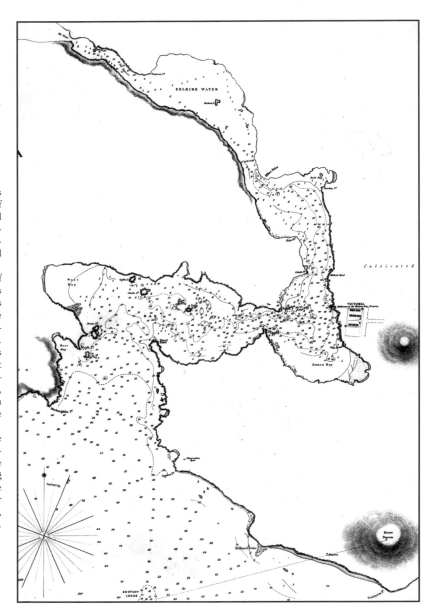

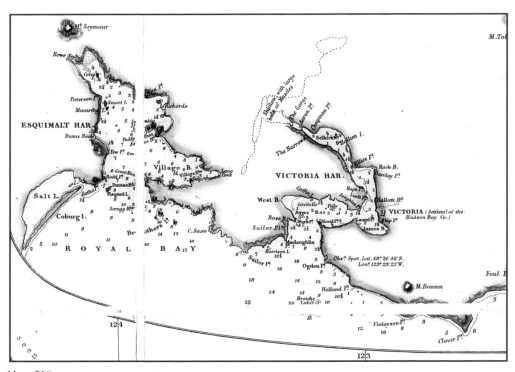

A bastion of Fort Victoria, c1860, the year it was demolished.

Map 210
Victoria District. Inset in: *Map of Vancouver Island And the Adjacent Coasts Compiled from the Surveys of Vancouver, Kellett, Simpson, Galiano, Valdes, etc. by J. Arrowsmith. 1849.*

Map 211 (right)
Esquimalt District Official Map, 1858.
Esquimalt, three miles from Victoria by road, had an excellent
harbor suitable for ships larger than those that could use Victoria
Harbour. This led to the establishment of a British naval yard in
1864. Fisgard Lighthouse guards the entrance (see page 160).

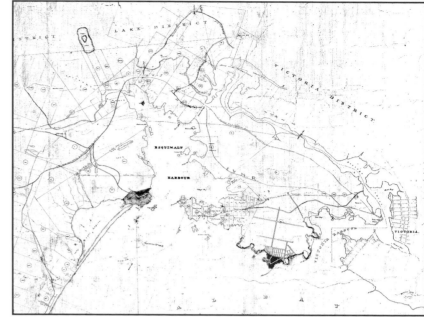

Esquimalt in the 1860s.

Map 212 (below)
Map of the City of Victoria, Vancouver Island
Numbered, revised and corrected from the Official Map and the best authorities. Published by Alfred Waddington, January, 1863.
The new "Government Buildings", the "birdcages", opened in 1860, are shown. The residence of Governor Douglas is shown, adjacent to James Bay. In 1904,
this part of the bay was filled in, and the Empress Hotel built on the reclaimed land, granted by the city to the Canadian Pacific Railway. The map shows the
boundaries of Victoria when it was incorporated as a city in 1862. The map was printed, not in Victoria, but in San Francisco.

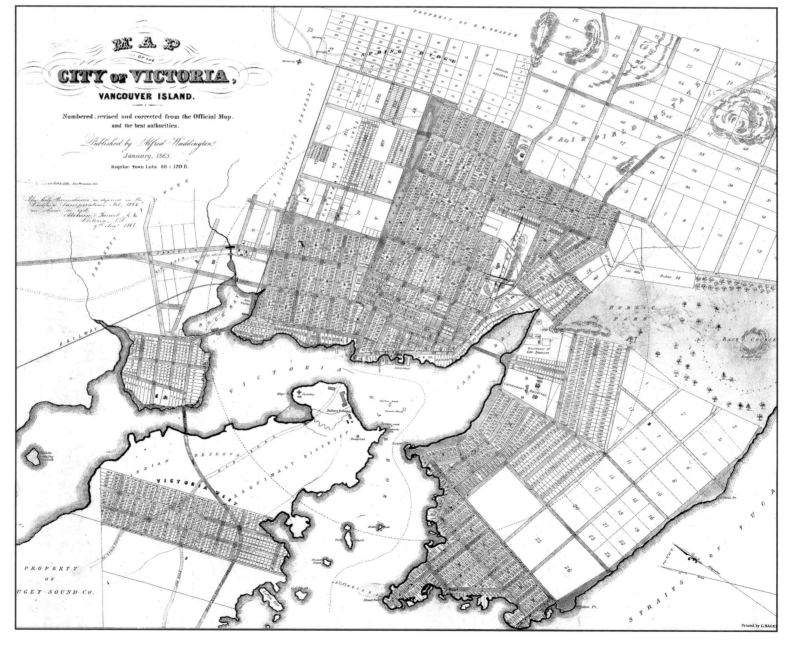

PORTLAND

Even before Oregon was officially American territory, the provisional government in Oregon City was accepting land claims in anticipation of the event.

Portland originated as such a land claim by Asa Lovejoy and William Overton in 1844, the latter, lacking the 25-cent filing fee giving half of his 260 ha (640 acre) claim to Lovejoy in return for the fee, thus trading 130 ha (320 acres) of what was to become downtown Portland for 25 cents!

Overton soon moved on, trading his interest to Francis Pettygrove, who with Lovejoy surveyed the townsite and cleared some land.

The name of the city was decided on a coin toss by the two; Lovejoy was from Massachusetts and wanted the name to be Boston, while Pettygrove was from Maine and wanted Portland. Needless to say, Pettygrove won, and Portland it was.

Portland both gained and lost from the discovery of gold in California in 1848. Many people left to go to the gold fields,

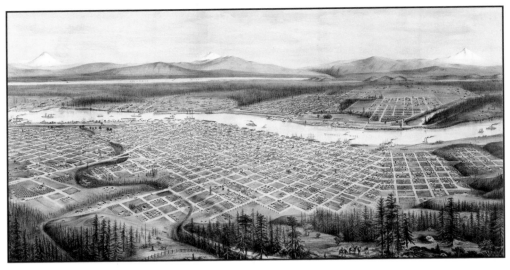

Map 213
Portland Oregon. Showing Also East Portland and the Cascade Mountains. J.K. Gill & Co. 1881.
This beautiful view of Portland in 1881 is towards the east and northeast, with (from left to right) Mt St. Helens, Mt Adams, and Mt Hood. East Portland lies across the river. This bird's-eye map originally sold for $10, a considerable sum in 1881. In the map margin, the population of Portland is reported to be 22,000, and East Portland, 4,250.

including Pettygrove, but those who stayed found they could make a good living supplying California with lumber and food.

By 1853, with the help of enterprising citizens, a newspaper, a plank road, and scheduled steamer service, Portland's survival seemed assured.

Map 214 (below)
Portland, Oregon. 1890. Clohessy and Strenghels. A superb promotional view, indeed a classic of the "bird's-eye genre". Maps such as this one often showed detailed views of individual houses or businesses around the edges. They were normally either paid promotional advertising or, because they were the residences of important local people, included to enhance the value of the map to others.

JAMES McI. WOOD.
REAL + ESTATE + AND + INVESTMENT + BROKER,
PORTLAND, OREGON.

SECRET BRITISH PREPARATIONS FOR WAR

In the mid-1840s, the Hudson's Bay Company became increasingly concerned about the possibility that hostilities might break out between Britain and the United States over the ownership of the Oregon country. Governor Simpson called for military aid in this event, and asked that an assessment be made of the military situation right away. In 1845, Lieutenants Mervin Vavasour and Henry Warre, military officers stationed in Lower Canada, were sent to do this assessment. Vavasour was an engineer who was able to survey and map, while Warre was an artist.

They were to make recommendations on how best to protect British interests in the Pacific Northwest. They were to advise on how to fortify the Columbia River, and how to protect various British forts against attack. They also had to assess the feasibility of transporting troops overland to the Pacific coast. Their true identity was kept secret, and they posed as what we today would call tourists.

Vavasour prepared maps of a number of British forts in the Oregon country, including the one of Fort Vancouver shown here (Map 215). He drew a map of the entrance to the Columbia, with suggestions for possible fortifications (Map 216). He traveled north to Nisqually, the location of the Puget Sound Agricultural Company, and again drew a map with defensive proposals shown (Map 217).

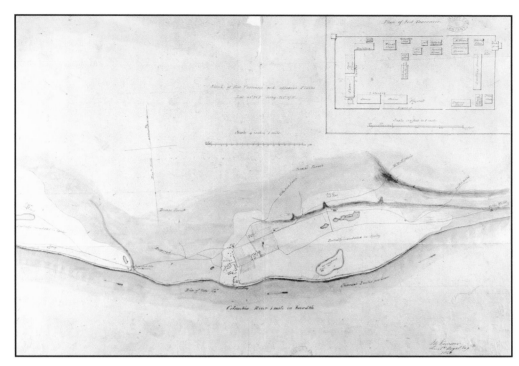

Map 215
Sketch of Fort Vancouver and adjacent plains Lat.45° 36'N. Long. 122° 37'W. M. Vavasour Lieutn. Royal Engr. 1845

Henry Warre produced a large number of paintings and drawings to illustrate his report written with Vavasour, one of which was this 1845 sketch of Fort Vancouver.

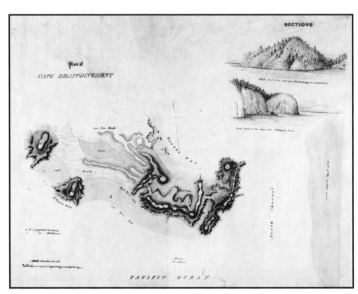

Map 216
Plan of Cape Disappointment. Mervin Vavasour, 1846.
This delightful little map of Cape Disappointment, on the north side of the mouth of the Columbia, was to suggest siting of fortifications. It is enhanced by views of the coast from the sea done by Henry Warre.

Map 217 (right)
Eye Sketch of the Plains and about Nisqually at the head of Pugets Sound. Mervin Vavasour, 1846.
In 1839, the Hudson's Bay Company had signed an agreement with the Russian-American Company to supply Russian America with wheat and other foodstuffs. To do this, they formed the Puget's Sound Agricultural Company and started farms at Cowlitz, and at Nisqually, the map of which was drawn by Vavasour, right. The agreement ran for ten years, but was not renewed by the Hudson's Bay Company due to the loss of much of its prime farming land, including Nisqually, after the boundary treaty of 1846. The island shown is named Kitsons Island, now Ketron Island. It was named by Charles Wilkes (see page 119), but misspelled on his maps, after William Kitsson, who supervised the construction of Fort Nisqually for the Hudson's Bay Company. Map 201, page 120, shows Ketron Island. Vavasour obviously attempted to put the spelling right, but got it wrong again!

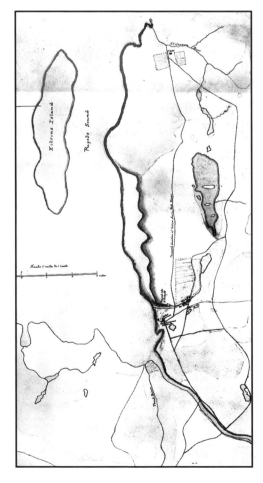

Vavasour and Warre also visited the new Hudson's Bay Company settlement at Fort Victoria, on Cammusan Harbour (now Victoria Harbour) at the south end of Vancouver Island, Vavasour producing another map on which he showed a plan of Fort Victoria as an inset (Map 218).

Before Vavasour and Warre could even return to Lower Canada, the British had decided not to run the risk of war with the United States, and had signed the 1846 treaty with the United States (see page 134), making Vavasour and Warre's work unnecessary.

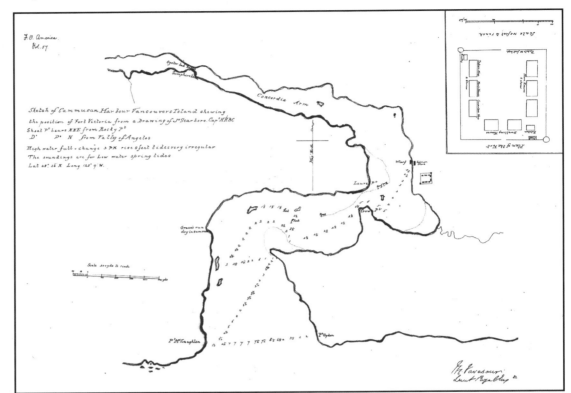

Map 218
Sketch of Cammusan Harbour, Vancouvers Island shewing the position of Fort Victoria, from a drawing of Js. Scarboro Capt. H.H.B.C. M. Vavasour Lieut. Royal Engrs
Inset: *Plan of the Fort.* 1846.

The plan of the fort, inexplicably upside down in relation to the rest of the map, was the only part of this map actually originated by Vavasour. The main map was copied from one done in 1842 by James Scarborough, the captain of the Hudson's Bay Company schooner *Cadboro*, which had brought James Douglas to the area to determine the site for Fort Victoria (see page 125). Scarborough's original map seems to have been lost.
A salmon store is shown near the fort.
Today's Laurel Point is labelled Crow Point, while Songhees Point opposite is labelled Laurel Point.

THE HUDSON'S BAY COMPANY SEEKS A BETTER ROUTE TO THE COAST

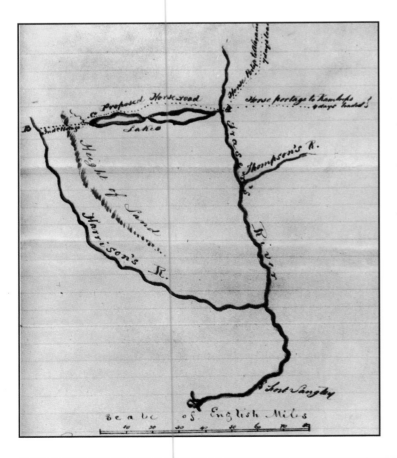

Map 219
Sketch map accompanying *Suggestions for the exploration of a new route of communication by which...the transport of the supplies and returns to and from the Districts of New Caledonia and Thompson's River might be advantageously carried on in connexion with Fort Langley and the new establishment of Victoria* Alexander C. Anderson, 1845.

Anderson Lake and Seton Lake are shown. The portage between these two lakes, today's Seton Portage, was the scene of British Columbia's first "railway" about 1861. Wooden rails faced with iron strips were used for horse-drawn wooden flat cars to haul the freight of miners on the way to the Cariboo goldfields.

The problem of transportation to and from the interior of what is now British Columbia became more critical when it became clear that Britain was not likely to hold on to the lower Columbia.

In 1846, Alexander C. Anderson, a Hudson's Bay Company officer at Fort Alexandria, was chosen to try to find an alternative fur-brigade route to New Caledonia from Fort Langley which avoided the virtually impassable Fraser Canyon.

In 1845, Anderson had written a report in which he had suggested a new route from Lilloet on the Fraser though Seton, Anderson, Lilloet, and Harrison Lakes to the lower Fraser River above Fort Langley. The map which accompanied this report is shown here (Map 219).

The route was not used by the Hudson's Bay Company at that time because of the short season for which it would be available, and the number of transportation-mode changes involved.

The route was later used, however, by James Douglas, who in 1858 was looking for a way to encourage mainly American gold miners to stay within British territory. A road was constructed by volunteer gold miners, directed by Alexander Anderson.

THE EVOLUTION OF THE BOUNDARY BETWEEN CANADA AND THE UNITED STATES

In the seventeenth century the French and the British had disputed the division of their territories in North America. The Hudson's Bay Company had suggested that the 49th parallel might be a boundary line between the British in the north and the French in Louisiana. The British member of an Anglo-French Commission in 1719 proposed the 49th parallel as the southern limit of Hudson's Bay Company territories, but since this would have excluded the French from the northwest quarter of the continent, they rejected it.

Another demarcation line which was suggested during the eighteenth century was the 45th parallel, which did become the boundary between Quebec and New York after the American Revolution. Alexander Mackenzie (see page 95) liked the 45th parallel and suggested in 1801 that it should be *"continued west, till it terminates in the Pacific Ocean, to the south of the Columbia."* Nothing came of this proposal, however.

After the American Revolution and the establishment of the new republic of the United States of America, the British were in possession of the northern territories formerly held by France, in addition to Rupert's Land, the Hudson's Bay Company territory, while the Americans adopted the viewpoint formerly held by Britain. The result was embodied in the Treaty of Paris, signed in 1783. This Treaty defined the New Brunswick – Maine boundary and also mentioned broadly a boundary towards the west extending from Lake of the Woods to the Mississippi. Not being prepared to accept a boundary which touched the Mississippi, the Americans came up with a proposal originally used by the British in their negotiations with the French: the 49th parallel. Britain accepted this and in October 1818 the United States and Britain signed a convention which defined the 49th parallel as the boundary *east of the Rockies,* but left the area west of the mountains as a territory for joint occupancy with free entry to both American and British citizens for ten years. This was the Oregon Country.

The ownership of the coastal area of the west and northwest was disputed by four nations: Spain, Russia, Great Britain, and the United States. They all used the same argument, that of prior exploration, to justify their claims. In 1819, Spain and the United States agreed that the northern limit of Spanish claims would be set at the 42nd parallel, and treaties between Russia and the United States in 1824, and

Map 220
United States
J.H. Young, 1830

Russia and Great Britain in 1825, set the southern limit of Russian territory at 54° 40'. Hence by 1825 only the United States and Britain were left as claimants to the region between Spanish and Russian territories.

The American claim was based on being the successors of Spain after the 1819 treaty. They therefore used the Spanish explorers as a basis for prior exploration claims, along with their own: Juan Pérez in 1774; Robert Gray in 1792; Meriwether Lewis and William Clark in 1805 and 1806; and the establishment of Astoria in 1811, and its *seizure* by the British in 1813 (see page 102-3).

The British in turn used for their claim James Cook in 1778; John Meares in 1786, 1787, and 1789; George Vancouver in 1792, 1793, and 1794; Alexander Mackenzie in 1793; David Thompson in 1807 and 1811; and Simon Fraser in 1808. To these the British added many fur traders and settlements belonging to the North West Company, and the *purchase* of Astoria by the North West Company in 1813.

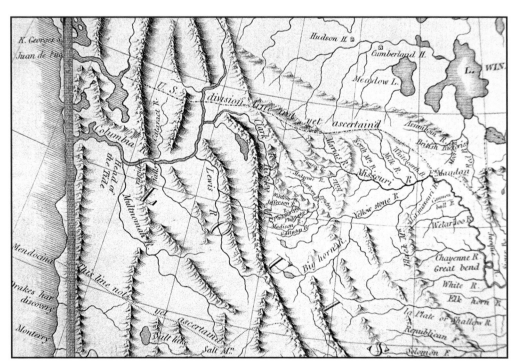

Map 221
Map of North America.
Inset in: *Map of the United States partly from new survey Dedicated to the citizens thereof by their humble servant Chas Varle Engineer & Geographer, 1817.*
Note the *"U.S. division line not yet ascertaind"* and a similar line to the south.

Whether the title of the United States to the countries situated between the fifty-first and sixtieth degrees of north latitude be well or ill founded... will, no doubt, be amicably determined whenever it shall be deemed of sufficient importance to claim the attention of those most interested in the issue.

Henry S. Tanner, *A New American Atlas,* 1823.

The United States wanted to establish its claims to the northwest coast because it valued the harbors for Pacific trade; there were few good harbors apart from those on Puget Sound and the lower part of the Columbia River.

The British position was essentially that of the Hudson's Bay Company. The land south of the Columbia was not considered valuable any more, as trapping had declined. But they wanted the Columbia Valley, as the main route for the export of furs and for the import of supplies for the Hudson's Bay Company posts in the interior.

In 1825, Sir John Pelly, the governor of the Hudson's Bay Company, proposed that the boundary between the British and American territories in the Oregon country should start at the 49th parallel and follow the crest of the Rockies south to where Lewis and Clark had crossed the mountains, and then along the Snake River and the south bank of the Columbia to the Pacific. Nothing came of this proposal. Twelve years later a similar boundary was proposed by the British Foreign Secretary, Lord Aberdeen, which was rejected by the Americans.

The United States government knew that its claims were weak historically, compared to those of the British. They therefore encouraged immigration to the disputed territory with the idea that ac-tual occupation would be hard to counter. In 1843, a senate committee which reported on the best means of promoting the colonization of Oregon stated,

The occupation and settlement of Oregon by American citizens will of itself operate to repel all European intruders, except those who come to enjoy the blessings of our laws; this would secure us more powerful arguments than any diplomacy could invent or use to assert and maintain our just rights in that country if war should ever be necessary to preserve and protect them.

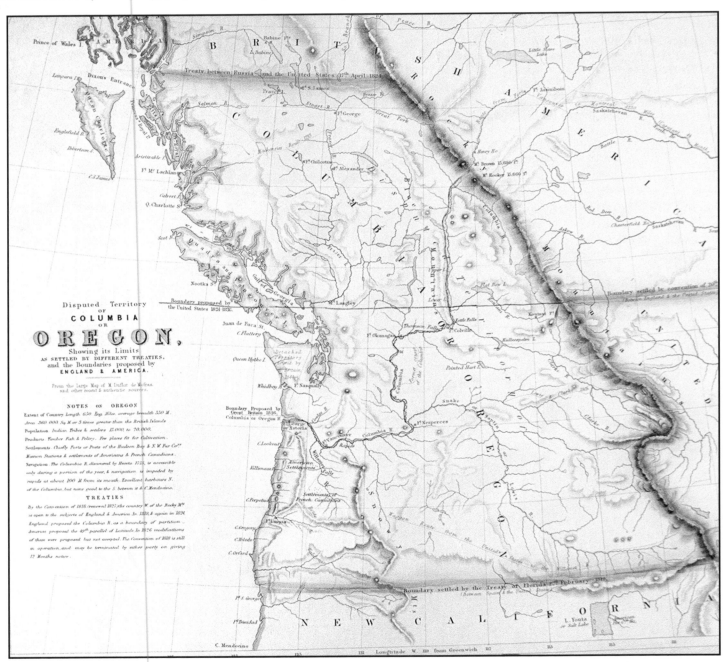

Map 222

Disputed Territory of Columbia or Oregon Showing its limits as settled by different treaties and the Boundaries proposed by England and America
From the large map of M. Duflot de Mofras and other recent & authentic sources. Published by W. & A.K. Johnston. 1st January 1846
This map shows three boundary proposals: the 49th parallel through Vancouver Island to the Pacific as the boundary proposed by the United States in 1824–1826; from the 49th parallel where it meets the Columbia and then down that river to the Pacific, as a British 1826 proposal; and an additional territory on the Olympic Peninsula as offered to the United States by Britain in 1844.

During the 1840s, many settlers migrated to Oregon, although they generally tended to settle south of the Columbia, in the Willamette Valley.

Thus the argument of settlement did not have much validity when negotiations started again between the United States and Britain in 1844. However, despite weak arguments, the Americans were more vociferous about their right to the Oregon Country than the British, whose perception was that the United States might resort to force. A senate committee did in fact hint at war in 1843.

In 1845, James Knox Polk, an expansionist, became President of the United States. The convention that nominated Polk in May 1844 adopted a declaration that *"our title to the whole of the territory is clear and unquestionable; that no portion of the same ought to be ceded to England, or any other power..."* A slogan of the ensuing campaign was *"Fifty Four Forty or Fight!"*

After his election Polk asked Congress for the authority to terminate the joint occupation agreement of 1818, and received it. Polk never intended to risk war with Britain over Oregon, because he was anticipating that the United States would soon be fighting Mexico over California.

The British Foreign Secretary, Lord Aberdeen, seemed to be intimidated by the threat of war in this difficult-to-supply region of the British Empire, and by the apparent determination of the Americans to control the whole Pacific coast. The British government of Sir Robert Peel at this time was in difficulty due to opposition to the repeal of the British Corn Laws, and the British cabinet wanted to be rid of what they saw as "the Oregon problem."

Aberdeen proposed a compromise to the American demand for 54° 40': the 49th parallel from the crest of the Rockies as far as the Columbia and then down the river. He also offered free port facilities for American ships north of this boundary. The Americans countered with a proposal for the 49th parallel straight to the Pacific Coast, right through Vancouver Island.

Map 224

A New Map of Texas, Oregon and California with the regions adjoining compiled from the most recent authorities

Philadelphia: Published by S. Augustus Mitchell

1846

Although the boundary proposals shown on the Johnston map (Map 222) are also shown on this map, they are downplayed as compared to the 54° 40' boundary; at first glance it looks like American territory extends north to include all of the Oregon Country.

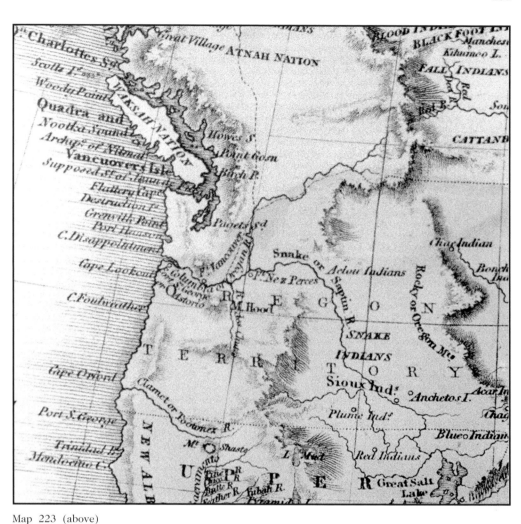

Map 223 (above)

Gall and Inglis' Map of North America, c1847.

This British map shows British territory south to the Columbia. The map was hopelessly out-of-date when it was published.

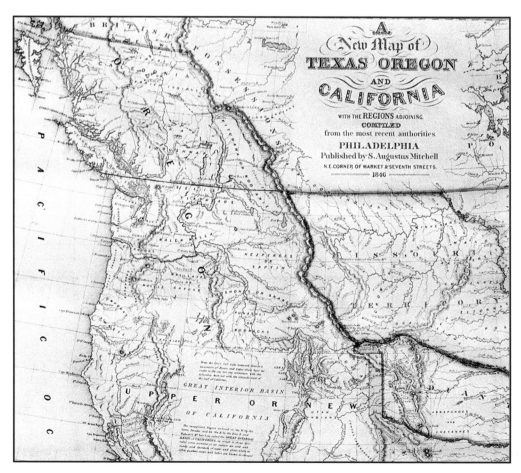

Not wanting to lose Vancouver Island, and knowing that the Hudson's Bay Company had retreated to Fort Victoria precisely because it was on an island, Lord Aberdeen then proposed the 49° N international boundary *except* for Vancouver Island. This President Polk accepted. Polk submitted the proposal to the Senate, which accepted it on 15 June 1846. Rather than "fifty-four forty or fight," the United States agreed to 49°N and no fight.

It took five months for the news to reach Oregon. The treaty, called by the British the Oregon Treaty and by the Americans the Treaty of Washington,

should have settled the matter. But the treaty contained a clause about the sea boundary following the *"middle of the channel"* with no indication as to which of the multiple channels in the southern Strait of Georgia was meant. This led later to a dispute over the true sea boundary, which was not settled until 1872 (see page 171).

When the terms were published, James Douglas wrote, *"It appears that the Oregon Boundary is finally settled, on a basis more favourable to the United States than we had reason to anticipate..."*

The next year, after some reflection, he was able to write,

All things considered, the yielding mood of the British ministry and the concessions made, we have come off better than expected. I looked for nothing short of an utter sacrifice of our interests.[134]

Douglas, however, took a long time to give up hope that one day the situation would be reversable. In December 1861, when the United States was embroiled in a Civil War, and it seemed possible that war could break out between Britain and the United States, Douglas proposed to the British Government that he use the troops at his disposal to retake the Puget Sound area, and, with the aid of another British regiment, the region as far south as the Columbia. Needless to say, the British Government turned his idea down.

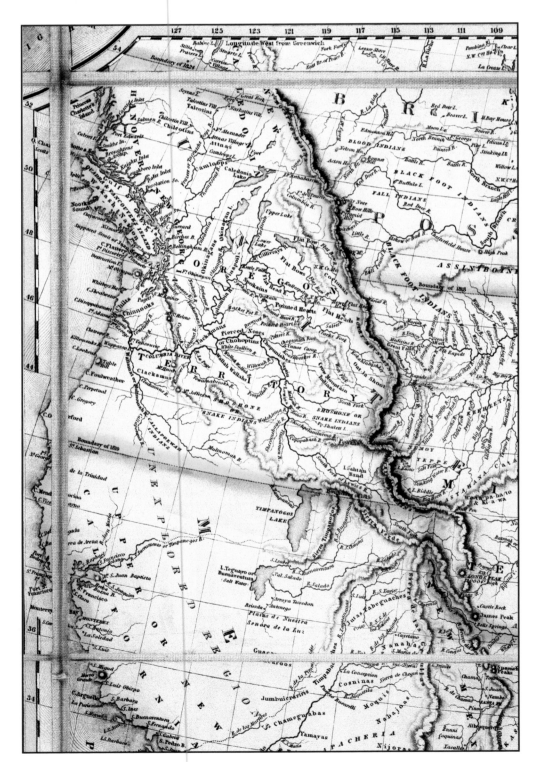

Map 226 (above)
British North America. Chapman & Hall, 1849. Shows the boundary as settled in 1846.

Map 225 (left)
General Map of the United States with the Contiguous British and Mexican Possessions
Inset in: *Mitchell's Reference and Distance Map of the United States J.H. Young. Published by S Augustus Mitchell, 1830*
Complete with cloth folds, the Oregon Country was shown on this map only as an inset, while the main map concentrated on the area east of the Mississippi. Shows the full extent of the Oregon Country, the area under dispute between the United States and Britain.
Note David Thompson's phantom "Caledonia River" is shown on this map, running to Puget Sound south of the Fraser (see page 105).

This sketch by artist Frederick Whymper was drawn about 1860 and shows the boundary line between the United States and the new Colony of British Columbia being cut through the forest near Yahk, B.C. (See: Fixing the Boundary, page 150.)

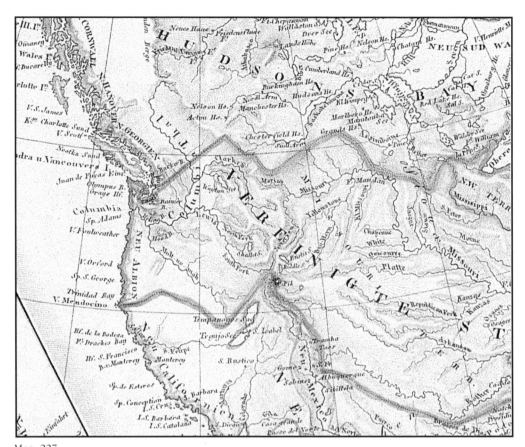

Map 227
Nord-America entw. u. gez. von C.G. Reichard. 1818.
This 1818 German map shows an erratic boundary between British and American territories; the 49th parallel east of the Rockies was not agreed upon until 1818, too late to show on this map. Parts of the boundary shown were copied from others, and were based on early American claims. Interestingly enough, the boundary is at about the 49th parallel at the point it reaches the Pacific. In the south, the 42° N boundary between Mexico and the United States is also undefined; this was agreed to in 1819. Note the confusion between the Columbia River and the Fraser.

Map 228
Nord-Amerika entw. u. gez von C.G. Reichard 1818 Revidire 1823.
From: *Stieler's Hand-Atlas Uber Alle Theile Der Erde und uber das Weltgebaude, 1827.*

In this edition of Reichard's map, updated to 1823, the 49th parallel is now shown as the boundary between British territory and the United States as far west as the Rocky Mountains, following the treaty of 1818. An "Oregan Terr" bulges north into what is now British Columbia, but not as far north as was usually shown as being the extent of the Oregon Country at this time, such as on Map 220, page 131, or Map 193, page 116.
What is now northern British Columbia is shown as "West Caledonia."
The inset shows George Vancouver's 1792 – 1794 survey of the northwest coast.

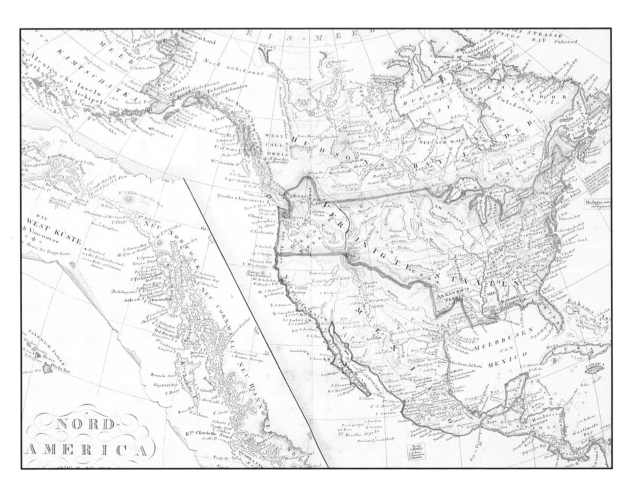

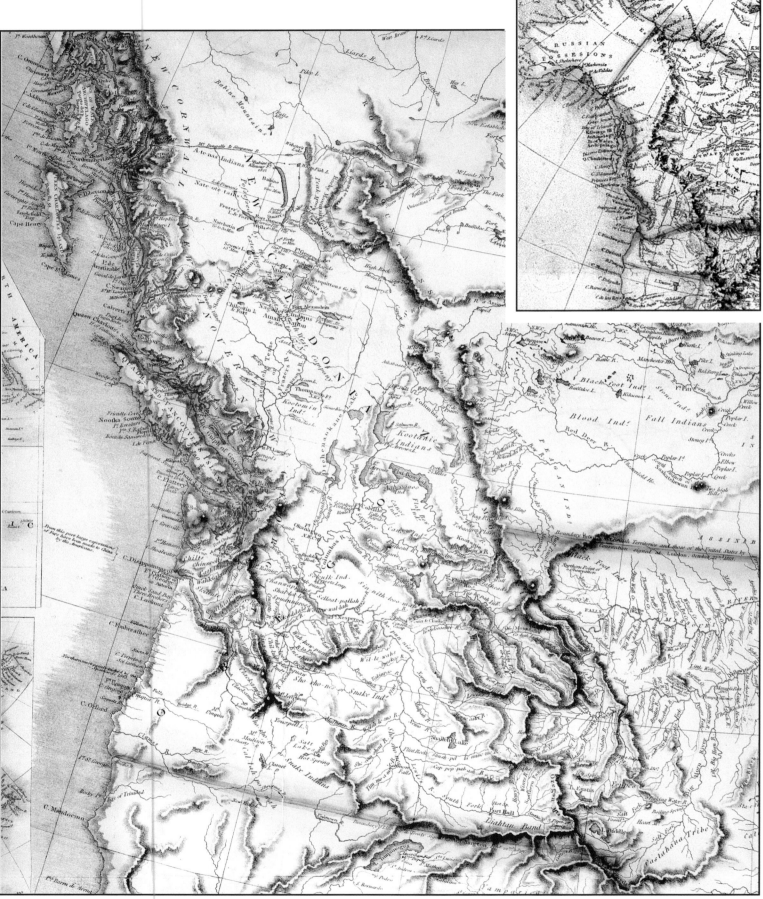

Map 229
Map of the Oregon Districts and the Adjacent Country. James Wyld, Geographer to the Queen 1843

This beautiful map by British mapmaker James Wyld shows the coast as British as far south as the entrance to the Columbia, but in the interior only shows the 49th parallel boundary ending at the Rocky Mountains, with no other boundary lines shown between them. "Oregon" and "New Caledonia" are both marked, but where one stops and the other starts is undefined.

Map 229A (Inset, top)
British Possessions in America. James Wyld, 1843.
Part of an inset map in Map 229.
The boundary of British territory is shown south to the mouth of the Columbia, more definitively than on the main map.

THE EVOLUTION OF THE BOUNDARIES
OF THE STATES OF WASHINGTON AND OREGON

In 1846 the Treaty of Oregon had awarded the United States the land south of the 49th parallel, except for Vancouver Island. In August 1848, the whole area between the Mexican boundary at 42°N and 49°N and eastwards to the Continental Divide was formed into Oregon Territory, and Joseph Lane, an Indiana politician, became the first governor.

The huge territory was never properly unified. The settlers north of the Columbia, in what was then termed Northern Oregon, thought that the more numerous settlers in the Willamette Valley dominated territorial affairs. The northern settlers met at Cowlitz landing in August 1851, and in November 1852 at Monticello, part of today's Longview, Washington, and drew up a petition to Congress for a new territory north of the Columbia. The rest of Oregon, including the governor, supported this request for partition because Oregon's chances of being accepted as a state were thought to be greater if its size was smaller than the largest existing state at that time.

They also hoped that the new territory, which they assumed would also eventually become a state, would increase the

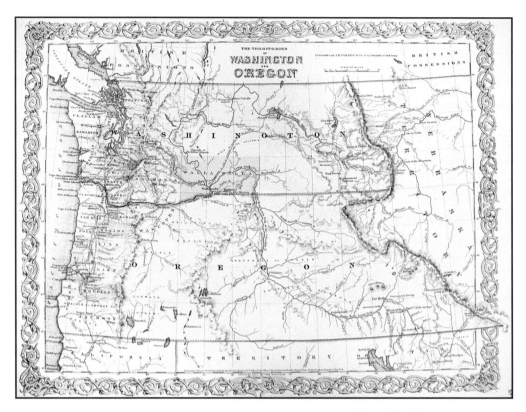

Map 230 *(above)*
The Territories of Washington and Oregon. J.H. Colton, 1853.

The first division of the American part of the Oregon Country after 1846 was in 1853, when what was then Northern Oregon became Washington Territory. Both territories stretched from the Pacific to the Continental Divide. This map shows the political divisions lasting from 1853 to 1859, when Oregon achieved statehood.

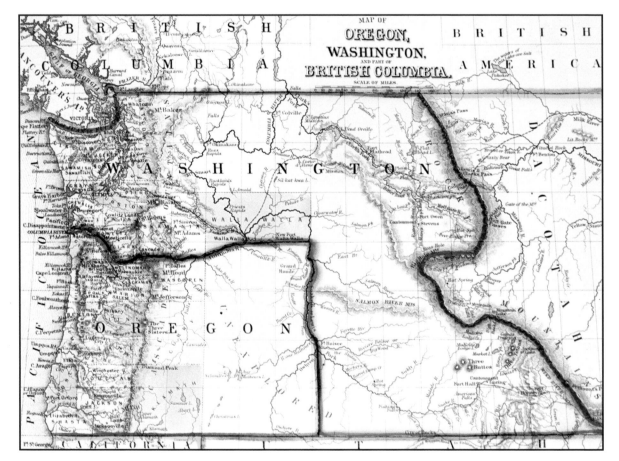

Map 231 (left)
Map of Oregon, Washington, and Part of British Columbia.
S. Augustus Mitchell, 1860
From: *Mitchell's New General Atlas,* Philadelphia, 1862.

This map shows the Territory of Washington and the new State of Oregon after the eastern part of the latter had been annexed to Washington Territory. Oregon was again made smaller to improve its chances of being admitted to statehood, which it was in 1859. These boundaries lasted from 1859 until 1863, when Idaho Territory was created.

representation of the Pacific Northwest in Washington, D.C., and further the chances for military appropriations and a transcontinental railroad.

President Franklin Pierce agreed to the requests of the settlers, and Washington became a territory in 1853.

The boundaries of both territories still stretched to the Continental Divide. Map 230 shows the extent of both at this time. The first governor of Washington Territory was Isaac Ingalls Stevens. He had fought in the Mexican War, and had served in the Corps of Engineers. He was also the Superintendent of Indian Affairs for the territory, and in addition he was given the job of surveying a northern route for a transcontinental railroad (see page 148).

In Oregon Territory in August 1857 a convention was held at Salem to draw up a constitution for a bid for statehood. As a preliminary to the bid for statehood, a series of surveys of the territory had been made; Map 195 (page 116) was one such survey, principally of the Willamette Valley, from a 54th Congress document in 1855.

Because of national politics at the time related to the issue of slavery (Oregon was to prohibit slavery, which was not liked by southern states), it took almost two years for Oregon to be admitted to the Union. Finally, in February 1859, Oregon became the thirty-third state by a narrow vote.

Oregon had again made itself smaller to improve its chances of being admitted as a state, still more than the 1853 reduction in size. In so doing, it made Washington Territory considerably larger, so that it embraced much of today's Idaho. Map 231 shows the boundaries of Washington Territory and the State of Oregon as they were from 1859 to 1863.

The large area of Washington Territory now made it difficult to govern effectively from Olympia, particularly when gold was discovered in the vicinity of today's Lewiston, Idaho. As a result of the mining boom, Walla Walla emerged as the largest city in Washington, and the residents of Olympia became concerned that it might replace their city as the territorial capital. They were glad when on 4 March 1863, Congress voted to combine the remote mining regions into a new territory called Idaho, which originally encompassed today's Idaho, Montana, and most of Wyoming, an area larger than Texas (Map 232). So large was this new territory that the first thing its new legislative assembly did was petition Congress to divide the territory, and in May 1864, Montana Territory was created.

Even after that, in the following years, the Idaho legislature petitioned four times to have the panhandle annexed to either Washington or Montana.

Map 233 shows the boundaries from 1864 to 1868. Map 234 shows the boundaries (except for San Juan Island, added to Washington Territory in 1872)

as they were after the creation of Wyoming Territory in July 1868.

Washington was a territory until 11 November 1889, when it became a state. In the end, the decision reached Olympia in a telegram to governor-elect Elisha P. Ferry which arrived collect. Ferry had to pay sixty-one cents to get the news!

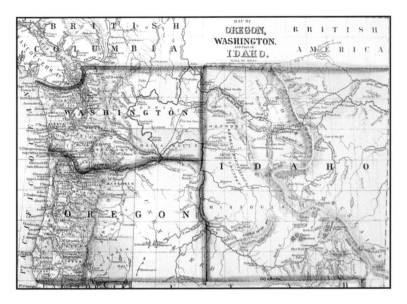

Map 232
Map of Oregon, Washington, and Part of Idaho.
S. Augustus Mitchell, 1863

With the formation of Idaho Territory in 1863, Washington Territory and the State of Oregon have almost reached their present-day boundaries

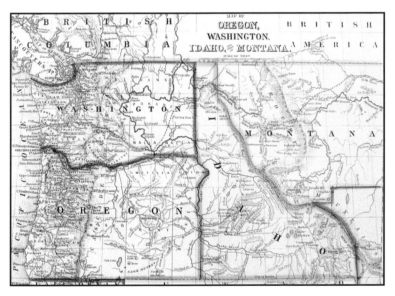

Map 233
Map of Oregon, Washington, Idaho, and part of Montana.
S. Augustus Mitchell, c1868

Shows boundaries as they were 1864 – 1868. Idaho Territory has been divided into Idaho, Montana, and Dakota Territory.

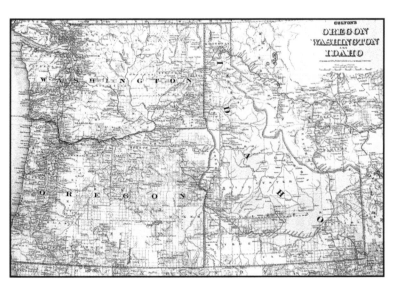

Map 234
Colton's Oregon, Washington and Idaho
1886
After the final adjustment to Washington's boundaries with the settling of the San Juan dispute in 1872, (see page 171) the territory achieved its current boundaries. Washington is still a territory, but will become a state in three years.

THE COLONY OF VANCOUVER ISLAND'S FIRST SETTLER

In 1849 the headquarters of the Hudson's Bay Company was moved from Fort Vancouver to Fort Victoria, and by the "Charter of Grant of Vancouver's Island" Vancouver Island was ceded to the Hudson's Bay Company, at a yearly rent of seven shillings.

The British government wanted to establish a colony as protection against American incursions, to avoid a possible repeat of what had happened in Oregon.

One of the conditions of the grant was that the company establish a settlement or settlements within five years or lose their rights.

In 1849, the Hudson's Bay Company employed Lieutenant Colonel Walter Colquhoun Grant as their first land sur-

veyor. He was also to be the island's first settler. At twenty-four, Grant had been the youngest captain in the British army, but had lost his fortune and was forced to leave the army by 1848. He decided to start anew in "the colonies" and negotiated with the Hudson's Bay Company for 200 acres, about 80 hectares of land. His initial foray onto Vancouver Island turned out to be a bit of a joke; he is reputed to have shot a cow on first landing, thinking it to be a buffalo.

Grant and eight other settlers established themselves at Sooke, southwest of Fort Victoria, the first residents, other than natives, not employed by the Hudson's Bay Company on Vancouver Island. Grant himself did not last long. He did

not appear to have the surveying skills required for the job, and he left in late 1850. He returned in 1853, but only stayed long enough to sell his land.

Grant did achieve one thing while he was on Vancouver Island, however. He prepared a detailed description of the physical characteristics, settlements, flora and fauna, natives, and trade of Vancouver Island which was later published in the *Journal of the Royal Geographical Society*, together with a map of the entire Island

Map 235
Map of Vancouver Island with the adjacent coast, to illustrate a description of the Island by Lt. Col. W.C. Grant, 1856. John Arrowsmith.
Published for the *Journal of the Royal Geographical Society* by J. Murray, Albemarle Str., London, 1857.

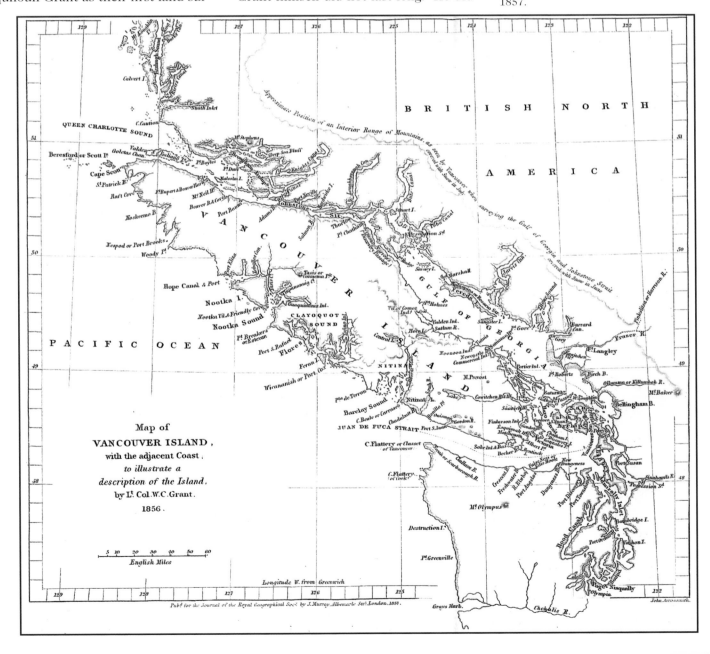

(Map 235, previous page). The map was drawn by John Arrowsmith.

Walter Colquhoun Grant's article in the *Journal of the Royal Geographical Society,* from which Map 235 comes, was entitled: "Description of Vancouver Island. By its first Colonist, W. Colquhoun Grant, Esq., F.R.G.S., of the 2nd Dragoon Guards, and late Lieut.-Col. of the Cavalry of the Turkish Contingent. Read, June 22nd, 1857."

"The position and natural advantages of Vancouver Island would appear eminently to adapt it for being the emporium of an extended commerce," the article began, in typical Victorian style.

Also typically for the times, Grant talks about the small population of Vancouver Island, completely ignoring native peoples:

The population of the Island in the end of the year 1853 was about 450 souls, men, women, and children; of these, 300 are at Victoria, and between it and Soke [now Sooke]; about 125 at Nanaimo; and the remainder at Fort Rupert [near today's Port Hardy; these were miners at the Hudson's Bay Company coal mine there].

Another map of the Colony of Vancouver Island, drawn by Edward Weller and published in a British atlas in 1856 is shown here (Map 236).

Map 235A (right)
Detail of Map 235: *A Map of Vancouver Island with the adjacent coast... W.C. Grant, 1856.*
Olympia and Nisqually are shown on Puget Sound, but not Seattle, which was founded in 1852. The Gulf Islands are incorrectly shown. The map was drawn by John Arrowsmith.

Map 236 (below)
Vancouver Island. Engraved by Edward Weller for an atlas plate. Edinburgh, Blackie and Son, 1856.

Virtually nothing is marked away from the coast. The Gulf Islands are shown, less accurately than on Grant's map (Map 235). Saltspring Island is shown as Chuan Island, an early name that did not stick. Grant's map shows the island as Saltspring. The San Juans are clearly shown as British red; it would not be until 1872 that their ownership would be finally decided (see page 171).

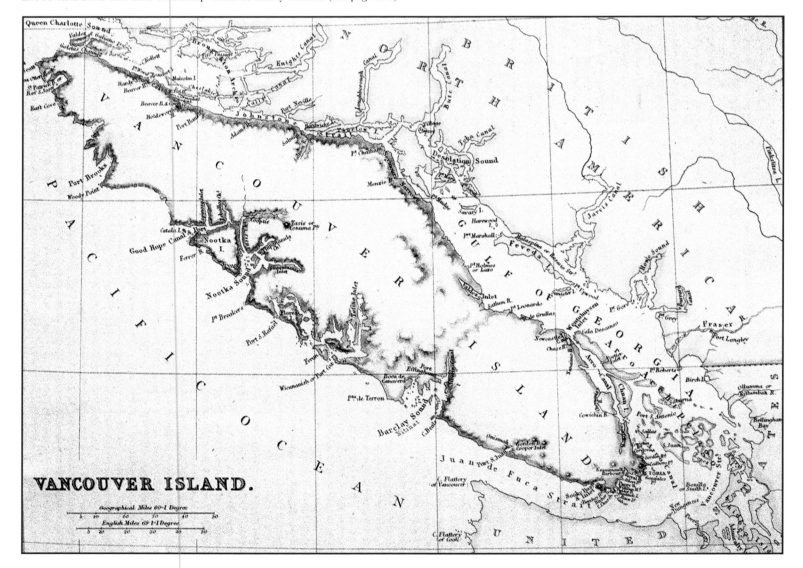

VANCOUVER ISLAND.

JOSEPH DESPARD PEMBERTON, SURVEYOR - GENERAL

After Grant left Vancouver Island, an English surveying professor named Joseph Despard Pemberton was appointed as the surveyor and mapmaker jointly for the new Colony of Vancouver Island and the Hudson's Bay Company.

Pemberton arrived in Victoria in 1851. He was charged with making surveys which would form the groundwork on which an accurate map of Vancouver Island was to be constructed. The object of this was to aid colonization. Maps that Pemberton drew were used as the basis for published maps by John Arrowsmith (Map 235, page 139).

Some of the maps that Pemberton drew were of the Nanaimo area (Map 237), where coal had been found. The coal seam was on the shores of what was known locally as Wentuhuysen Inlet (after the Spanish name, Boca de Winthuisen, on Map 128, page 78, for example), or Nanymo Bay, or the native name Syn-ny-mo. Then Pemberton mapped the area in 1853 and called it Nanaimo Harbour on his maps; after that, it was not long until Nanaimo supplanted the settlement's original name of Colvile Town, after Andrew Colvile, a Governor of the Hudson's Bay Company.

Map 238
Map of Nanaimo, c1860.
Note the coal shaft and "train way for coal waggons".

Map 237
Nanaimo Harbour and Part of the Surrounding Country
Joseph Despard Pemberton, 1853

Perhaps the first use of the name "Nanaimo" on a map.

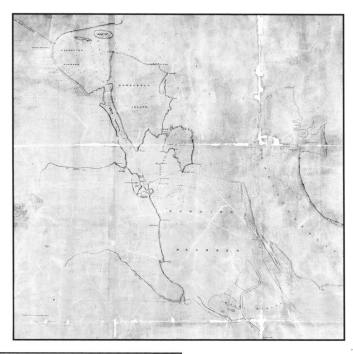

View of Nanaimo about 1860, showing the bastion, Hudson's Bay Company buildings, the coal loading wharf, and coal ships waiting in the harbor.
Although known to the natives, coal was discovered by the Hudson's Bay Company at Nanaimo in 1850, and mining began in 1852. Coal was provided to the British fleet during the Crimean War (1853–1856). The last coal mine was worked until 1950.

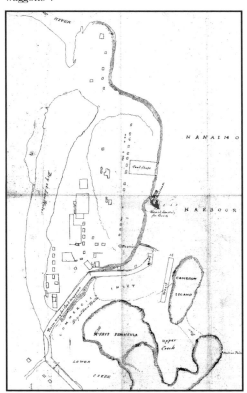

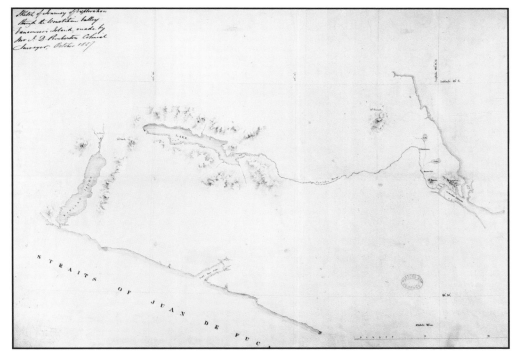

Map 239
Sketch of Journey of Exploration through the Cowetchin Valley Vancouver's Island, made by Mr. J.D. Pemberton Colonial Surveyor, October 1857

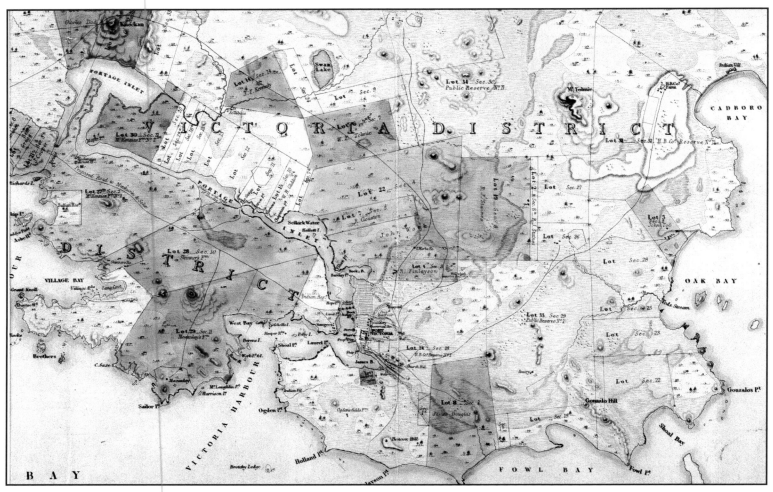

Map 240
Map of the Districts of Victoria and Esquimalt in Vancouver Island.
London. Pubᵈ 1854 by John Arrowsmith
A delightfully detailed map of Victoria eleven years after its establishment by the Hudson's Bay Company, copied from surveys of Joseph Despard Pemberton. Fort Victoria is shown. The names of many company employees and ex-employees are shown as the owners of land, including two, one on James Bay and one on Fowl Bay, belonging to the governor, James Douglas. A company farm is near Cadboro Bay.

In an effort to fulfill his mandate, Pemberton went on a number of exploring expeditions across Vancouver Island. One such expedition is illustrated by Map 239 (previous page) which shows a route he took along the Cowichan Valley from one coast to the other. During this trip, Pemberton damaged his instruments, and so this map is really only a compass sketch. He returned to Victoria by walking along the shore of the Strait of Juan de Fuca.

Pemberton served in his joint capacity for the Company and the Colony until 1859, when the Hudson's Bay Company gave up its rights to the Colony. Serving then only as colonial surveyor, he was appointed the first Surveyor-General of the Colony of Vancouver Island.

In 1860, Pemberton wrote a book for immigrants based on his knowledge, entitled *Facts and Figures Relating to Vancouver Island and British Columbia, showing what to expect and how to get there*. This contained several maps, including the one shown here (Map 241).

Map 241
British Columbia, Vancouver Island and part of United States
From: Joseph Despard Pemberton, *Facts & Figures Relating to Vancouver Island and British Columbia showing what to expect and how to get there,* 1860.
Pemberton's book was written as a guide for immigrants, *"the practical inquirer of the present day, for whose perusal these pages are intended."*

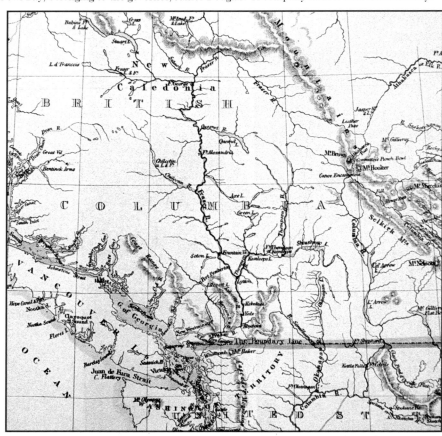

THE TEBENKOV ATLAS

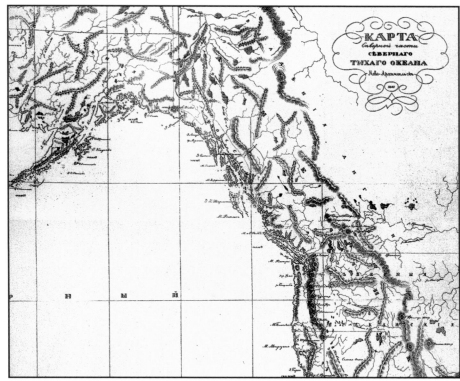

Mikhail Dimitrievich Tebenkov was a Russian naval officer who was manager of the Russian American Company from 1845 to 1850. In 1831, he had built Mikhailovskii redoubt, St Michaels, near the mouth of the Yukon River, where, sixty-six years later, gold seekers would board river steamers for the trip upriver to the Klondike (see page 185).

In the 1840s, Tebenkov organized several expeditions to survey the coasts of Russian America. Over a period of twenty-five years, he had collected hydrographic maps that he had drawn, and added them to maps from other sources. He also used ships' logs for information and verification.

In 1852, Tebenkov consolidated maps from these sources and published an atlas, which represents a fine collection of maps of the northwest coast from Russian sources.

Map 242 (top)
Map of the northern section of the North Pacific Ocean, Novo Archangel'sk, 1849.
From: Mikhail D. Tebenkov, *Atlas Severozapadnikh beregov Ameriki ot Beringova proliva do mysa i ostrov Aleutskikh,* 1852.

Map 243
Map of the northwest coast of America, to the north and south of the Columbia River, adjusted from George Vancouver, Novo Archangel'sk, 1848.
From: Mikhail D. Tebenkov, *Atlas Severozapadnikh beregov Ameriki ot Beringova proliva do mysa i ostrov Aleutskikh.*
(Atlas of the Northwest Coasts of America from Bering Strait to Cape Corrientes and the Aleutian Islands.)
1852.

The left-hand map is of the Washington and Oregon coasts, north and south of the mouth of the Columbia; the mouth of that river is shown at top right. Bottom right is Grays Harbor.

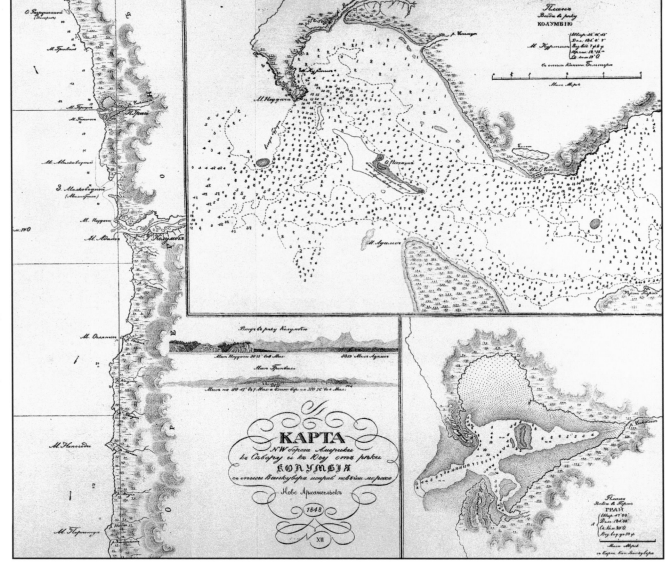

Map 244
Map of the Island of Quadra and Vancouver, Novo Archangel'sk, 1849.
From: Mikhail D. Tebenkov, *Atlas Severozapadnikh beregov Ameriki ot Beringova proliva do mysa i ostrov Aleutskikh*, 1852.

Fort Victoria is shown. This map was based on George Vancouver's map published in 1798 (Map 150, page 92), with updating. Vancouver's maps were at this time still the best maps of much of the northwest coast, including the west coast of Vancouver Island. Captain George Henry Richards surveyed the west coast of Vancouver Island in 1859 to 1862, filling in much detail that Vancouver had missed, and for the first time provided maps that were more reliable than Vancouver's.

His *Atlas of the Northwest Coasts of America from Bering Strait to Cape Corrientes and the Aleutian Islands...* was published in St. Petersburg on his return from Novo Archangel'sk.

The atlas contained a map of the entire northwest coast, drawn in 1849 (Map 242, previous page), contemporary with the one drawn by the American Charles Wilkes in 1844 (Map 202, page 120).

Perhaps the most interesting of the maps in this atlas was the map of the Oregon and Washington coasts, north and south of the Columbia estuary (Map 243, previous page). Included as insets are larger-scale maps of the mouth of the Columbia and of Grays Harbor.

In 1808, the Russians had intended to establish a colony on the Columbia, but their ship had been wrecked before reaching its destination. Nevertheless, Russian interest in the area continued. This map was drawn by Tebenkov in 1848.

Map 244 (left) is a part of a map of Vancouver Island and the adjacent mainland coast drawn in 1849.

Map 245 (below) is a map of an area of the Alaskan panhandle showing part of Chicagof Island, north of Peril Strait at the top of the map, and Baranof Island with Novo Archangel'sk, now Sitka. It was copied from a map drawn by George Vancouver in 1793, revised and corrected in 1849.

Map 245
Map of northern portion of the northwest coast of America from a copy of Vancouver's map, corrected for navigational purposes.
Novo Archangel'sk, 1849.
From: Mikhail D. Tebenkov, *Atlas Severozapadnikh beregov Ameriki ot Beringova proliva do mysa i ostrov Aleutskikh*, 1852.
This portion of the map shows Sitka Sound and Novo Archangel'sk (Sitka), the headquarters of the Russian-American Company.

SEATTLE AND THE COMING OF THE RAILROAD

As we have seen in the case of Portland (page 128), in the mid-nineteenth century, cities could be started by a land claim, platting out a town site, and promoting it to other settlers. Most of the ventures did not get off the ground, but one that did was Seattle.

Arthur A. Denny, Charles D. Boren, and William Bell marked out land claims to an area on the east side of Elliott Bay in Puget Sound in February 1852, where they were soon joined by others, including David S. Maynard and Henry L. Yesler, the latter a lumberman from Portland who wanted to establish a steam sawmill.

Within a few months of their claim, they decided to call their town "Seattle" after the local native chief.

Some of the plats in one land claim did not mesh with those in adjacent ones, leading to the necessity of jogs in street patterns.

Map 246, drawn in 1887, shows the original plats in the center of Seattle laid out by Denny, Boren and Maynard, showing the street discontinuities, together with later platted claims. These were only rectified following the Seattle fire of 6 June 1889.

Right from the beginning, Seattle residents were convinced that their city would be the logical terminus for any northern transcontinental railway, a feeling that was reinforced by the railroad surveys of 1853, which concluded that the Puget Sound ports had "great superiority" over those on the Columbia, because of the infamous bar at the river's entrance.

The first railway to Puget Sound, however, the Northern Pacific line running northwards from Portland, terminated at Commencement Bay, Tacoma. Although announced in 1873, due to poor economic conditions, the line did not reach Puget Sound until September 1883.

Map 246
Guide Map to the City of Seattle Washington Territory Compiled by Whitworth & Thomson, Surveyors 1887

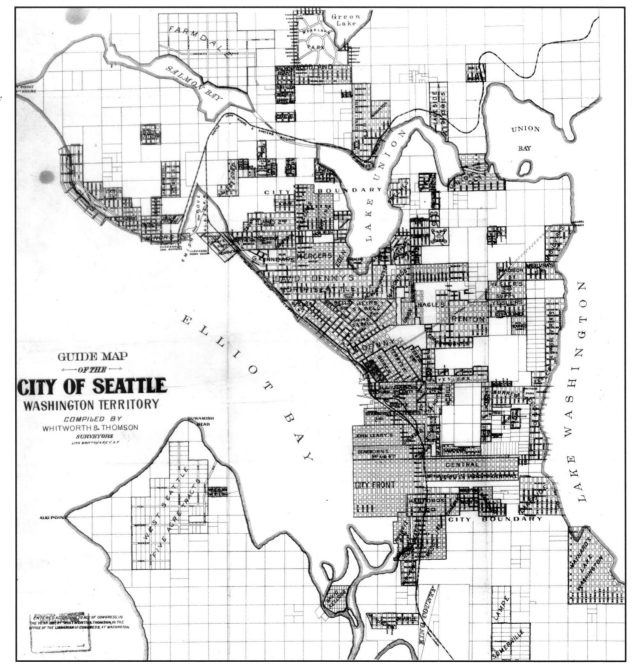

See also a superb "bird's-eye" view of Seattle in 1884 on page 181.

The commercial map of the Northern Pacific lines shown here (Map 247) was published by Rand McNally in 1883. It shows the Portland to Tacoma line as complete, with a line through the Cascades under construction. The distinction on the map between lines under construction and those that were complete seems deliberately confused, no doubt because Northern Pacific sought to portray themselves as having an extensive network of tracks. The map was, after all, published with the aim of attracting settlers to the areas it served.

The Northern Pacific did in fact extend the line northwards from Tacoma to Seattle in 1884, the year after this map was published.

The other major transcontinental railroad to reach Seattle was James J. Hill's Great Northern Railway, completed in 1893. The line across the Cascades was surveyed by John F. Stevens, after whom Stevens Pass is named.

Map 248 dates from 1890, when the track to the east had yet to be laid. The line was to join up with local railroads on Puget Sound. The Fairhaven and Southern Railroad was completed to the Canadian boundary in 1891, and the New Westminster and Southern provided a link into Vancouver, B.C., as well. Ultimately, the Great Northern system in Puget Sound was to be as shown on Map 249.

The Northern Pacific and Great Northern merged with the Chicago, Burlington and Quincy Railroad in 1970 to become Burlington Northern, and is now the Burlington Northern Santa Fe.

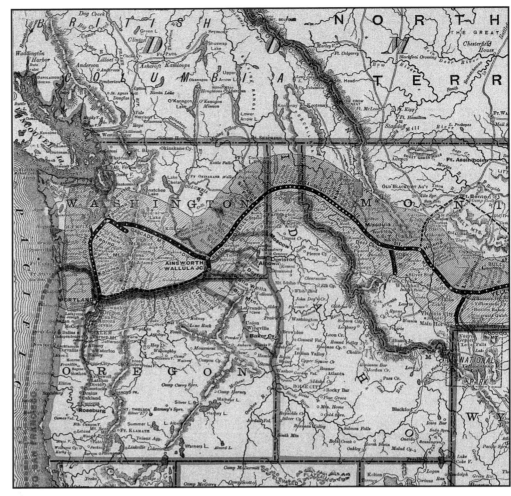

Map 247 (above)
New and Correct Map of the Lines of the Northern Pacific Railroad and Oregon Railway and Navigation Co.
Rand McNally and Co., Chicago, 1883

Map 249 (right)
Map of Pacific Coast Lines
(Great Northern Railway)
Poole Brothers, Chicago, 1912

Map 248 (below)
Great Northern Railway and Proprietary Lines. Poole Brothers, Chicago, 1890.
From: *First Annual Report of the Great Northern Railway Company,* St. Paul, Pioneer Press, 1890.

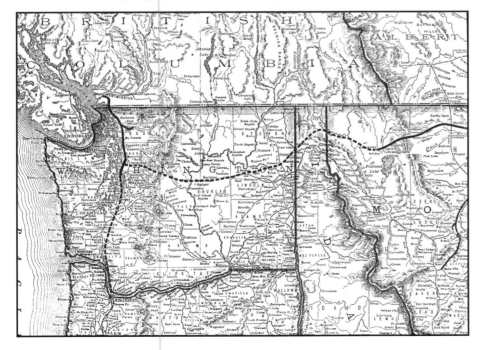

JOHNSTON SURVEYS A NORTHERN ROUTE

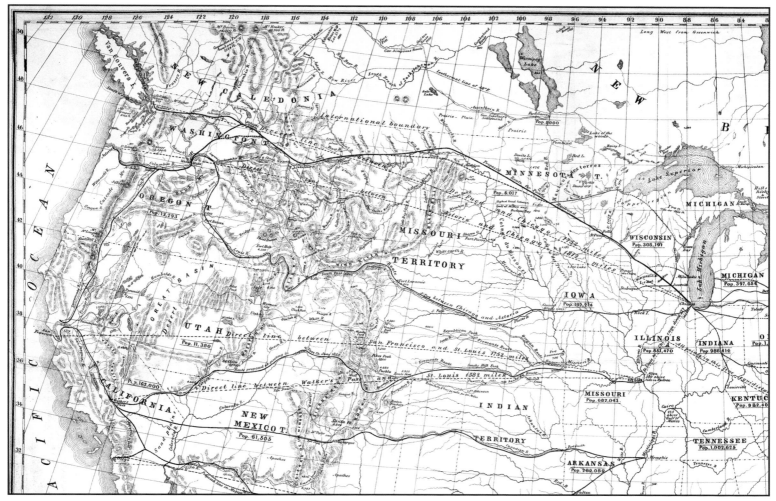

Map 250
Map of the Proposed Northern Route for a
Railroad to the Pacific by Edwin F. Johnson, C.E.
1853
From: *American Railroad Journal, Steam*
Navigation, Commerce, Mining, Manufacturers.
Vol IX No. 45–52, 1853.

In the mid-nineteenth century, a
number of schemes for rail lines to the
Pacific were advanced by private companies. One of those proposals came from
Edwin Ferry Johnson, one of the leading
railroad engineers of his day, who had suggested as early as 1862 that a line be constructed from the Hudson River westward.
Johnson became the chief engineer of the
Northern Pacific Railroad, which in 1883
reached Puget Sound at Tacoma (Map
247, opposite top).

Map 250 shows the routes Johnson
advocated in 1853, connecting Chicago
with Bellingham Bay and Astoria. Note
the dashed lines on the map showing a
direct line between Chicago and each location. Map 251 is a delightful later advertisement for the Northern Pacific
Route, completed to Puget Sound.

Map 251 (below)
Mark! When you want a pointer regarding your western trip...
(Advertisement for the Northern Pacific Railway Co.)
From: Olin D. Wheeler, *Wonderland 1902 Descriptive of that Part of the Northwest tributary to the*
Northern Pacific Railway, Chas. S. Fee, General Passenger and Ticket Agent, Northern Pacific Railway,
St. Paul, 1902.
Olin Wheeler was best known for writing the first fully illustrated book about the Lewis and Clark
expedition, *The Trail of Lewis and Clark*, published in 1904, but he also produced a series of travel
books for the Northern Pacific Railway.

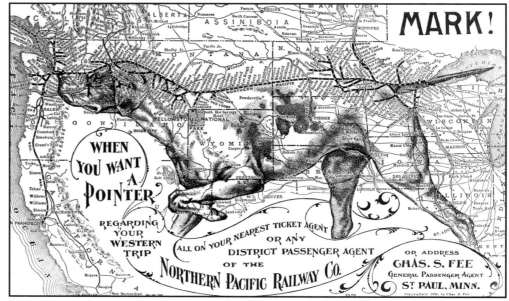

THE PACIFIC RAILROAD SURVEYS

In March 1853, the United States Congress authorized a survey by the government of all the principal potential railroad routes to the Pacific, having decided that it was strategically important that there be a rail connection from coast to coast. It was to be more a reconnaissance than a real survey, given the daunting magnitude of the task, but the object was to find the most practical and economical route.

The surveys were under the command of Jefferson Davis, then Secretary of War, and later to become the first and only president of the Confederate States of America, during the American Civil War. Four main parties were sent out. The survey of the northern routes into the Pacific Northwest between 47° and 49° N was led by Isaac I. Stevens, an army officer who had recently resigned to become governor of the newly created Wash-

ington Territory. The route he was to survey was westward from the Great Lakes via the Missouri to Puget Sound.

In his report to Jefferson Davis, Stevens was enthusiastic, as might be expected, about two routes he had located, which crossed the Rockies at Cadottes Pass (near Helena, Montana) and then diverged again, one following the Columbia and the Cowlitz to Puget Sound, and the other crossing the Cas-

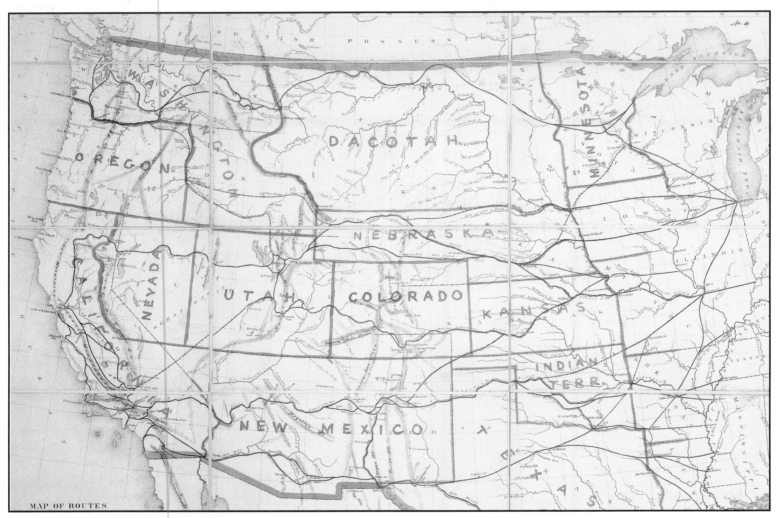

Map 252

Map of Routes for a Pacific Railroad Compiled to accompany the Report of the Hon. Jefferson Davis, Sec. of War In office of P. R. R. Surveys 1855
Gouverneur Kemble Warren, 1855. From: *Report of the Secretary...Communicating the Several Pacific Railroad Explorations*, Washington, 1855.
A note on the map states: *"This is a hurried compilation of all the authentic surveys and is designed to exhibit the relation of the different routes to each other; the topography represents only those great divides which form summits on the profiles of the routes."*
Lieutenant Warren revised this map in 1857, and again in 1858, adding detail to various areas including the interior of Oregon. Warren's maps of the American West remained the basic maps of the region for a generation, and were much copied. The state and territorial boundaries shown were superimposed onto the map at a later date; the boundaries of Washington Territory and the state of Oregon are those that prevailed between 1859 and 1863 (see page 137).

Top: Northern Pacific train, an 1883 Rand McNally engraving published with Map 247, page 146.

Map 253
Map of the United States West of the Mississippi Showing the Routes to Pike's Peak Overland Mail Route to California and Pacific Rail Road Surveys
D. McGowan and George H. Hildt, St. Louis, 1859.
The boundaries of Washington and Oregon Territories extend to the Rockies; they are the boundaries in effect between 1853 and 1859.

cades via the Yakima River and Snoqualmie Pass.

Stevens' report was not well received, even in the Pacific Northwest, and the legislature of Washington Territory commissioned a civilian engineer, Frederick West Lander, to survey another route from South Pass to Puget Sound. These reports were compiled into Davis' *Report of the Secretary...Communicating the Several Pacific Railroad Explorations*, published in 1855.

Included in this report was the map shown here (Map 252), drawn by Gouverneur Kemble Warren. Warren revised this map two years later, and that map, incorporating the Pacific railroad surveys, was widely used by commercial map publishers such as Joseph H. Colton and Rand McNally to revise their maps.

The map by D. McGowan and George H. Hildt, also shown here (Map 253), was a commercial map which used information from all of the Pacific railroad sur-

veys, and shows the route surveyed by Stevens to Puget Sound. A line marked "Puget Sound and St. Paul Route" is shown terminating at "Ft. Townsend" on the Strait of Juan de Fuca. This is near Port Townsend, which began with a land claim in 1851. Fort Townsend had been built in 1856 to protect Port Townsend, but the location is inaccurately shown on this map, as it is on Warren's (Map 252).

FIXING THE BOUNDARY

One of the responses of the British government to the expected influx of gold seekers after gold had been discovered on the Thompson River in 1856 was to suggest to the United States that the boundary between the two countries should be surveyed and marked. The Americans agreed, and both countries appointed boundary commissions to map the 49th parallel.

The American Boundary Commission, headed by Archibald Campbell, landed at Victoria in June 1857. In the absence of any suitable ship, especially the British survey vessel H.M.S. *Plumper*, nothing was done about defining the "middle of the channel" mentioned in the Oregon Treaty, or Treaty of Washington, of 1846, despite the fact that in 1853 a dispute had arisen over the ownership of San Juan Island and that this would leave the door open to further disputes in the future (see page 171).

Thus, Campbell's surveyors moved to the mainland where they started the work of determining the starting point of the survey on Point Roberts. They were joined the following year by the British Boundary Commission headed by Captain J.S. Hawkins, with a contingent of Royal Engineers.

The boundary commissions spent six years between 1857 and 1862 surveying, clearing, and marking the 49th parallel international boundary.

In June 1862, the British Boundary Commissioner J.S. Hawkins went to Washington D.C. to attempt to get the American commissioner, Archibald Campbell, to collaborate on the preparation of the final report, but co-operation was not forthcoming and the British and Americans drew up their own, separate reports. Only when, several years later, the two commission officials got together to prepare the final maps, was it discovered that there were discrepancies between them in some places. The method used to reconcile these differences was unusual. They simply split the difference and drew a mean line between the two. Since these boundaries were marked on the ground, settlers in the boundary areas often found two or three boundaries marked.

Even more astounding was that the original reports of *both* commissions were lost. A partial American report was made available in 1900, and in London, the missing report was found in the Royal Observatory in Greenwich. This discovery made it possible for the Canadian government to publish the missing report, which was dated 7 May 1869, in 1899. This report had been jointly signed by Hawkins and Campbell.

The publication of this report and the American one led both governments to undertake a new survey in order to ensure there were no more difficulties in defining where the boundary was. Between 1901 and 1907 the boundary was surveyed again.

New marker lines were cut, old ones cleared, and markers replaced if missing, but in general, relatively few corrections were necessary. This survey revealed the fact that much of the so-called 49th parallel boundary had been marked *not on the 49th parallel* but a few hundred yards north of it.

This error has been attributed not to poor surveying but to limitations in the surveying equipment of the day. However, the United States and Canadian governments were not about to continue to argue.

A new Treaty of Washington was signed on 11 April 1908, which defined the entire boundary between the United States and Canada from Passamaquoddy Bay on the Atlantic coast to the Pacific Ocean, and accepted the boundary as it was, inaccurately surveyed.

Charles Wilson, the secretary of the British Boundary Commission, returned to Britain where later he was for a time Director General of the Ordnance Survey, the British mapping organization famous for its accurate maps.

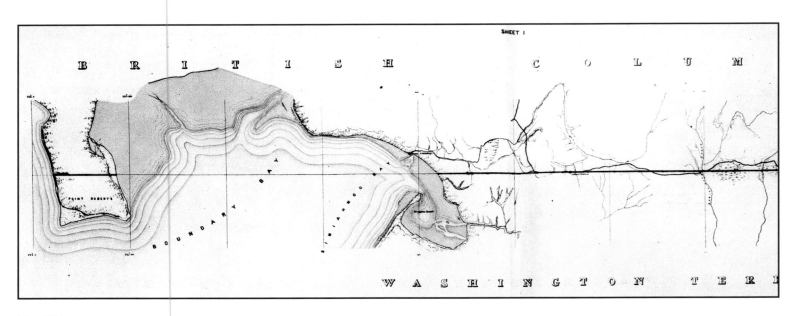

Map 254
Map of United States/British Possessions Boundary in and around Semiahmoo Bay.
From: *Maps of the Land Boundary between the British Possessions in North America and the United States as established by the Treaty of Washington, 15th June 1846 and surveyed & marked under the direction of the Joint Commission appointed to carry into effect the 1st Article of the Treaty.*
1" to 1 mile. Photozincographed at the Ordnance Survey Office, Southampton. 1869.

GOLD AND THE CREATION OF BRITISH COLUMBIA

In April 1858, James Douglas, the Governor of the Crown Colony of Vancouver Island, was concerned enough to write in his despatches to the Colonial Secretary in London that seventy or eighty American "adventurers" had been found to have gone up the Fraser River to look for gold, without any permissions being given by any British authority.

In May, Douglas reported that a thousand more had arrived, and by July he sent another despatch to report his belief that

this country and Fraser's River have gained an increase of 10,000 inhabitants within the last six weeks, and the tide of immigration continues to roll onward without any prospect of abatement.

In fact, before the year was out, between 25,000 and 30,000 gold seekers, mostly Americans, had flooded into the mainland. The gold rush was on!

Douglas, and the British government, represented at this time by the Colonial Secretary Sir Edward Bulwer Lytton (after whom Douglas named Lytton, B.C.), were concerned that the influx of Americans would challenge British sovereignty in the area; after all, it was the occupation of the Oregon country by American settlers which had been a deciding force in the British loss of that territory.

Lytton decided to create a new British colony on the mainland. The bill, as printed for the first reading in the British parliament, used Simon Fraser's name "New Caledonia," but Queen Victoria did not like the name, and after studying all the maps available, decided on the name "British Columbia," and it was this name that was on the final bill passed on 2 August 1858.

Map 259 (page 154) is from a newspaper report on the establishment of the new British colony published later that month, and is quite likely the first map to show and name the new Colony of British Columbia.

Colonial Secretary Lytton then asked Douglas to become Governor of the mainland colony in addition to Vancouver Island, but there was a condition attached: sever all connections with the Hudson's Bay Company. Douglas agreed, and on 19 November 1858, he was sworn in at Fort Langley.

A detachment of Royal Engineers was sent from England, as was a judge, Mat-

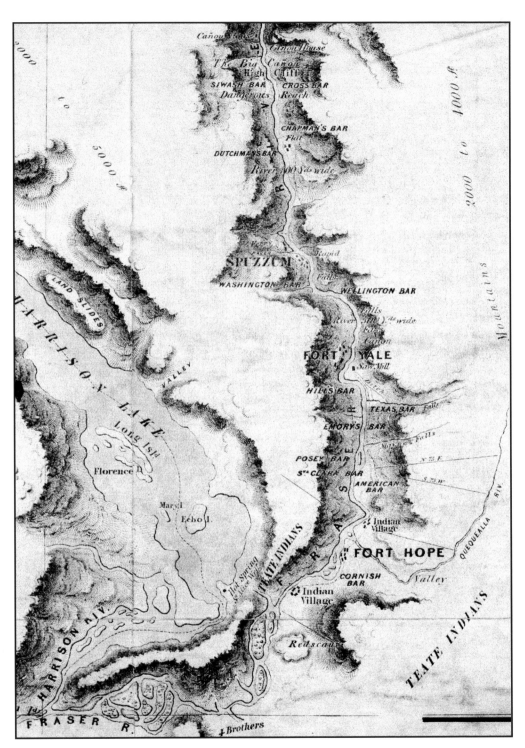

Map 255
Sketch of Part of British Columbia by Lieut. R.C. Mayne RN of HMS Plumper, c1860.

Shows the gold workings around Fort Hope, at the head of the lower Fraser Valley and the Fraser Canyon The variously named bars along the river are the sites of placer gold mining operations.
Fort Hope was named by the Hudson's Bay Company in 1848 because of the hope that they had finally found a route to the interior which did not involve traveling through what had recently become American territory.

thew Baillie Begbie. A Royal Navy ship, HMS *Ganges*, was ordered north from South American waters; it arrived at Esquimalt in October. Thus the British government, perhaps learning from its previous mistakes, quickly concentrated power and authority to ensure its sovereignty.

A number of maps were drawn at this time to promote the gold fields or show how to get to them. Three are shown here (Maps 256, 257, and 258, pages 152, 153, and 154).

Map 256 was published by Alfred Waddington, who came to Fort Victoria early in 1858 to open a grocery store; it was in his interest to encourage American miners to journey to Victoria, and no doubt the map was part of this promotion. Significantly, it was published in San Francisco.

Map 256
A correct map of the Northern Coal & Gold Regions comprehending Frazer River carefully compiled from the latest data and personal observation by A. Waddington. San Francisco, May 1858

Perhaps rather hopefully, the large yellow-colored area is labeled "Gold Formation". Nowadays it would be called subliminal advertising!

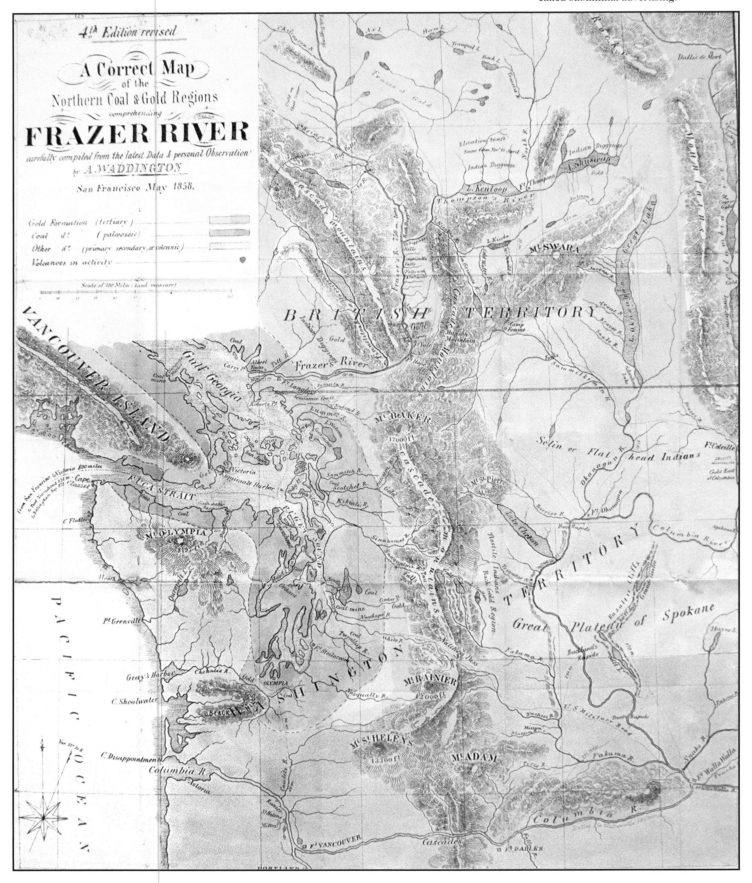

Map 257

Map of the Gold Regions of the Frazer River and the Washington Territory on the Western Coast of America. James Wyld, 1858.

In this rather beautiful map, British mapmaker James Wyld showed prospective gold seekers all the features of note. The area north of the 49th parallel boundary, on the mainland, is named "New Caledonia", the original name proposed for British Columbia before Queen Victoria changed it. In fact the map is dated exactly one week after British Columbia's official creation. New Westminster is marked "Albert City", again a proposed name that was never used, replaced by Queen Victoria. Close inspection of this map reveals the word "GOLD" rather liberally scattered. Note that the boundary between the United States and British Columbia and Vancouver Island is drawn so that the principal islands of the San Juan group fall into British territory. The dispute over the San Juans would not be resolved until 1872, and would nearly cause a war in the process (see page 171).

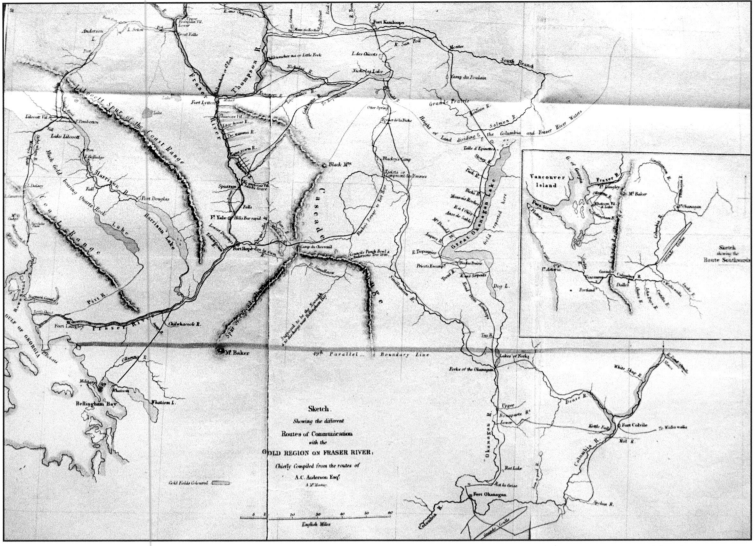

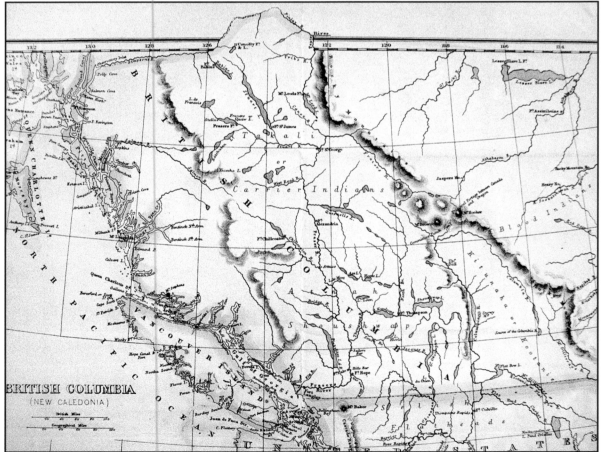

Map 258 (above)
Map showing the different Routes of Communication with the Gold Region on Frasers River. Alexander Anderson 1858, San Francisco. Inset: *Sketch of the Route Southwards.*
From: *Papers Relating to British Columbia, Part I, 18th February 1859.*

Map 259 (left)
British Columbia (New Caledonia)
From: *Weekly Dispatch Atlas*, Supplement to *Weekly Dispatch* for Sunday 29 August 1858. Edward Weller.
A map drawn to illustrate an article in a magazine on the creation of the separate Colony of British Columbia on 2 August 1858. It was possibly *the first map to show the new colony.* Note the northern boundaries, as initially established along the line of Simpson's (Stikine) River (incorrectly shown; see page 166–7) and Finlay River. The map was a quick adaptation of an earlier one. Today's Yellowhead Pass still retains the notation "Principal Portage between Canada and Oregon", despite the fact that the area had ceased to be part of the Oregon Country in 1846!

COLONEL MOODY'S SAPPERS
IN BRITISH COLUMBIA

Ever since the events leading up to the 1846 creation of the 49th parallel boundary between the United States and British territory, the British had sent Royal Engineers, their elite mapmakers and surveyors, to prepare maps in case of war with the United States.

Lieutenants Mervin Vavasour and Henry Warre had been in the region in 1845 and 1846 (page 129), and in 1850 Captain Elphinstone was sent to prepare a map of the region to provide information which might be useful if the United States invaded. The result was Map 260, which was also printed and sold to the public in Britain. Fort Langley is noted as having *"several hundred miles fit for cultivation"*, and trails, potential wagon roads, and portages are marked, as are Hudson's Bay Company forts.

The first major contingent of Royal Engineers had been sent from Britain in 1858 to form the British Boundary Commission (page 150). More were sent the same year to construct the roads, draw maps, and maintain British control after the discovery of gold on the Fraser had led to a gold rush (page 151).

The Royal Engineers, or "sappers" as they were known, were the cream of the British Army. Whenever Governor James Douglas required help to keep the peace among the miners, the Engineers were called upon. Whenever it seemed that a new road should be surveyed or built, the Engineers did it. And if towns needed to be platted, again the Engineers would do it. In this process they created, as might be expected, a number of maps.

Map 261 (right)
British Columbia New Westminster to Lilloett from a General Map in Preparation by the Royal Engineers. (With notations by Colonel Moody in handwriting.) August 1861.

Colonel Moody, as an engineer and military man, wrote notes all over this base map. On the lower Fraser valley he has written, *"Extensive Agricultural District and Open Agricultural District"*; at the head of Indian Arm *"Very deep water to the head of this Inlet"*; and just north of this location, *"It is said Communications Exist from hence to the Interior capable of being made into good roads"*.

In what seems like an attempt, or memo to himself, to change the name of the Island on which the City of Richmond now sits, Moody has written *"Palmer"* in front of the printed word *"Island"*, changing it from Lulu Island, its current name. It was reputedly named by Moody after a visiting actress, Lulu Sweet. Possibly Moody attempted to change the name later, feeling with sober second thought that *"Palmer"* might be viewed as more appropriate by his superiors! However, *Lulu* stuck; Palmer was obviously no match for her!

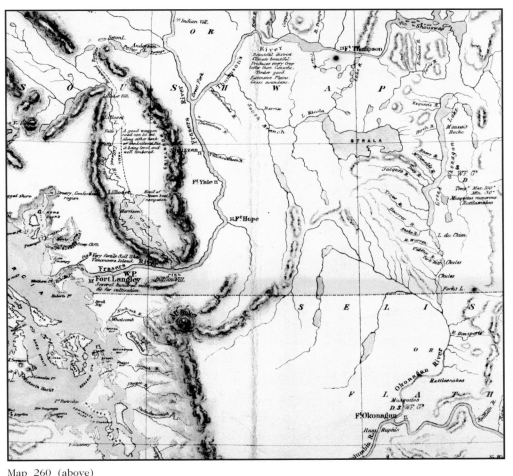

Map 260 (above)
North America. Sketch Map of Part of the British Possessions to the West of the Rocky Mountains. Lithographed & Printed at the Topographical Depot, War Department under the direction of Capt Elphinstone R.E. 1850. Agricultural and natural resources are marked with letters. W was for wheat, P for potatoes, WF for wildfowl, D for deer, G[R] for grouse, S for serviceberries. *"Musquitos"* are noted as numerous at Fort Okanagon and Great Okanagan Lake; the latter has temperatures *"Max 100 Min 30"* marked. Along Thompson's River, Elphinstone notes *"Beautiful District Climate Beautiful Produces every Crop better than Canada"*.

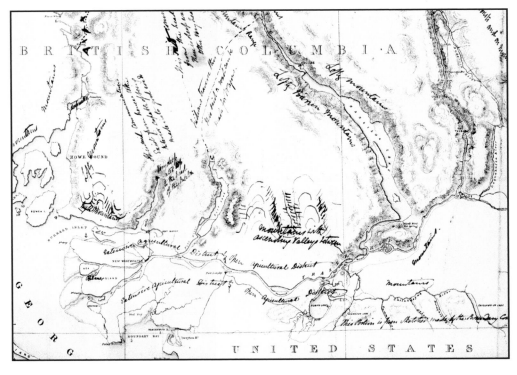

Map 262

Map of a Portion of British Columbia Compiled from the Surveys and Explorations of the Royal Navy and the Royal Engineers at the Camp New Westminster. 1859.

From: *Further Papers Relative to the Affairs of British Columbia, Pt. III, 1860.*

The lower Fraser has been surveyed by "HMS *Plumber*" (a spelling mistake; it is HMS *Plumper*), and Derby (the original site of Fort Langley) and the new colonial capital of New Westminster are shown. Detail of what is now the Lower Mainland of B.C. from a larger map.

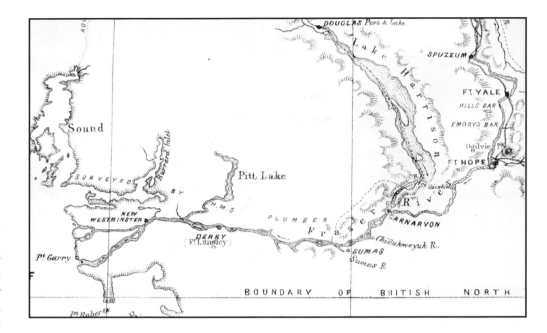

The Royal Engineers' commander, Colonel Richard Clement Moody, who had arrived at the end of 1858, first decided that the provisional capital of the new colony, Derby, near Fort Langley, where Engineers had already built some of their accommodations, was not suitable as a colonial capital, because it was not able to be defended against an American attack. It was Moody who, after a quick survey of the area, decided that the capital should be where New Westminster now stands. Initially, the settlement was called Queenborough, and it was Queen Victoria, hot on the heels of choosing the name "British Columbia", who selected the name "New Westminster."

Moody drew a quick and "extremely rough" sketch map of the area which is now the lower mainland of B.C. and Blaine, Washington, in February 1858, and on it the *"Proposed site of Capital"* is clearly marked (Map 263). This map looks like a map drawn by a military man assessing the terrain strategically. Other interesting features on this map are a *"proposed canal"* from Boundary Bay to the Fraser with a *"proposed pier"* in Boundary Bay. Although a good idea in principle, given the problems often encountered trying to enter the Fraser from the sea (see page 112), it would have been difficult to put into practice because of

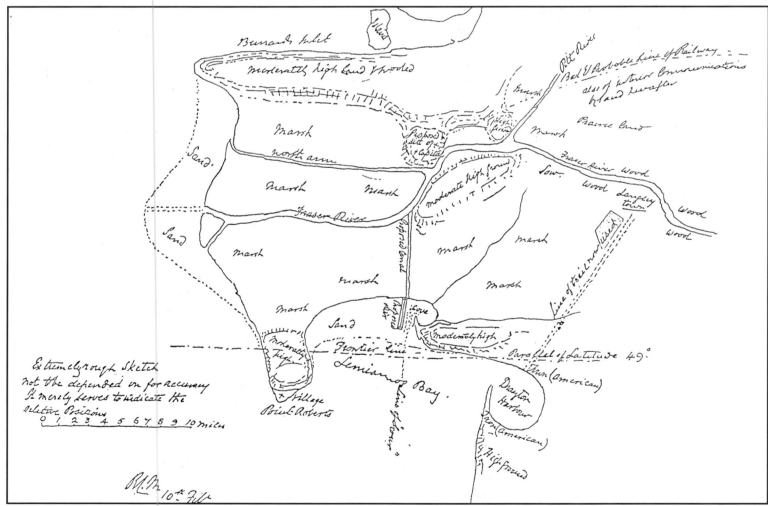

Map 263   *Extremely rough Sketch not to be depended on for accuracy. It merely serves to indicate the relative positions.*
Map of area of lower mainland of B.C., signed and dated *10th Feb.* Colonel Richard Clement Moody R.E., 1859.

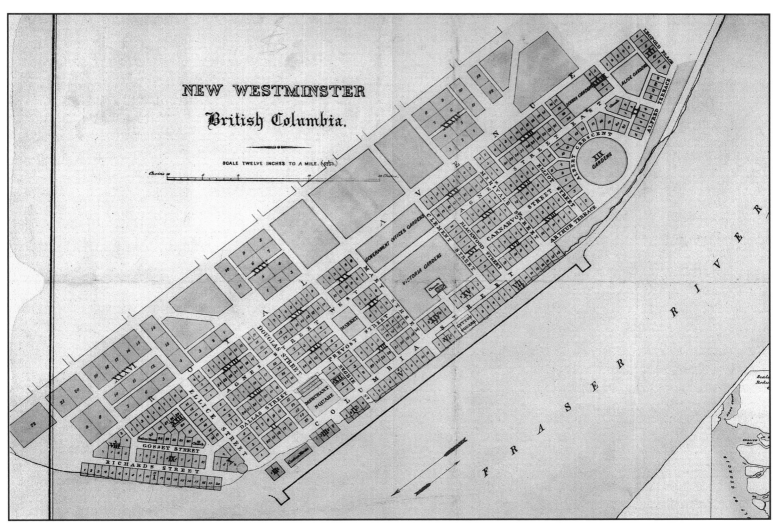

Map 264
New Westminster British Columbia. Lithographed at the Royal Engineer's Camp, New Westminster, May 1861, by order of Col. R.C. Moody R.E. 1861.
The plan for the newly established capital of the Colony of British Columbia, named by Queen Victoria. The plan had a distinctly English look to it, an attempt to recreate home in a faraway colony. Most of the lots shown on the map were empty at the time this plan was drawn, so that although it gives the impression of an instant city; in fact it was mainly just open ground or forest. The city would follow. Matthew Macfie, a contemporary writer, was not sure the site was a good one for a large city. *"It stands upon a slope inconveniently steep for extension into a great city,"* he wrote, *"though possessing facilities for anchorage by no means despicable. Should the colony of Vancouver Island be eventually united with British Columbia...New Westminster will serve admirably for the seat of government."* [157]

the shallowness of the bay. Moody's "cove", marked by today's Crescent Beach, had clearly not been examined in detail by him before he drew this map; he had in fact arrived only six weeks previously. Also marked, in the northeast part of the map, is the *"...Probable Line of Railway also of interior Communications by land and water"*, well away from the American boundary. Despite its crudeness, this is an interesting map indeed!

Having chosen a site for the new colonial capital, Moody then had his sappers lay out the town site. Map 264 shows the result.

For strategic reasons, Moody had a road constructed from New Westminster to Burrard Inlet, where Captain George Henry Richards named the eastern extremity of Burrard Inlet Port Moody after Colonel Moody in 1860.

View of New Westminster in 1864.[157/2]

British Colonial Secretary Sir Edward Bulwer Lytton had given Colonel Moody some instructions regarding site selection for a capital and other cities for the new colony:
You will consult with the Governor as to the choice of sites for a maritime town, probably at the mouth of Fraser's River, and for any more inland Capital to which the circumstances of the territory will suggest the most appropriate site. You will not fail to regard with a military eye the best position for such towns and cities, as well as for the engineering of roads and passes...[157]

In 1862, the difficulties of getting to the Cariboo gold fields led to the survey of another possible route, that from Bella Coola to the Fraser near today's Williams Lake.

Lieutenant Henry Spencer Palmer of the Royal Engineers was detailed to survey the route. At each of eighteen camps, Palmer fixed his position astronomically and by using a pocket chronometer set to New Westminster time. As a result, his survey was very accurate.

Part of the map he produced is shown here (Map 265). It shows North Bentinck Arm, the site of today's Bella Coola, which is where Alexander Mackenzie reached tidewater in 1793 (see page 95). Palmer followed the route used by Mackenzie to the Fraser. At one point Palmer narrowly escaped being attacked by natives; two years later a party of road builders (organized by Alfred Waddington; see Map 256, page 152) were massacred in this area. Mackenzie had also had problems dealing with unfriendly natives here. The attempt to build a wagon road, which failed, was made despite Palmer's recommendation, based on his survey, against use of the route for such a road because of the steep gradients.

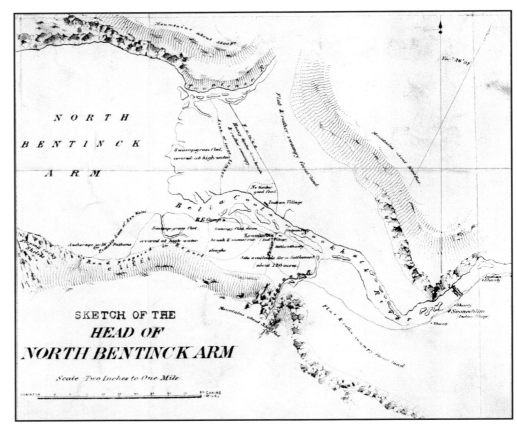

Map 266 (below)
British Columbia Thompson River District From a map in the possession of H.E. Gov. Douglas CB made in 1835 by S. Black Esq. H.B. Company's Service. The positions of New Westminster, Douglas and Hope are those determined by the Royal Engineers. Litho under direction of Capt W. Parsons RE By order of Colonel R.C. Moody July 1861

This interesting map from the British Colonial Office has handwritten notes on it, probably those of Colonel Moody. At top right, *"old HB Road"* is marked on a route from *"Tete Jaune Cache"* to *"Jasper's Ho."* (Jasper, Alberta), *"the direct and shortest road for miners from Canada to Cariboo, Antler and Bald Mountain."* The point at approximately today's Yellowhead Pass is marked with the notation *"2 or 3 days from future steamboat navigation on the Saskatchewan [River]."* Handwriting at the top of the map (north of Quesnel Lake) is *"The Great Gold Region Antler Creek Bald Mountain. Exceptionally Rich."* This was the Cariboo gold-mining area (see page 162).

Map 265
Sketch of the Head of North Bentinck Arm Inset in: *Sketch of the Route from North Bentinck Arm to Fort Alexander by Lieut H.S. Palmer R.E. To accompany Report of 24th November 1862*
The map was signed by Palmer, 18 February 1863, and by Col Moody.

North Bentinck Arm was the starting point for Palmer's survey. This is the point where Alexander Mackenzie reached the Pacific Ocean in 1793, becoming the first person to cross the North American continent from coast to coast (see page 95). It is the site of modern Bella Coola.

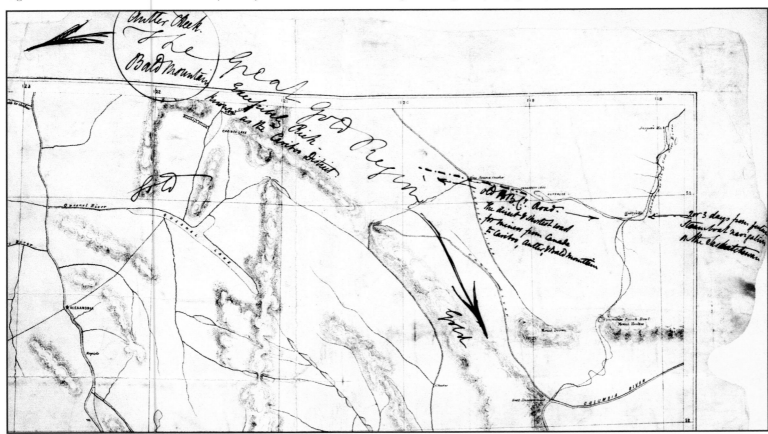

HYDROGRAPHIC SURVEYS OF THE BRITISH COLUMBIA COAST

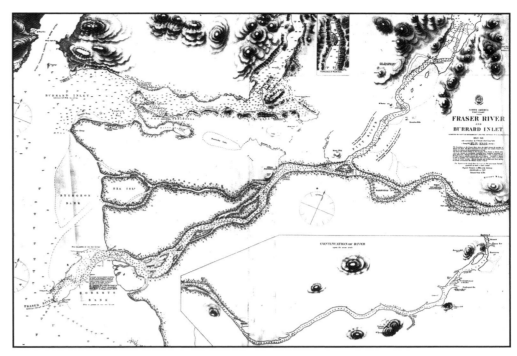

Map 267

Fraser River & Burrard Inlet Surveyed by Captain G.H. Richards, R.N. and the Officers of H.M.S. Plumper 1859–60. London: Hydrographic Office, 1860.

Hydrographic surveying, or surveying of water areas specifically for navigational purposes, had begun in earnest at the time of the gold rush to British Columbia in 1858, when many more ships were suddenly appearing on the coast.

Captains James Charles Prevost in HMS *Satellite* and Captain George Henry Richards in HMS *Plumper* had increased detailed navigational knowledge of the British Columbia coast, and had also been involved in surveying the water part of the boundary between the United States and British territory as part of the Boundary Commission of 1858. This in fact was the original motivation for the intensive surveying.

Richards had been appointed to hydrographic surveying in the Pacific Northwest after returning from the search for Sir John Franklin in the Arctic.

In 1858 and 1859, Richards had surveyed the coast of what is now the lower mainland of British Columbia in some detail, and the modern outline of Greater Vancouver emerged, shown in Map 267.

In 1860, HMS *Hecate* was sent to replace the small and defective *Plumper*; Richards continued as captain of the *Hecate* until 1863, when he was sent back to England.

Hydrographic surveying continued with Daniel Pender, master of the *Plumper* and then the *Hecate*, who was given com-

mand of the *Beaver*, which was leased from the Hudson's Bay Company and converted into a survey vessel.

One of the surveys Pender made was of the entrance to the Fraser River, which tended to change and therefore needed periodic resurveying (Map 268); this map was in fact incorporated into Map 267 as an update; the detailed pattern of soundings from Sandheads into the Fraser can be seen on that map as well.

A number of coastal place names in British Columbia date from the hydrographic surveying period of 1858 to 1870. Pender, Mayne, and Prevost Islands in the Gulf Island group were named by Richards after his officers and Captain

James Prevost, and Plumper Cove in Howe Sound and Hecate Strait between the Queen Charlottes and the mainland were also named by him after the ships involved, as was Satellite Channel off Saltspring Island, and many other features.

In addition to the charts of the Vancouver Island and British Columbia coasts that the British Admiralty began to publish in the early 1860s as a result of Richards' survey work was a volume of sailing directions. Such sailing directions are now used by many boaters; this volume, *The Vancouver Island Pilot,* was the first for the region. It was published in 1864, and authored by Richards himself.

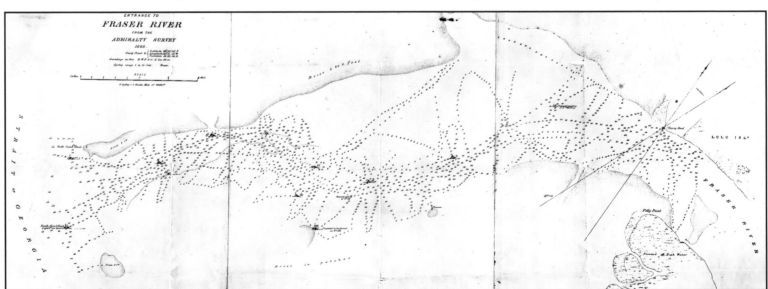

Map 268 *Entrance to Fraser River from the Admiralty Survey 1868*
A map of the thousands of soundings made in order to ensure safe access to the new capital city. The location of a new lightship, the South Sand Heads, is shown, as are the locations of existing and proposed new buoys. Richmond's Garry Point, at Steveston, is shown on the right; Westham Island to the south.

CHOOSING SITES FOR LIGHTHOUSES

With the increase in marine traffic after 1858, it was becoming clear that some navigation aids were necessary to guide ships into the British naval base at Esquimalt and into Victoria. Captain George Henry Richards, Captain of HMS *Plumper*, was instructed to determine the proper location for lighthouses.

Two lighthouses that he recommended were to guide naval ships into Esquimalt Harbour. The maps that he used to illustrate how they should be placed (Maps 269 and 270) were included in a later report included in a despatch from Governor Douglas to the British Colonial Office in July 1861. Richards was impressed with the harbor at Esquimalt, and observed that

from its position and capabilities, [it] would appear destined to become the emporium not only of Vancouver Island, but also in a great measure of the new colony which has just been called into existence under the name of British Columbia.

Beginning service in November 1860, Fisgard lighthouse became the first permanent light on the British Columbia coast. Race Rocks lighthouse was completed in December of the same year.

By the time Richards published his *Vancouver Island Pilot* in 1864, he was able to assure mariners that *"Esquimalt Harbour is a safe and excellent anchorage for ships of any size, and with the aid of the light on Fisgard island may be entered at all times with great facility."*

George Davies, Fisgard's first lighthouse keeper, arrived in the Colony of Vancouver Island in August 1860, after a journey from England round Cape Horn. The equipment for the actual light arrived with him, but it was not until November that the light was assembled and placed in the waiting lighthouse. Fisgard Lighthouse still stands at the entrance to Esquimalt Harbour, though the light itself is now automated. The lighthouse is a National Historic Site, open to visitors.

Map 269 (top)
South East part of Vancouver Island showing the proposed sites for Light Houses on the Great Race Rock and Fisgard Island
Captain George Henry Richards, 1858
In: *Papers Relative to British Columbia*, Pt II, Despatch from Governor Douglas C.B. to his Grace the Duke of Newcastle, K.G., Victoria, Vancouver Island, 27 October 1858.

Map 270 (bottom)
Entrance of Esquimalt Harbour showing the proposed site for a Light House on Fisgard Island
Captain George Henry Richards, 1858
In: *Papers Relative to British Columbia*, Pt II, Despatch from Governor Douglas C.B. to his Grace the Duke of Newcastle, K.G., Victoria, Vancouver Island, 27 October 1858.

Fisgard Island was named in 1847 after *HMS Fisgard*, which was stationed at Esquimalt between 1844 and 1847. Other points and islands around the harbor were all named after officers of the *Fisgard*.

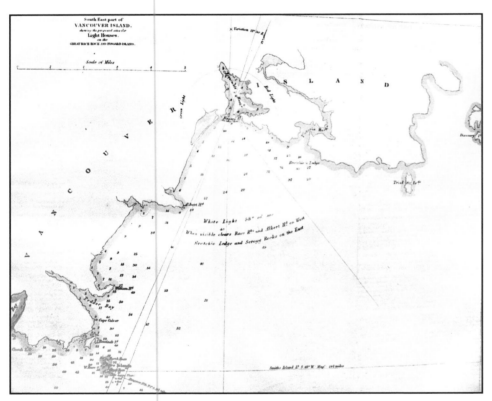

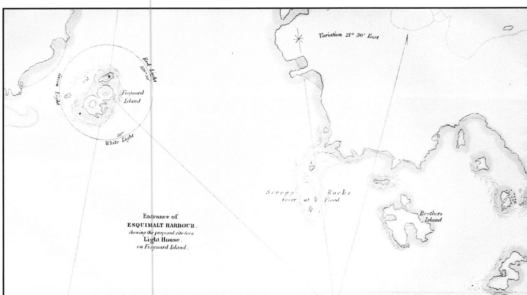

POINT ROBERTS – THE "INCONVENIENT APPENDAGE"

The acceptance of the 49th parallel as the international boundary by the British and American governments was done without detailed knowledge of the precise effects this might have. It was considered at the time more important to get the treaty signed than to worry about the boundary's exact location.

Later, when it came time for the Boundary Commission to survey and mark the boundary, the British government realized that if the boundary was accepted literally, it would leave to the United States the peninsula of land known as Point Roberts (named by Captain George Vancouver after Captain Henry Roberts, his predecessor on the *Discovery*) entirely cut off from the rest of American territory.

There are some very interesting instructions to Captain James Prevost, the British Boundary Commissioner, from the Foreign office, which were not communicated to Archibald Campbell, the American Boundary Commissioner. These secret instructions read:

Now there is reason to believe that a line thus drawn along 49° N will leave on the southern side of it soon after its Commencement a small promontory of low land [Point Roberts] forming the extreme headland to the West of a Bay [Boundary Bay] which is indented into the Continent. As this promontory would be entirely separated from the remainder of the United States Territory on the Continent, and inaccessible by land, except by passing through British territory, it would obviously be more convenient that it should belong to Great Britain; and as it cannot be of the slightest value to the United States, their Commissioner will probably not object to such an arrangement; and you will therefore propose that it should be left to Great Britain; but if he demurs to this course you will have to consider whether it may not be possible to offer him some equivalent compensation by a slight alteration of the Line of Boundary on the Mainland; and I should hope that in one way or the other you may be able to obtain his acquiescence in such an arrangement which would be attended with some convenience to this Country, while it would relieve the American Gov't from the inconvenient appendage to the territory of the Union of a patch of ground of little value in itself & inaccessible by land to the other territories of the Confederation, without passing through British Territory. [161]

It is not known what the reaction of the American Commissioner Campbell was to Prevost's proposal, but clearly the answer was not what the British government wanted, as Point Roberts remained American territory, now part of the state of Washington, and indeed, it does "inconvenience" the American government still as it is naturally more difficult to service. Utilities have to be purchased from British Columbia, and students are bused every day to Blaine, Washington, to attend school.

Ironically, part of Blaine itself would not have been in the United States had the boundary line been correctly surveyed on the 49th parallel (see page 150).

Map 271
A Part of the Strait of Georgia with the channels leading into the Strait of Fuca by the officers of HMS Plumper 1858.
Signed by Captain George Henry Richards.

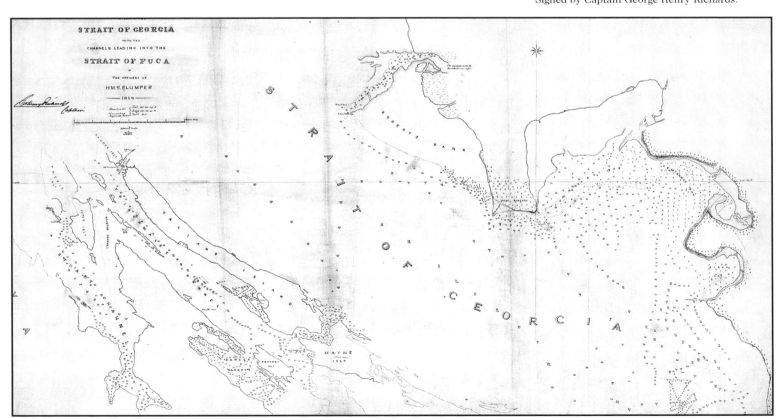

THE CARIBOO GOLD RUSH

The Gold Rush of 1858 had focused on the region between Fort Hope and Fort Yale; in 1859 it had moved to the area north of Lytton, and in 1860, gold seekers went eastwards from the Fraser at Quesnel, where unusually rich gold in gravel was found at Keithley Creek, in the Cariboo. More valuable gravel was discovered at Antler in 1861. The miners were encouraged to think that the further they pushed, the larger would be the nuggets.

The gold finds were publicized in Britain, and this led to more gold seekers arriving in British Columbia. In the spring of 1862, some five thousand more gold seekers arrived in the Cariboo. The hillsides were denuded, earthworks littered the land, and towns sprung up everywhere, especially on Williams Creek, another particularly rich area.

There was Richfield, Camerontown, Van Winkle and Lightning, and Barkerville. The latter town, named after Billy Barker, was perhaps the most famous. Barker hit pay dirt 16 m (52 ft) down in August 1862. And pay dirt it was. In a short period thereafter, Barker and his associates took out some $600,000 worth of gold, an absolute fortune.

The Cariboo gold region is shown quite well on an 1882 map of British Columbia by a Victoria publisher, R.T. Williams, a portion of which is shown here (Map 272). The region appears, as it was, relatively densely populated, though that did not last. In 1868, Barkerville burnt to the ground.

The Hudson's Bay Company plan showing the location of their warehouse in Barkerville (Map 273) was obviously surveyed before that date, as it is dated 13 October 1868, almost a month after the warehouse no longer existed!

Another map of British Columbia was published in 1865 by Matthew Macfie in a book called *Vancouver Island and British Columbia: Their History, Resources and Prospects*, a promotional book which, like that of Joseph Despard Pemberton (see page 142), was aimed principally at encouraging immigrants. As such it dwelt at length on the gold mining areas, and included a map of the colonies in which the word "GOLD" is rather liberally sprinkled across the map! Map 274 shows the Cariboo goldfields in some detail.

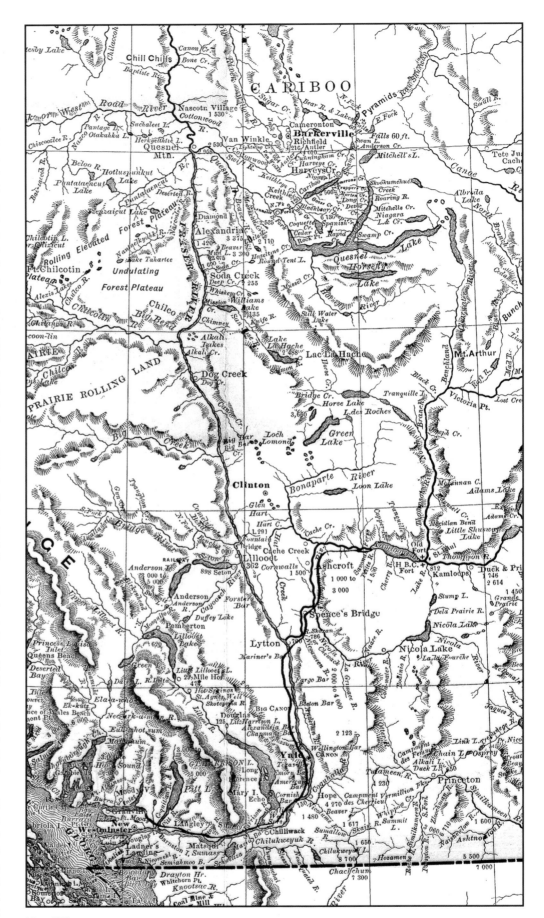

Map 272

New Map of British Columbia by R.T. Williams, Publisher, Victoria, 1882

Here are all the evocative names of the Cariboo gold rush. Just below the larger word "CARIBOO" are marked Keithley Creek and Lightning Creek, Harveys Creek and Richfield, Antler and Van Winkle, plus the larger center of Barkerville, of which Map 273 (top, opposite) is a plan. Today Barkerville has been reconstructed and is a popular tourist destination.

The Cariboo Road, near Spences Bridge, about 1867. The freight wagons are above the Thompson River, on their way to the Cariboo goldfields. The telegraph wires were strung in 1865 as Perry McDonough Collins' telegraph (see page 166) was progressing towards Alaska. The Cariboo Road, an initiative of Governor James Douglas, was built between 1862 and 1865, to service the goldfields.

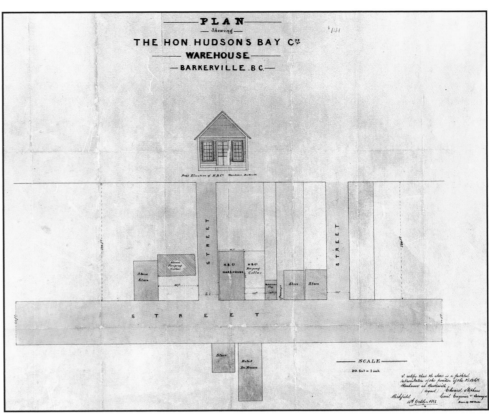

Map 273 (above)

Plan Shewing the Hon. Hudson Bay Cᵒˢ· Warehouse Barkerville, B.C. 13th October 1868 W.H. Newton
Obviously this plan of Barkerville was finished elsewhere, for the city had burned to the ground before this map was dated and finished.

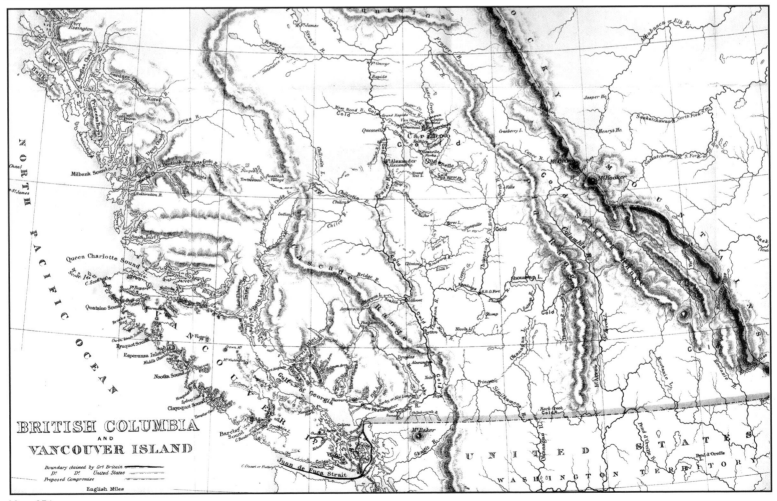

Map 274

British Columbia and Vancouver Island. Edward Weller.
From: Matthew Macfie, *Vancouver Island and British Columbia: Their History, Resources and Prospects,* 1865.
A map drawn for miners and prospective settlers to British Columbia. It shows the relatively dense area of settlement which was the Cariboo goldfields.

GOVERNOR DOUGLAS' DESPATCH

Map 275 was included in a dispatch, called a "despatch" in Victorian terminology, sent by James Douglas, in his capacity of Governor of the newly formed Colony of British Columbia, to the British Colonial Secretary, the Duke of Newcastle. The despatch described a journey Douglas took north of Lytton to Cayoosh (Lillooet) and Pavilion in June 1861.[164]

He reported on farming and the possibilities for irrigation in this drier district, and commented on the state of the gold mining areas:

The mining districts of Thompson's River, and of the Fraser below the Pavilion, have been almost abandoned by the white miners of the Colony, who have been generally carried away by the prevailing excitement to the Caribou and Antler Creek mines; and their claims are now occupied by Chinamen and native Indians, the latter especially exhibiting an unwonted degree of activity in mining. Their daily earnings sometimes reach the large sum of two pounds sterling, and never, as they assured me, fall short of eight shillings, so that they are becoming exceedingly valuable to the Colony, both as producers and as tax-paying population.

The protection of the gold that was being mined in the Cariboo was also dealt with:

The remoteness of the Caribou mines, and the large assemblage of people there, have rendered it necessary to establish a gold escort for the conveyance of treasure from Quesnel to New Westminster; and more especially with the view of strengthening the hands of the magistrates in those distant localities by the periodical exhibition of a small military force. This will put the colony to much expense, but I conceive it is an indispensable precaution that may prevent much future evil.

Douglas had a plan, explained in his despatch, to build roads to connect the upper reaches of the Columbia River with Hope, in the upper Fraser Valley, so as to provide a means of getting to the sea without going down the Columbia and through American territory.

Douglas ends his despatch in good Victorian style:

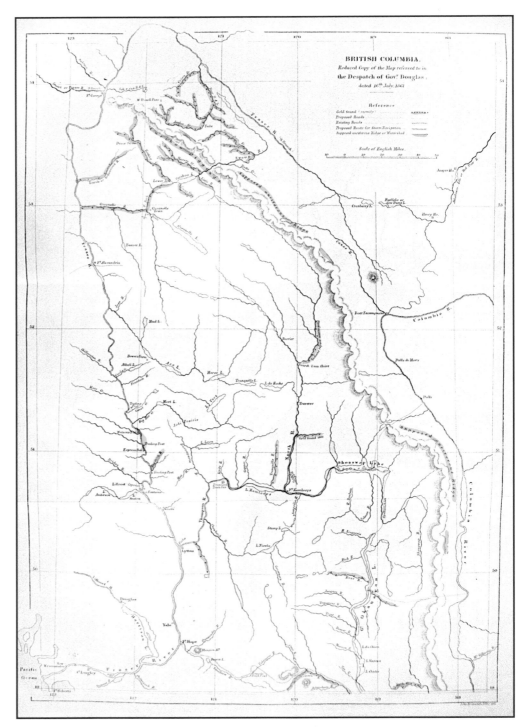

Map 275
British Columbia
Reduced copy of the Map Referred to in the Despatch of Gov.' Douglas dated 16th July 1861
In: *Further Papers Relating to the Affairs of British Columbia,* 1862.

Effort seems to have been made in this map to make British Columbia appear rich with gold all over. One mountain range bears the inscription "Supposed auriferous Ridge". The yellow areas are gold finds or simply where there were reports of gold, bearing labels such as "Gold found 1861" or "Indians report coarse gold". The concentration of yellow in northern British Columbia is the Cariboo goldfields (see page 162).

I returned to New Westminster on the 20th of June; and in conclusion it only remains for me to add the gratifying intelligence that peace and good order prevail throughout the Colony.

Sir James Douglas was Governor of the Colony of Vancouver Island from 1851 to 1864, and Governor of the mainland Colony of British Columbia from 1858 to 1864. Vancouver Island and British Columbia merged to form the Colony of British Columbia in 1866; British Columbia became part of Canada in 1871.

THE VANCOUVER ISLAND EXPLORING EXPEDITION

Robert Brown arrived in Victoria in 1863 as an agent for the Botanical Association of Edinburgh, Scotland. He had been sent by them to collect seeds. Not content with this, his relationship with his employer became strained, and in 1864 he accepted the leadership of the Vancouver Island Exploring Expedition.

This expedition had been ostensibly organized to fill in the still considerable unknown areas on the map of southern Vancouver Island. It was a private effort that obtained government support in the form of Arthur Edward Kennedy, who arrived to become Governor in March 1864. However, the main motivation behind the public's interest in the expedition was the hope that it might lead to the discovery of goldfields and in so doing revive the flagging fortunes of Victoria itself, which was not growing much after the decline of the 1858 gold rush. In 1863, a small amount of gold had been found at the appropriately named Goldstream, near Victoria, which had piqued the public's interest.

The expedition left Victoria in June 1864, and did indeed find some gold, but also collected a significant amount of information on the island's mineral and agricultural potential. Brown drew a map (Map 276) showing a cross section of the south-central part of Vancouver Island.

Map 276
Map of the Country Between Barclay Sound and Nanaimo By the V.I. Explor⁴ Expedⁿ 1864
Robert Brown, 1864.
A cross section of southern Vancouver Island, accompanying the report of the Vancouver Island Exploring Expedition.

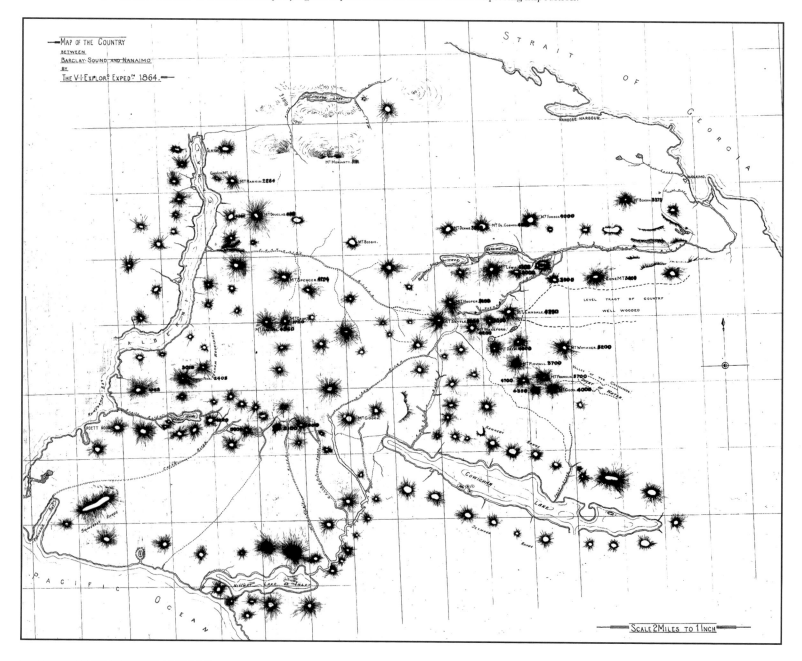

A TELEGRAPH LINE AROUND THE WORLD?

An American entrepreneur named Perry McDonough Collins was touring Russia in 1856 when he conceived of the idea of running a telegraph wire from the western United States through Canada and Russian Alaska, across the Bering Strait and linking with a Russian line to western Europe. This was surely easier, he reasoned, than laying a submarine transatlantic cable, which was being unsuccessfully attempted at this time.

Collins obtained permission from the Russians, the British, and the Americans to run his cable across their respective territories, and interested the Western Union Telegraph Company, which had just finished a transcontinental line, in 1861. In 1864, after the fifth attempt to lay the transatlantic cable had failed, Western Union started to survey and lay the line. The line was laid north from San Francisco and reached New Westminster in April 1865, in time to carry the news of the assassination of President Lincoln. It was then extended northwards to meet up with a section which was being laid in Alaska, but got only as far as Fort Stager, at the confluence of the Kispiox and the Skeena Rivers, near today's New Hazelton, when in July 1866 the news came that the sixth attempt to lay a transatlantic cable had succeeded, killing Collin's project. Some $3 million had been spent on the whole project, a staggering sum for the time.

In Alaska, the Western Union Telegraph Company had managed to lay only about 130 km (80 miles) of cable, but this earliest American attempt to explore Alaska did produce the first map of the entire 3200 km (2,000 mile) Yukon River. The Alaskan party, since they were working in isolation rather than extending an existing cable, did not learn of the completion of the transatlantic cable until July 1867, at the same time as they learned of the American purchase of Alaska (page 168).

Map 277 shows the projected line of the Collins Telegraph in the Pacific Northwest and beyond.

The telegraph line near Spences Bridge in British Columbia is shown in the photograph on page 163.

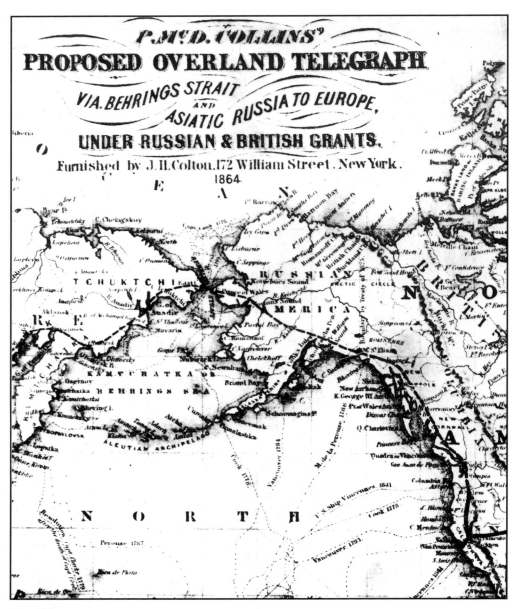

Map 277
P. Mc.D. Collins' Proposed Overland Telegraph via Behrings Strait and Asiatic Russia to Europe Under Russian and British Grants. J.H. Colton, 1864.

Map 278 (page 167, right)
Map showing some proposed northern boundaries for the new Colony of British Columbia.
James Wyld, 1858.

This rather beautiful three-dimensional-effect map was drawn by James Wyld, Queen Victoria's geographer, in July 1858, a month before the creation of the new colony. Found in British Colonial Office files, the map has a handwritten notation in the margin "Received from Mr Wyld July /58". The exact history of this map has not been traced, but it appears Wyld either offered or was asked to suggest what the northern boundaries of the colony should be. Wyld's proposed boundary follows the "Stickeen or Frances R." (Stickine), and then the "Dease or Nahoney R." (Dease), and finally the Liard. The confluence of the Dease and the Liard is almost at 60° N, the northern boundary of British Columbia today. The Finlay River is also shown: the final boundary selected by the Colonial Office followed the Skeena, then called Simpson's River, and the Finlay. Wyld has shown Simpson's River, but it is inaccurate, mixing up the Nass and Skeena Rivers. Although the boundaries suggested by Wyld were not used, because of his position as the Queen's geographer, the map was almost certainly consulted during the determination of British Columbia's first northern boundary. A further possible boundary was suggested by Wyld along the Pelly and Macmillan Rivers, much further north, also shown on this map.
Note that the boundaries of Russian America, the panhandle of Alaska, are shown the way the British would have liked them to be, and later would claim (see page 188), but not the way they were finally settled, by treaty, in 1903.

THE SHORT-LIVED STICKEEN TERRITORIES

In August 1858, when the original boundaries of the new Colony of British Columbia were established, the northern boundary was defined as *"Simpson's River* [Skeena and Nass Rivers] *and the Finlay branch of the Peace River,"* at about 57°N.

In July 1862, the discovery of gold led the British government to establish the Stickeen Territories, as the gold area was north of these northern boundaries of British Columbia. The Stickeen Territories extended to 62° N and west to 125° W. The gold discovery proved to be of minor importance, however, and so the new territory had a short existence. In July 1863, the area was incorporated into the new Colony of British Columbia.

In 1898, this time in response to the discovery of gold in the Klondike (see page 184) Yukon Territory was formed, separated from the Northwest Territories, with its southern boundary at 60° N.

Map 279, published by New York map publisher Alvin Jewett Johnson in 1867,

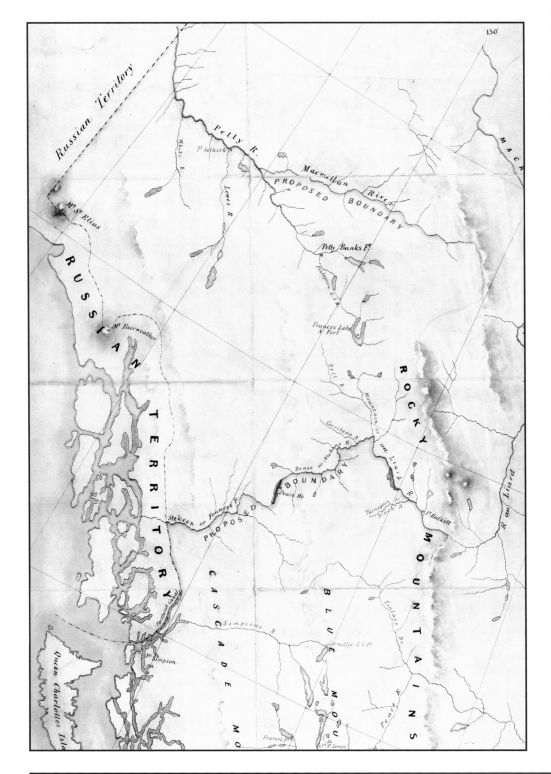

Map 279 (above)
Johnson's North America
Published by A.J. Johnson, New York 1867

shows the confused nature of boundaries in this region at the time. The northern boundary of British Columbia is shown at 54° 40' N, the southern boundary of Alaska (which had just that year become American territory), and from British Columbia north to the 141° W boundary with Alaska the map shows "New Columbia", which never existed! The map also shows, incorrectly, like Wyld's map (Map 278), Simpson's River, the initial British Columbia boundary; and the "Russo-American Telegraph Line" (previous page).

THE PURCHASE OF ALASKA BY THE UNITED STATES

In the nineteenth century, all Russian territories were viewed as the personal properties of the Tsar, his to dispose of at will.

The concept of selling Alaska, a remote part of this property, first came about in 1854, when Russia was on the verge of the Crimean War with England. The idea was that if Alaska was sold – temporarily – to a San Francisco company that imported Alaskan ice from the Russian-American Company, Britain would not attack American property. In fact, the British government signed a gentleman's agreement with Russia not to attack Alaska in return for Russia's assurance that it would not attack the Hudson's Bay Company. Nevertheless, this planted the seed of the idea of selling Alaska, which was revived after Russia's defeat in 1856.

Negotiations were opened with the United States government, but were derailed by the American Civil War.

By 1866, the Russian-American Company was almost bankrupt, and appealed to the Russian government to save it. The government was faced with the prospect of having to administer what they thought of as an unprofitable region. A sale to the United States would liquidate the Russian-American Company and free the Russian government of this potential burden.

On the American side, among those most wanting the purchase were the residents of Washington Territory, so as to acquire fishing rights. The territorial legislature adopted a memorial to this effect in the winter of 1866 and sent it to the president.

In December 1866, the Russians made a final decision to sell Alaska and instructed their ambassador in Washington, Baron Edouard de Stoekl, not to take less than five million dollars for it.

The American Secretary of State, William H. Seward, was an archexpansionist who was determined that the United States should own Alaska, and as a result, he did not negotiate with Stoekl as hard as he might, even at one point increasing his offer before receiving a counter-offer. As a result, he committed the United States to pay $7.2 million for Alaska. Even so, it was a bargain by any criteria: an area of 1,530,000 sq km (591,000 square miles) for about 5 cents a hectare (not quite 2 cents an acre). The twenty-seven-page treaty was signed at four in the morning on 30 March 1867. A long battle with the Congress then followed, but the sale was approved.

As historian Hubert Howe Bancroft put it in his 1886 classic, *History of Alaska*:

On the whole, the people of the United States have not paid an exorbitant price for the ground on which to build a nation. What we did not steal ourselves, we bought from those who did, and bought it cheap.

The actual transfer took place on the cool, misty afternoon of 18 October 1867, at Novo Archangel'sk, now Sitka. The money for the sale had not even changed hands at that point.

The map drawn by J.W. Lowry and published in an 1860 British atlas (Map 281) is a fine example of the way the political divisions of the Pacific Northwest looked just prior to the sale, with Alaska still shown as "Russian Territory." The map below, drawn by S. Augustus Mitchell in 1871, was designed specifically to show the area purchased (Map 280).

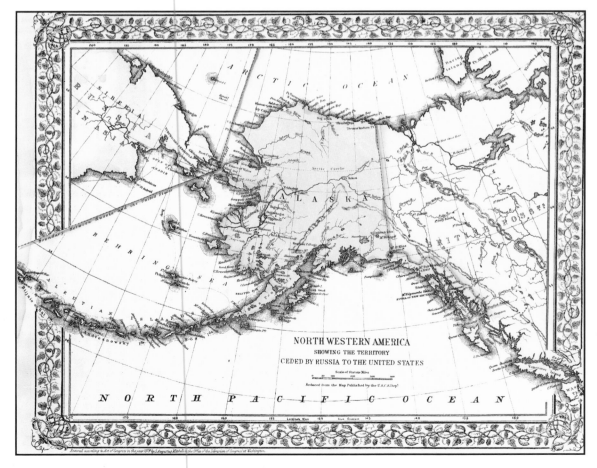

NORTH WESTERN AMERICA
SHOWING THE TERRITORY
CEDED BY RUSSIA TO THE UNITED STATES

Map 280 (left)
Northwestern America showing the territory ceded by Russia to the United States.
S. Augustus Mitchell, 1871

Map 281 (right)
*North America
Drawn & Engraved by J.W. Lowry.
Blackie & Son, Edinburgh, Scotland, 1860*

Alaska is shown as "Russian Territory" in this 1860 map; it would be seven more years before the purchase by the United States. The Territories of Washington and Oregon are shown, with the boundaries of both extending from the Pacific to the Rockies, encompassing all of today's Idaho. These were the boundaries in the period from the creation of Washington Territory from northern Oregon in 1853 to Oregon statehood in 1859. British Columbia is shown, following the creation of the new mainland colony in 1858. There is no northern boundary, with British Columbia merging into "British Territory," but "Simpson's R" is shown, which was defined as the northern boundary of British Columbia. This nonexistent river was the result of confusion between the Nass and Stikine Rivers.

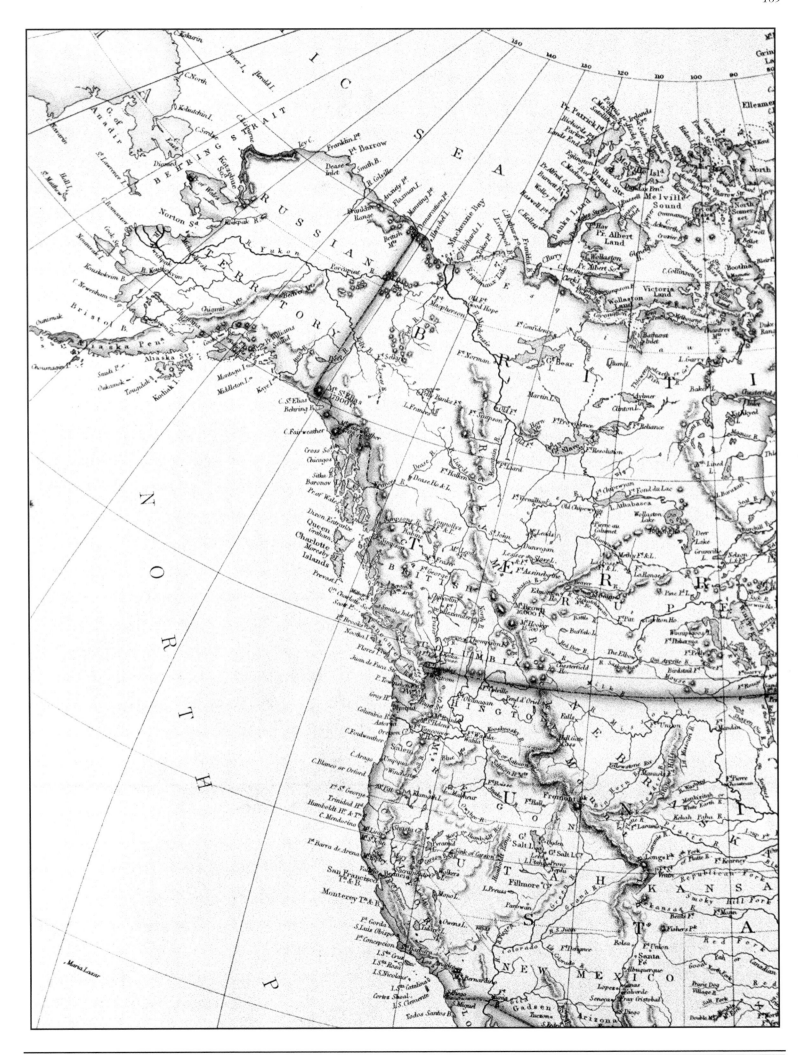

THE TRUTCH MAP OF 1871

After Colonel Moody and the sappers who did not settle had left British Columbia, Joseph W. Trutch was appointed the first surveyor-general of the mainland colony, and in 1866, with the amalgamation of the mainland with Vancouver Island, he became the first surveyor-general of the united colony of British Columbia.

He was responsible for the construction of this famous map, which is an excellent summary of geographic knowledge at the time of British Columbia's entry into Confederation. It was drawn at a scale of 25 miles to the inch.

As a summary map, it includes information from many sources. The area along the 49th parallel, the Thompson-Nicola area, and the Fraser-Harrison-Lillooet drainage area all reflect the work of the Royal Engineers (see page 155). In the Rocky Mountain area, information from the Palliser expedition of 1857 is incorporated.

On the coast, information from Lieutenant Henry Palmer (Map 265, page 158) is used, as are surveys of from the head of Bute Inlet by road builder Alfred Waddington.

The entire coast is shown in greater detail than any map since Vancouver's survey in 1792 – 1794. The southern part uses information from the hydrographic surveys of Captain George Henry Richards (see page 159); the northern part has much less information, though

notations on the Skeena such as "Steamer Mumford 1866" and "Ft. Stager" refer to activities associated with the Collins Overland Telegraph (Map 277, page 166). The line of that telegraph is shown from New Westminster to well beyond Ft. Stager.

Much detailed geographic information has been added as a result of the gold rush activities. The course of the Fraser River south of Prince George (Fort George) is shown accurately, and there is detail in the Cariboo goldfields area.

North of 56° N, the information shown on the map dwindles, reflecting the as yet largely unmapped nature of the region.

In 1871, Joseph Trutch became the first post-Confederation Lieutenant Governor of British Columbia.

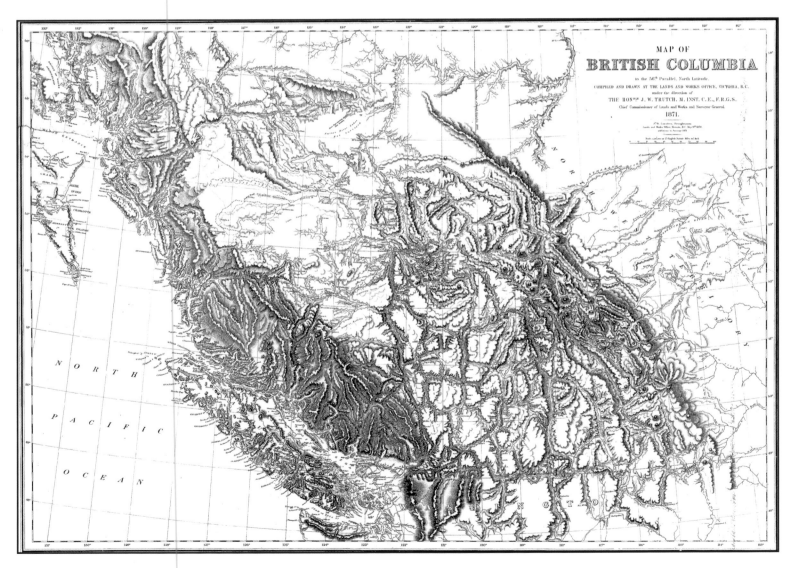

Map 282
Map of British Columbia to the 56th Parallel, North Latitude
Compiled and drawn at the Lands and Works Office, Victoria, B.C., under the direction of the Honourable J.W. Trutch. 1871.

THE SAN JUAN BOUNDARY DISPUTE

The San Juan Islands, where Georgia Strait meets the Strait of Juan de Fuca, were the scene of the final chapter in the resolution of the main continental boundary between the United States and Canada.

The 1846 Oregon Treaty, or Treaty of Washington, defined the boundary between British and American possessions. It was mainly straightforward in that it defined the boundary as the 49th parallel, but once the sea was reached the boundary became less clearly defined.

The boundary, the treaty stated,

shall be continued westward along the said forty-ninth parallel of north latitude to the middle of the channel which separates the continent from Vancouver's Island; and thence southerly through the middle of the said channel, and of Fuca's Straits to the Pacific Ocean; provided, however, that the navigation of the whole of the said channel and Straits south of the forty-ninth parallel of north latitude remain free and open to both Parties.

It was the term *"the middle of the channel which separates the continent from Vancouver's Island"* which was to give rise to problems.

When British Secretary of State Buchanan first studied the wording of the treaty he wrote to Louis McLane, the American Minister at London, that it

does not provide that the line shall pass through the Canal de Arro [Haro Strait], as stated in your despatch, [but] this would be the fair construction.
(6 June 1846) [171]

This suggests that the line intended by the British was through Haro Strait, yet there is some evidence that ambiguity was intentional, perhaps to satisfy the American demands at that point but keep open the possibility of renegotiation at some point in the future.

The geography of the region was not clearly known in 1846, particularly as it concerned the many islands. The maps most available and most in use in 1846 were George Vancouver's maps published

in 1798 (page 90 – 92), and Charles Wilkes' maps published in 1844 (page 119 – 120). These maps show some confusion between the southeastern coast of Vancouver Island and the Gulf Islands.

In 1856 it was decided jointly by the United States and Britain that a Boundary Commission should survey the boundary line between the territories of the two countries (see page 150). Captain James Charles Prevost and Captain George Henry Richards were appointed commissioners for Britain insofar as the water part of the boundary was concerned; Archibald Campbell was the American commissioner.

But how to define a boundary where there is no agreement as to its location? There were three possible boundaries through the San Juan Islands, shown on Map 283, below, and Map 287, page 173, both based on the surveys of Captain Richards on HMS *Plumper* in 1858 and 1859.

The British Foreign Office sent Captain Prevost a number of maps to help him argue his case that the boundary

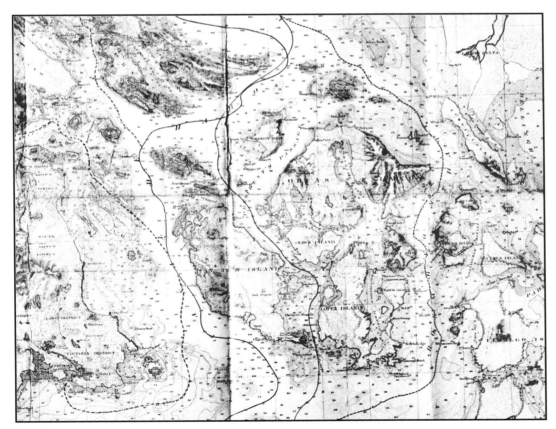

This American map shows all three of the boundaries in contention through the San Juan Islands. Naturally, the British wanted the easternmost one, the Americans the westernmost.

The key to the lines shown on the map is as follows:

Solid black line: *Boundary line contemplated by the Treaty as shown by contemporaneous evidence.*
Dashed black line: *Boundary line as claimed by the British Commissioner.*
Solid red line: *Boundary line proposed by the British Commissioner as a compromise between the Canal de Haro and Rosario Straits and rejected by the U.S. Commissioner as a violation of the Treaty.*
Dashed red line: *Boundary line in accordance with the strict letter of the Treaty, and also with the object of deflection from the 49th parallel as stated by Lord Aberdeen in his instructions to Mr. Pakenham viz. "thus giving to Great Britain the Whole of Vancouver's island and its harbors."*
Dashed blue line: *Track of steamers plying between Victoria and Fraser river since the discovery of gold.*

Map 283
Map Showing the Line of Boundary between the United States and British Possessions From the point where the 49th Parallel of North Latitude strikes the Western Coast of the Continent "to the middle of the channel which separates the Continent from Vancouver's Island and thence Southerly through the middle of said channel" and c. to Fuca's Straits, in accordance with Treaty of June 15th 1846
Bowen & Co. Lith. Philad[a]. c1872.

should be in Rosario Strait, the eastern-most of the three channels. One of these was

a tracing of a Map from a Survey by Col. Fremont which confirms the British claim to the possession of the islands, and in other Maps, equally of American origin, you will find a line drawn through Rosario Strait as the line between British and American Possessions.

This map from the British Foreign Office files is shown here (Map 284, below). It is a extract of Map 205, page 123. The fact that a prominent American mapmaker had shown the eastern boundary was to be used as evidence for the British argument.

But the commissioners could not agree on the water boundary.

Even while the British and American Boundary Commission surveys were taking place, a dispute over the ownership of San Juan Island broke out. In June, 1859, an American settler shot a pig belonging to the Hudson's Bay Company. He then refused to pay the $100 damages demanded by the Hudson's Bay Company. General W.S. Harney, the military commander of Oregon, landed troops on San Juan, and Captain George E. Pickett[172] issued a proclamation which said *"this being United States Territory, no laws, other than those of the United States,... will be recognized on this island."*

In response, Governor James Douglas sent two British ships and a detachment of Marines and Royal Engineers to the island. The resulting standoff was dubbed the "Pig War."

The American government was not pleased by Harney's actions, and sent General Winfield Scott to the coast to settle the matter. He and James Douglas

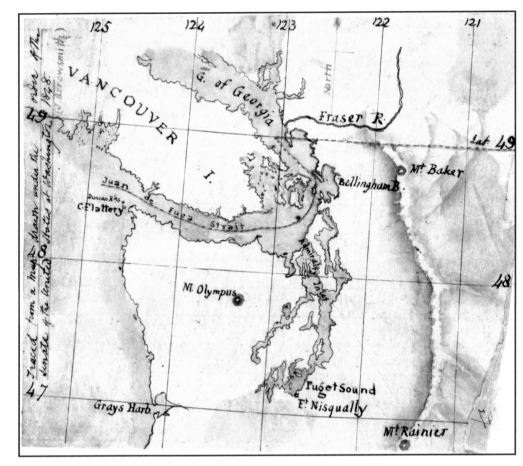

Map 285
Map of southern tip of Vancouver Island and Oregon Territory showing boundary line between possessions of Great Britain and United States Traced from a map drawn under the order of the Senate of the United States at Washington 1848 J. Arrowsmith, 1853

Map 287 (right, page 173)
*Haro and Rosario Straits
Surveyed by Captain G.H. Richards and the Officers of H.M.S. Plumper 1858–59
(with San Juan boundary options)*
Captain George H. Richards, 1859

Map 286 (right, below)
*A Diagram of a Portion of Oregon Territory
Surveyor Generals Office, Oregon City, October 21st 1852.*
Tracing by John Arrowsmith, 1856, and certified as true copy in handwriting.
This American map was copied by the British to try to show that even the American view was that the islands belonged to Britain.

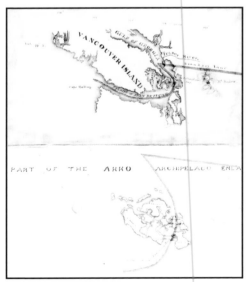

Map 284 (left)
Copy of 'Section of Map of Oregon & Upper California. From the surveys of John Charles Fremont And other Authorities. Drawn by Charles Preuss Under the Order of the Senate of the United States, Washington City, 1848' Exhibiting the boundary line between the possessions of Great Britain and the United States as therin laid down.
Inset: *A Part of the Arro Archipelago Enlarged.*
1853.

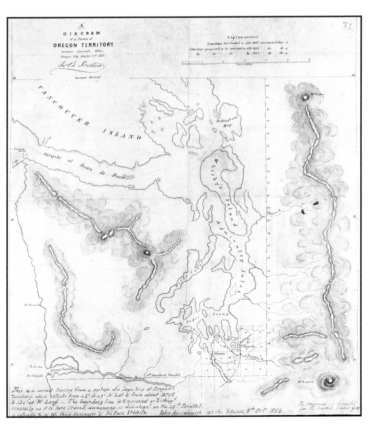

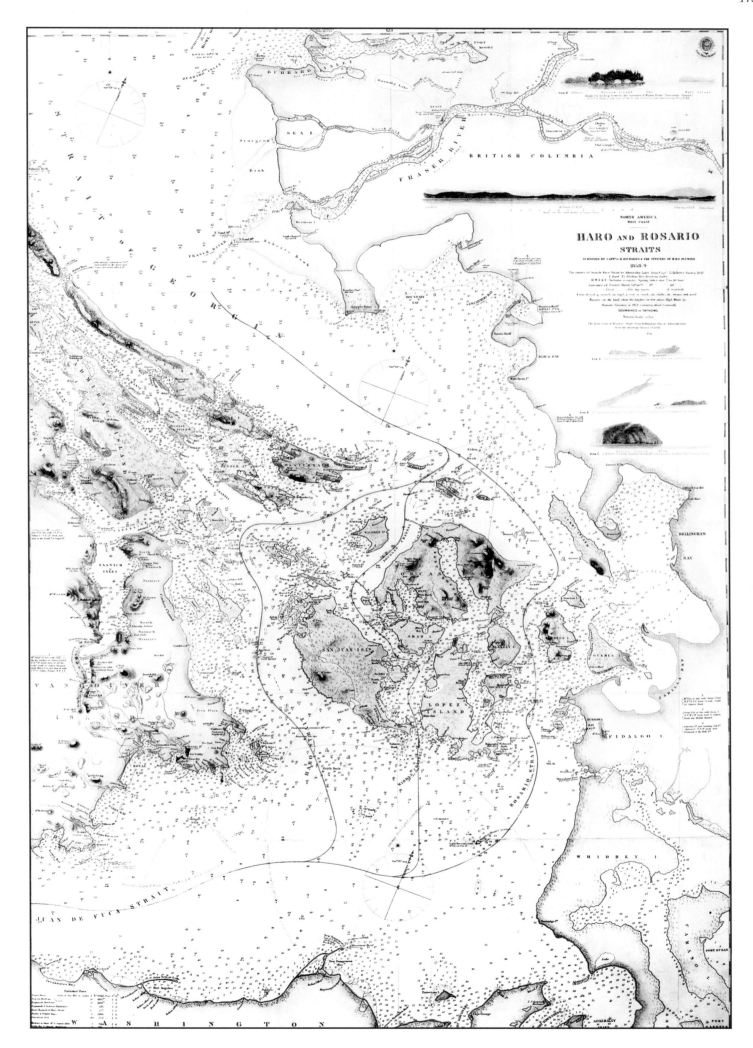

agreed to joint occupation of the island, and thus between 1860 and 1872 there were two military camps on San Juan Island, one British and one American.

The water boundary was finally settled in 1872, when both parties agreed to international arbitration in the form of Kaiser Wilhelm of Germany. One of the witnesses for the British side in Berlin was none other than now Rear Admiral Prevost. Map 289 was one of the maps sent to Prevost in Berlin.

But the British were to be disappointed; Kaiser Wilhelm, perhaps just to spite his cousin Queen Victoria, awarded the United States the boundary line it claimed. The popular magazine *Harper's Weekly* published in November 1872 an article describing the arbitration award, and included with it a map showing the boundary line as decided (Map 288).

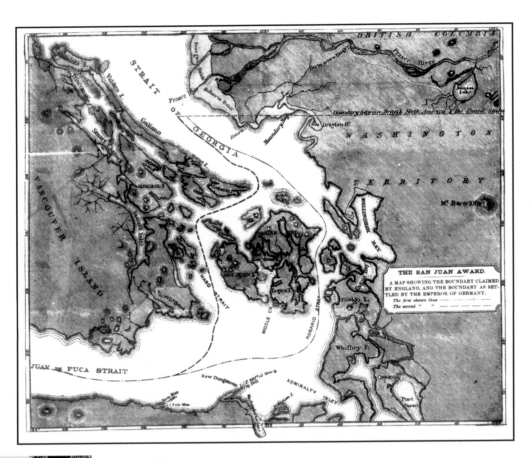

The site of the English Camp in Garrison Bay, San Juan Island, today. The blockhouse has been reconstructed, as has a knot garden. Clearly the English expected to be here for a considerable time.

Map 288
Map of the Boundary Between British and American Territory on the Pacific Coast, Settled by the Decision of the Emperor of Germany.
From: *Harper's Weekly*, 30 November 1872, p. 939.
Below: the text from the same article.

Map 289
Vancouver Island and the Gulf of Georgia
From the surveys of Captain G. Vancouver R.N., 1792, Captains D. Galiano and A. Valdes, 1792, Captain H. Kellett, R.N. 1849.
(Certified in handwriting *A True Copy of the Chart Published by Mr. Arrowsmith 28th February 1849* and signed by now Rear Admiral George Henry Richards, dated at the Admiralty, 21 May 1872.)

One of the maps used in the arbitration. Richards was appointed Hydrographer to the British Admiralty in 1870.

THE DISPUTED BOUNDARY LINE.

MANY of our readers will remember the old political rallying cry of "Fifty-four-forty or fight!" during the excitement about the disputed boundary line between British and American territory in the Northwest. At that time, prior to 1846, the boundary fixed at the 49th parallel ended at the Rocky Mountains, and was undefined beyond that point. At length Lord ABERDEEN proposed a compromise to President POLK, viz., to drive the 49th parallel due westward to the coast, and then to deflect to the south so as to give England the whole of Vancouver's Island, to which we laid no claim. The boundary was to pass through the middle of the channel between Vancouver's Island and the main-land. This sounds simple enough; but unfortunately there were islands in the strait, which broke up the passage into several channels. The result was that the English claimed that the boundary passed to the south of the islands, while we claimed that it passed to the north, and so the treaty remained in abeyance, and for years the island of San Juan has been occupied by a joint force of soldiers from either country.

The question being submitted to the arbitration of the Emperor of Germany, he has just decided that the boundary line runs through the Haro, or northern channel, and, therefore, that the island of San Juan belongs to the United States. A glance at the accompanying map will show the strategical importance of San Juan Island, and explain why the English take the Emperor's decision with such ill grace.

THE CANADIAN PACIFIC RAILWAY COMES TO BRITISH COLUMBIA

Sandford Fleming was an engineer with the Canadian Pacific Railway (CPR) who organized a transcontinental expedition in 1872 to determine a route across Canada for the new rail line to the Pacific.

Map 290 was used by Sandford Fleming to illustrate his report on the exploratory surveys for the Canadian Pacific Railway up to 1874. It shows both explored and unexplored routes at that point.

At Fort Edmonton, Fleming went south through Yellow Head Pass (marked on the *"line common to Route No's 1 to 6"*) to Kamloops, then southwest along "route No. 2" to the Fraser River, and then west to New Westminster. Other members of his expedition went north along the Peace River, and then to Fort St. James and the Pacific (Route No. 7 on the map).

The 1872 map (Map 291, overleaf) is part of a larger map covering the whole of southern Canada, but Fleming's proposed route is very clearly shown. This was not the route finally utilized by the CPR east of Kamloops, but that which would later be used by the Canadian Northern Railway, now Canadian National.

Neither of these maps shows the route east of Kamloops as built. It was not until 1882 that it was decided to use Kicking Horse Pass through the Rockies and Rogers Pass through the Selkirk Range (found by Major A. B. Rogers) instead of Yellowhead Pass. This route satisfied the criteria laid down by the Canadian government in a bill allowing the CPR to abandon Yellowhead Pass, that the new route had to be at least one hundred miles (160 km) from the United States boundary so as to afford some measure of protection in case of an American attack.

The construction of one of the most difficult parts of the British Columbia portion of the CPR route, the section through

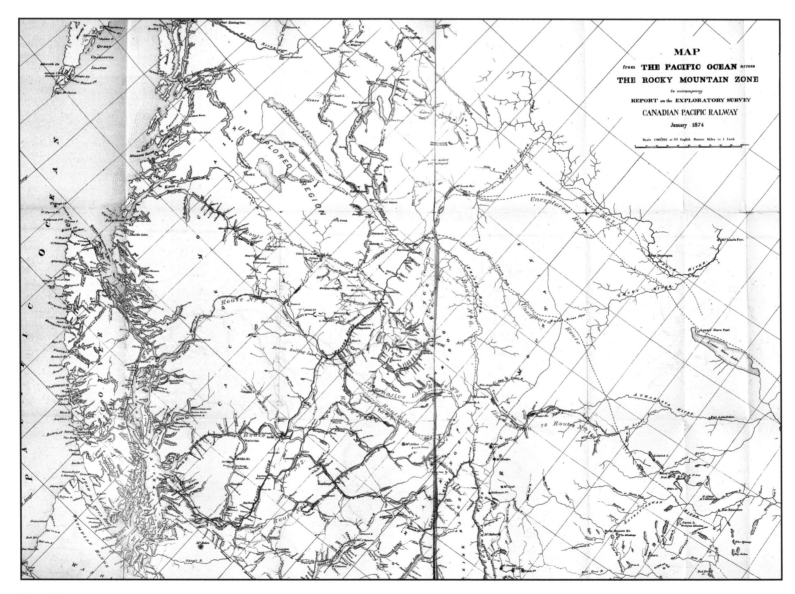

Map 290
Map from the Pacific Ocean across the Rocky Mountain Zone to accompany Report on the Exploratory Survey
Canadian Pacific Railway January 1874 Sheet No.8.
From: Sir Sandford Fleming, *Report of Progress on the Explorations and Surveys up to January 1874.* MacLean Roger and Co, Ottawa, 1874.

the Fraser canyon from Yale to Savona, had begun in May 1880, under the direction of an American engineer, Andrew Onderdonk. The part of the line from the British Columbia – Alberta boundary line westwards was built under the direction of CPR engineer James Ross. This section included the difficult western slope of the Kicking Horse Pass, where steeper gradients than normally permitted were used. This was the so-called "Big Hill" down to Field, British Columbia.

The two construction parties finally met at Craigellachie on 7 November 1885, and the main line to the Pacific was a reality.

Map 292, below, was produced by the Canadian Pacific Railway in 1893, just eight years after the completion of the main line to the coast. It shows the branch lines built in that time, plus lake steamer routes, and proposals for further railway construction.

One of the incentives the CPR was offered to build the main line to the Pacific coast was a huge grant of land either side of the right-of-way. Map 293, page 177, shows the surveys of these lands along the rail route.

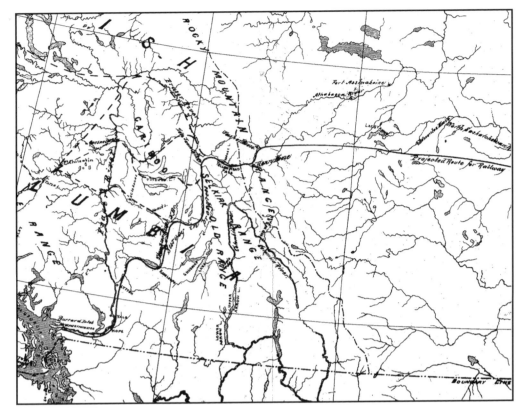

Map 291 (above)

Map to Accompany Progress Report on Surveys Canadian Pacific Railway April 10th 1872 Sandford Fleming, Engineer in Chief. Routes drawn by hand on printed map, 1872.

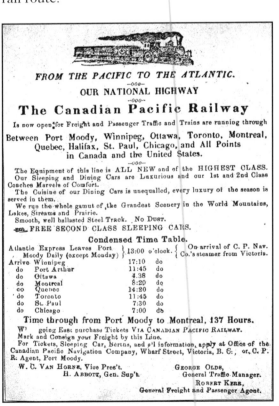

A Canadian Pacific advertisement and timetable, 1886.

Map 292 (right)

Map of the Canadian Pacific Railway showing the route (indicated by lines in red) followed by Early Fur Traders, from the Pacific Coast to the interior of New Caledonia and to the Hudson Bay and to Montreal; also the route taken by the Explorer, Sir Alexander Mackenzie, as he went toward the Pacific Coast from Athabasca, in 1793 1893.

Map 293

Map of the lands comprised within the Railway Belt, British Columbia as defined by the terms of union. c1895.

The Railway Belt was a strip of land about 32 km (20 miles) wide on each side of the rail line. The land shown in this map was given to the Canadian government by the new Province of British Columbia as part of the terms by which B.C. joined the Dominion. From these, the Canadian government was to grant lands to the CPR as one of the terms of its agreement with the CPR to build the rail line to the Pacific, signed in 1880 and ratified by the Canadian Parliament in 1881. The total land grant to the CPR was huge, amounting to 100 000 square km (39,000 square miles) of western Canada. The railway was allowed to select the land it wanted, and naturally it preferred to select land from the prairies that had more potential for farming, and thus settlement. No land was selected from the mountainous area of British Columbia. Lands not granted in British Columbia were returned to the Province in 1930.

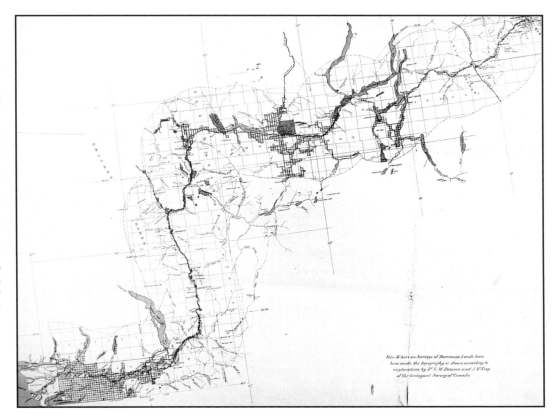

Sir Sandford Fleming on a Canadian stamp.

Map 294 (below)

Map showing the Canadian Pacific Routes in British Columbia, 1879.

In fact, this map shows *proposed* routes, reaching the Pacific in three places: at the site of today's Vancouver; a location near Prince Rupert; and Bute Inlet.

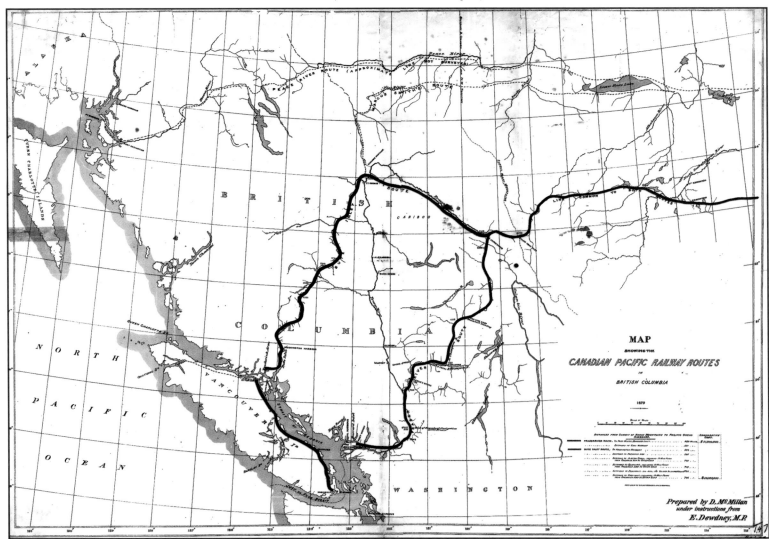

AMOR DE COSMOS AND
THE CASE FOR A VICTORIA TERMINUS

When it became clear to the British Columbia government that the Canadian Pacific Railway was to terminate on the mainland at Port Moody, it tried to interest them in building a rail line on Vancouver Island.

An elaborate argument and map was published in 1881 by Amor de Cosmos, a former British Columbia premier (1872–1874) to try to persuade the CPR that Victoria was strategically the better terminus for the transcontinental railway (Map 295, below).

The argument was that the Northern Pacific could establish a terminus which would be more convenient and less costly for inbound ships than Port Moody. The map showed a proposed extension of the CPR line from Port Moody to English Bay, and a connection by "Steam Railway Ferry" to Nanaimo. However, the CPR was not interested in de Cosmos' argument.

Since the CPR could not be persuaded to build a line on Vancouver Island, the B.C. government turned to a private syndicate led by Robert Dunsmuir, who had extensive coal mines in the Nanaimo area (Map 238, page 141), and thus had a vested interest in such a line to transport his coal to the Victoria market. The Esquimalt and Nanaimo Railway was completed in 1886, the same year the CPR completed the transcontinental line to tidewater at Port Moody.

Amor de Cosmos retired from politics in 1882, having been rejected by the voters for advocating Canadian independence. Ironically for de Cosmos, the extension of the rail line to English Bay, in Kitsilano, as he had advocated, was built, and a rail ferry to Nanaimo was also inaugurated.

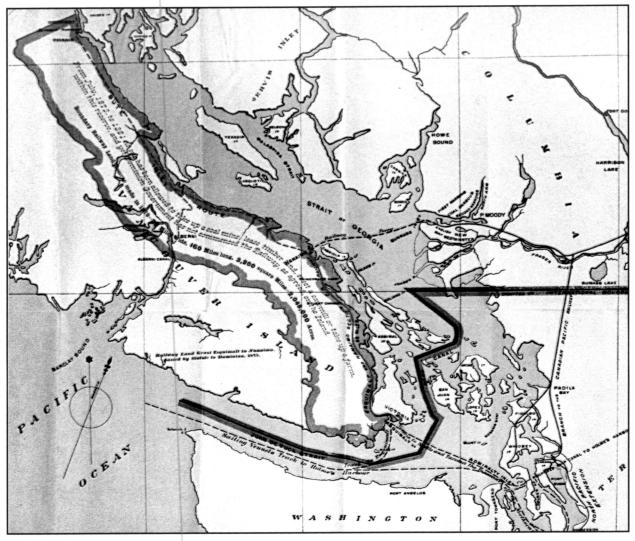

Amor de Cosmos' map was accompanied by an explanatory broadsheet.

"*This Map is intended to show that Port Moody is not the proper place for the Western Terminus of the Canadian Pacific Railway,*" it was headed.

His argument was that sailing ships required expensive tugs to get to Nanaimo or Vancouver, and that the Northern Pacific might build a new alternative port at "Holme's Harbor."

"*It is apparent, therefore, that a serious mistake has been made in selecting Port Moody as the Syndicate Terminus of the Canadian Pacific Railway.*

To remedy the mistake, it is necessary to extend the Railway from Port Moody to English Bay, which has excellent anchorage; then connect it with Nanaimo by a Steam Railway Ferry, and construct and operate the Esquimalt-Nanaimo section of the Canadian Pacific as part of the main trans-Continental line. Thus, expensive towage would be rendered wholly unnecessary, dangerous navigation, entailing extra rates of insurance, avoided, and the Northern Pacific prevented from building up a great commercial city, largely at the expense of Canada."

Map 295
Plan Showing Canadian Pacific Railway Terminus at Port Moody, and Railway Ferry between English Bay and Nanaimo; the Esquimalt Nanaimo section of the Pacific Railway; the extension of Northern Pacific from Tacoma to Seattle and to a terminus at Holme's Harbour opposite Port Townsend, and a branch connecting it with the Canadian Pacific Railway.
Compiled from Admiralty Chart by Henry A. Gray, Civil Engineer for A. De Cosmos Esqe. MP. (with memorandum and explanation) 1881
The proposals for a port at "Holmes Harbour" which de Cosmos thought the Northern Pacific Railway would build to compete against Vancouver, B.C., were nothing more than his suppositions; the Northern Pacific did no such thing. His proposals for a railway ferry from Vancouver to Nanaimo, however, were implemented by the CPR. The area of Vancouver Island outlined in red was a reserve for the CPR; de Cosmos' point was that new economic activity was excluded in this zone and yet the Canadian Government had not started to build the promised rail line.

THE CPR AND THE FOUNDING OF VANCOUVER

The Canadian Pacific Railway was completed to tidewater, at Port Moody, in late 1885, and the first scheduled passenger train from Montreal arrived on 4 July 1886. The following year the line was extended to the shores of Coal Harbour, and the first through passenger train from Montreal arrived in Vancouver on 23 May 1887. The announcement that the settlement of Granville was to be the western terminus of the CPR resulted in explosive growth. Population grew from a few hundred to 10,000 by the end of 1889, despite a fire which destroyed most of the new city in June 1886.

In return for the relocation of its terminal, the CPR acquired a huge area of land around the townsite, some 2550 hectares (6,000 acres). To create industry

CPR Engine No. 378, one of the first in service to the west coast.

to feed its freight service, the railway leased lands along the north shore of False Creek to industry at low rates and constructed a branch line to the area.

Map 296 shows the Canadian Pacific townsite in 1887. Although the city looks built up, the map is misleading in that it shows platted lots rather than actual buildings. False Creek is shown penetrating deep into the city; it was not until about 1914 that the eastern part of False Creek was filled in to provide railway yards and stations for the Canadian Northern

Pacific, in 1915, and Great Northern, in 1917. The CPR line runs through the city to English Bay, today's Kitsilano. At this point is the notation *"2909 $^7/_{13}$ miles from Montreal"*. The map also has an inset which shows an index plan. On it, the laying out of lots from New Westminster towards the north west can clearly be seen; this was the development pattern which occurred before the coming of the CPR, after the establishment of New Westminster in 1859.

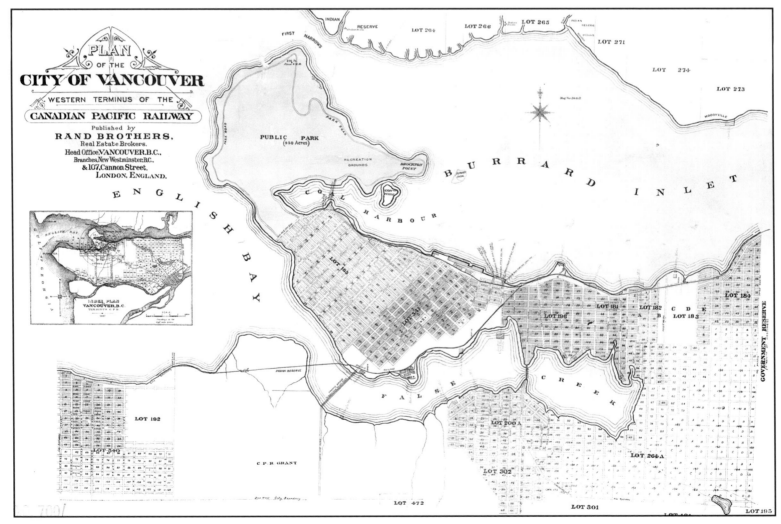

Map 296
Plan of the City of Vancouver Western Terminus of the Canadian Pacific Railway. Published by Rand Brothers. 1887
Inset: *Index Plan of Vancouver B.C. Terminus CPR 1887.*

False Creek extends considerably further eastwards than it does today. It was not until 1914 that the eastern section was filled in to make room for the Canadian Northern Railway station and yards, which could not otherwise find land close to Vancouver that was not already owned by its rival, the CPR.

THE CPR EXPANDS IN THE INTERIOR OF BRITISH COLUMBIA

From about 1888 onwards, deposits of silver, copper and lead were discovered in the southeastern part of British Columbia. This led to the construction of several local railways to move ore from the mines to the many lakes in the region and to the Columbia River.

Most of these lines were purchased by the CPR, in no small measure because of the fear that they would otherwise be used by the Great Northern to gain entry into Canada. The CPR also decided that it should build an east-west line to cut off American incursions and connect with a line through the Crowsnest Pass, where coal had been discovered.

Map 297 shows the CPR network of existing lines (solid), lake steamer routes (dashed), and projected lines (dashed, south of the lakes) in 1897. The terrain of the Kootenays made a system of combined rail lines and steamer routes the most practicable.

Mining or smelter towns that were established at this time include Rossland, Trail, Greenwood, and Nelson, all shown on this map.

In the Okanagan Valley, Vernon, Kelowna, and Penticton are shown, the latter two having been laid out as townsites in 1892, though a post office at Penticton was established in 1889; Vernon dates from two years earlier. On the CPR mainline, Revelstoke and Golden are shown, both settlements created by the railway.

Also shown on the main line, just north of Sicamous Junction, is Craigellachie, the place where the "last spike" was driven in the transcontinental railway on 7 November 1885.

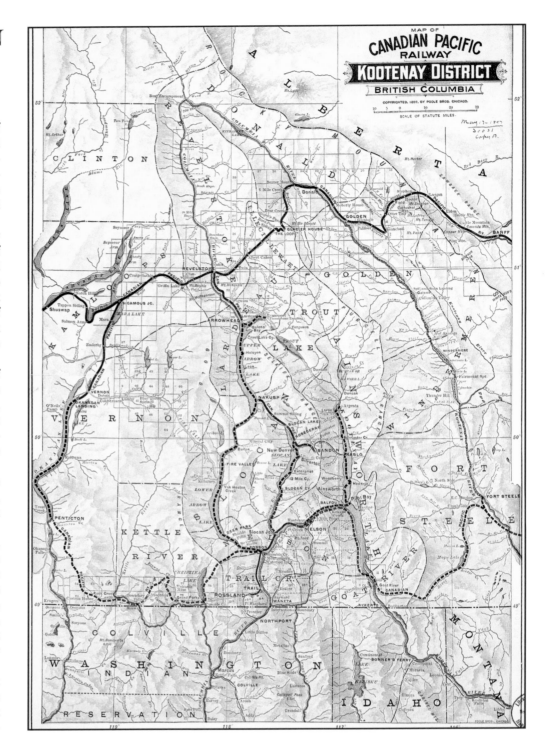

Map 297
Map of Canadian Pacific Railway Kootenay District British Columbia
Poole Brothers, Chicago, 1897

This rather beautiful topographic relief map extends into Washington and the extreme northwestern tip of Montana. It shows the network of rail lines and lake steamer routes established by the CPR to service this mountainous region.

A Canadian Pacific Railway train is met by SS *Nakusp* in the mid-1890s at Robson, on Lower Arrow lake, near today's Castlegar.
The SS *Nakusp* was a sternwheeler which entered service on the Lower Arrow Lake in 1894. It was very luxurious for its time, with electric lights, chandeliers in the dining room, steam heat, and hot and cold running water.

BIRD'S-EYE MAPS

Map 298 (below, top)
Bird's Eye View of the City of Seattle, W.T. Puget Sound. County Seat of King County 1884. J.J. Stoner, Madison, Wis. 1884.
The economic activity shown in this fine view of Seattle was perhaps nearer to the truth than in many bird's-eye maps of the period.

Map 299 (below, bottom)
Fairhaven: A Bird's-Eye View of the City and Harbor. 1890.
This fine panoramic view of today's Bellingham shows the city of Fairhaven in the foreground, and New Whatcom in the background, right. The view shows classically overdone economic activity.

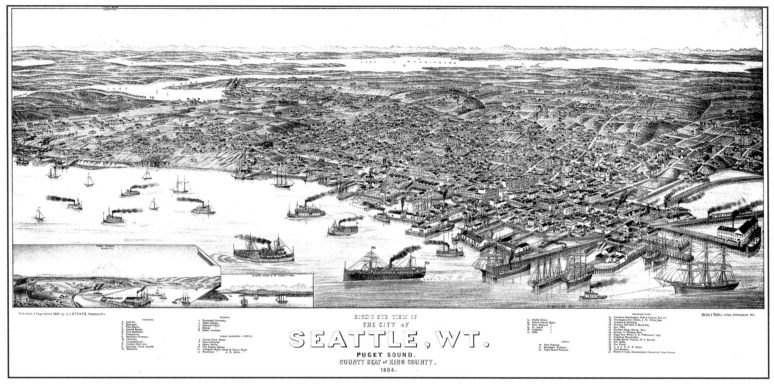

A popular cartographic form in the late nineteenth century was the panoramic map or bird's-eye view. These maps were not usually drawn to scale, but show street patterns, individual buildings, and landscape features in perspective.

They were often true works of art. Their preparation certainly involved a great deal of painstaking work.

First a framework of streets, in perspective, had to be prepared, and then the artist walked the streets, sketching trees, buildings and other features as though seen from an elevation of 600 to 900 metres (2,000 to 3,000 feet). No mean task with no means of actually looking at the scene from above! These sketches were then added to the framework of streets piece by piece.

Most panoramic maps were published individually, much like art prints might be today, rather than in atlases or books. They were often used for promotion by real estate companies or city fathers,

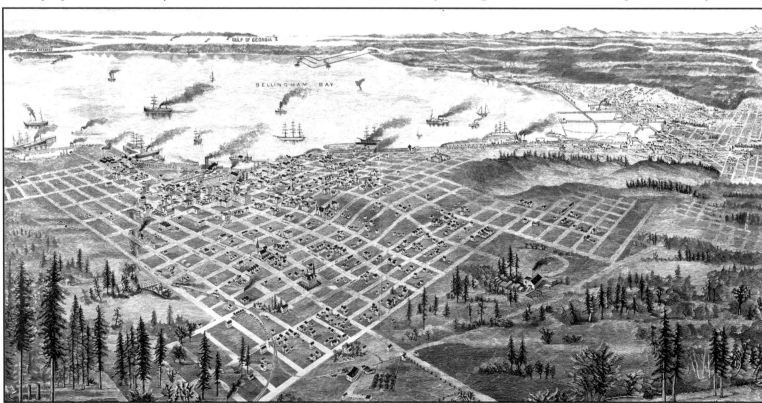

Map 300 (above)
Birds-Eye View of the Puget Sound Country An Accurate Perspective Projection, showing the Topography, Resources and Development of Northwestern Washington and British Columbia. Charles H. Baker Co. 1891.

Map 301 (below)
Panoramic View of the City of Vancouver, British Columbia 1898 J.C. McLagan.
Printed by Toronto Lithographic Co. Published by the Vancouver World Printing and Publishing Co. Ltd.

chambers of commerce or other civic organizations trying to sell the benefits of settling in their community. And of course, for selling purposes, it was best if the city looked prosperous and full of trains and boats and industry even if the city was in truth sleepy or undeveloped or even a dream, so most maps show cities bustling with activity.

Examples of panoramic or bird's-eye maps from the Pacific Northwest are shown here: Map 298 is of Seattle, Map 299 of Bellingham. Map 300 is of Puget Sound, in an unusual larger regional view taking in the entire area from Olympia to Vancouver, B.C. Quite an artistic feat without any actual means of viewing the scene from the air! Also shown is a magnificent view of Vancouver in 1898 (Map 301). It shows a typically exaggerated number of ships in the harbor; note the CPR ship *Empress of India* just docking. The map also shows the extent of the water area of the eastern part of False Creek very clearly.

Other bird's eye maps in this atlas are:
Victoria in 1878 (Map 303, right)
Portland in 1881 (Map 213, page 128)
Portland in 1890 (Map 214, page 128)
Dawson, Yukon Territory, in 1903
(Map 309, page 186)

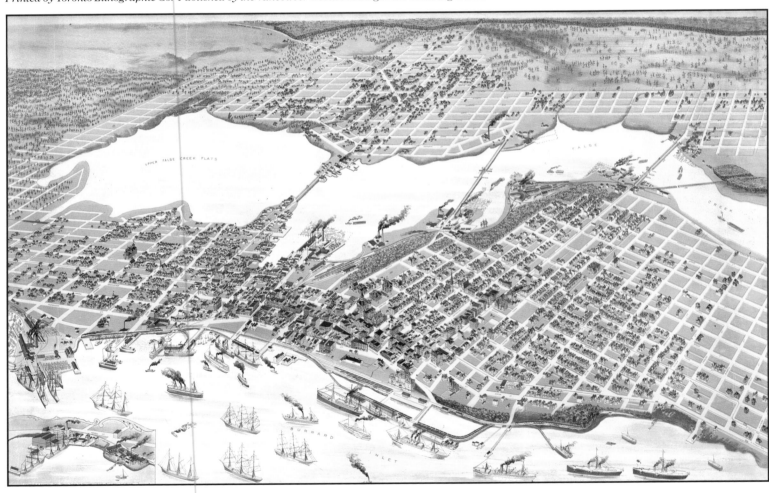

VICTORIA IN THE LATE NINETEENTH CENTURY

In 1871, Seattle had a population of 1,107 and Vancouver did not exist, but Victoria's population was 3,270. By 1911, the population of Seattle was 237,000, Vancouver had 100,000 persons, but Victoria only had 31,000.

In the intervening years, Victoria had changed from the primary urban center of the region to just another city. Its location on an island was primarily responsible. Once a strategic advantage, it was now a disadvantage to continued growth. New railroad schemes never got off the ground, and head offices moved to Vancouver. Tourism was thought of as a possible answer, and remains an important industry today.

Map 302 shows an early map aimed at tourists. It was a streetcar map published by B.C. Electric, which also built lines in Vancouver. Map 303 is a bird's-eye view of Victoria in 1878.

Map 302
Tourists & Visitors Guide to Victoria
Streetcar map, c1896. Electric streetcars arrived in Victoria in 1890, and Vancouver later the same year.

Front cover of Map 302. Not much different than today's tourist maps!

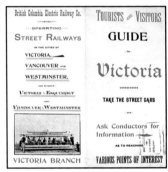

Map 303
Bird's-Eye View of Victoria, Vancouver Island, B.C. 1878 Drawn by E.S. Glover

GOLD RUSH TO THE KLONDIKE

Gold had been found in Alaska and the Yukon as early as 1804, when Aleksandr Baranov, the Russian manager of the Russian-American Company at Sitka, reportedly saw a hunter pull gold nuggets from his pockets. Baranov kept the incident quiet, fearing a gold rush by the British. But there was gold to be found.

Only the remoteness of the region explains why it took so long for a discovery to be made known to the world.

Gold seekers found gold on the Klondike River, a tributary of the Yukon River, in 1897, in apparently large quantities, and the rush was on.

Map 305 (below)
Map Showing the Two Routes to Dawson City.
Front page of *San Francisco Examiner,* Wednesday morning, 21 July 1897

Map 304 (above)
Map Showing the Yukon Country, With Klondike and Bonanza Creeks, Where the Recent Rich Discoveries Have Been Made. The Overland Route from Seattle, by Dyea, Chilkoot Pass, the Lakes and River, is Shown, as Well as the Outside Route by Way of Bering Sea, St. Michaels, and the Yukon River. The Dotted Line Shows the International Boundary.
Front Page of *Seattle Post-Intelligencer,* Saturday morning, 17 July 1897.

The front page of the newspaper, which included a hurriedly prepared map of Alaska and the Yukon, is shown here (Map 304). The sixty-eight passengers returning from the Klondike had a total of $700,000 worth of gold aboard. About the same time, the news hit San Francisco (Map 305).

Over the next year and a half, 100,000 gold seekers were to stampede to the Klondike. All required maps.

The first gold reached Seattle in July. *"At 3 o'clock this morning the Steamer Portland from St Michaels for Seattle, passed up [Puget] Sound with more than a ton of gold aboard..."* reported the *Seattle Post-Intelligencer* on 17 July 1897.

Anatomy of a Gold Rush
100 000 people set out for the Klondike from around the world
40 000 reached Dawson City
20 000 stayed to search for gold
4 000 found gold
300 found enough gold to be considered rich
50 managed to keep their new wealth[184]

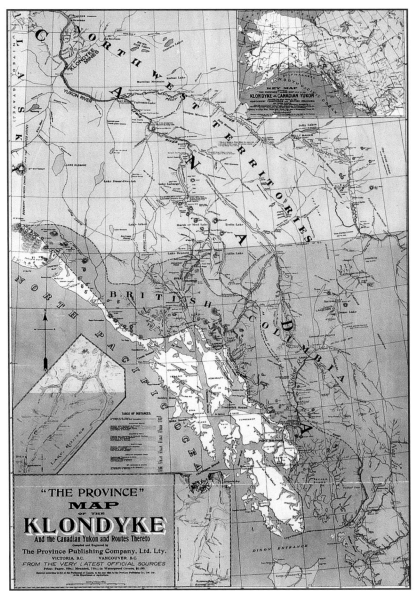

Map 306 (above)
"The Province" Map of the Klondyke and the Canadian Yukon and Routes Thereto
1897. Gold all over! Not-so-subliminal advertising.

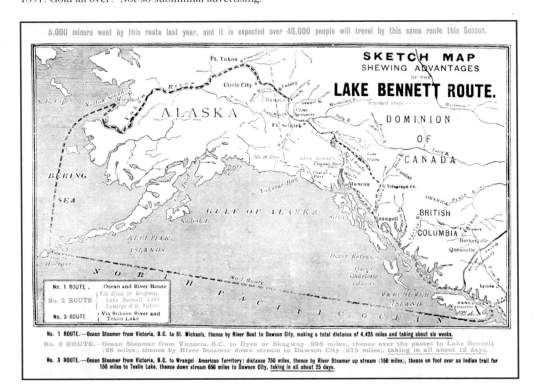

The Canadians, remembering how un-controlled influxes of Americans could lead to territorial challenges, dispatched a contingent of the North West Mounted Police to the Klondike to keep order, which they did relatively effectively considering the conditions.

Of the several routes to the Klondike, the most popular was by sea to Skagway and then over White Pass or Chilkoot Pass to Lake Bennett and the headwaters of the Yukon River. The passes were so steep that the gold seekers had to backpack their supplies themselves, and so many supplies were needed to survive in the interior that each person had to make twenty or more trips up the pass. The North West Mounted Police, stationed at the summit, enforced this; everyone had to have at least 520 kg (1,150 pounds) of solid food. This was in addition to tents, cooking utensils, and, of course, their gold mining equipment. The necessity of these multiple trips over the passes added some 950 km (600 miles) to the journey, a fact which was conveniently not noted on maps espousing this route.

Map 307 is such a map. Showing three possible routes, the Lake Bennett route is stated as taking only twelve days in total, when in fact it took at least six or seven weeks. The other routes shown were to St Michaels (now St Michael), north of the mouth of the Yukon River, where the change to a river steamer took place, and then up the Yukon to Dawson City, the site of the gold finds; and up the Stikine River and overland to Teslin Lake and River and the Yukon River. The map, like all gold rush maps, gives absolutely no indication of the hardships the gold seekers were likely to face on any of these routes.

The starting point for all the routes shown on this map is Victoria, B.C., so the map likely originated with merchants in Victoria who, of course, had a vested interest in supplying the miners with all their requirements.

Another map (Map 308, overleaf) likewise originated with Vancouver, B.C., commercial interests. To look at this map, one would think that Vancouver was the only starting point, when in fact it was Seattle that received the bulk of the Klondike trade. This map optimistically seeks to show Vancouver as the center for gold fields by adding the "Cariboo Mines," "Omineca Mines," and "Cassiar Mines" to the map, even those these fields had seen their producing days long gone by 1897.

Map 307
Sketch Map Shewing Advantages of the Lake Bennett Route. 1897.

Publishers rushed books, pamphets, and maps into print to capitalize on the public desire for knowledge and the gold seekers desire for information on how to get to the goldfields.

Many maps of the Klondike were printed in yellow or orange to subliminally suggest gold. The Province Publishing Company map (Map 306, previous page) was a good example. One of the first maps produced for gold seekers, it went through three editions in less than a year and sold over 100,000 copies.

The new Dawson City, which grew up on the site of the gold discoveries, struggled to survive in the aftermath of the gold rush. Map 309 is a bird's-eye view which portrays the city as well established and bustling with activity. It was an optimistic view designed to try to revive investor interest, which was quickly waning by the time this view was published, in 1903.

In fact, the Klondike gold rush had started to decline in 1898, when a few miners, waiting for the Yukon River to break up, found some gold in the vicinity of Nome, across Norton Sound from St Michaels, and for a short time set off a reverse gold rush from the Klondike to Nome.

Other gold finds were made along this coast, and continue to be made today. A map of the Nome, York, and Golofnin Bay gold areas is shown as an inset on Map 310, page 187.

The gold rush was a bonanza for map sellers too!

Map 308 (above)
Map of the Klondike, Cassiar and Cariboo Gold Fields Shewing Routes from Vancouver BC, the Base of Supplies. c1897.
A map produced by Vancouver interests to convince miners to outfit themselves in that city.

Map 309
Birdseye View of Dawson, Yukon Ter., 1903
M. Epting

This view of Dawson was published after the peak of the gold rush had past. It was an attempt to revive interest in the city.

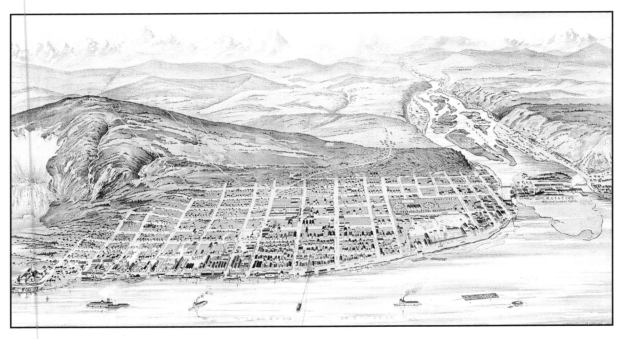

THE WHITE PASS AND YUKON RAILWAY

Demand from gold seekers for transportation to the Klondike soon led to the building of a railway. An "all-Canadian" route had been proposed and indeed contracted for on the Stikine River–Teslin Lake route, but this did not succeed. The successful railway was along the Lake Bennett route, the White Pass and Yukon. A 175 km (110 mile) narrow-gauge railway was built in two years between 1898 and 1900.

When it was complete, the Victoria *Colonist* reported:

It is no disparagement to other mountain railways to say that the construction of the White Pass and Yukon is among the most brilliant feats of railway engineering, in view of the tremendous difficulties to be encountered and the shortness of time in which the work was done.
(2 December 1900)

A map produced by the White Pass and Yukon Railway in 1919 shows that by that time the railway was trying to appeal to gold seekers all over Alaska, not just in the Klondike, as the gold rush there had diminished considerably after 1898 (Map 310).

An inset in this map shows the Nome, York, and Golofnin Bay gold region. The Nome goldfields, where gold was discovered on the beaches, caused a stampede out of Dawson once news reached that settlement.

Another map from the same White Pass and Yukon series shows the route of the railway in more detail (Map 311).

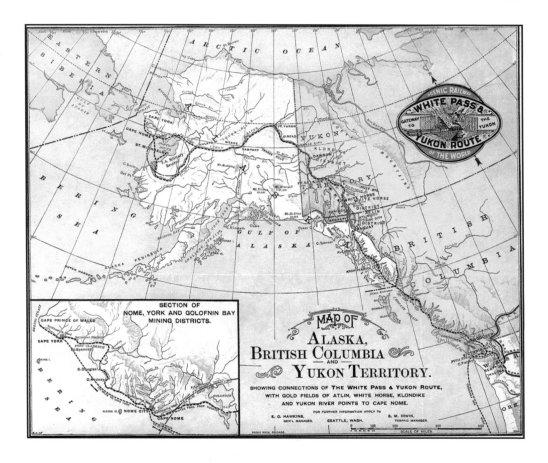

Map 310 (top)
Map of Alaska, British Columbia and Yukon Territory showing connections of the White Pass and Yukon Route with Gold Fields of Atlin, White Horse, Klondike and Yukon River points to Cape Nome
Inset: *Section of Nome, York and Golofnin Bay Mining Districts.*
Poole Brothers, Chicago, 1919

Map 311 (bottom)
Portions of Alaska, British Columbia and Yukon Territory reached by the White Pass and Yukon Route showing Atlin, White Horse, and other mining camps
Poole Brothers, Chicago, 1919

THE ALASKA BOUNDARY SETTLEMENT OF 1903

In 1825, the British and the Russians had come to an agreement as to the boundaries of their respective territories in the northwest part of North America (see page 108). Due to poor cartographic knowledge at that time, there were many ambiguities in the 1825 treaty.

When the United States purchased Alaska in 1867 (see page 168), it inherited the ambiguities; the area it had purchased was not defined exactly. During the latter part of the nineteenth century, there was some tension between Britain, and then Canada, and the United States over this issue, and several attempts were made to resolve it, without success.

In 1897, the influx of gold seekers during the Klondike gold rush brought the boundary problem to the fore again. In 1901, President Theodore Roosevelt, be-

coming president on the assassination of President William McKinley, made it clear that the only way the dispute could be settled was by arbitration with a tribunal made up of six legal experts, three from each side. This was thought to have little chance of success because decisions had to be made on the basis of a majority.

In January 1903, a convention was signed appointing the Alaska Boundary Tribunal, the first time ever that a boundary dispute was to be settled by a legal process in a quasi-court. The tribunal announced its decisions in October of that year.

One of the British judges had agreed with the Americans, and so the required majority was gained to give the Americans some of what they had claimed. The settlement appeared to divide the claims

more or less down the middle, but by excluding Canada from the inlets, it was in reality a decision perhaps more favorable to the United States. With this decision, which was met with disbelief in Canada, the final boundary in the Pacific Northwest was fixed.

Map 312, a 1898 Canadian Pacific Railway map showing the connections to the goldfields, illustrates the area of the Alaska panhandle which was in dispute.

Each side in this tribunal used copies of old maps to illustrate their cases, some of which are reproduced in this atlas; for example, Map 184, page 111, comes from the *British Case Alaska Boundary Atlas*. Map 313 (right) is a map produced for the American counter-claim.

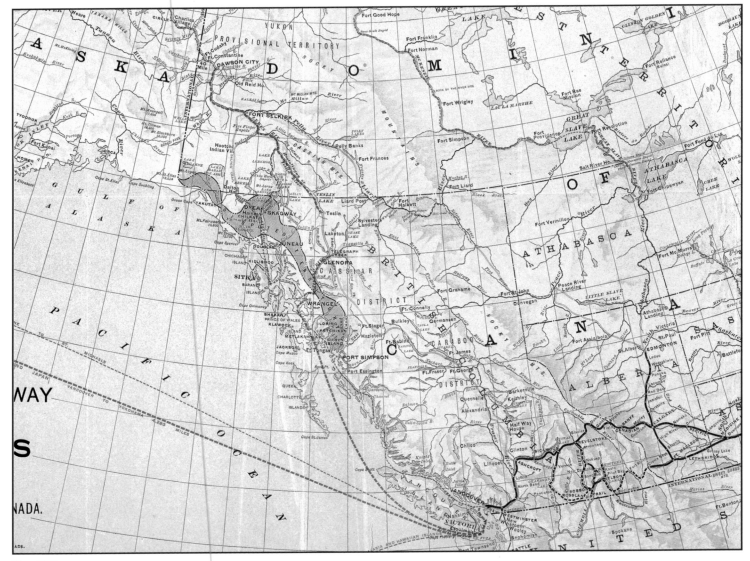

Map 312
Map of the Canadian Pacific Railway and Connections showing routes to the Yukon Gold Fields, Alaska, Klondike and the Northwestern Mining Territories of Canada. Poole Brothers, Chicago, 1898. The area of dispute is clearly marked.

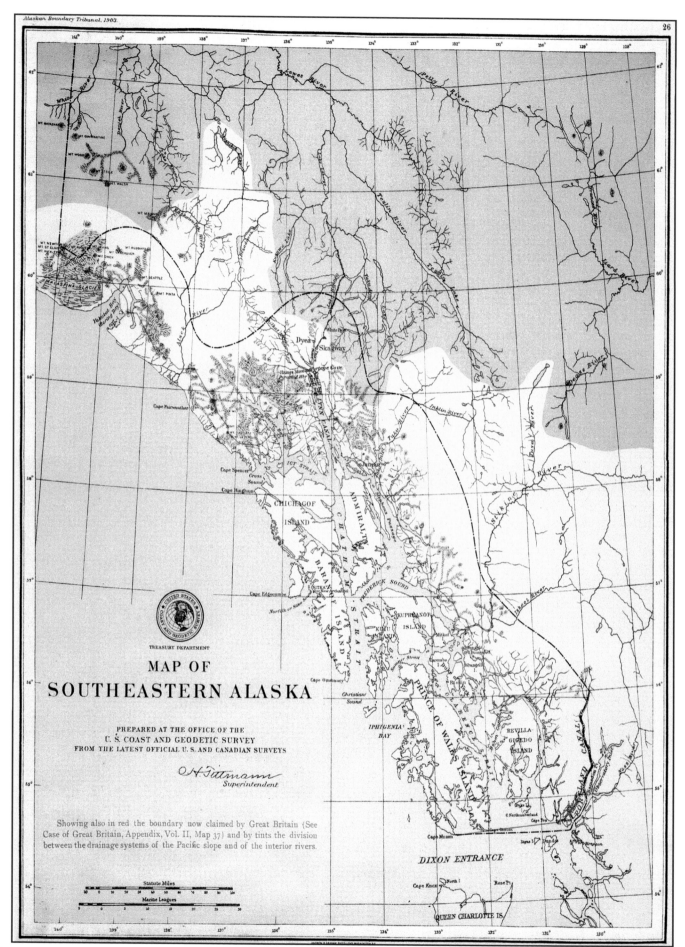

TREASURY DEPARTMENT

MAP OF
SOUTHEASTERN ALASKA

PREPARED AT THE OFFICE OF THE
U. S. COAST AND GEODETIC SURVEY
FROM THE LATEST OFFICIAL U. S. AND CANADIAN SURVEYS

H. Tittmann
Superintendent

Showing also in red the boundary now claimed by Great Britain (See
Case of Great Britain, Appendix, Vol. II, Map 37) and by tints the division
between the drainage systems of the Pacific slope and of the interior rivers.

Statute Miles

Marine Leagues

DIXON ENTRANCE

QUEEN CHARLOTTE IS.

Map 313
Map of Southeastern Alaska Prepared at the Office of the U.S. Coast and Geodetic Survey from the latest official U.S. and Canadian Surveys. Showing also in red
the boundary now claimed by Great Britain (See Case of Great Britain, Appendix, Vol. II, Map 37) and by tints the division between the drainage systems of the
Pacific Slope and of the interior rivers.
From: Alaska Boundary Tribunal, *Atlas accompanying the Counter Case of the United States before the Tribunal Convened at London under the Provisions of the*
Treaty between the United States of America and Great Britain, Concluded January 24th 1903. Washington DC 1903.

THE GRAND TRUNK PACIFIC AND THE NORTHERN ROUTE

A Grand Trunk Pacific passenger train ready to leave Prince Rupert for Winnipeg, 1915.

As the twentieth century began, the eastern based Grand Trunk Railway (GTR) came up with a scheme to build another transcontinental rail line to terminate at Port Simpson, at the entrance to the Portland Canal, at the boundary between British Columbia and Alaska. The route was to follow one of those surveyed by Sandford Fleming for the Canadian Pacific Railway (Map 290, page 175). The idea was to have a terminal which was nearer to Asia than Vancouver.

The Grand Trunk Pacific Railway was created as a subsidiary of the GTR, and the federal government became involved as a partner; the National Transcontinental Railway was to run from Moncton, New Brunswick to Port Simpson.

Construction started on the western division, from Winnipeg to Port Simpson, in 1905, and, after blasting away millions of tons of rock to create a roadbed, the Grand Trunk Pacific finally reached the Pacific terminal on April 9th 1914, thus becoming Canada's second transcontinental rail line.

It was not at Port Simpson, however. In 1906, a new terminal had been decided upon, which was named Prince Rupert, the winning entry in a contest held to select a name.

As a result of the 1903 Alaska boundary decision (page 188), Port Simpson was thought by Prime Minister Sir Wilfred Laurier to be too close to disputed territory, territory awarded to the United States due to the siding of one British member of the commission with the Americans, which led to a lot of Canadian resentment. President Theodore Roosevelt had indeed threatened to send an occupation force unless the Canadians ceased to clamor. The new site of Prince Rupert was in a more defensible location, in the lee of an island twenty miles north of the Skeena River.

Map 313 shows the rail line as it was in 1910, completed for some distance east from Prince Rupert, where construction had begun in 1908 to connect with that coming westwards.

This map also shows the Pacific Great Eastern as a projected line from Fort George, now Prince George, to Vancouver via Howe Sound. The PGE was a creation of the Grand Trunk Pacific designed to give the parent railway access to Vancouver. Two segments of the rail line were built from 1913 to 1915, but Howe Sound proved too difficult, and the PGE ran out of money. It operated as two disjointed lines in the 1920s, and the southern section was closed in 1928. It was not until 1956 that the two sections were finally joined and the line was complete to North Vancouver. Today it is the British Columbia Railway.

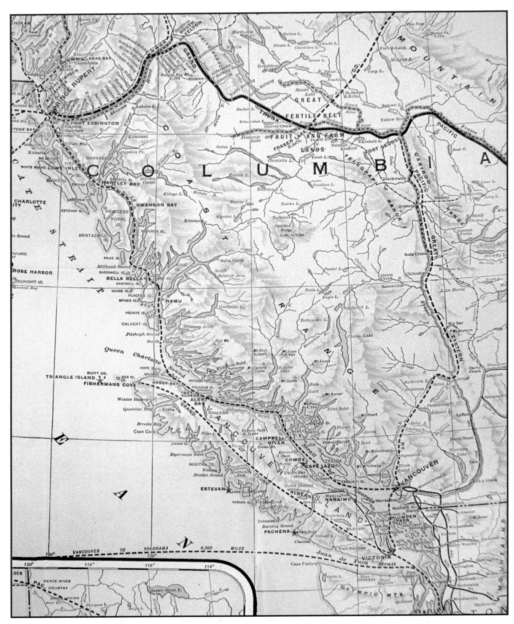

Map 314
Routes of Grand Trunk Pacific Steamships Pacific Coast Service
(with lines under construction and proposed, including Pacific Great Eastern) 1910

THE CANADIAN NORTHERN RAILWAY

Sir Donald Mann and Sir William Mackenzie were two successful contractors who had worked for the Canadian Pacific Railway who formed a partnership in the 1890s to acquire and build railroads in western Canada. In 1899, they amalgamated two railroads in Manitoba to form the Canadian Northern Railway Company. In 1909, they began to survey for a transcontinental rail line into British Columbia. Finding one of Sandford Fleming's tree-blaze markers, they followed his route quite closely, through the Yellowhead Pass and down the Thompson and Fraser Rivers (Map 290, page 175).

In Vancouver, the Canadian Pacific owned almost the entire waterfront. Mackenzie and Mann therefore purchased an area twelve miles up the Fraser from its mouth and announced that the Fraser was to be dredged to allow oceangoing ships to reach it. This was Port Mann, under what is now the Port Mann Bridge which carries the TransCanada Highway across the Fraser and into Vancouver.

However, they really needed access to Vancouver or they would be at a competitive disadvantage. Even the route of the Great Northern, which crossed the Fraser at New Westminster, made their path to the sea more difficult.

Mackenzie and Mann came up with a brilliant solution no one had thought of before. They offered to dam False Creek, thus recovering 66 hectares (164 acres), giving some to the city and keeping the rest for their station and yards. Thus the shape of the map of Vancouver was changed forever.

The last spike of the new transcontinental railway was driven on 23 January 1915, at Basque, British Columbia, almost a year after the Grand Trunk Pacific had reached Prince Rupert. It became, therefore, Canada's third transcontinental line.

Mackenzie and Mann were already thinking of a shorter route across the Rockies through the Crowsnest Pass, and

had embarked on its first leg, from Kamloops Junction to Kelowna. Map 315 shows the Canadian Northern Route in 1914, with the main line in operation to Vancouver, although through trains did not begin until the following year. The Kamloops to Kelowna line is shown under construction.

In 1918, after the First World War, the Canadian Northern was in poor economic condition, and was taken over by the Canadian government and amalgamated into the Canadian National Railway. It was followed a year later by the Grand Trunk Pacific.

A Canadian Northern train accelerates across a newly built wooden trestle bridge.

Map 315
Canadian Northern Railway in British Columbia 1914

The rail line is shown even though it was not completed until the following year.

NOTES TO TEXT

Numbers refer to the number in the text,
which is also the same as the page number

7   I am indebted to Professor William Lang of the Center for Columbia River History, Portland State University, for the point about global perspective.

11   R.P. Bishop, *Drake's Course in the North Pacific,* B. C. Historical Quarterly, 3, 1939.

15   Richard Hakluyt, *Principal Navigations...,* 1598–1600, 3 vols.

19   Jonathan Swift, *On Poetry, a Rhapsody,* Dublin, 1733.

22   Hubert Howe Bancroft, *History of Alaska 1730 – 1885,* 1886.

37   Translations are from Beals, Herbert K., *For Honor and Country,* 1985.

38   From Hezeta's diary, quoted in Beals, op. cit., page 86. Beals says "with this statement, Hezeta has a reasonably valid claim to being the European discoverer of the Columbia River."

39   Translations from Beals, op. cit.

42   James Cook's journal, 22 March 1778.

42/2   Instructions to Cook from the British Admiralty, dated 6 July 1776.

43   Cook's journal, 3 September 1778.

43/2   Cook's journal, 19 October 1778.

44   Cook's journal, 19 October 1778.

49   Instructions to Cook from the British Admiralty, dated 6 July 1776.

49/2   Letter from Sir James Harris to Lord Sandwich, 7/18 January 1780; quoted in Beaglehole, *Journals of Captain James Cook,* 1967, part 2, page 1553.

52   Translations from the Russian taken from Lydia Black, *The Lovtsov Atlas of the North Pacific Ocean,* 1990, University of Alaska.

57   George Dixon, *A Voyage Around the World,* London, 1789.

61   The international date line was not established by any law, but was the corollary to the establishment of a prime meridian (0°) passing through Greenwich, England, and an agreement to count degrees both east and west of that line. The prime meridian was established by an international conference in Washington, D.C., in 1884, and slowly adopted by most countries of the world.

62   Transcript of Frances Barkley's diary by Captain John T. Walbran. The original is thought to have been lost in a fire in 1909.

67   Henry R. Wagner, 1933, foreword, *Spanish Explorations in the Strait of Juan de Fuca.*

68   Warren Cook, *Flood Tide of Empire: Spain and the Pacific Northwest 1543 – 1819,* Yale University Press, 1973.

72   Francisco de Eliza, *Extracto de la navegacíon,* 1791, translated in Wagner, 1933/1971, page 152.

73   Dionisio Galiano and Cayetano Valdes, *Extracto del diarío de la campana ejecutada por las goletas Sutil y Mexicana,* Monterey, 21 October, 1792; Quoted in Wagner, 1933/1971, page 216.

76   Named "The Duke of Clarence's Strait" by George Vancouver in September 1793.

85   Vancouver's instructions, of 11 February 1791, are preserved in the Public Record Office, London, PRO CO 5/187.

85/2   See George Vancouver, *A Voyage of Discovery...,* 1798, Hakluyt Society edition, 1984, Appendix 4, page 1612.

86   George Vancouver, op. cit., page 580.

87   George Vancouver, op. cit., page 592.

88   Edward Bell, Journal, quoted in George Vancouver, op. cit., page 112.

91   William Watson Woollen, *The Inside Passage to Alaska, 1792 – 1920, with an Account of the North Pacific Coast from Cape Mendocino to Cook Inlet...,* 1924.

95   This is the location of Mackenzie Rock, now in Sir Alexander Mackenzie Provincial Park, east of Elcho Point, Dean Channel. The location was found by Captain R.P. Bishop, a surveyor, in 1923; he would later calculate Francis Drake's course in the Pacific Ocean (page 11 and footnote 11).

97   Jefferson had been interested in the idea of a route to the Pacific coast since 1782 or 1783. He helped organize an expedition in 1793 by botanist Andre Michaux "to find the shortest and most convenient route of communication between the U.S. and the Pacific Ocean."

97/2   Quoted in E.W. Gilbert, *The Exploration of Western America 1800 – 1850,* 1933, reprinted 1966, page 106.

99   Samuel Lewis was not related to Meriwether Lewis.

99/2   Even the Cascades had been considered to be part of the Rockies by some geographers at this time, and it seems likely that Thomas Jefferson believed it.

99/3   Elliott Coues, *History of the Lewis and Clark Expedition,* page 421.

100   Quoted in Elliott Coues, op. cit., page 930.

103   James Ronda, *Astoria and Empire,* 1990.

104   Richard Glover (ed.), *David Thompson's Narrative 1784 – 1812,* 1962, page 358.

112   The quote is from Archibald McDonald, *Journal of the voyage from Fort Vancouver to Fraser's River and of the establishment of Fort Langley* (1827), but this part was probably written by James McMillan.

113   Fort Langley was moved upriver in 1839, to a site nearer the company farm.

134   Letters written 4 November 1846 and 19 April 1847 to Dr. W.F. Tolmie; *BC Archives Report,* 1913, v, pages 82–85, quoted in W. N. Sage, *Sir James Douglas and British Columbia,* 1930, page 139.

157   Matthew Macfie, *Vancouver Island and British Columbia Their History, Resources and Prospects.* Longman et al, London, 1865.

157/2   This photo was taken by Richard Maynard, who had come to British Columbia to look for gold in 1859. With his wife, he set up a photography business in Victoria, and took many historical photographs. BCARS A-3330

161   Public Record Office, London FO 5/810.

164   James Douglas, *Copy of Despatch from Governor Douglas...,* 1861.

171   David Hunter Miller, *San Juan Archipelago: Study of the Joint Occupation of San Juan Island,* 1943.

172   George Edward Pickett was the Confederate general who led a disastrous charge during the battle of Gettysburg, in the American Civil War, in July 1863.

184   Information from Klondike Gold Rush National Historical Park, Seattle Unit, U.S. National Park Service, web site http://www.nps.gov/klse/klse_vvc.htm

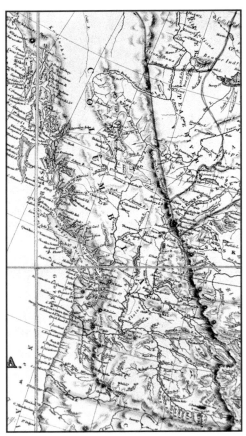

Map 316
British North America by permission dedicated to the Honble Hudson's Bay Company containing the latest information which these documents furnish. By their obedient servant J. Arrowsmith. London. Pub^d 15 Feb^r 1832 by J. Arrowsmith
This is a hand-colored version of the 1832 John Arrowsmith map illustrated on page 114 (Map189), with more of the northwest coast shown.

Select Bibliography

While it was the intention in this atlas to present historical maps together with their background, it was not intended to even attempt to be a comprehensive history of the Pacific Northwest. The following list of books includes both some original sources referred to in the notes, and modern comprehensive overviews that may be of interest to anyone seeking to learn more.

It is recommended that this atlas be read in conjunction with good modern maps such as can be found in the De Lorme series of state atlases for Alaska, Washington, and Oregon; and the *British Columbia Recreational Atlas.*

Allen, John Logan
Lewis and Clark and the Image of the American Northwest. Dover, Mineola, NY, 1991. (Originally publ. as *Passage Through the Garden: Lewis and Clark and the Image of the American Northwest,* University of Illinois Press, Urbana, 1975.)

Bancroft, Hubert Howe
History of the Northwest Coast
Bancroft & Co., San Francisco, 1884

Bancroft, Hubert Howe
History of Alaska 1730 – 1885
Bancroft & Co., San Francisco, 1886

Barkan, Frances B. (Ed.)
The Wilkes Expedition: Puget Sound and the Oregon Country. Washington State Capital Museum, Olympia, Washington, 1987.

Barratt, Glynn
Russia in Pacific Waters, 1715 – 1825
University of British Columbia Press, Vancouver, 1981

Beaglehole, John C. (Ed.)
The Journals of Captain James Cook on His Voyages of Discovery: The Voyage of the Resolution and the Discovery 1776-1780 Vol 3.
Hakluyt Society, Cambridge, 1967

Beaglehole, John C.
The Life of Captain James Cook
Hakluyt Society, London, 1974

Beals, Herbert K.
(Translation and Annotation) *Juan Pérez on the Northwest Coast. Six Documents of His Expedition in 1774*
Oregon Historical Society Press, Portland, 1989

Beals, Herbert K.
(Translation and annotation) *For Honor and Country The Diary of Bruno De Hezeta*
Western Imprints The Press of the Oregon Historical Society, Portland, 1985

Bishop, R.P., Captain.
Drake's Course in the North Pacific
British Columbia Historical Quarterly 3, 1939

Black, Lydia
The Lovtsov Atlas of the North Pacific Ocean by Vasilii Fedorovich Lovtsov. Translation with an introduction by Lydia Black. Limestone Press, Kingston Ontario, 1991.

Carey, Charles H.
General History of Oregon. Binfords and Mort, Portland, 1971 (Originally published in 1922).

Carver, J.
Travels Through the Interior Parts of North America in the Years 1766,1767, and 1768
Walter and Crowder, London, 1778

Cook, Warren L.
Flood Tide of Empire Spain and the Pacific Northwest, 1543 – 1819
Yale University Press, New Haven, 1973

Coues, Elliot (Ed.)
The History of the Lewis and Clark Expedition
Meriwether Lewis and William Clark
Dover, New York, 3 vols., no date. Originally published Francis P. Harper, 4 vols., 1893.

Cutright, Paul Russell
A History of the Lewis and Clark Journals
University of Oklahoma Press, Norman, 1976

Cutter, Donald C.
Malaspina and Galiano: Spanish Voyages to the North-west Coast, 1791 and 1792
Douglas and McIntyre, Vancouver, 1991

Dixon, George
A Voyage Around the World but More Particularly to the North West Coast of America
G. Goulding, London, 1789

Divin, Vasilii A.
The Great Russian Navigator, A. I. Chirikov
Translated and annotated by Raymond H. Fisher
University of Alaska Press, Fairbanks, 1993

Dmytryshyn, Basil, and Crownhart-Vaughan, E.A.P. (translation and notes)
Colonial Russian America: Kyrill T. Khlebnikov's Reports 1817 – 1832
Oregon Historical Society, Portland, 1976

Dodds, Gordon B.
The American Northwest: A History of Oregon and Washington. The Forum Press, Arlington Heights, Illinois, 1986.

Douglas, James
Copy of Despatch from Governor Douglas, C.B. to his Grace the Duke of Newcastle. Papers Relating to British Columbia, Part IV, No 21, p. 54 – 56, 1861. BCARS NW 971K G786

Duncan, Dayton
Lewis and Clark: The Journey of the Corps of Discovery. Knopf, New York, 1997.

Efimov, A.V.
Atlas of Geographical Discoveries in Siberia and Northwestern America, Nauka, Moscow, 1964.

Falk, Marvin W.
Mapping Russian America
In: Russia in North America. Proceedings of 2nd International Conference on Russian America, Sitka, Alaska, 19 – 22 August 1987.

Fisher, Raymond H.
Bering's Voyages: Whither and Why
University of Washington Press, Seattle, 1977

Fisher, Raymond H.
The Voyage of Semen Deshnev in 1648: Bering's Precursor; with selected documents
Hakluyt Society, London, 1981

Fisher, Robin
Vancouver's Voyage:
Charting the Northwest Coast, 1791 – 1795
Douglas and McIntyre, Vancouver/University of Washington Press, Seattle, 1992

Fisher, Robin, and Johnston, Hugh (eds)
From Maps to Metaphors: The Pacific World of George Vancouver
UBC Press, Vancouver, 1993

Gilbert, E.W.
The Exploration of Western America 1800 – 1850
Cambridge University Press, 1933. Reprinted 1966, Cooper Square Publishers, New York.

Glover, Richard (Ed.)
David Thompson's Narrative 1784 – 1812
Champlain Society, Toronto, 1962

Goetzmann, William H.
Exploration and Empire
W.W. Norton and Company, New York, 1978

Goetzmann, William H. and Williams, Glyndwr
The Atlas of North American Exploration From the Norse Voyages to the Race to the Pole
Prentice Hall, New York, 1992

Golder, Frank A.
Russian Expansion in the Pacific, 1641 – 1850
Arthur H. Clark, Cleveland, 1914

Golovin, Pavel Nikolaevich
The End of Russian America
Captain P. N. Golovin's Last Report, 1862
Trans. and introduction, Basil Dmytryshyn and E. A. P. Crownhart-Vaughan, Oregon Historical Society, 1971

Goss, John
The Mapping of North America: Three Centuries of Map-making 1500 – 1860
Wellfleet Press, New Jersey, 1990

Gough, Barry M.
The Northwest Coast: British Navigation, Trade and Discoveries to 1812
UBC Press, Vancouver, 1992

Grant, Walter Colquhoun
Description of Vancouver Island. By its first Colonist. Journal of the Royal Geographical Society, pages 268 – 320, 1857

Gray, William Henry
A History of Oregon 1792 – 1849. 1870

Hayman, John (Ed.)
Robert Brown and the Vancouver Island Exploring Expedition. UBC Press, Vancouver, 1989.

Hebert, John R., and Dempsey, Patrick E.
Panoramic Maps of Cities in the United States and Canada
Library of Congress, Washington, 1984

Ingraham, Joseph
Journal of the Brigantine Hope on a Voyage to the Northwest Coast of North America 1790 – 92
Facsimile edition, edited/introduction: Mark D. Kaplanoff, Imprint Society, Barre, MA 1971 (Original in Library of Congress.)

Hill, Beth
Sappers: The Royal Engineers in British Columbia
Horsdal and Schubart, Ganges, B.C., 1987

Hopwood, Victor (Ed.)
Travels in Western North America 1784 – 1812, David Thompson. Macmillan, Toronto, 1971.

Hough, Richard
Captain James Cook: A Biography
Hodder and Stoughton, London, 1994

Howay, F.W.
British Columbia from the Earliest Times to the Present
Volume 2 of 4 volumes by E.O.S Scholefield and F.W. Howay, S.J. Clarke Publishing Co., Vancouver and Chicago, 1914.

Hussey, John A.
The History of Fort Vancouver and its Physical Structure
Washington State Historical Society, 1957

Kendrick, John
The Men with Wooden Feet:
The Spanish Exploration of the Pacific Northwest
NC Press, Toronto, 1986

Kendrick, John (trans and intro)
The Voyage of Sutil and Mexicana 1792:
The last Spanish exploration of the Northwest Coast of America
Arthur H. Clark Co., Spokane, Wa. 1991

Kohl, J.G.
History of Discovery and Exploration on the Coasts of the United States.
US Coast and Geodetic Survey, Washington DC 1885

Lamb, W. Kaye (Ed.)
The Journals and Letters of Sir Alexander Mackenzie
Macmillan, Toronto, and Cambridge University Press, London, 1970

Leonard, Frank
A Thousand Blunders: The Grand Trunk Pacific Railway and Northern British Columbia.
UBC Press, Vancouver, 1996

Lillard, Charles
Seven Shillings a Year:
The History of Vancouver Island.
Horsdal and Schubart, Ganges, B.C., 1986

Longenbaugh, Dee
From Anian to Alaschka:
The mapping of Alaska to 1778
Map Collector, No. 29, December 1984, p. 28

McArthur, Lewis A.
Oregon Geographic Names
Oregon Historical Society Press, Portland Sixth edition, 1992

McDonald, Archibald
Journal of the voyage from Fort Vancouver to Fraser's River and of the establishment of Fort Langley. Typescript manuscript, Special Collections, Vancouver Public Library, no date. (Only the part from 16 Oct 1828 is by McDonald, the author of the rest is unknown, but is probably James McMillan.)

McDonald, Norbert
Distant Neighbors: A Comparative History of Seattle and Vancouver
University of Nebraska Press, Lincoln, 1987

Mackenzie, Alexander
Voyages from Montreal on the River St. Laurence, through the Continent of North America to the Frozen and Pacific Oceans In the Years 1789 and 1793
Alexander Mackenzie, London, 1801

Mackie, Richard Somerset
Trading Beyond the Mountains:
The British Fur Trade on the Pacific 1793 – 1843
UBC Press, Vancouver, 1997

Mathes, W. Michael
Vizcaíno and Spanish Exploration in the Pacific Ocean, 1580 – 1630
California Historical Society, San Francisco, 1968

Meares, John
Voyages Made in the Years 1788 and 1789 from China to the North West Coast of America.
Logographic Press, London, 1790

Miller, David Hunter
San Juan Archipelago: Study of the Joint Occupation of San Juan Island
No imprint, 1943

Milton, William Fitzwilliam, Viscount
A History of the San Juan Water Boundary Question as affecting the division of territory between Great Britain and the United States
Cassell, Petter, Galpin, London & New York, 1869

Ministerio de Defensa, Museo Naval.
La Expedición Malaspina 1789 – 1794
2 Vols. Barcelona, 1987/1993

Minter, Roy
The White Pass: Gateway to the Klondike
McClelland and Stewart, Toronto, 1987

Mourelle, Francisco Antonio
(as translated by the Hon. Daines Barrington)
Voyage of the Sonora from the 1775 Journal.
From Daines Barrington, *Miscellanies,* 1781, reprinted by Thomas C. Russell, San Francisco 1920; also reprint of this edition by Ye Galleon Press, Fairfield, Washington, no date.

Müller, Gerhard Friedrich
Voyages from Asia to America, for Completing the Discoveries of the North West Coast of America
Trans. T. Jefferys, London, 1764

Müller, Gerhard Friedrich
Bering's Voyages: The Reports from Russia
Trans. of: *Nachricten von Seareisen,* St. Petersburg, 1758; with commentary by Carol Urness, University of Alaska Press, Fairbanks, 1986

Murray, Jeffrey S.
Going for Gold
In: *Mercator's World,* Vol. 2, No. 4, July/August 1997, page 37–42

Nisbet, Jack.
Sources of the River: Tracking David Thompson Across Western North America.
Sasquatch Books, Seattle, 1994

Nuffield, Edward W.
The Pacific Northwest: Its discovery and early exploration by sea, land, and river
Hancock House Publishers, Surrey and Blaine, 1990

Ormsby, Margaret A.
British Columbia: A History
Macmillan, Toronto, 1958

Pallas, Peter Simon
Neue nordische Beyträge 1781-3
Trans. by Masterson, James R. and Brower, Helen, in *Bering's Successors 1745-1780* University of Washington Press, Seattle, 1948

Pemberton, Joseph Despard
Facts and Figures Relating to Vancouver Island and British Columbia, showing what to expect and how to get there.
Longman, Green, Longman and Roberts, London, 1860

Pethick, Derek
Vancouver: The Pioneer Years 1774 – 1886
Sunfire Publications, Langley, B.C., 1984

Pethick, Derek
First Approaches to the Northwest Coast
J.J. Douglas, Vancouver, 1976

Pethick, Derek
The Nootka Connection: Europe and the Northwest Coast, 1790 – 1795
Douglas and McIntyre, Vancouver, 1980

Phillips, James W.
Washington State Place Names
University of Washington Press, Seattle, 1971

Portinaro, Pierluigi, and Knirsch, Franco
The Cartography of North America 1500 – 1800
Crescent Books, New York, 1987

Portlock, Nathaniel
A Voyage Around the World: But more particularly to the North West Coast of America
London, 1789

Richards, George Henry
Report to Governor James Douglas, 1861. Papers Relating to British Columbia, II, p.13, 1861.
British Columbia Archives NW 971K G786

Richards, George Henry
The Vancouver Island Pilot containing Sailing Directions for the Coasts of Vancouver Island; and part of British Columbia compiled from the Surveys made by Captain George Henry Richards RN in HM ships Plumper and Hecate, between the Years 1858 and 1864
Hydrographic Office, Admiralty, London, 1864

Ronda, James
Astoria and Empire
University of Nebraska, Lincoln, 1990

Ruggles, Richard
A Country so Interesting: The Hudson's Bay Company and Two Centuries of Mapping 1670 – 1870. McGill-Queens University, Montreal, 1991.

Sage, Walter N.
Sir James Douglas and British Columbia
University of Toronto Press, Toronto, 1930

Schwantes, Carlos Arnaldo
The Pacific Northwest: An Interpretive History
University of Nebraska Press, Lincoln, 1996

Schwantes, Carlos Arnaldo, et al.
Washington: Images of a State's Heritage
Melior Publications, Spokane, 1988

Schwartz, Seymour I., and Ehrenberg, Ralph E.
The Mapping of America
Harry N. Abrams Inc., New York, 1980

Sherry, Frank
Pacific Passions:
The European Struggle for Power in the Great Ocean in the Age of Exploration
William Morrow, New York, 1994

Stanley, George F.G. (Ed.)
Mapping the Frontier: Charles Wilson's Diary of the Survey of the 49th Parallel 1858 – 1862, while Secretary of the British Boundary Commission.
Macmillan, 1970

Stanton, William
The Great United States Exploring Expedition
University of California Press, Berkeley and Los Angeles, 1975

Strange, James
James Strange's Journal and Narrative of the Commercial Expedition from Bombay to the North-West Coast of America
Government Press, Madras, 1928

Stuart-Stubbs, B.
Maps Relating to Alexander Mackenzie.
A keepsake distributed at a meeting of the Bibliographical Society of Canada, Jasper Park, June 1968.

Svet, Yakov M., and Fedorova, Svetlana G.
Captain Cook and the Russians
Pacific Studies, Vol II, 1, Fall 1978, pages 1–19

Thrower, Norman J.W. (Ed.)
Sir Francis Drake and the Famous Voyage 1577 – 1580
University of California Press, 1984

Thwaites, Reuben Gold (Ed.)
Original Journals of the Lewis and Clark Expedition
8 vols. Dodd, Mead, New York, 1904
Also reprint: Arno Press, New York, 1969

Tompkins, S.R. and Moorhead, M.L.
Russia's Approach to America.
B.C. Historical Quarterly, XIII,
April, July and October 1949

Tooley, R.V.
Maps and Map-Makers
Seventh edition, Dorset Press, 1987

Tyrrell, J.B. (Ed.)
David Thompson: Narrative of his Explorations in Western North America, 1784 – 1812
Champlain Society, Toronto, 1916

United States, Department of State
Papers Relating to the Treaty of Washington
Six volumes. Government Printing Office, Washington DC, 1872 and 1874.

Vancouver, George
A Voyage of Discovery to the North Pacific Ocean and Round the World 1791–1795
4 Vols. Ed. W. Kaye Lamb, Hakluyt Society, London, 1984.
Also original edition, London, 1798.

Vaughan, Thomas, Crownhart-Vaughan, E.A.P., and Palau de Iglesias, Mercedes
Voyages of Enlightenment: Malaspina on the Northwest Coast 1791/1792
Oregon Historical Society, 1977

Verner, Coolie, and Stuart-Stubbs, Basil
The Northpart of America
Academic Press, Toronto, 1979

Wagner, Henry R.
Spanish Explorations in the Strait of Juan de Fuca
Santa Ana, 1933; reprinted AMS Press, New York, 1971

Wagner, Henry R.
Cartography of the Northwest Coast to the Year 1800
University of California Press, 1937

Wagner, Henry R.
Spanish Voyages to the Northwest Coast in the Sixteenth Century
California Historical Society, San Francisco, 1929

Walbran, John T., Captain
British Columbia Coast Names: Their Origin and History
Govt. Printing Bureau, Ottawa, 1909. Reprinted, Douglas and McIntyre, Vancouver, 1971.

Warhus, Mark
Another America: Native American Maps and the History of Our Land
St. Martin's Press, New York, 1997

Whitfield, Peter
The Image of the World: 20 Centuries of World Maps
Pomegranate Artbooks, San Francisco, and the British Library, 1994

Wilkes, Charles
Narrative of the United States Exploring Expedition During the Years 1838, 1839, 1840, 1841, 1842.
Lea and Blanchard, Philadelphia, 1845

Williams, Glyndwr
The British Search for the North West Passage in the Eighteenth Century
Longmans, Green, London, 1962

Wolff, Hans (editor)
America: Early Maps of the New World
Prestel, Munich, 1992

Wroth, Lawrence C.
The Early Cartography of the Pacific
In: *Bibliographical Society of America Papers*, Vol 38, No. 2 (June 1944) pp 87–268

Map 317
Sketch Map of Quadra and Vancouver's Island and the adjacent mainland coast.
Meriwether Lewis, c1803.

It is interesting that Meriwether Lewis should have prepared a map of the Pacific coast so far north of the objective of the Lewis and Clark Expedition, the Columbia River. The map has been copied from George Vancouver's published map of 1798. Complaining that Vancouver's work was both too costly and too heavy to carry, Lewis copied parts of the maps the book contained to assist with the compilation of a base map of the west incorporating all known information at the time, which was prepared by Nicholas King, a Philadelphia mapmaker, in 1803. This map was part of a collection belonging to William Clark's granddaughter rediscovered by Reuben Gold Thwaites in 1903. The map may have been carried with the Lewis and Clark Expedition or it may have simply come into Clark's possession afterwards, as he collected together information for the construction of his large map of 1810 (Map 165, page 99).

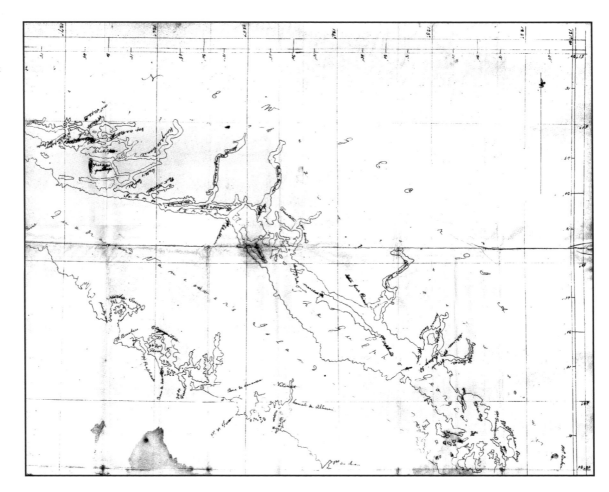

Map Sources

The maps in this atlas are reproductions of original hand-drawn or engraved and printed maps. They have been collected from archives and libraries all over the world. Sources are noted with the listing of each map in the Map Catalog which follows. The full addresses of these sources are given below. Where the source for a map or illustration is not noted it is from the author's collection or other private collections; in a few cases the maps are from secondary sources where the original sources are unknown. I apologise for any omissions. I am indebted to the librarians and archivists of these institutions for their assistance.

Source locations

American Geographical Society
The American Geographical Society Collection of the University of Wisconsin – Milwaukee Library
University of Wisconsin – Milwaukee
The Golda Meir Library, PO Box 399
Milwaukee, WI 53201

American Philosophical Society
American Philosophical Society Library
105 South South Fifth Street
Philadelphia, PA 19106-3386

Archivo General de Indias
Archivo General de Indias,
Avda de Constitucion s/n 41004
Sevilla, Espana (Spain)

Bancroft Library
The Bancroft Library
University of California
Berkeley, CA 94720-6000

Beinecke Library
The Beinecke Rare Book and Manuscript Library
Yale University, PO Box 208240
New Haven, CT 06520-82240

Bibliothèque nationale
Bibliothèque nationale de France,
58 rue de Richelieu,
75002 Paris, France

BCARS
British Columbia Archives and Records Service,
655 Belleville Street,
Victoria, BC V8V 1X4

British Library
The British Library,
96 Euston Road,
London NW1 2DE England

HBCA
Hudson's Bay Company Archives
Provincial Archives of Manitoba
200 Vaughan Street,
Winnipeg, Manitoba R3C 1T5

John Carter Brown Library
John Carter Brown Library
Brown University, Box 1894
Providence RI 02912

Library of Congress
Library of Congress
Geography and Map Division
James Madison Memorial Building
101 Independence Avenue SE
Washington, DC 20540

Museo Naval
Museo Naval, Paseo del Prado 5
ES – 28014, Madrid, Espana (Spain)

Map 318
Carta general de quanto asta hoy se ha descubierto y examinado por los Espanoles en la Costa Septentrional de California, formada...por D. Juan Francisco de la Bodega y Quadra Ano de 1791

This map is a detail from Map 121, page 74, and is a detailed summary of Spanish knowledge of the west coast of North America in 1791. This was the year before the final Spanish voyage of exploration, that of Dionisio Galiano and Cayetano Valdes, and that of George Vancouver, whose surveys of 1792 to 1794 were to define the outline of the coast enough to prevent further speculation about a Northwest Passage.
The map was drawn by the Spanish commander at Nootka, Juan Francisco Bodega y Quadra. The map shows Vancouver Island as part of the mainland, though it shows the beginnings of a passage northwards (today's Strait of Georgia); the Queen Charlotte Islands are shown as islands, and there are two tentative coastlines which could have been northwest passages.

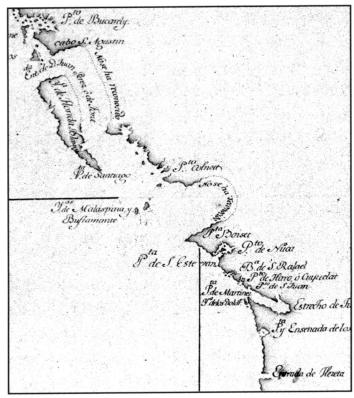

National Archives of Canada
National Archives of Canada
395 Wellington Street
Ottawa, Ontario K1A 0N3

National Maritime Museum
National Maritime Museum
Greenwich, London SE10 9NF England

New Westminster Public Library
New Westminster Public Library
716 6th Avenue
New Westminster, BC V3M 2B3

New York Public Library
Map Division, The New York Public Library
Fifth Avenue and 42nd Street
New York, NY 10018-2788

Newberry Library
The Newberry Library
60 West Walton Street,
Chicago, IL 60610-3380

OHS
Oregon Historical Society
1200 SW Park Avenue
Portland, OR 97205-2441

PRO
Public Record Office, Ruskin Avenue, Kew
Richmond, Surrey TW9 4DU England

Spokane Public Library
Northwest Room, Spokane Public Library
906 West Main
Spokane WA

University of British Columbia
Special Collections Division
University of British Columbia Library
1956 Main Mall, Vancouver, BC V6T 1Z1

University of Washington
Special Collections and Preservation Division
Allen Library
University of Washington Libraries
Box 352900, Seattle WA 98195-2900

UKHO
United Kingdom Hydrographic Office
Admiralty Way, Taunton, Somerset
TA1 2DN England

U.S. National Archives
The National Archives, Cartographic Branch
8601 Adelphi Road, College Park, MD 20740

Vancouver City Archives
Vancouver City Archives
1150 Chestnut Street, Vancouver, BC V6J 3J9

Vancouver Public Library
Special Collections Division
Vancouver Public Library, 350 Georgia Street
Vancouver, BC V6B 6B1

Western Washington University
Center for North West Studies
Western Washington University
Bellingham, WA 98225

Other Sources

Page 42   Painting of Captain James Cook, by Nathaniel Dance.
National Maritime Museum BHC2628

Page 85   Painting of George Vancouver, artist unknown, by courtesy of the National Portrait Gallery, London, Reg No. 503

Page 87   George Vancouver's letter.
PRO CO 5/187

Page 157   New Westminster about 1864.
BCARS A-03330

Page 163   Wagons on Cariboo Road about 1867.
BCARS A-00350

Page 180   CPR train meets SS *Nakusp* at Robson.
BCARS A-00571

Page 190   Grand Trunk Pacific train at Prince Rupert, 1915
National Archives of Canada PA-011231

Page 191   Canadian Northern train.
Vancouver Public Library, Photo 12984

MAP CATALOG
MAP TITLES AND SOURCES BY MAP NUMBER, IN ORDER OF APPEARANCE

For explanations of abbreviated source names, see page 196

(i) *America*
From: *Thomson's New General Atlas,*
John Thomson, 1817

(ii) *Nuove Scoperte de' Russi al Nord del Mare del Sud si nell' Asia, che nell America*
Venezia 1776, Antonio Zatta.

(iii) *A Map Exhibiting all the New Discoveries in the Interior Parts of North America. Inscribed by permission To the Honourable Governor and Company of Adventurers of England Trading Into Hudsons Bay.* Aaron Arrowsmith, 1795.
BCARS W61 1/4

1 *Nova et Aucta Orbis Terrae Descriptio ad Usum Navigantium emendate accomodata*
World Map of Gerard Mercator, 1569.
Bibliothèque nationale

2 *Il Disegno del Discoperto della nova Franza, ilquale s'è hauuto ultimamente dalla novissima navigatione de Franzesi; in quel luogo: Nel quale si vedono tutti L'Isole, Porti, Capi, et luoghi fra terra che in quella sono venetijs aneis formis Bolognini Zalterij Anno MDLXVI*
British Library K. Top. 118.23

3 *Vera Totius Expeditionis Nauticae descriptio D. Franc. Draci ... Addita est etiam viva delineatio navigationes Thomea Caundish ... Iudocus Hondius* (Incl. 2A, Inset: *Portius Nova Albionis,* and 2B, part of main map.)
Joducus Hondius, Amsterdam, 1589
Bancroft Library G3200 1589 H6 Case C

4 *La Herdike (sic, Heroike) Enterprinse Faict par de Signeur Draeck d'avoir Cirquit Toute la Terre* ("The French Drake Map")
Nicola van Sype c.1583
British Library Maps Cs.a7(1)

5 *Carta particolare della stretto di Iezo Pra l'America e l'Isola Iezo*
D'America Carta XXXIII Robert Dudley, 1647
From *"Dell Arcano del Mare"* (atlas),
Florence, 1647.
National Maritime Museum Neg. No. B 5752

6 *Illustri Viro, Domino Philippo Sidnaes Michael Lok Civis Londinensis Hanc Chartam Dedicabat: 1582*
From: Richard Hakluyt, *Divers Voyages touching the Discoverie of America,* London, 1582.

7 *Orbis Terrae Compendiosa Descriptio*
Rumold Mercator, Geneva 1587

8 *Quivirae Regnu cum alijs versus Borea*
From *Speculum Orbis Terrae*
Atlas of Cornelis de Jode, Antwerp, 1593
Ayer Collection, Newberry Library, Chicago
No. 135 J9 1593 Vol 1 fol. 11-12

9 *Septentrio America*
Joducus Hondius, 1606

10 *Limes Occidentis Quiuira et Anian 1597*
From: *"Descriptionis Ptolemaicae Augmentum sive Occidentis Notitia Breui commentario illustrata studio et opera... MDXCVIII"* 1597, Cornelius Wytfliet
British Library 146e.14

11 *Carta de los reconociemientos hechos en 1602 por El Capitan Sebastian Vizcayno Formaoa por los Planos que hizo el mismo durante su comision* (Map of the reconnaisance carried out in 1602 by Sebastian Vizcayno.) *Relación del Viage...* Atlas No.4
Vancouver Public Library SPA 970P E77r2

12 Map of Cape Mendocino from Vizcaíno 1602 voyage, perhaps by Fray Antonio de la Ascension
Archivo General de Indias, M 372. Copy in Kohl, J.G., *History of Discovery and Exploration on the Coasts of the US,* USCGS, 1885

13 *A mapp of Virginia discovered to ye Falls.*
John Farrer. From: Edward Bland, *The Discovery of New Brittaine,* 1651. British Library 278.a.3

14 Map of the Pacific Ocean
Johannes van Keulen, Amsterdam, c1700.

15 *Mappe-Monde geographique ou description general du globe terrestre et aquatique*
Nicholas Sanson, c.1705
Pierre Mortier, Amsterdam
BCARS CM B191

16 The northwest coast according to Jonathan Swift in 1726. From *Gullivers Travels* 1726–1766 ed.

17 *Diese Charte uber Siberien nimt isren aufang zu Tobolske Ostwerts bis au die enferste Grentze von Sutotsky gemacst unter dem commendo des Capt Comandeurs Bering Ao 1729*
(German copy of 1729 map of Bering's discoveries drawn by P.A. Chaplin.)
British Library K.Top 114.43 (1)

18 Map by Martin Spanberg of voyage of Mikhail Gwosdev
1732
Central State Archives of Military History, Moscow

19 Sketch illustrating Bering's first voyage in 1728. Drawn by Joseph-Nicolas de L'Isle based on his conversation with Bering. c 1732
From de L'Isle Manuscripts, xxv, 6.
Archives nationale, Paris.

20 Sketch illustrating Gwosdev's voyage in 1732. Drawn by Joseph-Nicolas de L'Isle, c1732
From de L'Isle Manuscripts xxv, 16, A.
Archives nationale, Paris.

21 *A Map of the Country which Capt[n] Beerings past through in his Journey from Tobolsk to Kamtschatka*
(Map drawn by J.N. de L'Isle after Jean-Baptiste Bourguignon d'Anville.)
From: Jean Baptiste du Halde, *The General History of China,* vol 4, p.429. London, 1736.

22 *Carte Dressee en 1731 Pour Servir a la recherche des Terres et des Mers Situees Au Nord de la Mer du Sud.* Joseph Nicholas De L'Isle, 1731.
BCARS CM A607

23 *Nova et Accuratissima Totius Terrarum Orbis Tabula Auctoribus R en 1 Ottens Amsterdam 1745* From: *Atlas van Zeevaert en Koophandel door de Geheele Weereldt,* 1745.
PRO FO 925 4022

24 Fleet master Sofron Khitrov's Sketch Map of St. Elias (Kayak) Island, 1741.
From: F.A. Golder: *Bering's Voyages,* American Geographical Society, New York, 1925, Vol.2, Fig.3, p.42., reproduced from Sololov, Zapiski Hydrogr. Depart., Vol 9, St. Petersburg 1851.

25 Fleet Master Sofron Khitrov's Sketch Map of the Shumagin Islands, with log entries, 1741.
From: F.A. Golder: *Bering's Voyages,* American Geographical Society, New York, 1922, Vol 1, Fig 11, p.148.

26 Map of the known land of America, with the islands newly discovered under the command of the former Captain Commander Bering, 1742.

27 Map of the voyage of Chirikov's expedition on the St Paul to America in 1741 and the discoveries of a number of Aleutian Islands and a part of the Alaskan coast, 1741.

28 *Carte de L'Amerique Septentionale Pour servir a l'Histoire de la Nouvelle France*
Jacques-Nicholas Bellin, 1743

29 *Carte de Amerique et des Mers Voisines*
From: J.N. Bellin, *La Petit Atlas Maritime Recueil de Cartes et Plans des Quatre Parties du Monde en Cinq Volumes, Vol 1, Amerique Septentrionale et Isles Antilles,* 1764, Map 2, 1763.

30 *Carte Reduite du Globe Terrestre*
From: J.N. Bellin, *La Petit Atlas Maritime Recueil de Cartes et Plans des Quatre Parties du Monde en Cinq Volumes, Vol 1, Amerique Septentrionale et Isles Antilles,* 1764, Map 1, no date.

31 *Carte Reduite des Parties Connues Du Globe Terrestre Dressee au Depost des Cartes, Plans et Journaux de la Marine. Por les service des vaisseaux Du Roy.* J. N. Bellin 1784.

32 *Carte Reduite de L'Ocean Septentrional*
Jacques Nicholas Bellin, 1766.
BCARS CM B194

33 *A New Map of Part of North America From The Latitude of 40 to 68 Degrees. Including the late discoveries made on Board the Furnace Bomb Ketch in 1742. And the Western Rivers & Lakes falling into Nelson River in Hudson's Bay as described by Joseph La France a French Canadese Indian who Travaled into those Countries and Lakes for 3 years from 1739 to 1742.* From: Arthur Dobbs, *An Account of the Countries Adjoining to Hudsons Bay,* London, 1744.
BCARS NW 971 H D632 1744

34 *Carte Generale Des Decouvertes de l'Amiral de Fonte et autres navigateurs Espagnols Anglois et Russes pour la recherche du passage a la Mer du Sud. pas M. De L'Isle de l'Academie des Sciences etc.* Robert De Vaugondy, 1752.
From: Diderot, *Encyclopédie.*

35 *Carte Des Nouvelles Decouvertes dresse par Phil Bauche, Pr. Geographer du Roi, presentee a L'Accad des Sciences le 9 Aoust 1752 et approuvee dans son assemblee de 6 Septembre suivant.* 1752.
BCARS CM A1489

36 *Carte Générale des Découvertes de L'Amiral de Fonte representant la grande probabilité d'un Passage au Nord Ouest par Thomas Jefferys Géographe du Roi à Londres 1768*
From Denis Diderot, *Encyclopedié...,* 1780 edition.

37 *Mappe Monde ou Globe Terrestre en deux Plans Hemispheres. Dressee sur les observations de Mrss de L'Academie Royal Des Sciences*
Jean Covens and Corneille Mortier, c1780
New York Public Library

38 *A Chart containing the coasts of California, New Albion, and Russian Discoveries to the North with the Peninsula of Kamschatka, Asia, opposite thereto And Islands dispersed over the Pacific Ocean to the North of the line*
John Green, 1753
Published by Thomas Jefferys, London 1753
British Library Maps C11.d22 (3)

39 *Chart containing part of the Icy Sea with the adjacent coasts of Asia and America*
John Green, 1753. Published by Thomas Jefferys, London 1753.
British Library Maps C11.d22 (1)

40 *Nouvelle Carte des decouvertes faites par des vaisseaux Russiens aux cotes inconnues de l'Amerique Septentrionale avec les pais adjacents. St. Petersbourg a l'Academie Imperiale des Sciences 1758*

41 Carte Des Nouvelles Decouvertes Au Nord De La Mer Tant a l'Est de la Siberie et du Kamtchatka Qu'a l'ouest de la Nouvelle France Dressee sur las Memoires de Mr Del'isle, Professeur Royale et de l'Academie des Sciences Par Philippe Buache de la meme Academie et Presentee a l'Academie, dans son Assemblee Publique de 8 Avril 1750 Par Mr Del'isle 1752

42 A General Map of the Discoveries of Admiral De Fonte and other Navigators, Spanish, English and Russian in Quest of a Passage to the South Sea By Mr De L'isle Sept 1752
From: Thomas Jefferys, Voyages From Asia to America For Completing the Discoveries of the North West Coast of America, 1764.
VPL 970P V22

43 An Exact Map of North America from the best authorities. J. Lodge, 1778.
BCARS CM A561

44 The Asiatic Part of the Russian Empire with the adjacent coast of North America from D'Anvilles map, Robert Sayer, March 1772.
BCARS CM B1221

45 A Map of the Discoveries made by the Russians on the North West Coast of America. Published by the Royal Academy of Sciences at Petersburg
London: Printed for Carington Bowles 1771
BCARS CM B961

46 Map of the explorations of Lieut. Ivan Synd 1764–1768.
Library of the Academy of Sciences, Moscow

47 A Map of the New Northern Archipelago discover'd by the Russians in the seas of Kamtschatka and Anadir. Jacob von Stählin, 1774.
BCARS NW 970P S778

48 Geographical map showing discoveries of Russian seagoing vessels on the northern part of America. Gerhard Friedrich Müller, Imperial Academy of Learning, St. Petersburg.
Russian edition, 1773.
The John Carter Brown Library, Brown University

49 Carte des parties nord et ouest de l'Amerique dressee d'apres les relations les plus authentiques par M en 1764. Nouvelle edition reduie pas M. de Vaugondy en 1772.

50 Map of Krenitsin and Levashev's Voyage to the Fox Islands in 1768 and 1769 Published April 13th 1780 by T. Cadell. Engr by T. Kitchin.
From: William Coxe An Account of the Russian Discoveries between Asia and America,
London, 1803.
Vancouver Public Library 970 C87a

51 Map of northeast Asia and northwest America.
V. Krasilnikov, 1777.

52 A New Map of North America From the Latest Discoveries 1778 Engrav'd for Carvers Travels
From: Jonathan Carver, Travels through the Interior Parts of North America in the Years 1766, 1767 and 1768, London 1778.

53 The Heads of Origan, detail from A Plan of Captain Carver's Travels in the interior parts of North America in 1766 and 1767
From: Jonathan Carver, op. cit., 1778.

54 Map of North America Showing all the New Discoveries From: The American Gazeteer Exhibiting a Full Account of the Civil Divisions, Rivers, Harbours, Indian Tribes, etc. of the American Continent. Compiled from the best authorities by Jedediah Morse Author of the American Universal Geography.
Boston, 1804
BCARS NW 910.3 M885

55 A new map of the whole continent of America: divided into North and South and West Indies...
London: Printed for Robert Sayer, 1786
OHS Negative # 27392

56 A chart containing the coasts of California, New Albion, and Russian Discoveries to the North with the Peninsula of Kamschatka, Asia, opposite thereto And Islands dispersed over the Pacific Ocean to the North of the line
From: An American Atlas... Engraved on 48 copper plates by the late Thomas Jefferys Geographer to the King, and others. London 1775.
BCARS NW 912.7 J45am (1)

56A Carta Reducida del Oceano Asiatico õ Mar del Sur que contiene la Costa de la California comprehendida desde el Puerto de Monterrey. hta la Punta de Sta. Maria Magdelena hecha segun las observaciones y Demarcasiones del Aljerez de Fragata de la Rl Armada y Primer Piloto de este Departamento Dn Juan Perez por Dn Josef de Cañizares. 1774

57 Chart containing part of the Icy Sea with the adjacent Coast of Asia and America. Western half of A Chart of North and South America including the Atlantic and Pacific Oceans with the nearest coasts of Europe, Africa and Asia
From: An American Atlas, 1775
BCARS NW 912.7 J45am (1)

58 The Russian Discoveries from the Map Published by the Imperial Academy of St. Petersburg. London. Printed for Robt Sayer Map and Printseller No 53 in Fleet Street. Published as the Act Directs March 2nd 1775
From: An American Atlas..., 1775
BCARS NW 912.7 J45AM (1)

59 Plano de la Rada de Bucareli
Bruno Hezeta y Dudagoitia, July 1775
Archivo General de Indias, Sevilla
MP, Mexico 532 (OHS negative #67613)

60 Plano de la Bahia de la Asunción
Bruno Hezeta y Dudagoitia, August 1775
Archivo General de Indias, Sevilla
MP, Mexico 306 (OHS Negative #48234)

61 Map of the northwest coast from the voyage of Juan Francisco Bodega y Quadra, 1775, Francisco Antonio Mourelle.
From Daines Barrington, Miscellanies, London, 1781, page 489.

62 Carta reducida de las costas, y mares septentrionales de California construida bajo las observaciones, y demarcaciones hechas por...de Fragata Don Juan Francisco de la Vodega y Quadra commandante de la goleta Sonora y por el piloto Don Francisco Antonio Maurelle
Archivo General de Indias, Sevilla
MP, Mexico 581 (OHS Negative #49258)

63 Carta reducida que comprehende las costas septentrionales de la California contenidas el grado 36 y 61 de latitud Norte descubiertas en al ano 1775 y en el de 1779 en las expediaciones que de orden del Soberano...Dn Bruno de Hezeta...Dn Juan Francisco de la Bodega y Quadra ... D. Ignacio Arteaga...Dn Juan Fran. de la Bodega y Quadra
PRO FO 925/1650 (8)

64 Carta Reducida que comprende las costas septentrionales de la California
D. Tomas Mauricio Lopez, Madrid 1796

65 Carta Reducida de las Costas y Mares Septentrionales de California
Watercolour, c1779
Archivo General de Indias, Sevilla
MP, Mexico 359

66 Chart of part of the N W Coast of America Explored by Capt. J. Cook in 1778
Map enclosed with Cook's letter to Philip Stephens, Secretary of the Admiralty, from Unalaska, sent 20 Oct 1778 (21 in Cook's Journal), received in London 6 March 1780.
PRO MPI 83 (removed from ADM 1/1621)

67 Chart of the NW Coast of America and the NE Coast of Asia explored in the years 1778 and 1779 The unshaded parts of the coast of Asia are taken from a MS chart received from the Russians.
From: James Cook, Voyage to the Pacific Ocean, 1784.

68 Chart of the New Northern Archipelago discovered by the Russians in the seas of Kamtschatka and Anadir. Jacob von Stählin, 1774. Engraved for Millar's New Universal System of Geography.
London: Alex Hogg, 1782–83.

69 Sketch of Nootka Sound A. Ship Cove 1778
From: James Cook, Voyage to the Pacific Ocean, 1784.

70 Chart of Norton Sound and of Bherings Strait made by the East Cape of Asia and the West Point of America. 1778/1779.
From: James Cook, Voyage to the Pacific Ocean, 1784.

71 Chart of Cooks River in the N W Part of America 1778
From: James Cook, Voyage to the Pacific Ocean, 1784.

72 Sandwich Sound and the Gulf of Good Hope (Prince William Sound & Cook Inlet).
Map by Henry Roberts for John Gore's journal, 1778.
PRO MPI 82/2, removed from ADM 55/120

73 Sketch of King Georges Sound.
By Henry Roberts for John Gore's journal, 1778.
PRO MPI 81/1, removed from ADM 55/120

74 General Chart exhibiting the discoveries made by Capt. James Cook in this and his preceding two voyages, with the tracks of the ships under his command. Wm. Faden
BCARS CM B1189

75 Chart of the N.W. Coast of America and the N.E. Coast of Asia explored in the years 1778 and 1779. Prepared by Lieutenant Henry Roberts under the immediate inspection of Capt Cook Wm Faden 1784
PRO FO 925 4062 Part 2, Map 21

76 Track from first making the Continent, March 7th, to Anchoring in King George's Sound.
From: Journal of James Burney, 1778.
PRO ADM 51/4528

77 Sketch of King George's Sound
From: Journal of James Burney, 1778.
PRO ADM 51/4528

78 Chart showing the Tracks of the Ships employed in Capt. Cook's last voyage to the Pacific Ocean in the Years 1776, 1777, 1778 and 1779
John Ledyard. From: Journal of Captain Cook's last Voyage to the Pacific, Hartford, 1783.

79 Chart of New [sic] Coast of America and New [sic] Coast of Asia explored in the years 1778 and 1779. (Russian copy of Cook's chart.)

80 Chart of the NW Coast of America and part of the NE of Asia [sic] with the track of his Majestys Sloops Resolution & Discovery from May to October 1778 by George Vancouver
American Geographical Society Collection, University of Wisconsin, Milwaukee.

81 Carte Der Entdekvn Zwischen Siberien und America bis auf das jahr 1780
Peter Simon Pallas 1781
From: Neue nordische Beyträge, ed. P.S. Pallas, St. Petersburg & Leipzig, Vol l. 1781.

82 Chart of the New Discoveries in the Eastern Ocean. E. Khudyakov, 1781.

83 Map of Bering Strait and adjacent coasts, with inset: Representation of the Southernmost Kurile Islands. From: P.S. Pallas Neue nordische Beyträge, Vol.IV, 1783.

84 A-E Charts 10, 11, 12, 13 & 14 from: Atlas, by Navigator Lovtsov composed by him while wintering at the Bol'sheretsk ostrog in the year 1782
Vasilii Fedorovich Lovtsov, watercolours, 1782.
BCARS NW 912.722 L922

85 Charts 8A and 8B, Bering Strait, from Lovtsov
   Atlas, as Map 84.
   BCARS NW 912.722 L922

86 *North America with the new discoveries, by*
   William Faden, Geographer to the King
   MDCCLXXXV. 1785.
   BCARS CM A175

87 *Plan of St. Patrick's Bay by Capt. James Hanna*
   1786 Publ. by A. Dalrymple, March 29th 1789
   UBC G3350 D34 1789 (SP)

88 *Chart of Part of the N.W. Coast of America by Capt.*
   James Hanna in Snow Sea Otter 1786
   Publ. by A Dalrymple, March 29th 1789
   UBC G3350 D34 1789 (SP)

89 *Chart Exhibiting the Route of the Experiment Snow*
   in the years 1785 and 1786
   S. Wedgbrough.
   From: *Strange's Journal and Narrative 1786 –*
   1787, Madras Survey Office, reprinted 1928.
   BCARS NW 970P S897

90 *Track of the Snow "Experiment" In Company with*
   the "Captain Cook" by S. Wedgbrough
   Publ. by A Dalrymple March 29th 1789
   UBC G3350 D34 1789 (SP)

91 *Chart of the World on Mercator's projection,*
   exhibiting all the new discoveries to the present
   Time, with the Tracks of the most distinguished
   Navigators since the year 1790, carefully collected
   from the best charts, maps, voyages, etc extant
   And regulated from the accurate astronomical
   observations made in three Voyages Perform'd
   under the command of Captn. James Cook, in the
   years 1768, 69, 70, 71, 72, 73, 74, 75, 76, 77, 78,
   79 and 80. Compiled & Published by A.
   Arrowsmith. London: 1st April 1790
   BCARS CM X12, 1/4

92 *Chart of the North West Coast of America with the*
   Tracks of the King George and Queen Charlotte in
   1786 – 1787. From: Nathaniel Portlock: *Voyage*
   around the World but more Particularly to the
   North-West Coast of America Performed in 1785,
   1786, 1787 and 1788 in the King George and
   Queen Charlotte. London, 1789.

93 *Chart of the North West Coast of America with*
   Tracks of the King George and Queen Charlotte in
   1786 and 1787. From: George Dixon, *A Voyage*
   Around the World, 1789.

94 *A Chart of the Interior Part of North America*
   Demonstrating the very great probability of an
   Inland Navigation from Hudson's Bay to the West
   Coast. From: John Meares, *Voyages made in the*
   years 1788 and 1789 from China to the North West
   Coast of America to which are prefixed An
   Introductory Narrative of a Voyage performed in
   1786, from Bengal in the Ship Nootka; observa-
   tions on the probable existence of a Northwest
   Passage and some account of the Trade Between
   the North West Coast of America & China, and the
   latter country & Great Britain. J. Meares, 1790.

95 *Chart of the N.W. Coast of America and the N.E.*
   Coast of Asia, explored in the Years 1778 and
   1779 by Capt Cook and further explored, in 1788,
   and 1789. From: John Meares, *Voyages, op. cit.,*
   1790.

96 *A Sketch of Raft-Cove taken by Mr. Funter, Master*
   of the North West American. 1788
   From: J. Meares, *Voyages, op. cit.,* 1790.

97 *A Sketch of Port Cox in the District of Wicananish*
   1787. From: John Meares, *Voyages, op. cit.,* 1790.

98 *A Plan of Port Effingham in Berkley's Sound*
   1787. From: John Meares, *Voyages, op. cit.,* 1790.

99 Map of Pacific Northwest compiled from Grigorii
   Shelikov's directions, c1793.

100 *Sketch of the Entrance of the Strait of Juan de Fuca*
    by Charles Duncan Master in the Royal Navy 15th
    August 1788
    Alexander Dalrymple, publ.
    BCARS CM A442

101 *Carte des Decouvertes Faites par Les Russes et par*
    le Captaine Anglais Jacques Cook dans la Mer de
    Sud. Alexander Wilbrecht, 1787.
    British Library 981.(5)

102 Map of Western Canada presented to Lord
    Hamilton 1785, by Peter Pond.
    PRO MPG 425

103 *A Map shewing the communication of the Lakes*
    and the Rivers between Lake Superior & Slave
    Lake in North America
    From: *Gentleman's Magazine,* March 1790.

104 *Chart of the Coasts of America and Asia from*
    California to Macao according to the discoveries
    made in 1786 and 1787 by the Boussole and
    Astrolabe. G. G. & J. Robinson, November 1798.
    UBC Ms Coll Verner L1798N

105 Mercator Map Showing the Northeast Portion of
    Siberia, the Arctic Ocean, Eastern Ocean, and
    Northwest Coasts of North America
    G.A. Sarychev, 1802. From: *Puteshesvie flota*
    kapitana Sarycheva po severovostochnoi chasti
    Sibiri, Ledovitomu moriu, i Vostochnomu okeanu,
    v prodolzhenie os' mi let, pri Geograficheskoi i
    Astronomicheskoi ekspeditsii pod nachal' stvom
    flota kapitana Billingsa s 1785 po 1793 god,
    2 volumes, St Petersburg, 1802.
    UBC G9285 S2 1954 loc4

106 *Map of marine discoveries by Russian Navigators*
    in the Pacific & Frozen Oceans, made in various
    years. Compiled & corrected according to the
    latest observations of foreign navigators &
    engraved in the year 1802 at the Map Depot of His
    Imperial Majesty. Enclosure in Sir C. Bagot's
    Despatch no.56, 17 November 1821.
    British case, Alaska Boundary, Atlas of Maps,
    Appendix Vol II.
    Vancouver City Archives A365 No. 5

107 *Carta reducida que contiene la costa septentrional*
    de la California asta los 62 grados de latitud Norte
    correjida y en mendada en la expedicion que
    hicieron los dos buques de S.M. la fragata Princesa
    y el paquebot San Carlos desde el Puerto de San
    Blas asta las latitud Norte de 60 grados y 11
    minutos en el ano de 1788
    Gonzalo Lopez de Haro, 1788

108 *Plano de la Cala De Los Amigos situada en la*
    parte occidental de la entrada de Nutka.
    Ano 1791. From: *Relación,* Atlas, 1802.
    Vancouver Public Library SPA 970P E77r2

109 *Numero 3 Continuacion de los reconocimientos*
    hechos En La Costa No. De America por los buques
    de S.M. en varias Campanas desde 1774 a 1792
    From: *Relación,* Atlas, 1802.
    Vancouver Public Library SPA 970P E77r2

110 *Plano de la Bahía de Núñez Gaona, situada en la*
    costa del Sur del Estrecho de Fuca.
    Manuel Quimper, 1790.

111 *Plano de Puerto de Córdova situado en la Costa*
    del Nort del Estrecho de Fuca.
    Manuel Quimper, 1790.

112 *Carta reducida que comprehende parte de la Costa*
    Septentrional de California, corrigida y
    enmendada hasta la Boca de Estrecho de
    Fuca...Dn Manuel Quimper en el ano de 1790.
    Construida por su primer Piloto Dn Gonzalo
    Lopez de Haro 1790. (Map sent to G. Vancouver.)
    PRO MPK 203 (2)

113 *Plano del Estrecho de Fuca reconicido y le bantado*
    en el ano 1790
    Lopez de Haro (attrib), 1790.
    BCARS CM A447

114 *Carta des las Costas Reconocidas al Norueste de*
    la California, 1792.

115 *Carta del la Costas Reconocidas al Norueste de la*
    California. 1792.
    PRO FO 925 1650 (7)

116 *Plano del Archipelago de Clayocuat.*
    Juan Pantoja y Arriaga, 1791.
    BCARS CM A1413, sh 1 & 2

117 *Carta que comprehende los interiers y veril de la*
    costa desde los 48° de Latitud N hasta los 50°.
    1791. Juan Carrasco, 1791.
    Museo Naval, Madrid / BCARS CM A438, 1 – 6

118 *Plano de Archipelago de Nitinat o Carrasco.*
    Jose Maria Narvaez, 1791.
    BCARS CM A1415

119 A tracing by an English draughtsman of a Spanish
    survey of Vancouver Island from Nootka to Cape
    Classet and the Straight of Georgia; with plans of
    Pto. Clayocaut, Pto de Nuestro Sd de los Angles,
    Pto de la Sta Cruz and Pto San Rafael.
    UKHO 355/2 on Ac 1 fol.1

120 *Plano reducida que comprehende parte de la Costa*
    Septentrional.
    Lopez de Haro, 1792.
    BCARS CM A446

121 *Carta general de quanto asta hoy se ha*
    descubierto y examinado por los Espanoles en la
    Costa Septentrional de California, formada...por
    D. Juan Francisco de la Bodega y Quadra Ano de
    1791
    Museo Naval, Madrid.

122 *Plano Del Puerto De Mulgrave Frabasado a bordo*
    de las Corvetas Descubierta y Atrevida de la
    Marina Real Ano 1791
    From: *Relación.* Atlas, 1802.
    Vancouver Public Library SPA 970P E77r2

123 *Num 9 Plano del Puerto del Desengano Trabasdo*
    de Orden del Rey. From: *Relación.* Atlas, 1802.
    Vancouver Public Library SPA 970P E77r2

124 *Plano de los Canales Imediatos a Nutka y de la*
    Navegation [sic] hecha para su reconocimiento
    por las lanchos de las corvetas Descubierta y
    Atrevide en el Ano 1791 Pasa el uso de
    Mendendez. (Map given to George Vancouver by
    Bodega y Quadra, and sent via Lieut. Broughton
    to England in 1792.)
    UKHO 355/1 on Ac11

125 *Carta Reducida que manifiesta parte de la Costa*
    de la nueva Cantabria con sus Yslas adjacenta...
    Don Jacinto Caamano fio con la Fragata
    Aranzasu en el ano de 1792.
    From: Journal of Don Jacinto Caamaño, 1792.

126 *Chart of the West Coast of North America, with the*
    Isles adjacent from the Latde 50 45'N & Longde.
    30 [sic] copied from one constructed...by Dn.
    Caamano...in...1792
    (Traced by an English draughtsman.)
    UKHO 355/3 on Ac 1

127 *Carta Esferica de la parte de la Costa No. de*
    America Comprehendida entre la Entrada de Juan
    de Fuca, y la Salidas de las Goletas con algunos
    Canales interiores arroglada segun los resultados
    de las operaciones hechos por los Commandantes
    y Officiales de las Goletas Sutil y Mexicana desde
    5 de Junio a 31 de Agosto de 1792
    Dionisio Galiano, 1792.
    PRO FO 925 1650 (13)

128 *Num. 2 Carta Esferica de los Reconocimientos*
    hechos en la Costa N.O. De America en 1791 y 92
    por las Goletas Sutil y Mexicana y otres Bruques
    de S.M.
    Dionisio Galiano, 1792.
    From: *Relación.* Atlas, 1802.

129 *Carta esferica de la reconocimientos hechos en*
    1792 en la costa N. O. de America para examinar
    la entrada de Juan de Fuca y la internacion de sus
    Canales navegables levantada de orden Del Rey
    Nuestro Senor abordo de las Goletas Sutil y
    Mexicana Por D. Dionisio Galiano y D. Cayetano
    Valdes Capitaines de la Navio de la Rl. Armada
    Ano de 1793. 1795.
    BCARS CM A176
    Carta Reducida de la Costa Septentrional desde

130 *Carta Reducida de la Costa Septentrional desde
el Puerto de Acapulco hasta la Isla de Unalaska*
Bodega y Quadra, 1792
BCARS B1173 sheet 1

131 *Plano del Puerto de Gray*
Bodega y Quadra, 1792
OHS Neg #74106

132 *Carta de los Descubrimientos en la Costa N.O.
Americana Septentrional por las Embarcaciones
de S. Blas y noticias adquirados en este viage*
(Map of the discoveries made on the N W coast of
America by the ships of San Blas and information
acquired on this voyage.) Bodega y Quadra, 1792.
OHS Neg #67563

133 *Plano del estrecho de Juan de Fuca descuvierto el
ano 1592, reconocido en 1789 por Dⁿ Jose
Narvaez en el de 90...Dⁿ Manuel Quimper, en 91...
Dⁿ Franᶜᵒ Eliza y concluido en...el Comandame
Vancouver y Dionisio Galiano en el qual sedenetan
con el color negro los descubrim los hechos...con el
ecarnado los Vancouver y con elasul los de
Galiano.* Bodega y Quadra, 1792.
OHS Neg #097867

134 *Hydrographical Chart of the Known Parts of the
Globe Between the Seventieth Parallel North and
the Sixtieth South to illustrate the Voyage round the
world performed in 1790, 1791 and 1792 by
Captain Etienne Marchand.*
From: *Voyage Around the World,* Etienne
Marchand (Translated from the French edition of
C.P. Claret Fleurieu), London, 1801.

135 *Sketch of Cloak-Bay and Cox's Strait (Queen
Charlotte's Islands) By Capt. Prosper Chanal,
Sept. 1791.* From: *Voyage Around the World,*
Etienne Marchand, 1801, op. cit.

136 Chart of the N.W. Coast of North America from
Cape Maddison to Cape Flattery.
Joseph Ingraham, 1792
BCARS CM A785

137 Chart of the N.W. Coast of North America from
Cape Maddison to Cape Flattery, south at top of
map, Joseph Ingraham, 1792.
Library of Congress, Marine Miscellany,
Manuscript Division.

138 And 138A Quadra's Isles
From: Journal of the *Hope,*
Joseph Ingraham, 1792.
Library of Congress, Marine Miscellany,
Manuscript Division.

139 Washington's Isles
From: Journal of the *Hope,*
Joseph Ingraham, 1792
BCARS CM A318

140 Washington's Isles
Joseph Ingraham, September 1791
BCARS CM A783

141 And 141A. Preliminary chart of N.W. Coast of
America from George Vancouver's landfall to
Cape Mudge, including the first mapping of Puget
Sound.
PRO MPG 557 (4), removed from CO 5/187

142 *Chart of the Coast of N W America and islands
adjacent north Westward of the Gulf of Georgia as
explored by His Majesty's ships Discovery &
Chatham in the months of July & August 1792*
(Preliminary chart of N W Coast of America, Cape
Mudge to Queen Charlotte Sound.)
PRO MPG 557 (3), removed from CO 5/187

143 James Johnstone's first survey of Johnstone Strait
and Loughborough Inlet, 1792.
UKHO 231/4 Ac 1

144 *Columbia's River*
PRO MPG 557 (1), removed from CO 5/187

145 *A Sketch of the Columbia River Explored in His
Majesty's Arm'd Brig Chatham Lieut Broughton
Commander in October 1792*
UKHO 229 on Rv

146 *Plan of the River Oregan from an Actual Survey*
London: Published 1st Nov 1798 by A. Arrowsmith
BCARS CM A1347

147 *A Chart of the Western Coast of N. America in
which the continental shore from the Latde. of 42°
30' N and Longde. 230° 30' E. to the latde. 52° 15'
N and longde 288° 03'; E. has been finally traced
and determined by His Majesty's Sloop Discovery
and armed tender Chatham under the Command
of George Vancouver Esqr. in the Summer of 1792.
The parts of the Coast red, are copied from
Spanish Charts constructed by the Officers under
the order of Senres. Quadra and Malaspina.
Prepared by Lieut. Jos. Baker, under the immediate
inspection of Captn. Vancouver.*
UKHO 228 on 82

148 *A Chart shewing part of the Coast of N.W. America
with the tracks of His Majesty's Sloop Discovery
and Armed Tender Chatham Commanded by
George Vancouver Esq...The parts not shaded are
taken from Russian Authority.* (Cook Inlet)
Plate 12 of Atlas, *A Voyage of Discovery to the
North Pacific Ocean and Around the World*
George Vancouver, 1798.

149 *A Chart shewing part of the N.W. Coast of North
America with the Tracks of His Majesty's Sloop
Discovery and Armed Tender Chatham...*
(Summary map of west coast)
Plate 14 of Atlas, *A Voyage of Discovery to the
North Pacific Ocean and Around the World*
George Vancouver, 1798.

150 *A Chart shewing part of the Coast of N.W. America
with the tracks of His Majesty's Sloop Discovery
and Armed Tender Chatham Commanded by
George Vancouver Esq. ... The parts not shaded
are taken from Spanish Authorities.* (Vancouver
Island and adjacent coast.) Plate 5 of Atlas, *A
Voyage of Discovery to the North Pacific Ocean
and Around the World.* George Vancouver, 1798.

151 *A Chart shewing part of the Coast of N.W. America
with the tracks of His Majesty's Sloop Discovery
and Armed tender Chatham...* (North coast of B.C.
and the Alaska panhandle.) Plate 7 of Atlas, *A
Voyage of Discovery to the North Pacific Ocean
and Around the World* George Vancouver, 1798.

152 *A Chart shewing part of the Coast of N.W. America
...with the tracks of His Majesty's Sloop Discovery
and Armed tender Chatham...* (Prince William
Sound.) Plate 11 of Atlas, *A Voyage of Discovery
to the North Pacific Ocean and Around the World.*
George Vancouver, 1798.

153 *A Chart shewing part of the Coast of N.W. America
with the tracks of His Majesty's Sloop Discovery
and Armed Tender Chatham Commanded by
George Vancouver Esq. and prepared under his
immediate inspection by Lieut. Joseph Baker...
The parts not shaded are taken from Spanish
Authorities.*
Compilation chart for Plate 5 of the Atlas for *A
Voyage of Discovery to the North Pacific Ocean
and Around the World,* George Vancouver, 1798.
PRO CO 700 British Columbia 1

154 *Chart on Mercator's Projection, exhibiting the
track of Maldonado and De Fonte in 1598 and
1640, compared with the modern discoveries.*
From: William Goldson, *Observations on the
Passage between the Atlantic and Pacific Oceans,*
1793.
BCARS NW 970 G624

155 *An Indian map of the different tribes, that inhabit the
East and West side of the Rocky Mountains with all
the rivers and other remarkable places, also the
number of tents. Drawn by the Feathers or Ac ko
mok ki a Blackfoot chief 7th Feby 1801*
From the Journal of Peter Fidler, 1801.
HBCA G1/25 (N9259)

156 *A Map of Mackenzie's Track from Fort Chipewyan
to the Pacific Ocean in 1793*
From: *Voyages from Montreal,*
Alexander Mackenzie, London, 1801.

157 *Chart of the Coast from Behrings Bay to Sea Otter
Bay with different settlements of the natives.
Surveyed by Captain Lisiansky. (1804) Engr.
under the direction of Mr. Arrowsmith.*
From: Urey Lisianskii, *Voyage Around the World in
the Years 1803, 1804, 1805 and 1806,* London,
English translation publ by John Booth 1814.

158 *Map of the Globe, incorporating the latest
descriptions from the Lisianskii fleet, with a
display of the route of the Neva from 1803 - 1806*
From: *Collection of Maps and Drawings Relating to
the Voyage of the Fleet of Captain (1st Order) and
Gentleman Urei Lisianskii of the ship Neva.*
St Petersburg, 1812.
PRO FO 925 4062

159 *Chart of the World on Mercator's projection,
exhibiting all the new discoveries to the present
time, with the track of the most distinguished
navigators since the year 1790...*
Aaron Arrowsmith. London: 1st April 1790.
BCARS CM X12, 1/4

160 (Part of double hemisphere world map, no title)
Aaron Arrowsmith, 1794, updated to c1798
BCARS CM B1188 sh.1

161 *Chart of the World...* (Title as Map 159.)
A. Arrowsmith. 1790, updated to c1800.
BCARS CM W134

162 Sketch map of the mouth of the Columbia River,
northern and southern parts. William Clark, 1806.
Beinecke Library, Yale University

163 Page 152 from William Clark's journal, showing
Cape Disappointment and the north shore of the
Columbia River. November 1805.
American Philosophical Society,
Codex I, p.152, Neg. 913

164 *A Map of part of the Continent of North America...
Compiled from the information of the best
informed travellers through that quarter of the
globe...* William Clark, 1810.
Beinecke Library, Yale University

165 *A Map of part of the Continent of North America,
Between the 35th & 51st degrees of North Latitude,
and extending from the 89 degrees of West
Longitude to the Pacific Ocean. Compiled from the
Authorities of the best informed travellers, by M.
Lewis 1805-6 Copied by Nicholas King, 1808*
Records of the Office of the Chief of Engineers,
National Archives, Washington, D.C.

166 *Sketch of the Columbia River from the forks, & the
19th of October 1805 to the 1st of Janʸ on the Pacific
Ocean.* From: R.G. Thwaites, *The Original Journals
of the Lewis and Clark Expedition,* Vol. 8, Atlas.

167 [Map of the Multnomah and Columbia] *rivers
furnished Capt C. by an old and inteligent Indian.*
Meriwether Lewis, April 3rd 1806
(Copy of: *A Sketch of the Multnomah River given
by several different Tribes of Indians near its
entrance into the Columbia,* William Clark, 1806.)
American Philosophical Society
Lewis and Clark Journals, Codex K, pp 28-29.

168 *A Map of Lewis & Clark's Track, Across the
Western Portion of North America from the
Mississippi to the Pacific Ocean; By Order of the
Executive of the United States, in 1807, 5 and 6
Copied by Samuel Lewis from the original drawing
of Wm Clark, 1814*
Geography and Map Division, Library of Congress,
Washington, D.C.

169 *Sketch of the Routes of Hunt & Stuart*
From: Irving Washington, *Astoria,* 1836.

170 *Columbia River 1825
British War Office, 1826
Printed at the Lithographic Establishment, Quarter
Master Generals Office, Horse Guards, Octʳ 1826*
(Western part of map)
PRO FO 925 1379

171 *A New Map of America from the Latest Authorities*
John Cary, Engraver, 1803
BCARS CM B1037

172 Map of the North-West Territory of the Province of Canada from actual survey during the years 1782 to 1812. This map, made for the North West Company in 1813 and 1814 embraces the region lying between 45 and 60 degrees North latitude and 84 and 124 West longitude comprising the surveys and discoveries of 20 years, namely the discovery and survey of the Oregon Territory to the Pacific Ocean, the survey of the Athabasca Lake, Slave River and Lake from which flows Mackenzie's River to the Arctic Sea by Mr. Phillip Turner the route of Sir Alexander Mackenzie in 1792 down part of Frasers River together with the survey of this river to the Pacific Ocean by the late John Stewart of the North West Company, by David Thompson, Astronomer and Surveyor. Sgd. David Thompson
BCARS CM C110

173 A Map of America between the latitudes 40 and 70, and longitudes 45 and 180 west Exhibiting Mackenzie's Track from Montreal to Fort Chipewyan and from thence to the North Sea in 1789 and to the West Pacific Ocean in 1793.
From: Voyages from Montreal, Alexander Mackenzie, London, 1801.

174 A Map of America between Latitudes 40 and 70 North and Longitudes 80 and 150 West Exhibiting the Principal Trading Stations of the North West Company. (Drawn by David Thompson, 1812, but uncredited.)
National Archives of Canada NMC 6763

175 Untitled hand-drawn map of part of western British North America by David Thompson, 1843.
PRO FO 925 4622 sheets 15 & 16

176 A Map Exhibiting all the New Discoveries in the Interior Parts of North America. Inscribed by Permission to the Honourable Governor and Company of Adventurers of England Trading into Hudson Bay. In testimony of their liberal Communications To their most Obedient and Humble Servant. A. Arrowsmith Jan 1 1795 Additions to 1811, 18, 19, 20, 24. 1824.
BCARS CM W10, 1/2

177 Map of Russian Possessions in North America. From: Vasili Nikolayevich Berkh, Atlas geograficheskikh otkrytii v Sibiri i v Severo-Zapadnoi Ameriki. 1821.

178 Map of the Fort Ross area.
1817

179 Gulf of Sitka as described under the observations of the fleet of Urei Lisianskii, Captain and Gentleman, 1805 Novo Archangel'sk. From: Collection of Maps and Drawings... (as Map 158)
PRO FO 925 4062

180 Carte des Possessions Russes, dressee par Pierron, d'apres la carte de Mr. Brue 1825
BCARS CM B349

181 North America
A & S Arrowsmith 1825
BCARS CM A540

182 North America
D.F. Robinson, 1829
BCARS CM A573

183 British Possessions in North America
For Montgomery Martin's History of New British Colonies Vol III – Possessions in North America. Drawn & Engraved by J & C. Walker, 1834.
Vancouver City Archives, Map 287

184 Map of the Frozen Ocean & the Eastern Ocean. Compiled from the latest documents in the Hydrographic Dept. of the Ministry of Marine 1844.
From: British Case, Alaska Boundary Atlas.
Vancouver City Archives A365, No. 15

185 Map of the approaches to Novo Archangel'sk. Mikhail Tebenkov, 1850.

186 Northwest coast of America from Lat 52 to Lat 57 30'. Hudson's Bay Company map, cartographer unknown.
HBCA G1/158

187 Fraser River from a drawing by Mr. Emilius Simpson in HBC Schooner Cadboro 1827
London: Hydrographic Office 1849, Chart 1922.
National Archives of Canada NMC 106388

188 A Sketch of Thompson's River District 1827 by Archibald McDonald
HBCA B97/a/2, fo.40

189 British North America by permission dedicated to the Honᵇˡᵉ Hudson's Bay Company containing the latest information which these documents furnish. By their obedient servant J. Arrowsmith. London. Pubᵈ 15 Febʳ 1832 by J. Arrowsmith
BCARS CM B199

190 The Northwest Coast of North America and adjacent Territories
Compiled from the Best Authorities under the direction of Robert Greenhow to accompany his Memoir on the Northwest Coast published by order of the Senate of the United States drawn by David H. Burr. 1839.
From: Robert Greenhow, Memoir, Historical and Political, on the Northwest Coast of North America and the adjacent territories, 1840.

191 Map of Oregon
From: A Geographical Sketch of that part of North America, called Oregon, Hall J. Kelley 1830

192 Site plan of Hall J. Kelley's proposed city at the confluence of the Multinomah (Willamette) and Columbia Rivers
From: Hall J. Kelley, General Circular, 1830.

193 Oregon Territory
Entered according to act of Congress in the year 1833 by Illman and Pillbrow in the Clerk's Office of the District Court of the Southern District of New York. David H. Burr, 1833.
University of Washington N 979.5 Map 71

194 Map of Oregon City as surveyed in the spring of the year 1844. Adolphus Lee Lewes, 1844.
HBCA G1/121

195 Map of Oregon Territory West of the Cascade Mountains. Surveyor Generals Office, Salem, O.T. Oct.1st 1855. C.K. Gardiner, Surveyor General Sen.Ex. Doc No 1, 54th Cong. 1st Sess.
BCARS CM A1237

196 The United States and the Relative Position of The Oregon and Texas by James Wyld, Charing Cross East. 1845 .
PRO FO 925 1200

197 A map of the United States Territory of Oregon West of the Rocky Mountains Exhibiting the various Trading Depots or Forts occupied by the British Hudsons Bay Company, connected with the Western and northwestern Fur Trade Captain Washington Hood 1838
BCARS CM A200

198 Map of North America
Publ. by R. Cadell Edinburgh 1833
Vancouver City Archives Map No. 289

199 Map of the Oregon Territory by the U.S. Ex.Ex. Charles Wilkes Esq. Commander 1841 Inset: Columbia River, Reduced from a Survey Made by the U.S. Ex.Ex. 1841. Charles Wilkes, 1845.
PRO FO 925/1380

200 Archipelago of Arro, Gulf of Georgia, Ringgolds Channel and Straits of Fuca Oregon Territory By the U.S. Ex.Ex. 1841. Charles Wilkes, 1845.

201 Chart of Puget Sound Its Inlets and Anchorages by the U.S. Ex.Ex. 1841. Charles Wilkes, 1845.

202 Chart of the Pacific Ocean, Exhibiting the Tracks & Research of the U.S. Exploring Expedition With Corrections to the Year 1844
Charles Wilkes, 1845.

203 Map of an Exploring Expedition to the Rocky Mountains in the Year 1842, and to Oregon & North California in the Years 1843–1844 Brevet Captain J.C. Fremont of the Corps of Topographical Engineers. Drawn by Charles Preuss, 1845.
From: Report of the Exploring Expedition to the Rocky Mountains in the Year 1842, and to Oregon & North California in the Years 1843–44.
Library of Congress

204 Topographical Map of the Road from Missouri to Oregon Commencing at the Mouth of the Kansas in the Missouri River and Ending at the Mouth of the Wallah-Wallah in the Columbia 10 miles to 1 inch Drawn by Charles Preuss in 7 sections.
Sheet 7, Wallah-Wallah, 1846.
Library of Congress

205 Map of Oregon and Upper California From the Surveys of John Charles Fremont And other Authorities. Drawn by Charles Preuss Under the order of the Senate of the United States, Washington City 1845.
From: John Charles Fremont, Geographical Memoir Upon Upper California in Illustration of His Map of Oregon and California, 1848.
Library of Congress

206 Columbia River 1825
British War Office, 1826
Printed at the Lithographic Establishment, Quarter Master Generals Office, Horse Guards, Octʳ 1826 (Eastern part of map.)
PRO FO 925 1379

207 Sketch of the Environs of Fort Vancouver embracing a section of about 16 miles in length, showing the course of the great Conflagration, by which the Fort was nearly destroyed, on the 27th day of September 1844.
Henry Newnsham Peers, 1844
HBCA G1/125

208 Ground Plan of Portion of Vancouvers Island Selected for New Establishment Taken by James Douglas Esqr.
James Douglas and Adolphus Lee Lewes, 1842
HBCA G2/25

209 Victoria Harbour
Henry Kellett 1847
London: Hydrographic Office. 1848
National Archives of Canada NMC 106384

210 Victoria District. Inset in: Map of Vancouver Island and the Adjacent Coasts Compiled from the Surveys of Vancouver, Kellett, Simpson, Galiano, Valdes, etc. by J. Arrowsmith. 1849.

211 Esquimalt District – Official Map, 1858.
BCARS CM C64

212 Map of the City of Victoria, Vancouver Island Numbered, revised and corrected from the Official Map and the best authorities.
Published by Alfred Waddington, January, 1863
BCARS CM B274

213 Portland Oregon. Showing Also East Portland and the Cascade Mountains. J.K. Gill & Co. 1881.
OHS Neg. No. ORHI 99984

214 Portland, Oregon 1890
Cloughessy and Strenghels, 1890
Library of Congress

215 Sketch of Fort Vancouver and adjacent plains Lat.45° 36'N. Long. 122° 37'W.
M. Vavasour Lieutn. Royal Engr. 1845
HBCA G1/195

216 Plan of Cape Disappointment. Mervin Vavasour, 1846. HBCA G1/201

217 Eye Sketch of the Plains and about Nisqually at the head of Pugets Sound. Mervin Vavasour, 1846
BCARS CM B893

218 Sketch of Cammusan Harbour, Vancouvers Island. shewing the position of Fort Victoria...
M. Vavasour Lieut. Royal Engrs
Inset: Plan of the Fort. 1846.
BCARS CM B205

266 *British Columbia Thompson River District*
From a map in the possession of H.E. Gov.
Douglas CB made in 1835 by S. Black Esq. H.B.
Company's Service. The positions of New
Westminster, Douglas and Hope are those
determined by the Royal Engineers.
Litho under direction of Capt W. Parsons RE By
order of Colonel R.C. Moody July 1861
(With handwritten notes.)
PRO CO 700 British Columbia 8, 5

267 *Fraser River & Burrard Inlet*
Surveyed by Captain G.H. Richards, R.N. and the
Officers of H.M.S. Plumper 1859–60.
London: Hydrographic Office, 1860.
Vancouver City Archives Map 530

268 *Entrance to Fraser River from the Admiralty*
Survey 1868
BCARS CM C718

269 *South East part of Vancouver Island showing the*
proposed sites for Light Houses on the Great Race
Rock and Fisgard Island
Captain George Henry Richards, 1858
In: *Papers Relative to British Columbia*, Pt II,
Despatch from Governor Douglas C.B. to his
Grace the Duke of Newcastle, K.G., Victoria,
Vancouver Island, 27 October 1858.
BCARS NW 971K G786

270 *Entrance of Esquimalt Harbour showing the*
proposed site for a Light House on Fisgard Island
Captain George Henry Richards, 1858
In: *Papers Relative to British Columbia*, Pt II,
Despatch from Governor Douglas C.B. to his
Grace the Duke of Newcastle, K.G., Victoria,
Vancouver Island, 27 October 1858.
BCARS NW 971K G786

271 *A Part of the Strait of Georgia with the channels*
leading into the Strait of Fuca by the officers of
HMS Plumper 1858. (Signed by Captain Henry
Richards.)
PRO 925 1650, 36

272 *New Map of British Columbia by R.T. Williams,*
Publisher, Victoria, 1882
BCARS CM A132

273 *Plan Shewing the Hon. Hudson Bay Cos.*
Warehouse Barkerville, B.C.
13th October 1868. W.H. Newton
HBCA A10/77, fo.141

274 *British Columbia and Vancouver Island*
Edward Weller
From: Matthew Macfie,*Vancouver Island and*
British Columbia Their History, Resources and
Prospects. 1865.

275 *British Columbia*
Reduced copy of the Map Referred to in the
Despatch of Govr Douglas dated 16th July 1861
In: *Further Papers Relating to the Affairs of British*
Columbia, 1862.
BCARS NW 971K G786

276 *Map of the Country Between Barclay Sound and*
Nanaimo By the V.I. Explorᵈ Expedⁿ 1864
Robert Brown, 1864
BCARS CM C704

277 *P. Mc. D. Collins' Proposed Overland Telegraph via*
Behrings Strait and Asiatic Russia to Europe
Under Russian and British Grants
Furnished by J.H. Colton, 172 William Street, New
York. 1864
J.H. Colton, 1864
BCARS CM B313

278 Map of proposed northern boundaries for British
Columbia. Sent to British Colonial Office in July
1858 by James Wyld.
PRO CO 700 British Columbia 4

279 *Johnson's North America*
Published by A.J. Johnson, New York 1867
Vancouver City Archives Map 1153

280 *Northwestern America showing the territory ceded*
by Russia to the United States.
S. Augustus Mitchell, 1871

281 *North America*
Drawn & Engraved by J.W. Cowry.
Blackie & Son, Edinburgh 1860

282 *Map of British Columbia to the 56th Parallel, North*
Latitude
Compiled and drawn at the Lands and Works
Office, Victoria, B.C., under the direction of the
Honourable J.W. Trutch. 1871
BCARS CM A1557

283 *Map Showing the Line of Boundary between the*
United States and British Possessions From the
point where the 49th Parallel of North Latitude
strikes the Western Coast of the Continent "to the
middle of the channel which separates the
Continent from Vancouver's Island and thence
Southerly through the middle of said channel" and
c. to Fuca's Straits, in accordance with Treaty of
June 15th 1846
Bowen & Co. Lith. Philadᵃ
Vancouver City Archives Map 8a

284 *Copy of 'Section of Map of Oregon & Upper*
California. From the surveys of John Charles
Fremont And other Authorities. Drawn by Charles
Preuss Under the Order of the Senate of the United
States, Washington City, 1848' Exhibiting the
boundary line between the possessions of Great
Britain and the United States as therin laid down.
Inset: *A Part of the Arro Archipelago Enlarged.*
1853.
HBCA G1/155

285 *Map of southern tip of Vancouver Island and*
Oregon Territory showing boundary line between
possessions of Great Britain and United States.
Traced from a map drawn under the order of the
Senate of the United States at Washington 1848.
J. Arrowsmith, 1853
HBCA G1/156

286 *A Diagram of a Portion of Oregon Territory*
Surveyor Generals Office, Oregon City, October
21st 1852.
Tracing by John Arrowsmith, 1856, and certified
as true copy in handwriting.
PRO FO 925 1650, 30

287 *Haro and Rosario Straits*
Surveyed by Captain G.H. Richards and the
Officers of H.M.S. Plumper 1858–59
(with San Juan boundary options)
Captain George H. Richards, 1859
PRO FO 925 1650, 38

288 *Map of the Boundary Between British and*
American Territory on the Pacific Coast, Settled by
the Decision of the Emperor of Germany.
From: *Harper's Weekly,* 30 November 1872,
p. 939.
BCARS CM A1229 1/2

289 *Vancouver Island and the Gulf of Georgia*
From the surveys of Captain G. Vancouver R.N.,
1792, Captains D. Galiano and A. Valdes, 1792,
Captain H. Kellett, R.N. 1849. (Certified in
handwriting *A True Copy of the Chart Published by*
Mr. Arrowsmith 28th February 1849 and signed by
Rear Admiral George Henry Richards, dated at
the Admiralty, 21st May 1872.)
PRO FO 925 1650, 26

290 *Map from the Pacific Ocean across the Rocky*
Mountain Zone to accompany Report on the
Exploratory Survey
Canadian Pacific Railway
January 1874 Sheet No.8.
From: Sir Sandford Fleming: *Report of Progress on*
the Explorations and Surveys up to January 1874
Ottawa, MacLean Roger and Co, 1874.
Library of Congress

291 *Map to Accompany Progress Report on Surveys*
Canadian Pacific Railway April 10th 1872
Sandford Fleming, Engineer in Chief.
Routes drawn by hand on printed map, 1872.
BCARS CM C107

292 *Map of the Canadian Pacific Railway showing the*
route... 1893.
BCARS CM B372

Map 318
Carte de l'Empire Russe Par M. Bonne Ingenieur
– Hydrographe de la Marine. c1776.

A copy of the work of Jacob von Stählin by French
geographer Rigobert Bonne.
Compare with Map 47, page 31.
Alaska appears as an island, *I. Alaschka,* following
the voyage of Russian explorer Ivan Synd (see
pages 29 – 32).

293 *Map of the lands comprised within the Railway*
Belt, British Columbia as defined by the terms of
union. c1895.
BCARS CM B1235

294 *Map showing the Canadian Pacific Routes in*
British Columbia, 1879.
National Archives of Canada NMC 119640

295 *Plan Showing Canadian Pacific Railway Terminus*
at Port Moody, and Railway Ferry between English
Bay and Nanaimo; the Esquimalt Nanaimo section
of the Pacific Railway; the extension of Northern
Pacific from Tacoma to Seattle and to a terminus
at Holme's Harbour opposite Port Townsend, and
a branch connecting it with the Canadian Pacific
Railway.
Compiled from Admiralty Chart by Henry A. Gray,
Civil Engineer for A. De Cosmos Esqe. MP. (with
memorandum and explanation) 1881
BCARS CM B679

296 *Plan of the City of Vancouver Western Terminus of*
the Canadian Pacific Railway. Published by Rand
Brothers. 1887. Inset: *Index Plan of Vancouver*
B.C. Terminus CPR 1887.
PRO CO 700 British Columbia 17

297 *Map of Canadian Pacific Railway Kootenay*
District British Columbia
Poole Brothers, Chicago, 1897
Library of Congress

298 *Bird's Eye View of the City of Seattle, W.T. Puget*
Sound. County Seat of King County 1884
J.J. Stoner, Madison, Wis. 1884
Library of Congress

299 *Fairhaven:*
A Bird's-Eye View of the City and Harbor
1890
Galen Biery Papers,
Center for Pacific Northwest Studies,
Western Washington University.

300 *Birds-Eye View of the Puget Sound Country*
An Accurate Perspective Projection, showing the
Topography, Resources and Development of
Northwestern Washington and British Columbia.
Charles H. Baker Co. 1891
BCARS CM B886

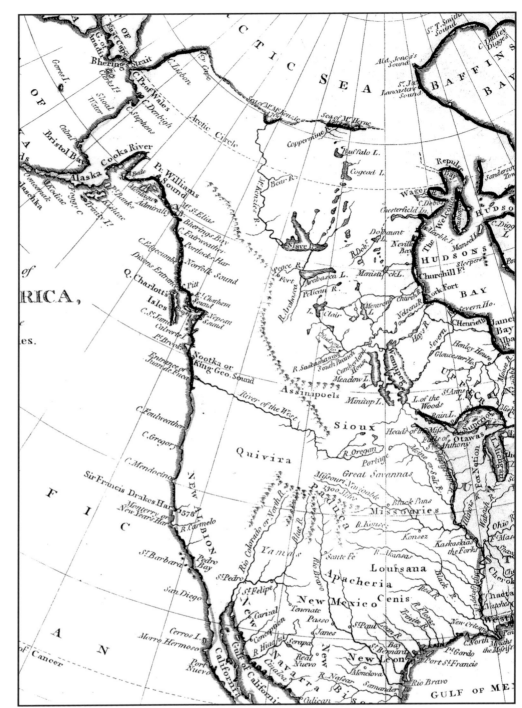

Map 320

A New Map of North America agreeable to the Latest Discoveries
London, Published Jany 1st 1794 by R. Wilkinson, No. 58, Cornhill.
Shows James Cook's discoveries, but none yet of George Vancouver's; the information from the latter voyage will not be published for another four years. Note the "R. Oregan" and "River of the West" flowing to the Pacific at the "Entrance of Juan de Fuca".

Index

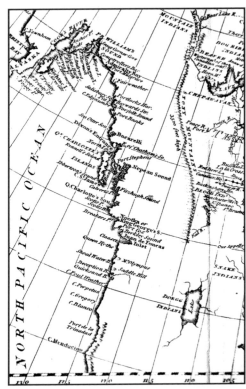

Map 321
British Colonies in North America from the best Authorities
Published November 29th 1797 by C. Dilly and G.G. & J. Robinson.
This map by Dilly was published by the same publishers that in only another nine months would publish George Vancouver's monumental work, *Voyage to the North Pacific and Round the World.* The Robinsons quite possibly knew full well that this map was hopelessly inaccurate even as they published it.